The Common-Sense Guide
to American Colleges
1991–1992

The Common-Sense Guide to American Colleges 1991–1992

Executive Editor
Charles Horner

Editor
Patty Pyott

Associate Editor
Steven B. Loux

Editorial Advisors
Chester E. Finn, Jr.
Leslie Lenkowsky
Stephen H. Balch

The Madison Center for Educational Affairs
Washington, D.C.

Madison Books
Lanham • New York • London

Published by Madison Books
4720 Boston Way
Lanham, Maryland 20706

3 Henrietta Street
London WC2E 8LU England

Distributed by National Book Network

The paper used in this publication meets the minimum
requirements of American National Standard for
Information Sciences—Permanence of Paper for
Printed Library Materials, ANSI Z39.48–1984. ∞ ™
Manufactured in the United States of America.

ISBN 0-8191-8244-3 (paperback : alk. paper)

British Cataloging in Publication Information Available

To the parents who pay the freight

Acknowledgments

Hundreds of students and professors around the country helped in the completion of this project, and it is impossible to thank them all individually here. However, the Madison Center especially appreciates the assistance of Chester E. Finn, Jr., professor of education and public policy at Vanderbilt University, and Leslie Lenkowsky, president of the Hudson Institute. We also wish to note the contributions of writers and editors of the Collegiate Network, a nationwide association of student publications. Additionally, we are grateful for the assistance of Stephen H. Balch, president of the National Association of Scholars, and to many of his NAS associates who, in their individual and private capacities, provided us with useful information, insight, and perspective. Members of the staff of the Madison Center in Washington were invariably helpful, especially David Bernstein, Kim Bowling, Tana Bowling, Robert Lukefahr, Hilda Maness, Janet O'Connor, and Mary Scalia.

Contents

Introduction

Every spring, about two and a half million young Americans graduate from high school, and about one and a half million of them go on to some form of higher education. Many head for a college near home. Many apply only to one institution. In recent years, however, more and more students and their families have come to give the most careful consideration to their choice of a college.

Higher education is an increasingly expensive investment and yet, of all the major commitments a family will make, there seems to be less reliable information about college than there is about less costly purchases. Moreover, colleges can change quickly. Students are supposed to come and go in four years, but within that brief time undergraduate conditions can alter so much that even a near-instant book could be out of date by the time it appears.

Of course, the prospective student already knows that the *quantity* of information available is not the problem. There is no shortage of books, newspaper articles, video tapes, magazine features and good old-fashioned word-of-mouth. In fact, colleges themselves go to enormous lengths to produce handsome materials about themselves. Why then, did the Madison Center for Educational Affairs feel a need to create *The Common-Sense Guide to American Colleges*?

In our view, something was missing from other available references. The encyclopedic tomes, for all their heft, were never designed to capture the essence of the institutions for which they provided a thumbnail sketch. The existing narrative guides, we thought, were either too accepting of the idea that "every college is good in its own way," or "it doesn't really matter where you go; good education is available everywhere if you work at it." It seemed to us that this value-free view was intended only to make the student feel happy about his final college destination, wherever that might be. Nor were we satisfied with assessments of institutions based on reports about the "hot" schools of the moment. Nor did we think that rankings and evaluations based on surveys were especially helpful—other than in reminding the prospective student that higher education is in its own way a very competitive business.

1

In this volume, the first of its kind, we evaluate a group of American colleges with a special focus on the undergraduate liberal arts education that they offer and a special emphasis on the general social and ethical climate that they foster. We have a point of view which may fairly be termed traditional. "Quality," "excellence," and "achievement" are words we like. One might even say we cherish the values they connote. We also have a generally high opinion of our civilization, our culture, and our country; we think that one important measure of any college or university—though surely not the only measure—is whether it values them also.

We pay special attention to the liberal arts, because it is through their teaching and study that a society reveals and passes on its deepest values. Mastery of these subjects may not lead to any particular professional competency or career path, but an understanding of them provides the real basis for professional, social, and civic ethics. Thus, we have a high regard for the standards of excellence that have developed in the liberal arts across the centuries, and we are disturbed by their cavalier dismissal in too many of our colleges today. Moreover, we feel that there is a relationship between the decline of standards in academic and intellectual life and the growing vulgarity and tastelessness that is increasingly prevalent in American society. Accordingly, we believe that the burden of proof rests on the advocates of radical departures from the tried and true. We think that their slogans, no matter how loudly chanted, are no substitute for reasoned argument. Thus, while we intend this guide primarily as a reference work, we do not disguise our hope that it will also play some role in the discussion of these basic issues.

Still, our purpose in publishing *The Common-Sense Guide* is not to make a case. In the United States as a whole, there are some 3,400 institutions of higher learning of every size, shape, and description, and only a tiny fraction of them are discussed in this book. The institutions we do evaluate were not selected via any scientific process. We picked colleges and universities that we thought people would want to know more about. As it happens, all sorts of places are represented—large and small, public and private, east, west, north and south, secular and religious—but mostly good and bad or, more precisely, better and worse.

Yet, even if we had not known of large national trends in higher education, this examination of individual institutions would itself have offered reason to ponder the condition of our colleges. Just as the guide offers prospective students, their families, and their counselors useful information and perspective, close readers will also not fail to notice as well the pressures on liberal arts education today. For example, our discussion of some of the schools reminds us of the sheer size of the enterprise. Americans have created some enormous universities, each enrolling tens of thousands of students whereas, in decades past, the characteristic mode of instruction was the smaller institution with a smaller student body. The reader will also notice the pressure that comes from the creation of the modern large research university. Toward the end of the last century, the research university established itself in this country, and it is now a model, especially for ambitious administrators. These huge institutions do not usually excel in the education of undergraduates in the traditional liberal arts. Moreover, some of the smaller private universities have decided that their own futures are best secured by developing themselves as research entities.

To these structural pressures against the liberal arts, the public must now add all those things which fall under the almost unpronounceable term "politicization." Higher education, both as an industry and as a profession, has become increasingly influenced by a left-of-center political agenda, now famous under the ironic term "political correctness." Its pressure on the teaching of the liberal arts, in particular, is manifest when college curricula are altered to reflect that political outlook, and when academic and intellectual decisions are made in accordance with, or in furtherance of, these same political objectives.

Contrary opinions are unwelcome. "Nowhere is the first amendment more imperiled than on college campus," wrote *Time's* Nancy Gibbs. Other writers have also spotted what *Newsweek* has called the campus "thought police." By the middle of 1991 these developments were receiving sustained national attention. But while newspapers, magazines, and books provide useful examples of general trends, they still do not allow the prospective student to consider how any particular institution is faring. Indeed, it is the relationship between general trends on the one hand, and how individual colleges fit into the larger picture on the other, which ought to influence practical decisions by students and their families.

The left-of-center politically correct outlook now infects almost every aspect of higher education, from investment decisions to hiring practices to the selection—and reception—of guest speakers. But now that the consumers of higher education—especially those who pay for it—are becoming more aware of the problem, it is possible that greater public attention will prompt a necessary and useful countertrend.

Meanwhile, the colleges and universities work hard to keep the larger public from fathoming the depth and the breadth of politically correct influences. We, however, do not share their reticence and intend this volume to cast some needed light on these developments.

But it is not only the quality of instruction that has suffered from the willingness of college administrators to alter curricula and hire faculty in accordance with prevalent political trends. The "quality of life" for undergraduates has also been affected. Relations among individuals, the conduct of campus debates, and human relations on the campus generally have all been influenced by larger political agendas. In particular, students tell us that, almost universally, the single most difficult problem affecting the campuses is race relations. The academic manifestation of the tension is reflected in debates about "multiculturalism" in the curriculum; non-academic aspects are subsumed into discussions of "diversity" in the student body and, more recently, in the faculty. Unfortunately, race-based definitions of intellectual quality and personal worth have become more conspicuous. The notion that rights inhere in groups, not in individuals, is more and more accepted as the basis of citizenship on the campus if not yet in the polity.

Whatever the merits of these arguments philosophically, there is a near consensus that divisions among the races on campus are, in fact, widening. While widely reported efforts in behalf of feminist, gender, and homosexual studies are certainly useless distractions, they are not yet as corrosive as the newly enshrined racialism. Overall, we have found that college administrators have responded weakly, if at all, to these debilitating trends. There are some exceptions, of course, but the general passivity of educators in the face of serious threats to instructional quality and even ordinary civility is very disturbing.

While these are general conclusions that emerge from our examination of campuses, our purpose, we repeat, is not to generalize— quite the contrary. We have sought to evaluate institutions on their individual merits, and have tried to take them as we have found them. We were often surprised by what we discovered, both for better and worse. We spent a year gathering information from students, teachers, and educational administrators, and we have also benefited from press accounts, college publications, books, and essays—all of which have given us different insights into the condition of the colleges and universities we discuss.

The reader will see that for each institution we provide a few basic statistics culled from the enormous quantity available today, and then give a description designed to convey our best sense of the things which interest us. There is always more to be learned, of course, and while we hope that prospective students will make good use of this guide, we recommend them also to make use of other sources. We especially encourage campus visits and, even more, we urge the asking of pointed questions.

In the months this guide has been in preparation, we have gained confidence in the fairness, balance, and general accuracy of the judgments we offer; they are based on the best reading of the evidence available to us. Doubtless we would have benefited from additional data; it is also true that another group of writers and editors, in evaluating the same body of information, might have reached different conclusions. Thus, though we are often pointed in our criticisms, we expect pointed criticism in return. Indeed, we expect the partisans, advocates, and employees of many campuses to dispute our conclusions, whether out of self-interest or deep philosophical disagreement. But if, in the process of give and take, our readers come to learn more about America's colleges and their virtues and vices, we shall feel we have accomplished our purpose.

Charles Horner
Washington, D.C.

Amherst College

Dean of Admissions, Amherst College
Amherst, MA 01002 (413) 542-2328

Type: Private and Secular			**Costs and Aid:**	
			Tuition and fees	$15,790
Students:			Room and Board	4,400
1,578 undergraduates			Scholarships:	
872 men			Academic	No
706 women			Athletic	No
Applications:			Minority	No
Closing date: January 1			Financial Aid:	
22% of applicants accepted			Freshmen	59%
	Applied	*Accepted*	*Enrolled*	Upperclassmen 50%
men	2,354	527	232	
women	2,150	468	189	**Library:** 466,204 titles
SAT or ACT required				
Score reported by: February 15			**ROTC:** Yes	
Mid 50% of freshman scores:			**Study Abroad:** Yes	
SAT-Math	N/A			
SAT-Verbal	N/A			

Amherst College is reputed outside its immediate circle to be a small, expensive, top-ranked, liberal arts school. But to those who know it better, Amherst is an institution caught between a past it cannot escape, but would rather forget, and a future that poses significant threats to its idyllic image. Like many similar schools, Amherst not only abandoned its traditional core curriculum during the Vietnam war period, but also jettisoned other practices that gave the college its distinctive character and personality. Once proudly all male, in 1976 Amherst began admitting women, who now make up close to half the student body of just under 1,600; eight years later the college abolished the fraternity system around which social life had revolved for decades.

Amherst was founded in 1821, oddly enough by a group of professors from Williams College, which by then had been struggling to survive for almost 30 years. The defectors despaired of Williams's longevity due to its inaccessibility near the Vermont border during winter, and began to look around for a more promising alternative. They discovered it in the rolling farmlands of the Connecticut River valley, which had no institution of higher learning and so welcomed them with open arms. Amherst began as a Congregationalist college

7

with strict standards about what a Christian gentleman should study to become an educated man.

Today, by contrast, there is no religious atmosphere at the college, and there are no required courses either—aside from an "Introduction to Liberal Studies," which entering freshmen must take. Distribution requirements are also nonexistent, except those imposed by individual departments for the major. Students are encouraged to take classes in different fields, but in the absence of a formal framework the goal of a traditional liberal education must be deliberately sought, and may also be deliberately avoided. A student can graduate without any laboratory work, without a single class in either Western civilization or history, and without any study of philosophy. All disciplines are considered equal and none is therefore indispensable.

1990–91 Catalog:
Sociology 44—Sport and Society.
Professor Allen Guttman

"A cross-cultural study of sport in its social context. Topics will include the philosophy of play, games, contests, and sport; the evolution of modern sport in industrial society; Marxist and Neo-Marxist interpretations of sport; economic, legal, racial and sexual aspects of sport; national character and sport, social mobility and sport; sport in literature and film."

In terms of faculty, resources, and general programs of study, some departments outshine others. One commonly cited standout is the department of economics, which, in addition to an excellent faculty, has the most stringent grading and honors requirements outside the "hard" sciences. The well-regarded English department, the largest at Amherst, offers an extensive menu of courses in literature and composition. The Russian department has a number of talented professors. The science departments have very capable faculty and are well-equipped for a small college. Honors work in the sciences is often quite advanced and sometimes brilliant.

On the other hand, following fad, Amherst has created a department of black studies and one of women's and gender studies (WAGS). Students can take such courses as "Race and Sex" and "War." The new departments are openly ideological, not scholarly—especially WAGS—and neither has been able to establish itself as seriously

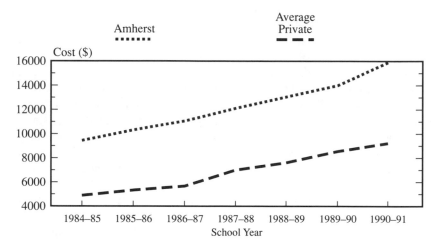

TUITION AND FEES INCREASE
Average Increase/Year: Private = 11.15%, Amherst = 8.83%

Source: The College Entrance Examination Board

academic. The department of political science also houses avowed radical teachers and others who display an embarrassing preoccupation with "sexual politics." Nevertheless, teaching at Amherst takes pride of place over research. Most of the faculty are bright, academically accomplished, and seriously interested in working with intelligent undergraduates, in which Amherst abounds. They come from almost all the states, plus nearly 50 foreign countries. About 25 percent are from minority groups.

The size of classes ranges widely from under 10 to 120. There is, in practice, no clear line between seminar and lecture classes and, especially in the humanities and social sciences, the classes feature both student discussion and presentations by the professor. Science courses often involve class lectures and laboratory work guided by teaching assistants; the teaching assistant is seldom encountered at Amherst outside these labs.

Students have an opportunity for "special topics" study in courses of individual research and reading, devised with one or more faculty members. There are also interdisciplinary major programs that can be individually tailored. Honors programs vary in requirements, but do not seem particularly demanding. More than half of all students graduate with honors.

The vast majority of the Amherst community lives on campus in coed dorms, although there are a few single-sex floors. Typically, freshmen are placed in older hall-type dormitories, and most share rooms. At the end of their first year they enter the room lottery; some end up in the "social dorms," built in the 1960s with four-, six-, and eight-student suites. The former fraternity houses contain most of the single rooms and, as choice housing, are reserved for upperclassmen. There are "theme houses" for foreign languages and the artistically inclined, with selection among the applicants by residential committee.

Outdoors, the nearby mountains create a picturesque background for the college's mellow brick buildings, and the scenery almost compensates for the clinical structures erected on the 1,000-acre campus during the last 40 years. Amherst lies at a crossroads with four other institutions—all-female Smith and Mount Holyoke, "experimental" Hampshire College, and the sprawling Amherst campus of the

DISTRIBUTION OF UNDERGRADUATE AID
1989–90 School Year

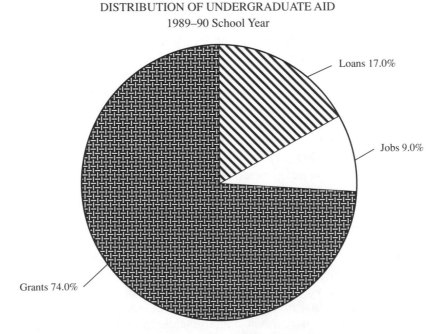

Loans 17.0%

Jobs 9.0%

Grants 74.0%

Source: The College Entrance Examination Board, 1990

University of Massachusetts. This consortium enables students to take classes at any of the other schools. Amherst's own small-town character has been seriously affected by the expansion of UMass since the late 1950s. Many businesses directed at the expanding student market have sprung up on the outskirts of the old village, and the non-student population continues to grow.

In spite of these degradations, the college manages to retain its high culture and elevated pastimes—its own collection of art and antiques, a varied and interesting concert series that regularly brings major classical and baroque performers to the campus, and recitals and performances by students in the departments of music, theater and dance. Lower on the cultural scale, drinking is also widespread and is the most common way to blow off steam or avoid work. The rite of draining several kegs of beer in the upperclass houses is observed on Wednesday and Thursday nights; Fridays and Saturdays may see better organized parties. Small, impromptu gatherings also abound, and five-college festivities attract many. The college, in response to the heavy drinking, has issued new restrictions on party planning and tries strictly to enforce state drinking laws. The new campus center, which was built to replace fraternities as the social beehive of the college, houses the snack bar, post office, tiny movie theater, miniature ballroom, and several living rooms, but has yet to attract large numbers of students.

Despite its small size, Amherst supports 15 intercollegiate teams for men and 14 for women, as well as several coed intramurals and club teams. There are two gymnasiums, a pool, and the usual complement of fields and courts. Williams is the archrival no matter what the sport.

During the past 15 years, Amherst has become increasingly self-conscious about its masculine, "elitist" history. Currently, the political position of the student body is somewhat left of moderate, and equally right of radical, though generally smug. Conservatism is not a socially acceptable option, and is widely supposed to reflect either intellectual inferiority or misanthropy. About a quarter of the students seem without political inclinations. The character of the campus is defined by a small but very noisy and determined cadre of apparently genuine radical leftists, to whose demands the administration usually acquiesces.

As a result, college life is dominated by a politically correct orthodoxy, a hybrid of Marxism, feminism, black nationalism, advocacy of homosexuality, and so on. These elements have seized the initiative and the high ground. For example, CIA recruiters have been banished from campus, and Coca-Cola is banned because of that company's ties with South Africa.

Today's Amherst seems hell-bent on dissolving a guilt complex stemming from its history as an exclusive institution. For example, the college is strongly committed to affirmative action in its admissions policy. Though the college gives the usual doublespeak, it appears that members of minority groups (as defined by the college) are accorded preferential consideration over white males. "It is absolutely untrue," states Dean of Admissions Jane E. Reynolds, "that Amherst is lowering its academic standards in admission" for students of color. However, she also states in this regard:

> Statistical measurements . . . should not be the only standards for evaluating students; we're interested in what they did with the opportunities they had. We look for evidence of potential, discipline, achievement, energy, motivation, leadership . . .

This preoccupation with "potential" has far-reaching effects on the character and quality of the student body. Apart from the predictable defensiveness by the beneficiaries of such preferences, there are also social repercussions.

Minority groups, who have the option of living in the separate housing which they demanded, form discrete and even isolated social blocs. The college increasingly consists not of one community but of a number of sanctioned subgroups, which lose no opportunity to shout out their "rights." They seldom mention their responsibilities. This seems to be a perversion of the administration's original intention of encouraging a diversified student body whose members would unite in harmony and mutual respect. Moreover, radical particularism is abetted by the college's implicit expectation that minority members serve as representatives of their groups' "viewpoint," instead of being present as individuals. Therefore, places are reserved on one of the three student governing bodies for representatives of various factions, including homosexuals and the Black Student Union. But selective indignation, politically motivated application of college regulations, and racially based decision-making are important, principally, in their implications for educational quality. At the moment, however, an Amherst degree is a definite plus-factor for employers and graduate schools.

But there are now serious questions as to whether the status quo will continue. Some leading faculty members have been lured away in recent years to other institutions without replacement. Further, the evermore important affirmative action component of student selection dilutes present standards and trades them for short-term political considerations and the promise of "potential." Meanwhile, as group preferences and "representativeness" compete with merit in faculty hiring, educational excellence is also likely to deteriorate in that quarter. The political atmosphere of the college, moreover, inhibits critical discussion of these problems. If all this continues to dilute the quality of learning at Amherst, future graduates are likely to find fewer open doors, diminished esteem, and good reason to wonder what it was they really paid for.

Assumption College

Vice President for Enrollment Management/
Dean of Admissions and Financial Aid
Assumption College, 500 Salisbury Street
Worcester, MA 01615-0005 (508) 752-5615 ext.285

Type: Private and Catholic

Students:
1,830 undergraduates
 760 men
 1,070 women
 385 graduate students

Applications:
Closing date: March 1
68% of applicants accepted

	Applied	Accepted	Enrolled
men	1,110	740	205
women	1,540	1,050	332

SAT or ACT required (SAT preferred)
 Score reported by: March 1
 Mid 50% of freshman scores:
  SAT-Math 430–550
  SAT-Verbal 400–550

Costs and Aid:

Tuition and fees	$9,210
Room and Board	4,700

Scholarships:
Academic	No
Athletic	Yes
Minority	No

Financial Aid:
Freshmen	56%
Upperclassmen	65%

Library:	175,000 titles
ROTC:	Yes
Study Abroad:	Yes

"Assumption College is a Catholic institution of higher learning founded by and conducted under the auspices of the Augustinians of the Assumption. It seeks to educate the student in the traditions of Christianity and liberal arts and to promote Christian living."

These are the first lines in the Assumption College catalog. Students considering Assumption should weigh them carefully. They capture in a nutshell everything the college is about—from the curriculum to the faculty, from the campus to the students. Yet the college's Catholicism is not rigidly rightist, nor does it embrace left-wing positions, such as liberation theology, at the other end of the spectrum. Instead, Assumption's Catholicism seems to be both inquiring and inclusionary; it seeks to learn from other cultures and faiths, and welcomes their contributions and insights. Nevertheless, because the administration and faculty do believe that ultimate truth is invested in the Christian faith, Assumption instills with passion as well as intellect

15

the history, culture, and values of Western civilization. It does not pretend to be either neutral or objective; it is frankly partisan.

Founded in 1904 by a religious order that was then educating young Catholics in France and Belgium, Assumption maintained a bilingual curriculum in English and French until the late 1940s. In 1953, a tornado destroyed the campus, which was moved to another part of Worcester shortly thereafter. In 1968, in the heady aftermath of Vatican II, Assumption began to admit young women as students and laypersons as trustees. Today the college maintains an undergraduate enrollment of approximately 1,800, slightly more than half of whom are from Massachusetts with most of the rest from the Middle Atlantic states. There is also a small graduate contingent of almost 400 students matriculating in one of four programs: Business Studies; Psychology and Education; Religious Studies; and Social and Rehabilitation Services. About 80 percent of all students are Roman Catholic.

Assumption operates on the semester system and requires 120 credits for graduation. The general education requirements almost amount to a genuine core curriculum in the liberal arts, because the choice of courses is limited both in number and subject matter. First, students must pass one specified English composition course and one "writing emphasis" course in a subject of their own choosing (this can be any course whose major evaluations come from papers rather than from exams). Next, there are the philosophy and theology requirements. All students must take "Introduction to Philosophy" and a course in the Bible; in addition they must complete one more course in each department, chosen from a list of five. (In philosophy, the choices are: "The Philosophy of Nature"; "Philosophical Psychology"; "Ethics"; "Logic"; and "Foundations—Philosophy and Religion." In theology, the list is: "The Problem of God"; "The Challenge of Moral Responsibility"; "History of the Early Christian Community"; "Catholicism Today"; or again, "Philosophy and Religion.")

Students are also required to pass one course from two of the following three areas: mathematics at the elementary level; physics, chemistry, or biology (with laboratory); a foreign language at the intermediate level. In the humanities, students must pass one course in the fine arts, music, or the theater arts (from a choice of 12), as well as one course of a two-course sequence in either "The History of Western Civilization," or "The History of Modern Europe and the United States." In addition, students must take "Introduction to Literature." After that, they have the option of a second course in literature or the second course in the history sequence mentioned

TUITION AND FEES INCREASE

Average Increase/Year: Private = 11.15%, Assumption = 8.25%

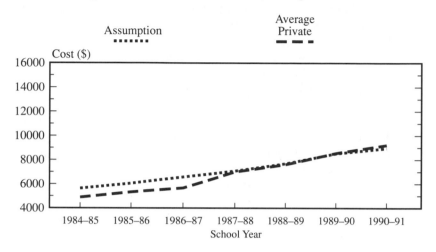

Source: The College Entrance Examination Board

above. In the social sciences, students must complete three courses in three different departments out of nine listed. These are the "breadth" requirements.

The "depth" requirements include three courses in three different categories from a selection of six: mathematics and computer science and statistics; foreign languages; philosophy and theology; literature; history; science.

For freshmen and sophomores wishing an interdisciplinary approach to the study of Western civilization, Assumption has developed a program called the Foundations of Fine Arts, Politics, Philosophy and Theology. Under a pilot grant from the National Endowment for the Humanities, four professors from four different disciplines pioneered the program to help students "reflect upon the heritage of the Western world." Freshmen study the politics and art of cities from ancient Athens to modern Washington, D.C.; sophomores try to find answers to questions raised in the first year by concentrating upon religion and philosophy and their evolution over the centuries. Two professors are present during each class, and guest speakers visit to stimulate discussion. Approximately 70 to 80 freshmen and sophomores are involved annually in the Foundations Program.

Another interdisciplinary program, also supported by the National Endowment for the Humanities, involves studying communities. Its aim is to demonstrate to students how they can utilize geography, history and sociology to "penetrate the workings of human communities." The project is carried out in Worcester, where 15-20 students concentrate on the social history of smaller ethnic or parish neighborhoods to find out what makes them tick. The program is popular with future social workers, health professionals, and urban planners.

Accepting that students should be exposed to wider horizons than their own, Assumption has also instituted a Third World studies program in which lowerclassmen take courses in anthropology, economics, history, and geography, in order to better understand the peoples living in Africa, Asia, and Latin America. About 20 juniors and seniors each year follow through with an interdisciplinary seminar that considers particular problems and issues, such as colonialism, hunger, health care, cultural systems, and trade relations with the West.

DISTRIBUTION OF UNDERGRADUATE AID
1989–90 School Year

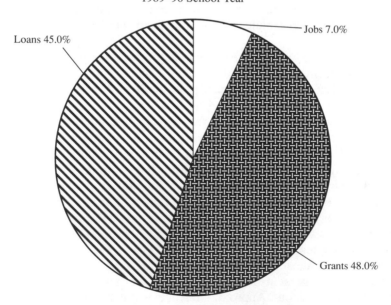

Loans 45.0%

Jobs 7.0%

Grants 48.0%

Source: The College Entrance Examination Board, 1990

In the same practical vein, the college has established a system of off-campus internships, which give approximately 25 students a year hands-on experience in preparation for a career. Students work as congressional aides in Washington or with state legislatures, in personnel positions, in labor-management relations, as well as in museums and in health care. The college's Internship Committee must approve individual projects, which usually carry from three to six (equivalent of one or two courses) academic credits. Each student is allowed only one internship, for which he must submit a formal proposal to a faculty sponsor to whom he reports regularly once he begins work. Internships usually last a semester and finish with a written report.

Students praise the advisory system and report that professors are uniformly accessible, helpful, and genuinely interested in student welfare. Most are immediately approachable when spotted on campus, so formal appointments are seldom needed. The college assigns advisors to freshmen, who may later substitute others if they wish. Since the primary business of Assumption is education not research, all faculty are required to give first priority to teaching; graduate students are not used to instruct classes. However, the college does employ a number of permanent part-time faculty, who act as section discussion leaders.

Outstanding departments are theology, philosophy, and political science. Some would add psychology and biology. The fine arts and foreign languages, with the exception of French, are considered to be weaker, the latter because of the paucity of languages available. Although Latin and Greek are offered along with German and the Romance languages, Asian and Slavic languages are not. It may be possible to fill in the gaps, however, by taking courses at other area colleges. Assumption is a member of the Worcester Consortium for Higher Education, which includes Clark University and Holy Cross, among others.

Housing on Assumption's pretty 150-acre campus is guaranteed for all four years; about 90 percent of students live in the college residences, which are coed and single-sex. The school is in the process of upgrading all dorms to what it calls the "pod configuration." Pods accommodate 24 students, three or four to a room, in independent suites linked by a common living room and a separate study area. Currently, upperclass students may opt for modern townhouses, or apartments for four to six persons. These have modern kitchens.

In spite of an absence of fraternities and sororities, social and extracurricular life is lively at Assumption. Much of it happens at the

Campus Center, the meeting place for 40 college-recognized groups and organizations, and much takes place in Worcester itself, New England's second largest city. Boston, New England's largest metropolis, is only an hour away. Cape Cod and even the Maine coast are within weekending distance. On campus, drinking is something of a problem, though drugs (except for occasional offenses) are not. Campus crime is virtually non-existent, and the affluent neighborhood is regarded as very safe.

Sports play a big part in Assumption life, and almost everyone participates in the popular intramurals or in the 10 intercollegiate teams for men and 9 for women. The college encourages "team spirit" over individual accomplishment. Everyone is a "Greyhound"; but men are called simply "Hounds," while women players are stuck with the genteel if awkward tag, "Lady Hounds." Ice and field hockey, basketball, soccer and lacrosse are all popular. All sports are Division II except football, which is Division III.

Politics as such are almost non-existent at Assumption. Only 4 percent of students are minorities, mostly Hispanic from the island of Puerto Rico. A smattering of foreign students hail from an eclectic array of countries including Taiwan, Lebanon, Portugal, Iceland, Uganda, Peru, Laos, and Vietnam. There is a multicultural program, which sponsors events like "World Fair" and Martin Luther King, Jr. Commemoration Day, as well as foreign films and guest speakers; however, antiharassment and sensitivity codes don't exist, because the issues involved simply don't arise—except when it comes to abortion. Recently, pro-choice activists demonstrated during a pro-life mass, and shortly thereafter obtained official university recognition.

On the whole, Assumption may be too conservative and Catholic in its orientation, providing students with insufficient exposure to other points of view. Because they take their conservatism and their Catholicism for granted, some students don't necessarily understand why they think and believe as they do, nor do they learn how effectively to defend their traditional principles against attack. In certain cases, it has simply never occurred to Assumption students that there is any other way to live. This is a relief to many, no doubt, but it may not be the best preparation for life in the real world outside the college cocoon.

Birmingham-Southern College

Vice President for Admissions Services
Birmingham-Southern College
900 Arkadelphia Road, Birmingham, AL 35254 (205) 226-4686

Type: Private and Protestant

Students:
1,849 undergraduates
  811 men
  1,038 women
  88 graduate students

Applications:
Priority date: December 1
Closing date: March 1
81% of applicants accepted

	Applied	Accepted	Enrolled
men	400	335	175
women	514	409	199

SAT or ACT required
  Score reported by: February 15
  Mid 50% of freshman scores:
    SAT-Math   450–670
    SAT-Verbal 440–660

Costs and Aid:

Tuition and fees	$9,000
Room and Board	3,440

Scholarships:
Academic	Yes
Athletic	Yes
Minority	No

Financial Aid:
Freshmen	84%
Upperclassmen	77%

Library:	153,067 titles
ROTC:	Yes
Study Abroad:	Yes

This small Methodist college, whose vital signs were weak and faltering 15 years ago, has since recovered its academic health, and today offers a robust, well-regarded liberal arts education to approximately 1,800 students. Under the leadership of a dynamic president and a faculty that cares more about teaching than research, "Southern," as the college is known to its nearest and dearest, overcame debt and declining enrollment to emerge as affectionate alma mater to a bevy of well-behaved offspring, who are mostly middle class, mostly white, mostly Protestant and mostly Alabaman.

Located on 185 acres in the heart of the Bible belt, the college, which was founded in 1856, draws three-quarters of its students from Alabama and the rest from more than 30 states, as well as three or four foreign countries.

Not surprisingly, the mood of the campus is generally conservative, although students seldom get fired up over non-campus politics and causes, conservative or radical. Ethnic and racial issues are non-issues, although 10 percent of students are minorities, mostly black. The races coexist harmoniously, though seldom seek each other out socially. The college says it does not practice affirmative action by reducing admissions standards. It does, however, prohibit "physical or verbal abuse" against all students.

Southern operates on a system of two four-month semesters with an interim semester of one month in January. Students generally take four courses of four hours a week during the long semesters, and one course during the interim term. (Alternatively, this "course" may also consist of an internship or a month abroad.) For the bachelor's degree, undergraduates must complete 144 hours of credit, including the interim term. There is no common core curriculum, but distribution requirements include: one writing course; one laboratory science course; one course in philosophy or religion; two in a foreign language; one each in literature, the arts, and history, as well as one in the social or behavioral sciences. Students must also complete a second course in a natural or computer science, or in mathematics, as well as an additional course in a second and different social science. Finally, they must take two more courses in the arts or humanities, plus two of their choice outside the major and minor fields.

Birmingham-Southern is solid in the liberal arts, but business administration, in which a quarter of the students major, has been plagued by frequent faculty turnover and is deemed to be weak. Biology, English, psychology, theater, and music are all strong. There are no departments of women's or Afro-American studies, and sensitivity training is not thought necessary on a campus where good manners and trust predominate. Students voted in an honor code, which prohibits academic cheating and dishonesty in all campus activities. By and large, it is respectfully observed. Professors, not teaching assistants, lead the classes, which usually enroll 30 or fewer. Faculty are easily accessible at other times, routinely give out their home as well as office telephone numbers, and seem eager to act not only as academic advisors, but also as friends and mentors to their students.

On a more mundane level, an aggressive fundraising drive has given a much-needed face lift to the school's physical plant, which boasts several new buildings, including up-to-date computer and laboratory facilities, as well as a modern dormitory for women. The college is proud of its small art gallery and its planetarium. Improved playing fields have recently been added. The library, however, only contains

TUITION AND FEES INCREASE
Average Increase/Year: Private = 11.15%, B.-S. = 9.58%

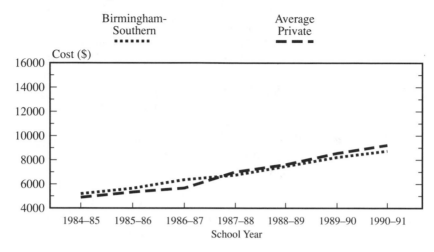

Source: The College Entrance Examination Board

between 150,000 and 160,000 volumes, and, if it is to fit the college's bright, new image, clearly needs expanding.

Housing, which is single-sex, is guaranteed for all four years and allotted on a first-come basis to the 90 percent of students who live on campus. There are seven dorms, on-campus apartments, and married-student quarters. Students decide visitation policies, which vary from house to house.

Southern is too small to worship at the shrine of big-time sports, and it lacks a football team; but the college tries to compensate with intercollegiate teams in men's soccer, basketball, and baseball, the last being first class. Men's and women's tennis are also excellent. Less high-powered athletes choose from six intramural sports for each sex.

Social life, which is serious business at Southern, generally revolves around the Greek system in a dozen sororities and fraternities, to which about 65 percent of the undergraduates belong. Although drugs are not a problem, many students drink to excess, especially on weekends. In addition to the fraternities and sororities, there are 80 groups and organizations which offer a wide choice of extracurricular activities; band concerts and plays are especially popular, and deserv-

edly so, because the quality of Southern's drama, dance and music is
much higher than you would expect in a college of its size.

Southern's small-school insularity is also relieved by its proximity
to Birmingham, Alabama's largest city, which abounds in good restaurants, pretty parks, museums and other cultural opportunities. The
campus itself—called the Hilltop—is green and attractive, with a mix
of modern and traditional buildings. It is, however, literally fenced off
from its immediate neighborhood, an urban slum. On weekends, some
students escape to more scenic surroundings at the beach or the
mountains, each about a five-hour drive.

Although the intellectual atmosphere at Birmingham-Southern is
not intense enough to nurture a community of true scholars, it is
serious enough to sustain interest in a sturdy liberal arts education for
a homogeneous, career-oriented student body. This loyalty to the
traditional liberal arts is a big plus in higher education these days; but
Southern's uniformity and conformity has a downside as well. The
college's undergrads often miss out on the spirited, intellectual debate

---

DISTRIBUTION OF UNDERGRADUATE AID
1989–90 School Year

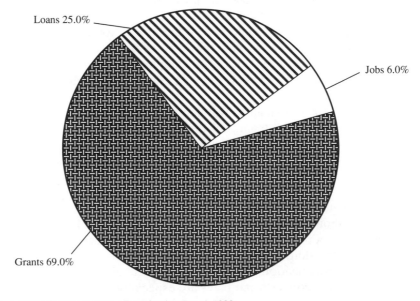

Loans 25.0%

Jobs 6.0%

Grants 69.0%

Source: The College Entrance Examination Board, 1990

sparked by sharp differences on other campuses, and they don't get many chances to practice the old American art of getting-along-with-all-kinds. In short, students here might benefit from a little less Southern comfort and a little more Northern aggression.

Boston College

Director of Undergraduate Admissions, Boston College
Lyons Hall 120, Chestnut Hill, MA 02167-3804 (617) 552-3100

Type: Private and Catholic

Students:
10,326 undergraduates
  4,552 men
  5,774 women
  4,123 graduate students

Applications:
Closing date: February 1
37% of applicants accepted

	Applied	Accepted	Enrolled
men	5,973	2,201	866
women	7,553	2,868	1,252

SAT or ACT required
  Score reported by: February 1
  Mid 50% of freshman scores:
    SAT-Math   580–680
    SAT-Verbal 520–620

Costs and Aid:

Tuition and fees	$13,080
Room and Board	5,830

Scholarships:
Academic	No
Athletic	Yes
Minority	No

Financial Aid:
Freshmen	63%
Upperclassmen	70%

Library: 1,094,523 titles

ROTC: Yes

Study Abroad: Yes

Boston College was started in 1863 by the Society of Jesus with the nickels and dimes of Boston's Irish Catholic immigrants, who were often poor and victims of religious discrimination. Their hope was to build a college where their children could be educated to compete in the new world with their old-world faith and heritage intact. Today, Boston College is still conscious of the plight of the poor and continues to open its doors to all qualified students, regardless of race, creed, color, or national origin. But its emphasis on Catholic morality has weakened and, in a broader sense, the campus is divided between loyalty to a liberal arts education centered on Western civilization and an education that gives equal, if not superior, value to other peoples and cultures.

Although three-quarters of BC students are still nominally Catholic and often mildly conservative, only about 10 percent of the faculty are Jesuits (some are politically very liberal), and the atmosphere on campus is becoming increasingly secular. This situation creates tension between religious students, who arrive expecting BC to give them an old-fashioned Catholic education, and the rest who, whether Catholic or not, subscribe to the new ethic of relative values.

The result of this dichotomy is reflected in student life where drinking is the number one recreational activity, in spite of a crackdown in on-campus consumption, and where sexual activity and attitudes defy Church teaching. Left-wing radicals—who often openly acknowledge their contempt for the Church—are as vocal at BC as they are on any modern campus, and often get their way. Ironically in a Catholic college, a kind of reverse discrimination against Catholicism has gradually polluted the atmosphere on campus.

1990–1991 Undergraduate Catalog:
Sociology 092—Peace or War? The United States and the Third World
Professor Charles K. Derber

"The Third World—where most of the world's population lives—has become increasingly important to the world's economy, but remains a seething cauldron of revolution and war. While not well understood by the American public, the United States has been a major player in the wars of the Third World. This course explores the bloody, often covert, entanglements that have defined—and continue to characterize—our own government's relations to Central America, Southern Africa, the Middle East, and Southeastern Asia. We will explore 'secret wars,' conducted by the CIA, that are the heart of today's most important regional conflicts. We will consider the motives for our own involvement and then focus on how such wars can be stopped and avoided in the future."

For example, the practice of abortion referrals at the university health service—a clear violation of university policy and Catholic teaching—was exposed by an investigative report in the conservative *Boston College Observer* in 1989. The overwhelming response of the college community to these revelations was, "Shoot the messenger." Given the current campus ethos, there was no particular surprise that abortions were condoned, but there was outrage that the policy was made public. Student pro-life activists were opposed by university officials, while pro-abortion feminists, who are extremely influential on campus, received encouragement. In spite of such hypocrisy, it is possible to get a first-rate education at Boston College. In the fall of 1990, no fewer than 76 percent of admitted freshmen were ranked in the top 10 percent of their high school classes.

"Boston College is one of the oldest Jesuit-founded *universities* (emphasis added) in the United States," the catalog states. (But it

TUITION AND FEES INCREASE
Average Increase/Year: Private = 11.15%, Boston C. = 9.25%

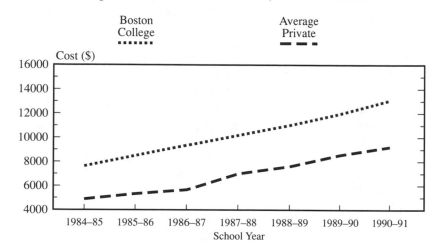

Source: The College Entrance Examination Board

---

definitely is not to be confused with nearby Boston University, over which Dr. John Silber presides.) Since its founding, BC has gradually added schools and colleges on several Massachusetts campuses and now enrolls more than 14,000 students, approximately 10,000 of whom are undergraduates; 14 percent are minorities.

Located on the Chestnut Hill campus are the School of Arts and Sciences, the Wallace E. Carroll School of Management, the School of Education, and the School of Nursing, as well as the Law School and the Graduate School of Social Work. There is a College of Liberal Arts in Lenox and Schools of Philosophy and Theology in Weston.

Of BC's undergraduates, approximately 5,400 matriculate in the School of Arts and Sciences. Thirty-eight one-semester courses are needed for graduation. Although the college says students must satisfy the "core" to graduate, they do have a choice of courses within the various divisions—which turns the core into a system of distribution requirements. Two courses each are mandated in English, European history, philosophy, theology, the natural sciences, the social sciences, and either two in mathematics or one course each in fine arts and in speech communication and theater. In addition, there is a foreign or classical language requirement, which may be met by examination or by completion of two semesters of course work at the intermediate level or one semester above the intermediate level. If this requirement is met by a proficiency examination, students do not obtain course credits.

One optional program, which satisfies both the theology and philosophy requirements, is called "Perspectives on Western Culture." Professor Allan Bloom, of the University of Chicago and author of *The Closing of the American Mind,* helped in its formulation and in the training seminars for professors. The program is based on the Great Books model, and is designed to provide an overview of Western civilization, culture, and tradition. Of course, much depends on the professor, and there have been complaints about injections of personal agendas, such as Marxism and feminism. But it is rare to find an American university these days where this isn't a problem and, overall, the program receives excellent reports from students.

An honors program is open to about 7 percent of entering A&S freshmen, who are selected on the basis of their high school records,

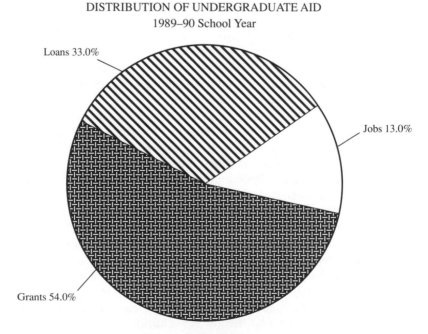

DISTRIBUTION OF UNDERGRADUATE AID
1989–90 School Year

Loans 33.0%

Jobs 13.0%

Grants 54.0%

Source: The College Entrance Examination Board, 1990

SAT scores, and teacher recommendations. They must complete majors in one of the regular departments and, in addition, must take an intensive course in "Western Cultural Tradition." This two-year course is good for six credits per semester, 24 credits in all. It substitutes for the normal distribution requirements in theology, philosophy, English, and for non-majors in social science. The course uses original texts (in translation) and ranges from Greek, Roman, Hebrew and Christian thought through medieval times and the Renaissance to the Enlightenment and the 20th century. The course is conducted in seminars with approximately 15 students, and attendance is mandatory.

The glories of Western civilization are not, of course, the only priorities at BC. Students may minor in black or women's studies, both interdisciplinary programs. On a more celestial level, the school has given a new twist to a minor on the peace-and-justice theme. Students may choose "Faith, Peace and Justice Studies," for which they design their own interdisciplinary programs, in order to examine "the power of God to heal worldly divisions and to promise various forms of reconciliation to earthly strife." The minor is "organized to explore how these attestations and promises relate to the work for peace and justice."

Back on the purely earthly plane, students may opt for a no-holds-barred course called "Inequality in America," which examines "strategies used by the rich for maintaining the status quo . . . and obstacles that are used to keep the poor in their place." Or, they may enroll in "Peace or War? The United States in the Third World," an offering which "explores secret wars, conducted by the CIA, that are at the heart of today's most important regional conflicts."

When they want to escape from the dark iniquities and inequities of the United States, students seek fun and frolic in 124 extracurricular activities in the form of clubs and groups of every description. One of the most notable is the University Chorale, which has performed for Pope John Paul II at the Vatican and all over the world. Community service is strongly emphasized, and is organized by the Chaplaincy both locally and in such far-flung places as Appalachia and Haiti. There are no fraternities or sororities, but social life is active.

Sports are important at BC. The college sponsors 16 intercollegiate teams for men and 15 for women, as well as 7 intramurals for men and 6 for women. Facilities are excellent, including a 32,000-seat stadium, an 8,600-seat arena for basketball and ice hockey, and a large recreation complex. The whole student body is football mad and shouts itself hoarse during home games.

Housing at BC is guaranteed for three years for students admitted as residents (some are admitted as commuters). Sixty-seven percent of students live on campus. The college is in the process of adding residential space and hopes soon to be able to offer three years of housing to all students, eliminating the distinction in admissions between residents and commuters. Accommodation is mostly coed, very comfortable, and includes honors, special-interest and language houses, as well as "quiet" dorms and single-sex halls for freshmen.

The suburban campuses in Chestnut Hill and nearby Newton are very attractive and just a trolley ride away from Boston's nightlife and cultural activities. The campus is quite safe, although there have been scattered incidents of sexual assaults on women, usually involving intruders from off campus. University police offer frequent instruction in personal safety, and provide an escort service with marked vans and uniformed security officers as drivers.

In sum, Boston College has arrived at a crossroads. Academically, it still stresses the culture of Western civilization, which has been so intertwined over the centuries with the history and staying power of the Roman Catholic Church. But when faculty and students choose to genuflect before the altar of political correctness both in and out of the classroom, the college also undermines the very values its Church was so instrumental in creating. Sooner or later, Boston College will have to resolve this identity crisis. Meanwhile, for students with strong intellects and characters, it still provides a solid grounding in the liberal arts.

Boston University

Director of Admissions, Boston University
121 Bay State Road, Boston, MA 02215 (617) 353-2300

Type: Private and Secular		**Costs and Aid:**	
		Tuition and fees	$15,190
Students:		Room and Board	5,960
14,564 undergraduates		Scholarships:	
6,911 men		Academic	Yes
7,653 women		Athletic	Yes
10,165 graduate students		Minority	Yes
Applications:		Financial Aid:	
Priority date: January 15		Freshmen	62%
66% of applicants accepted		Upperclassmen	53%

	Applied	Accepted	Enrolled
men	9,210	6,017	1,628
women	9,549	6,388	1,867

SAT or ACT required (SAT preferred)
Score reported by: March 15
Mid 50% of freshman scores:

SAT-Math	550–650
SAT-Verbal	500–600

Library:	1,711,000 titles
ROTC:	Yes
Study Abroad:	Yes

President John R. Silber. Any serious discussion of Boston University must start with this man, who has ruled his school and its students with an iron fist during a period when most university heads wore a velvet glove. The would-be governor of Massachusetts, who last year almost added a state to his domain, took over BU 20 years ago, and has provided excitement and provoked controversy ever since.

In 1989, BU celebrated its 150th anniversary. Only 20 years earlier, however, the school had celebrated its 120th anniversary. The president, ignoring charges that he couldn't count, justified the sesquicentennial celebration by triumphantly tracing the origins of BU back to a small school in New Hampshire 150 years before. Undaunted by that tempest-in-a-teapot, Silber survived several protests by disgruntled faculty members, strikes by food and maintenance workers, and accusations of infringements on students' First Amendment rights (disallowing the hanging of banners outside of dorm windows).

One of the most recent brouhahas involved new residence hall visitation policies. After receiving a complaint from a parent whose

33

daughter ended up sharing a room with her roommate's boyfriend as well as the roommate, Silber appointed a group to examine dormitory policies. As a result, students must now sign in visitors, who must leave by 1 a.m. Mondays through Fridays and by 2:30 a.m. Saturdays and Sundays. No overnight visitors are allowed unless they are family members, or of the same sex as the student host.

Moreover, students who are legally of drinking age may bring in no more than one six-pack of beer a day or a liter of alcohol. Predictably, all this "parenting" has been greeted by howls of protest from outraged students and a reduction in numbers signing up for on-campus housing. At this writing, however, Silber is standing pat.

On a less controversial note, even Silber's critics generally credit him with lifting BU out of both the academic and financial doldrums. Since his arrival, the endowment has climbed to more than $218 million, and, symbolic of its new academic prestige, the university attracted two presidents, George Bush and François Mitterrand, to its 1989 commencement exercises. Silber has also tightened admissions standards and drawn new talent onto the faculty, including Nobel Prize winner Elie Wiesel.

Boston University is composed of approximately 25,000 students and an array of graduate and undergraduate schools and colleges. The 10 undergraduate schools are: the College of Liberal Arts; the School for the Arts; the College of Basic Studies; the College of Communications; the School of Education; the College of Engineering; the School of Management; the Metropolitan College; the Sargent College of Allied Health Professions; and BU's equivalent of an honors program, the University Professors Program—"an independent degree-granting college, designed for a select group of students whose backgrounds, aptitudes, motivation, and promise warrant the creation of special and highly individualized programs of study." This group is select indeed, and usually numbers only slightly more than 60 top students.

Professionally, there is a School of Medicine including a School of Public Health, a School of Law, a School of Social Work, and a School of Theology. At the undergraduate level, there are close to 15,000 students, about 70 percent of whom are from the other 49 states. Eighty foreign countries are represented. About 13 percent of students are minorities. While BU does have a reputation for attracting affluent students, a large proportion is currently on some form of financial aid.

The College of the Liberal Arts, described in institutional literature as the core of the university, enrolls approximately 6,200 students.

TUITION AND FEES INCREASE
Average Increase/Year: Private = 11.15%, Boston U. = 8.89%

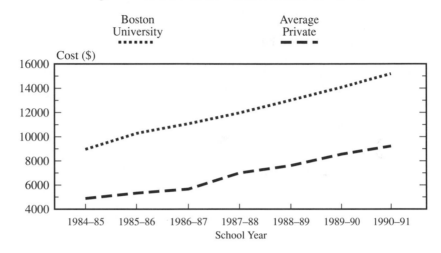

Source: The College Entrance Examination Board

It operates on the semester system and requires 32 courses for graduation. Students have the option of completing distribution (divisional) requirements, or a core curriculum of "historically-based, integrated courses providing an in-depth study of classic works in the humanities, great ideas in sciences, and significant social concerns in the contemporary world."

Those who go the divisional route must complete two semester courses from an approved and limited list in each of the three major divisions of the liberal arts: humanities, natural sciences, and social sciences. They must also take or test out of English composition and mathematics, and must "demonstrate proficiency at the advanced level in a language other than their own."

Students who opt for the core curriculum must also satisfy the English composition, math, and foreign language requirements, and take the following courses: "The Ancient World"; "Late Antiquity to the Medieval World"; "The Renaissance and the Enlightenment"; "The Modern World"; "Evolution of the Universe and Life"; "The Making of the Contemporary World"; "The Individual and the World."

Strong departments, generally cited, are history, physics, biology, and English. Some say economics and sociology are the weakest, though eight new professors have recently been brought in to buttress the former and strengthen its public finance focus.

As you might expect, some classes consist of large lectures with 100 to 200 students, but these are usually broken down into discussion sections with 20 to 25 students led by teaching assistants who, on the whole, seem competent. Professors are accessible, holding office hours to supplement their lectures, but some do complain of pressure to concentrate more heavily on research.

The BU campus, located on the Charles River in Boston's Back Bay, is small (99 acres) and bisected by a trolley line, but students don't seem to mind, perhaps because they consider all of Boston their bailiwick. Housing for underclassmen is usually in high rises; freshmen tend to live in Warren Towers, popularly known as the "Zoo," which has a capacity of 1,500. Other housing includes fraternities and sororities; honors, language, and special-interest houses; and dorms, both co-ed and single-sex.

DISTRIBUTION OF UNDERGRADUATE AID
1989–90 School Year

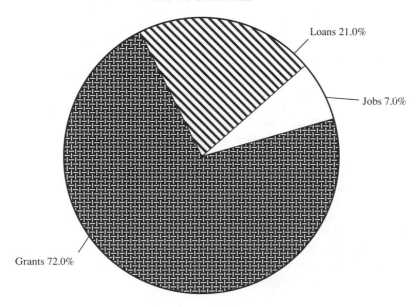

Loans 21.0%

Jobs 7.0%

Grants 72.0%

Source: The College Entrance Examination Board, 1990

Although housing is now guaranteed for all four years, only about 55 percent of students live on campus. Juniors and seniors typically move off campus to the surrounding areas of Allston, Brighton, Brookline, Back Bay, and Fenway. Naturally enough, conflicts sometimes arise between the students and the residents of these communities, but the BU Office of Community Relations does a good job of mediating disputes and keeping town-gown relations on an even keel.

Security has become a problem of late as the result of rising crime rates in Boston, which is no exception to this American blight. The university has acted expeditiously to safeguard the campus, however, and the BU police force now boasts a two-minute response time to emergency calls. There is an escort service; additional lighting and emergency phones are being installed where needed.

Socially, there is plenty to do, not only in the big city, but also within the university community itself. Between 10 and 15 percent of all undergraduates join fraternities and sororities and, both for those who do and those who don't, there is an array of 300 organized activities to choose from. As so many live off campus, students also become involved in community service, participating in neighborhood literacy, education, and preservation projects. The administration is proud of their dedication and does its best to foster this outreach.

Favorite campus hangouts are the George Sherman Union, which has a gamesroom, a deli-snack bar, and a cafeteria, the Science Center (with another snack bar), and the lawn of the College of Communications. Due to the university's huge size and its urban environment, however, students do tend to socialize in small groups with those they meet in their majors or clubs, and this can interfere with a sense of university identity.

Sports, however, definitely constitute a unifying force. Students enthusiastically support their often excellent teams, particularly in basketball and ice hockey. There are 12 intercollegiate and 10 intramural sports for men, and 10 intercollegiate and 19 intramural teams for women. Facilities include an athletic center, a 2,500-seat gymnasium, a 17,000-seat stadium, a swimming pool, a large ice arena, and a park for track and field. The university takes pride in the high academic standards of its varsity athletes.

Student government is not strong at BU, partly because President Silber (who returned early in 1991 after a leave of absence for his foray into politics) largely disregards it. He once lost patience with the Student Union and compared it to a four-year old. In 1989, only 17 percent of the student body bothered to vote in student government elections. Two special-interest groups in particular, however, have been active in trying to further their respective goals. Umoja (a black organization) keeps pushing minority issues, and the Lesbian/Gay Alliance has been fighting to have members' lifestyles specifically included in anti-harassment policies. So far the Alliance has failed, so that homosexuals in general have a much harder time advancing their agenda at BU than they do on many other campuses. The Martin Luther King, Jr. Center, named after BU's famous alumnus, helps students with academic and social problems, as well as job placements and internships. It also has a minority affairs division and a disability service center.

On the whole, the political climate on campus is not highly charged, with students about equally divided between Democrats and Republicans. The faculty is more liberal, but by no means radical. One wag has declared, however, that the most popular political party on campus is the Apathy Party. Students do not appear to be very interested in issues that divide other campuses, such as the battle against "Eurocentrism" (a popular major is Western European studies) and sensitivity and harassment codes, so there is no significant grass-roots movement to institute the latter. At present, the university has not proclaimed official policies on these subjects, nor has it initiated programs to indoctrinate students about how they should think and what they should, or should not, say to whom.

Although Boston University may not be a hotbed of controversy or a cauldron of excitement (except when President Silber mounts his charger), it does offer all the amenities of a most interesting and historic city, as well as a superb educational grounding for those who would rather hit the books than beat the drums for the latest cause.

Brandeis University

Dean of Admissions, Brandeis University, 415 South Street
Waltham, MA 02254-9110 (617) 736-3500, (800) 622-0622

Type: Private and Secular

Students:
2,941 undergraduates
  1,404 men
  1,537 women
  839 graduate students

Applications:
Closing date: February 1
69% of applicants accepted

Applied	Accepted	Enrolled
3,888	2,688	765

SAT or ACT required
  Score reported by: February 15
  Mid 50% of freshman scores:
    SAT-Math   N/A
    SAT-Verbal N/A

Costs and Aid:

Tuition and fees	$15,320
Room and Board	5,960

Scholarships:
Academic	Yes
Athletic	No
Minority	No

Financial Aid:
Freshmen	42%
Upperclassmen	42%

Library: 850,000 titles

ROTC: No

Study Abroad: Yes

Founded in 1948, Brandeis is doubly unique because it is the only Jewish-sponsored, nonsectarian university in the United States, as well as the nation's newest, major research university. From its inception, Brandeis, named after the distinguished Supreme Court Justice, was intended to serve as a proud symbol of the achievements of American Jewry, and to some extent it still does. But of late, the school has begun to seem somewhat embarrassed by its Jewish roots. In fact, during the tenure of President Evelyn Handler, who announced her resignation effective in June 1991, the administration initiated policies which have since been dubbed "dejudaization." These provoked considerable controversy in the Brandeis community and are reputed to be a factor in her resignation. President Handler's successor is Samuel Thier, M.D., formerly the president of the Institute of Medicine in Washington, D.C.

The thrust toward dejudaization reflects the university's efforts to "diversify" the largely Jewish student body by downplaying its Jewish character, in a sense misleading applicants. The school calendar has been changed to replace the names of religious holidays on which no classes are scheduled with the phrase, "No University Exercises."

Important university events, such as Convocation and Founders' Day, are often scheduled on Saturday mornings, excluding the participation of observant Jewish students, and no kosher food is served at such events. Most controversial of all was the introduction of pork and shellfish on campus in the fall of 1987. Despite student protests, dejudaization continues. In deference to religious students, however, Brandeis does maintain a large kosher dining hall, and classes are not scheduled on Jewish holidays. But these seem increasingly to be token gestures, and ones which more determined efforts at diversification may imperil.

The school's status as the nation's youngest major research university has also been a source of problems. Brandeis has invested heavily in order to acquire national prominence in research. The university maintains a medical research facility; science majors and pre-meds work with state-of-the-art equipment; the physics department boasts a Nobel laureate, and NASA astronauts have been hosted at its Spatial Orientation Laboratory. Ironically, the quest for scientific excellence has brought the university to an educational crossroads—whether to emphasize research or the liberal arts. Since its beginnings, Brandeis has believed it could do both, and has prided itself on being one of a very few liberal arts colleges able to offer the resources of a great research institution to undergraduates. Now it is rapidly losing that ability.

The debate between research and liberal arts revolves around money. The endowment of this young university of close to 3,900 students is small and, despite a fairly successful capital campaign to raise $200 million by 1991, the budget is very tight. Consequently, Brandeis relies heavily upon tuition fees—consistently among the highest in the nation.

Nonetheless, in May 1990, the administration published a "Strategic Plan" intended to eliminate a $51.4 million deficit by 1997. This plan, by augmenting the number of students, raising tuition by a further 20 percent, and increasing the student-faculty ratio, aims to produce a healthier balance sheet. Presumably, more students will bring in more money, but will it be enough, without substantial endowment, to maintain excellence both in research and teaching? Will Brandeis, in the end, have to sacrifice one or the other?

Whatever the future holds, undeniable academic advantages persist at Brandeis today. The faculty is top-notch and all professors teach, even the "stars" (who are always accessible to undergraduates). Although the Florence Heller School for Advanced Studies in Social

TUITION AND FEES INCREASE
Average Increase/Year: Private = 11.15%, Brandeis = 8.13%

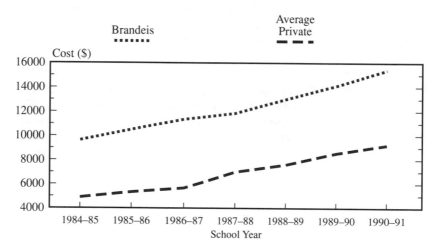

Source: The College Entrance Examination Board

Work is the university's only separate graduate school, there are four undergraduate units, which also confer graduate degrees. They are the Schools of Science, Social Science, Humanities and Creative Arts, which together form the College of Arts and Sciences. Among them, they enroll approximately 3,000 students, who come from 50 states and 50 foreign countries with a majority from the Northeast. About 15 percent are minorities.

The schools maintain an average class size of under 20; only a few introductory classes exceed 100 students, and they split into small sections to provide a more intimate setting. Near Eastern and Judaic studies and biochemistry are as good as any in the U.S.A., and pre-meds are pampered with special advisors and their own premedical center. Politics, history, English, and American studies are also outstanding. Philosophy, on the other hand, is notably weak.

Course registration offers a popular two-week "shopping period," during which students may audit classes and then make their final decisions. The registration process itself runs smoothly with almost all students gaining admission to their first-choice classes. International programs are also very successful, with more than one-third of the junior class going abroad. The most favored destinations are Israel and

England where Brandeis participates in a student-exchange program with Oxford University.

Academic standards at Brandeis are rigorous. Professors generally do not hesitate to give out Fs, and grading is uniformly tough. The old Ivy League maxim that "the hardest part is getting in" undergoes a reversal at Brandeis; admission is not very difficult, but graduating can be. While most comparable schools offer a one-to two-week reading period before finals, for example, Brandeis generally allows one day, and there is often no break between classes and finals.

Brandeis has no core curriculum, but it does have a system of distribution requirements called the "University Studies" program, which has recently been revised to add non-Western and comparative studies. To graduate, students must complete 32 semester courses, seven of which must be taken in the six university studies program areas: the humanities; science and mathematics; creative arts; historical studies; social analysis; and non-Western and comparative studies.

In the humanities, students must choose in sequence two courses

DISTRIBUTION OF UNDERGRADUATE AID
1989–90 School Year

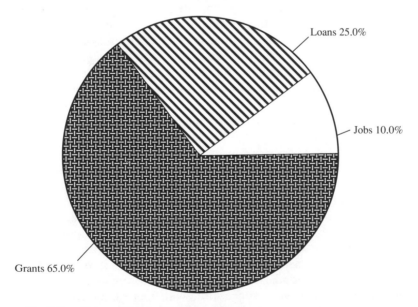

Loans 25.0%

Jobs 10.0%

Grants 65.0%

Source: The College Entrance Examination Board, 1990

(step one and step two) that deal first with ancient texts from the earliest through the classical Christian era, and then go on to reflect new elements in later Western civilization. Examples are: "Conflict and Moral Choice" as related to Greek, Roman and Biblical texts; "The Canon"; "Understanding Evil and Human Destiny"; and "Self-Images of the Modern Age." Three papers and two essay examinations are assigned in each course.

In mathematics and science, two courses are required from among three options—two courses in biology, chemistry, or biochemistry (usually selected by science or pre-med majors); one in physical or chemical science and one in biological or biochemical science (usually chosen by students weak in science); one in mathematics or computer science and one from any of the offerings in options one and two.

In historical studies, social analysis, and non-Western and comparative studies, students must enroll in one course each from two of the three areas. All courses are designed to explore themes in the development of Western civilization, from "Faith and Reason in Human Culture," and "An Intellectual History of Modern Europe and America" to "The History of the Family," "Africa and the West," and "Nationalism and Ethnicity in the Modern World." To top off, students must elect one course in the creative arts and must fulfill a writing requirement unless they can place out of it through examination or satisfactory advanced placement scores. Two physical education courses and a swim test are also mandatory for graduation.

Brandeis has never been a school for jocks—which may explain the physical education requirement—but the university is finally beginning to flex its athletic muscles. Although it has always had adequate teams in basketball, soccer, and track, its facilities have been antiquated. In 1989, the university began a total overhaul of its crumbling Shapiro Gymnasium. The facility is to undergo a $25 million face-lift, to include new gyms, indoor tennis courts, squash and racquetball courts, and state-of-the-art weight training equipment. The planned Red Auerbach Sports and Convocation Center will be a welcome addition to the campus, as well as future host to the Boston Celtics's practices. Presently, there are 11 intercollegiate and 10 intramural teams for men, and 10 intercollegiates and 9 intramurals for women.

Undergraduates have a choice of coed housing through a lottery every spring. Students submit a list of choices, which is then processed by computer, and housing assignments are thus generated. Except for freshmen, students can live wherever they choose on the 235-acre campus, although upperclassmen do have preference. The options vary from singles and doubles to suites of up to eight, to off-campus apartments and condominiums owned by the university. The most spectacular residence is certainly Brandeis's replica of a castle, with winding stairs and oddly shaped rooms. Under 10 percent of students live off campus in easily available, affordable private housing.

Students gripe justifiably about the social life. Alcohol is prohibited at non-university sponsored parties, and even these are few and far between. A student-run group, Student Events (SE), is in charge of the major social activities on campus, and all students contribute a fee toward its budget. SE sponsors pre-finals party weekends, concerts, and occasional dances; yet these events are often ill-conceived and poorly attended. More often than not, students are responsible for their own social lives, and this results in a fairly cliquish campus. A few Jewish fraternities and sororities have recently sprung up. They are unrecognized and even reviled by the administration, and are met with general hostility by the student body. The groups do give weekly parties, seemingly the principle attraction of membership. For the most part though, weekends are quiet at Brandeis, and students use them to play catch-up with their studies.

The remarkably rich, extracurricular life compensates for the weaknesses in social life. New clubs are chartered weekly, and Brandeis's "non-exclusionary rule" mandates that all groups have open membership. The university has 11 student-run publications, an active Hillel chapter, myriad student musical groups, and dozens of special-interest, minority, and political clubs.

It is on the political front that Brandeis's extracurricular activities gain greatest momentum, and it is also here that the university's traditional liberalism takes a sharp left turn. Except for one conservative magazine and the College Republicans, Brandeis's political groups are uniformly left-wing. Triskelion, the homosexual advocacy group, is reputedly the largest student organization on campus, followed by the increasingly radical reproductive rights group, Brandeis Voice for Choice. The Brandeis Black Student Organization is also very powerful despite the relatively small black population.

In March 1990, black students alleged that the campus bookstore had a "racist" policy concerning customers "of color." They boycotted the store and clamored for the "removal" of the bookstore's two managers. Ultimately the managers were removed. This incident has since generated major student backlash and considerable ill will. Yet Brandeis is not without its dissenters from the general, radical political tone. College Republicans has more than 250 members, and the conservative publication (*The Brandeisian*) is now the most active magazine on campus. Indeed, activism subscribes to a modified boom-bust cycle: Apathy—left-wing protest—resolution—moderate back-lash—apathy. Each incidence of backlash helps to strengthen the conservative presence.

Although the Brandeis *ambience* is decidedly left of center, the university's Jewish heritage still saves its academics from conquest by the new barbarians. But Brandeis's ambivalence about its Jewish character and mission versus its secular aspirations is taking a toll. The new administration will need to resolve this tension if Brandeis's future is to shine as brightly as its brief past.

Brown University

Dean of Admission and Financial Aid, Brown University
P.O. Box 1876, Providence, RI 02912 (401) 863-2378

				Costs and Aid:	
Type: Private and Secular				Tuition and Fees	$15,870
Students:				Room and Board	4,980
5,970 undergraduates				Scholarships:	
3,178 men				Academic	No
2,792 women				Athletic	No
1,618 graduate students				Minority	No
Applications:				Financial Aid:	
Closing date: January 1				Freshmen	36%
24% of applicants accepted				Upperclassmen	32%
	Applied	*Accepted*	*Enrolled*		
men	6,057	1,435	730	**Library:**	2,116,673 titles
women	5,660	1,355	681	**ROTC:**	No
SAT or ACT required				**Study Abroad:**	Yes
Score reported by: March 1					
Mid 50% of freshman scores:					
SAT-Math	620–730				
SAT-Verbal	560–680				

About 20 years ago, Brown was an afterthought in the Ivy League, but its fortunes have taken a turn for the better since. Without doubt, its popularity among prospective undergraduates derived from its then new policy of having a non-curriculum. At the new Brown, there were to be no requirements and a generous use of the pass/fail system. Before then, there had been requirements of various kinds, but the reformers believed they interfered with the goals of liberal education. Fortuitously, the 20th anniversary of this innovation coincided with the arrival of a new university president, Vartan Gregorian, who commissioned a retrospective analysis. In general, the school has announced itself satisfied with the status quo. The core curriculum, the president says, is more appropriate to the high school than the college. And besides, there is no arguing with the fact that, while applications may be down at other institutions, they are holding firm, indeed increasing, at Brown.

Without doubt, Brown's decision to abandon its older approach, and its subsequent successes in the applications marketplace (it's now called "enrollment management" at some colleges), had a profound

47

influence throughout American undergraduate education. It caught, rather nicely, the spirit of the age, namely that the expression of feelings might legitimately be substituted for intellectual exercise, thus making life easier for both student and teacher by making it virtuous to be, well, lazy.

Success, however, creates problems of its own, for it is now difficult for Brown to be at the cutting edge, or to be a trendsetter, from its current lofty perch. For instance, Brown would be less than true to its 1970s self if it were to *require* the study of one or another of the new academic fads—homosexual studies, for example—but it just might come to that. The Gregorian era searches for innovations uniquely its own, and it is starting to find them, even if they are not turning out in the manner intended.

Catalog of the University for the years 1989–91:
Political Science 114—Justice and Gender
Professor Nancy Rosenblum

"Course discusses the relevancy of gender for justice. We ask whether women are capable of being just, how men and women define the goods to be distributed, and what a just distribution would be."

English 39B—Lesbian and Gay Literature: Post Structuralist and Literary Theory
Mr. Kopelson

"Twentieth-century lesbian and gay literary texts and selected issues in contemporary literary theory."

Brown is beginning to become famous once again, not so much as an innovator, but as a kind of *reductio ad absurdum*. Without meaning to, it has launched a nationwide debate. It started, amusingly enough, in the fall of 1990, when the interfraternity council decided to ban ethnic theme parties, after complaints that a "South of the Border" party had offended an Hispanic sophomore. This case of self-imposed sensitivity training provoked a bit of a backlash, and led to the popularization of the term "politically correct" as a description of the grab-bag of leftist causes. The term, it seems, was first popularized by Jeffrey Shesol, a cartoonist for the student newspaper, whose parodies of this sophomoric left-wing earnestness soon became renowned throughout the country.

TUITION AND FEES INCREASE
Average Increase/Year: Private = 11.15%, Brown = 7.63%

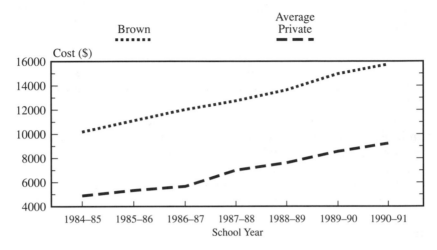

Source: The College Entrance Examination Board

And, as if on cue, President Gregorian, a successful academic adept and not usually the victim of a tin ear on matters of this kind, decided that he needed to turn himself into a real-life example of young Shesol's parody. In a case that drew nationwide attention in the spring of 1991, Gregorian announced the expulsion of a student for violations of Brown's "hate speech" rules. Apparently the young man, while drunk, in the middle of the night shouted out some ugly racial epithets to any of the 20 percent minority population who might have been listening. As the argument about the student's fate raged, Gregorian decided that what he was punishing was not speech, but conduct. So, what began as a campus disciplinary matter somehow managed to lead to an op-ed piece in the *New York Times* where in convoluted—some would say Orwellian—prose, President Gregorian tried to talk himself and his school out of the predicament into which his desire to prove his right-mindedness had led. This dispute, though silly in itself (except for the victim, of course), reveals what happens when a college, having decided that there is not much left for it to do educationally, still tries to fill up time.

Such typical modernism would not necessarily please the band of Baptists who started little Rhode Island College in Warren in 1765.

Brown, as it was renamed in 1804, is thus older than the United States, and like the other venerable Ivy League colleges encapsulates the history of higher education in the country. Brown added graduate studies in the 1880s, women in the 1890s (Pembroke, Brown's renowned coordinate college for women, disappeared in 1971 by merger), and a full-fledged medical school in 1973. But Brown is different from many of the others in that undergraduates still predominate—there are only about 1,600 graduate students in an overall population of about 7,500.

Interestingly, there has been an unheralded but significant build-up in Brown's capacities to offer instruction in science and engineering, even as its traditional liberal arts programs have become trendily flaccid. (The B.S. program in engineering, an unlikely Ivy League option to begin with, is outstanding, confirming a general national trend that the sciences remain relatively unaffected by the debasement of the curriculum in the humanities and social sciences—so far.) Ironically, Brown seems well-designed to concentrate its resources on

DISTRIBUTION OF UNDERGRADUATE AID
1989–90 School Year

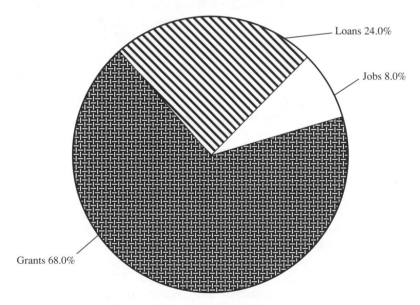

Source: The College Entrance Examination Board, 1990

undergraduate liberal arts instruction and yet, paradoxically, the school encourages a minimum amount of "adult" intervention in the process.

This minimalism leads to inconsistent reactions and impressions on the part of students. Some swear by the system; some leave with the conviction that they have been seriously shortchanged, that it may have been fun while it lasted, but that not much more than the memory lingers. This, too, may explain the difficulties in getting consensus opinions about the strength of departments. Significantly, three thought by some to be among the best—geology, computer science, and economics—are "harder" disciplines, less vulnerable to ideological corruptions. The departments thought by many to be the worst— history, political science, and religious studies—are also disciplines which have proved less capable of defending themselves against corrosive attack.

Though Brown may be atypical, even by contemporary standards, in its devil-may-care approach to the college's instructional responsibility toward its students, it is amusingly typical in its self-absorption, in its obsession with "caring," "awareness," "concern," "diversity," "sharing," "dialogue," and other such empty concepts. (About 15 years ago, the faculty, perhaps too tired from mere "thinking," created a whole series of courses concerned with "modes of thought"; similarly, there is a companion known generally as "modes of analysis." The purpose is to give students "new awareness.")

The main areas for the application of this terminology are relationships between the sexes and among the races. The former is, of course, a perennial problem. The latter results from the fact that about a quarter of the undergraduates are now of minority background. As at other places, the "adjustment" implicit in this seems extraordinarily difficult to make, even though it should not be. Some students report that, left to their own devices, they themselves would be able to work things out, as young people always have. But the administration, they claim, is committed to harping on the subject at every available opportunity, as if to make sure that problems never go away, but are perpetuated. Indeed, as at many other colleges, a Brown bureaucracy has grown up whose job is to "manage diversity"; there is thus a vested interest in insuring that things always seem to be going badly. This is now a permanent feature of college life.

Brown's compact 146-acre Providence campus contributes to a kind of inward-looking also. The city is not especially stimulating. Almost all undergraduates live on campus, mostly in the dormitories, though there are some who join the 11 fraternities and single sorority, especially now that the coed fraternity chapter has appeared. To cut costs, the school decided in the spring of 1991 to drop four of its 32 intercollegiate teams (men's golf and water polo; women's gymnastics and volleyball), but there are still plenty of activities for jocks, and a myriad of intramural sports. As on any active and lively campus, there are dozens (150) of extracurricular activities and plenty of opportunities for writing or performing.

Brown's habits are now ingrained enough so that their effect is pervasive. Most campuses report some dissent from the reigning liberal orthodoxies, and there is some at Brown too, but even the conservative backlash, such as it is, is of the soggy Brown sort. Indeed, so far as the intrastudent body debate is concerned, the conservative wing finds itself as much committed to individual expression and non-conformity as the opponents with whom it appears to be arguing. Thus, students who feel inspired to become part of a truly feisty minority at Brown will probably be disappointed.

In the spring of 1991, prospective graduates from prestigious institutions like Brown began to report substantial difficulties in finding jobs in the "real world." The job crunch highlighted once again the old arguments about the value of liberal arts training in general, and the unusually delicate Brown variant of it in particular. So far, developments within the academy have not provided much of a corrective to the trends that have stressed not knowledge of anything but "knowing" in general, not learning but "approaches" to it—and all the rest of Brown's high-tuition cant. Whether the market can do what criticism has failed to accomplish remains to be seen. But for Brown, the growing estrangement between the ivory tower and the real world is not a problem, but still a source of pride.

Bryn Mawr College

Director of Admissions, Bryn Mawr College
Bryn Mawr, PA 19010 (215) 526-5152

			Costs and Aid:	
Type: Private and Secular			Tuition and Fees	$14,580
Students:			Room and Board	5,500
1,312 undergraduates			Scholarships:	
1,280 women			Academic	No
32 men			Athletic	No
527 graduate students			Minority	No
Applications:			Financial Aid:	
Closing date: January 15			Freshmen	48%
57% of applicants accepted			Upperclassmen	48%
	Applied	*Accepted*	*Enrolled*	
women	1,423	804	327	**Library:** 850,000 titles
SAT required				
Score reported by: February 15			**ROTC:**	Yes
Mid 50% of freshman scores:			**Study Abroad:**	Yes
SAT-Math	580–670		**Percentage of courses that can**	
SAT-Verbal	570–680		**be used to fulfill distribution**	
			requirements:	73.7

Bryn Mawr College, situated on a beautiful Gothic campus outside Philadelphia, was founded in 1885 to offer a higher education to conservative Quaker women. It is currently nonsectarian, still all female, but definitely no longer conservative. Today Bryn Mawr is a tight little island of feminism and political correctness. Long recognized as one of the best liberal arts colleges in the country, the school still ranks high academically, but its radical atmosphere and small size don't leave much breathing room for those who won't conform to the prevailing orthodoxy.

Even though Bryn Mawr is top-ranked academically, the undergraduate admissions office turns down no more than half its applicants. This is partly because single-sex education is generally unpopular, but also because applying to Bryn Mawr is a process of self-selection; on the whole, only those young women who are very serious about their work and their causes want to go there. As a result, the student body is highly motivated both in and out of the classroom.

Many of the approximately 1,300 Bryn Mawr women come from educated and sometimes affluent backgrounds. Most are from the

53

Middle Atlantic states, but all states are usually represented, as well as 40 to 50 foreign countries. Twenty percent are minorities; 5 percent are Asian or Asian-American. Bryn Mawr operates on the semester system and requires 32 courses (units) for graduation. The college offers graduate degrees in the liberal arts and in social work; as far as undergraduate work goes, the most popular majors are English, economics, and the natural and physical sciences.

The Undergraduate College Catalog and Calendar, 1990–91:
Feminist and Gender Studies

"The bi-college [Bryn Mawr and Haverford] concentration in feminist and gender studies is committed to the interdisciplinary study of women and gender. The program includes courses on women's experiences considered both historically and cross-culturally, on literature by and about women, on gender roles and gender socialization, and on gender bias in theories and theoretical aspects of attempts to account for gender differences. Students plan their programs in consultation with the feminist and gender studies adviser on their home campus and members of the Faculty Committee on Feminism and Gender Studies."

There is no core curriculum and the distribution requirements are complex. In addition to departmental requirements in the major, the general components are: two courses in English composition, unless exempted; one in quantitative skills; seven to meet the "divisional" requirement, which involves two in the social sciences, two in the natural sciences, and three in the humanities; a foreign language requirement, which mandates demonstrated competency through examination, or obtaining a C average in two courses above the elementary level. Students must also pass with a C two courses in the same language at the advanced level, or "attain knowledge of a second foreign language," or (this is still part of the *foreign language* requirement) complete two courses in mathematics, including at least one semester of calculus. In addition, Mawrters (as students are generally known) must complete eight terms (half a semester each) of physical education, and pass a swimming test.

One major advantage of the small-school atmosphere is the intimate relationship between faculty and students, which persists in spite of faculty interest in research. Professors seldom turn their classes over to teaching assistants, and are accessible and eager to help the

TUITION AND FEES INCREASE
Average Increase/Year: Private = 11.15%, Bryn Mawr = 8.16%

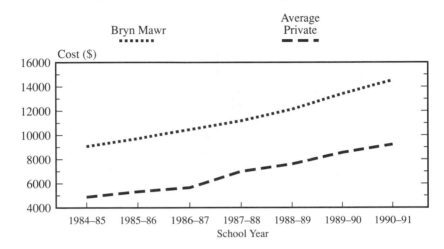

Source: The College Entrance Examination Board

students. For their senior projects, women work closely with their advising professors, often sharing research and sources. The administration at Bryn Mawr is also surprisingly approachable. The deans serve as both professors and curriculum advisers, and the president of the college often mingles with the students at sports and social events. At the first party of each year the students become acquainted with the deans and president while enjoying the rare pleasure of being served food and drink by them.

Housing at Bryn Mawr is guaranteed for all four years and ranges from older, comfortable dorms to unattractive, modern buildings. Dorms hold between 60 and 80 students and all classes are mixed. As well as language and special-interest houses, there are two coed dorms for visiting students from Swarthmore and Haverford, with whom the school has traditionally had close relationships. In order to offer a wider range of courses and activities than would otherwise be possible at such a small college, Bryn Mawr runs an exchange program with both Swarthmore and Haverford, which allows students to take classes and to live for considerable periods on any of the three campuses. It is also possible to choose courses at the University of Pennsylvania, although the ride into downtown Philadelphia discourages many students from taking advantage of the larger school.

The general tone on the Bryn Mawr campus is strictly academic; the work is very intense and the students immerse themselves in it. There is often a line in front of the main library on weekends and few study tables are free before midnight. Mawrters are generally considered uptight about their work but are not cutthroat about it. The students' own honor code forbids discussion of grades and exams, a practice the administration feels only adds to tension and causes unnecessary competition among students.

The honor code is one way in which students at Bryn Mawr are given control over their community. Each representative to the Honor Board is elected by the student body and presides over confidential cases of violations of both the academic and the social honor codes. Many examinations are self-scheduled and cheating is rare. Students do not use the code as a form of policing so much as a method for confronting behavior they find harmful to the college community.

DISTRIBUTION OF UNDERGRADUATE AID
1989–90 School Year

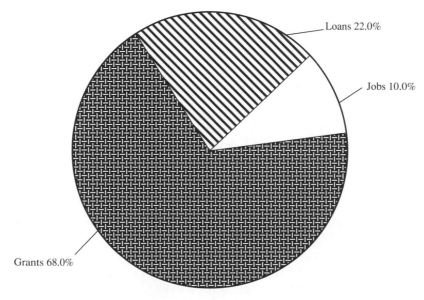

Loans 22.0%

Jobs 10.0%

Grants 68.0%

Source: The College Entrance Examination Board, 1990

Bryn Mawr's Student Government Association was one of the first student-run governments to be established in the country. All policies affecting the community are drafted by it and must be approved by the student body. Recently, in response to Pennsylvania's crackdown on alcohol abuse, the students voluntarily restricted their own drinking and are expected to monitor that restriction, as regulated by the honor code.

As you might guess, social life at Bryn Mawr is limited. Before the new alcohol policy went into effect, each dormitory gave one party a semester, and private groups were always willing to open their doors to the college community. Although the legal drinking age was 21, the law was not enforced. Now alcohol is allowed only at private parties in students' rooms and the crowds they attract often cause noise-conscious security officers to break them up early.

Bryn Mawr has yet to establish an effective social committee to arrange alternative entertainment to the popular, college-sponsored, all-campus parties. Students are forced to rely on the closed, private parties, or—due to lack of parking space—to go into Philadelphia on one of the nation's most expensive public transportation systems. The unsatisfactory social scene is not helped by the tension that began between Haverford and Bryn Mawr when Haverford went coed a number of years ago. Since a single-sex college cannot provide the same level of social life as a coed school, jealousies tend to reinforce the stereotypes of the boring, uptight Mawrter and the giggling, airhead "Ford" woman, thus keeping a lot of students away from bi-college activities. The exception is perhaps at Step Sing, one of the many traditions carried over from early years that still act as a unifying element enjoyed by both colleges.

Athletics, like social life, play a strictly secondary role to academics at Bryn Mawr. Students may either take part in self-paced exercise, or play on a varsity team to satisfy their gym requirements. The physical education department has raised its standards during the last few years, so that students of lesser athletic ability may now be cut from teams which were previously open to all. There are eight intercollegiate sports, and several intramurals. Facilities include a new gymnasium and an Olympic-size swimming pool. Much to everyone's surprise, Mawrters have recently won district titles in several sports. These successes put added pressure on the players, however, who are now forced to make choices between studying and sports, a state of affairs that was previously inconceivable at Bryn Mawr.

Except in academics and the use of alcohol, the administration is reluctant to interfere in any aspect of student life. Bryn Mawr women tend to be very determined and vocal about what they believe; the prevailing ideology is overwhelmingly leftist and militantly feminist with definite lesbian overtones. Minority groups, such as the Sisterhood (the black students' association) and the lesbian and bisexual groups, are very prominent on campus, and issues concerning these and other minorities form the focus of campus discussion. Most students are also active in supporting their pet political causes, and because the student body is so cause-oriented it is easy to raise volunteers for almost any project, the less conventional the better.

The college often calls itself "diverse," and "pluralism" is a campus ideal. Pluralism workshops were begun several years ago in answer to the growing number of reports of discrimination against minorities, including not only the few blacks on campus and the larger number of Asian-Americans, but also a substantial representation from India. These workshops are mandatory for all freshmen and aim to give the newcomers a chance to discuss sensitive issues, such as racism and homophobia, with various members of the faculty and administration.

What often happens, however, is that freshmen are told just how a Mawrter should think. The Mawrter image is a very powerful symbol, and one must be PC, that is, politically correct, to truly belong. The college's student handbook trumpets this attitude in an exposition of the honor code: "We recognize that acts of discrimination and harassment, including but NOT [capitals in the text] limited to acts of racism, homophobia, classism, ableism and discrimination against religious and political minorities are devoid of respect and therefore, by definition violate this Code."

Diversity at Bryn Mawr is generally understood to be a characteristic of groups not individuals; if you can show that you support rights and special privileges for minority groups you will be embraced at Bryn Mawr. Respect for individuals seems to be based upon how far they diverge from the mainstream, as evidenced by the popularity of campus cults, such as the Pagans, the Witches, and the Werewolves. These are tantamount to secret societies, the precise nature of whose activities is generally a mystery to nonmembers. The only exceptions are the Werewolves, who go very public when they regularly wake up the campus in the dead of night by baying loudly at the moon. Tolerant though the rest of the Mawrters may be, they need their sleep after grinding so hard, and a few brave voices have been weakly raised in protest against the howling.

Christians, on the other hand, are not regarded as being respectably "diverse"; they are forced to practice their religion privately, making many feel not like Mawrters but like martyrs instead. The conventionally religious are often accused of proselytizing when they advertise their faith, unlike the cults which are merely exercising their "rights." An example of anti-religious sentiment occurred during Eastertide 1990, when Christians put up small-sized notices announcing Christ's Resurrection and the joy of Easter. This caused a tremendous uproar; protesters tore down the notices and, outraged at what they called "Christian oppression," loudly chastised and ridiculed those who had dared to mount them. In contrast, cult signs, regularly displayed, were accepted without objection.

If the college could bring itself to concentrate on arranging for a less incestuous and more interesting social life, perhaps Mawrters would channel their energies and vivid imaginations into more constructive outlets, instead of getting their kicks out of wailing like werewolves and rebelling indiscriminately against conventional society. The admissions policy would also benefit by recruiting women from more varied economic backgrounds, so that the college community could draw on the common sense, knowledge, and experience of those from different levels of American society.

The good news is that, however radical the personal views of faculty and administration, Bryn Mawr's traditional respect for academic rigor has prevented most professors from using the classroom lectern as a bully pulpit. Except in red-flagged areas like sociology, peace, and feminist and gender studies, courses are not rewritten to discredit Western civilization and dead white males. So, if she chooses her academics carefully and escapes the cloistered radicals often enough when the working day is done, the Mawrter can still achieve a superb liberal arts education.

University of California at Berkeley

Director of Admissions and Records
University of California at Berkeley
120 Sproul Hall, Berkeley, CA 94720 (415) 642-0200

Type: Public

Students:
22,248 undergraduates
  11,772 men
  10,476 women
  8,873 graduate students

Applications:
Priority date: November 1
Closing date: November 30
37% of applicants accepted
SAT or ACT required
  Score reported by: January 1
  Mid 50% of freshman scores:
    SAT-Math   630–720
    SAT-Verbal 470–550

Costs and Aid:

Tuition and fees:		
In state		$1,640
Out of state		7,560
Room and Board		5,570
Scholarships:		
Academic		Yes
Athletic		Yes
Minority		Yes
Financial Aid:		
Freshmen		41%
Upperclassmen		48%
Library:		6,504,230 titles
ROTC:		Yes
Study Abroad:		Yes
Percentage of courses that can be used to fulfill distribution requirements:		65.9

Call it Cal, UC-Berkeley, the University of California at Berkeley, UCB, or even California. But whatever you do, don't call it just plain Berkeley anymore. The university, while still leaning leftward, no longer appreciates being identified with the city that has become a showcase for radical activists and the political stamping ground of former hippies and flower children. In the 1990s, UC-Berkeley is trying instead for a mainstream public image, while continuing to promote its own radical agenda among students, who are generally more moderate than their peers who made headlines a generation ago.

Founded without much regard for politics back in 1868, the future flagship of the UC system modestly opened its doors five years later on 160 acres, and less modestly sought to emulate Harvard and Yale by requiring core courses for its 191 students in Latin, Greek, English, mathematics, history, and natural history. Today, more than 166,000 students and 7,000 full-time faculty rush to and fro on nine campuses,

61

and choose from thousands of courses on almost every imaginable topic.

The Berkeley campus, which has grown to more than 1,200 acres, hosts 31,000 of these students, 22,000 of whom are undergraduates. The university's original creed—that a sound liberal arts education must be based on a common core of knowledge—is now as outdated at Berkeley as the California gold rush. Instead, students peruse the academic menu, decide what looks tasty, and then choose their own courses—with one notable exception.

In addition to the 120 hours needed for graduation, one of the few common requisites for undergraduates is the new and controversial American Cultures Program, which began in the autumn of 1991. This obliges underclassmen to choose one course in the history and culture of at least three of five racial and ethnic groups on offer (Euro-Americans, blacks, Hispanics, Asians, and American Indians). There are also demands for more minority faculty hiring.

In addition to the American Cultures requirement, Letters and Science (L&S) students are required to take one semester of math, one semester of U.S. history (a campus-wide requirement), and two semesters of a foreign language. The latter two requirements can be waived through high school work, and all can be waived by examination. A year-long reading and composition sequence is required, as well as six courses outside the field of the major (i.e., social science majors must take courses in humanities and science, etc.).

In spite of the de-emphasis on Western civilization and values, at one of the nation's pre-eminent public universities the anti-establishment 1960s are over at last. To be sure, popular political causes, demonstrations on Sproul Plaza, and daily activist speeches never cease, but these events, seldom attracting more than 30 participants each, are viewed as noontime entertainment by the majority of under-graduates and as a distraction by the university.

Today, the administration seeks to concentrate the white glare of publicity not on the student body's political differences but on its ethnic, racial, and sexual diversity instead. Those who oppose this unrelenting focus on dissimilarities rather than commonalities are automatically and arrogantly tarred with the brush of racism, homo-phobia, or just plain stupidity. The radicals, among faculty, administra-tors, and students alike, exercise more influence on policy than their relatively small numbers would indicate, probably because of the political indifference of most of their fellows, 86 percent of whom

TUITION AND FEES INCREASE
Average Increase/Year: Public = 8.30%, UC-Berkeley = 3.40%

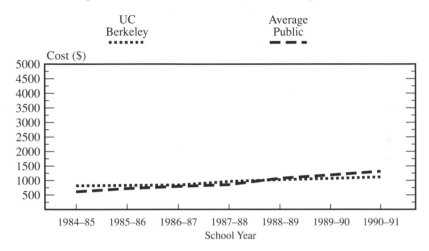

Source: The College Entrance Examination Board

---

come from California, with the rest from every state in the Union and 100 foreign countries.

Even though most students are politically apathetic, a sensitivity code prohibiting "fighting words" has been put in place to punish the politically incorrect. Students say its specific provisions are not widely publicized, though everyone knows the code exists. The policy defines fighting words as harassment

> when the circumstances of their utterance create a hostile and intimidating environment which the student uttering them should reasonably know will interfere with the victim's ability to pursue effectively his or her education or otherwise to participate fully in University programs and activities.

Penalties are imposed for violations by the Student Conduct Office, which sometimes behaves like the old Nazi Gestapo.

In one recent incident, a fraternity member, who had been partying, impulsively pinned the Confederate flag on the outside of the fraternity house. Politically correct students reported him to the administration, and the whole fraternity was subjected to a compulsory sensitivity training session, and asked to seek out more minority members.

Another incident produced a very different result. Two female members of the Jewish Student Union were recruiting for the organization when members of the Black Muslim Union spotted them, and began loudly harassing them with anti-Semitic remarks. A small crowd gathered and egged the Muslims on. The women, in tears, fled and reported the incident to the Student Conduct Office, wanting the fighting words code invoked. They were told that they ought to develop "thicker skins" and nothing was done. No sensitivity-awareness training was thought necessary for the Black Muslim bigots.

"Excellence and Diversity" is the current campus litany, and although efforts are made to achieve both, the university clearly puts diversity first and foremost, regardless of the consequences. As the general catalog proudly states, "The student body can *best* (emphasis added) be characterized by its diversity . . ."

State-mandated policy presently requires that 40 percent of the

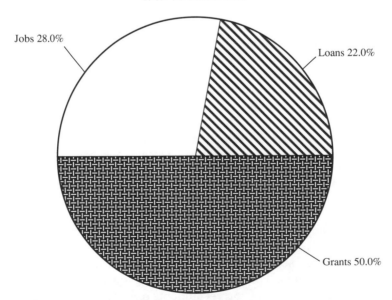

DISTRIBUTION OF UNDERGRADUATE AID
1989–90 School Year

Jobs 28.0%

Loans 22.0%

Grants 50.0%

Source: The College Entrance Examination Board, 1990

incoming freshman class be admitted under affirmative action. Of this group 25 percent are admitted under minimum University of California standards; the rest come in under Special Admissions, which waives these standards. Special Admissions includes athletes, the disabled, and children of alumni, along with minority groups. The rest of the freshman class is accepted by grades and test scores only (40 percent), or a combination of the application essay and extracurricular activities (20 percent). All this adds up to only 40 percent of students being admitted by academic criteria alone.

The result of this policy is that Cal is now fully integrated, in the sense that no single ethnic or racial group constitutes a majority, and it is achieving this result by the bald use of quotas. Since 1980, the percentage of white students has dropped from 66 percent to less than 45 percent; 27 percent are Asian, 13 percent are Hispanic.

Although the administration is well satisfied with this arrangement, for different reasons many students are not. On the one hand, some claim unfair reverse discrimination against white and Asian applicants, who are rejected in spite of possessing higher academic qualifications than many who are accepted. On the other hand, minority students complain that no matter how hard they work, they are not esteemed by their fellows because, as one black student put it, "I feel like I have affirmative action stamped on my forehead." Tension and dissension arise, therefore, between the groups protected by affirmative action and those which are not.

Besides undermining student relations and the old-fashioned spirit of collegiality that once was deemed essential to learning, the quotas policy raises questions about another sort of relationship—between excellence and diversity. If admissions standards are systematically lowered for a substantial number of students in pursuit of diversity, can the university over time maintain its other standard, excellence?

For now, the University of California is still riding high in terms of academic reputation in research and graduate studies. UC-Berkeley alone boasts 9 Nobel laureates, 94 members of the National Academy of Sciences, and 60 members of the National Academy of Engineering. Stars like these make the university ideal for the bright, assertive student, who may be uncertain about a future career but who wants to be assured of a high-quality education no matter what he studies. But less aggressive—and less well-prepared—students may get lost in the shuffle.

For many colleges, the story goes, once a student receives an acceptance letter, the most difficult stage is over—but at Berkeley, admission is only the first challenge. As a huge public university Cal offers an overwhelming variety of student services, social and extra-curricular activities, faculty contacts and opportunities—but you are left to discover and utilize the university system and resources on your own. You get very little help. The two most common frustrations are crowded classes and lack of housing. By the end of his Cal career, a student has either acquired the survival skills of resourcefulness and persistence, or has transferred elsewhere.

On the academic side, it is not unusual for a student—particularly a freshman—to be denied entry to all his first-choice courses due to overcrowding. Many lower-division undergraduate courses are huge (a few with more than 500 students). A peculiar phenomenon at Cal is that the large lecture courses are usually jammed with literally hundreds of students, while the small, more intimate classes are proportionately not so popular. Nobody seems to know why. The large courses, however, usually break down into discussion groups led by teaching assistants, who are often well on their way to their doctorates. Although their teaching ability varies, they are generally knowledgeable, friendly, and accessible to students outside of class.

This does not compensate, however, for the overcrowding. Required composition and writing courses are often in such short supply that many students are given until their junior or senior years to fulfill the requirement. The average age for all undergraduates is 23 and it is common to take five years to graduate. Long lines also plague students. Queues for registration, financial aid, and adds/drops are daunting, wasting time and fraying tempers. The university, however, is working hard to improve this situation.

Even in so large and bureaucratic a community, however, opportunities do exist to meet the faculty through brown-bag seminars and office hours. Though few students regularly take advantage of these extras, those who do describe their experiences as rewarding. All this, combined with the flexibility in most programs, is a definite plus for motivated self-starters.

The Berkeley library system deserves special mention because it is world class, not far behind Harvard and Yale for total volumes (seven million). Besides the two main libraries, two dozen specialized libraries are dotted around the campus. Many of the materials, including everything that was acquired since 1970, are catalogued in an easy-to-use computer database, but the wealth of information can be confusing to the novice.

The housing crisis can also be confusing, as well as annoying, to the new student. Not even freshmen are guaranteed housing. The university provides space for close to 10,000 students, who are chosen by lottery, with preference given to lower-division students. Residence halls are single-sex and coed, and include language and special-interest houses, dormitories, and co-ops. Those who must live off campus are left to compete in Berkeley's limited housing market—afflicted by the double jeopardy of the city's firm no-growth policy and rent control. Living quarters do exist, of course, but it takes energy and ingenuity to find them.

Even when you do, most units are old and/or very small. Streets have many potholes, and homeless vagrants roam them panhandling students in large numbers. Crime is especially high in southwest Berkeley and near People's Park. Women are advised not to walk alone on campus at night. For the past two or three years there have been riots, looting, and vandalism nearby.

When they tire of studying, leaping over potholes, or recalling the 1960s, students can find much to keep their minds and bodies active. The campus itself is a green oasis in the middle of built-up, urban Berkeley. Few cars are allowed on the premises (the disabled can park on campus), and there are lots of pleasant, tree-lined walkways. The buildings are an eye-catching mix of architectural styles, often in white or black granite. (No brick is used, as it is susceptible to earthquake damage.) With its two creeks and shady groves of redwood and eucalyptus trees, the Berkeley campus is an inviting place to study out of doors, or to participate in sports and extracurricular activities.

Athletes may compete in 13 intercollegiate sports for men and 11 intercollegiate sports for women. There are also 30 intramural sports, some coed, some single-sex, and many sports clubs. Besides the usual facilities, there are no fewer than seven swimming pools in competition with nearby beaches.

San Francisco, with its theaters, shopping, and restaurants, is only a short trip on BART (the light rail system). Berkeley's academic café scene reinforces the 1960s time warp atmosphere, resulting in a unique cultural and social flavor. On campus, students face an array of 370 organizations and clubs—ranging from the Gay-Lesbian-Bisexual Alliance and the Young Spartacus League to the Berkeley College Republicans.

Cal hosts 42 fraternities and 15 sororities, so a vibrant Greek life exists for those who wish to partake of it (roughly a quarter of the student body), but this does not dominate the social scene. In fact, no one aspect of life at Cal could be called dominant. In many ways the campus accurately reflects the California lifestyle—sweats and T-shirts are just as prevalent as stylish fashions. Intellectual discussions over espresso occur directly across the street from loud demonstrations. The heavy-drinking meat eaters coexist with the abstinent vegetarians. The political wolves, when exhausted from their exertions, occasionally lie down with the apathetic lambs.

But in the end, all fight for survival at Berkeley. Those who don't fall by the wayside still graduate with a highly respected degree; but this may not be the case for long if the university continues to dilute the academic quality of its student body through an admissions policy that puts diversity before excellence, and in many cases civility as well.

University of California at San Diego

Registrar and Admissions Officer
University of California at San Diego
Student Center, Building B, B-037, La Jolla, CA 92093-0037
(619) 534-4831

Type: Public

Students:
14,324 undergraduates
  7,596 men
  6,728 women
2,087 graduate students

Applications:
Closing date: November 30
55% of applicants accepted

	Applied	Accepted	Enrolled
men	9,339	5,193	1,342
women	9,682	5,293	1,398

SAT or ACT required
  Score reported by: January 15
  Mid 50% of freshman scores:
    SAT-Math 530–660
    SAT-Verbal 440–570

Costs and Aid:
Tuition and fees

In state	$1,730
Out of state	7,650
Room and Board	5,530

Scholarships:

Academic	Yes
Athletic	No
Minority	No

Financial Aid:

Freshmen	39%
Upperclassmen	31%

Library: 1,538,951 titles

ROTC: Yes

Study Abroad: Yes

The University of California at San Diego (UCSD) is comparatively new, having first opened its doors in 1959. Today, just over 30 years later, UCSD has achieved powerhouse status as a research institution, and on the undergraduate level boasts an unusual collegiate system based on the English Oxbridge model. Candidates for admission choose one of five colleges, each with different educational goals and requirements for graduation.

UCSD differs from most of its American counterparts in that its colleges do not specialize in specific disciplines (such as business, engineering, etc.); instead all five colleges offer all available majors. They differ from one another in atmosphere, educational philosophy, and student interests. The object is to personalize undergraduate education within a big university environment; therefore students apply to the college where they will feel most comfortable, the one most compatible with their interests and goals.

Before developing into a branch of the California university system, the San Diego campus had been a marine field station that eventually grew into the world-famous Scripps Institution of Oceanography, now affiliated with the university. The first new college to open was Revelle, named after distinguished oceanographer and scientist Roger Revelle—who continued to teach occasionally until his death in July 1991 at the age of 82.

Revelle specializes in the humanities, and is the most traditional college at UCSD, stressing breadth in general education. Matriculating students are required to take a five-quarter humanities sequence, which concentrates on writing and introduces them to some of the great works of literature, philosophy, and history. Though often described as too difficult, this sequence is highly valued by most Revelle students—who are also required to take four quarters of physics and chemistry (with at least one quarter in each); one of biology; three of calculus; three in the social sciences; and one in fine arts. They must also show proficiency in a foreign language. Those who support traditional liberal education take comfort from Revelle's curriculum, while the critical left complains about its lack of ethnic studies. According to one student, the typical undergraduate would note that Revelle is "the toughest college at UCSD . . . a nerd college . . . a well-respected college."

1990-91 General Catalog:
Sociology 133—Comparative Sex Stratification

"Utilizing a new theory of factors affecting female status, we examine topics including women in evolutionary perspective; Third World women and modernization; women's changing position in the USSR, Israeli kibbutz, and especially the U.S.A.; and the political economy of sex stratification. *(Satisfies area V.)*"

Muir College appeared hard on Revelle's heels, in 1967, and was named for the environmentalist John Muir. It is the largest of the five and is designed for exceptionally able students with well-defined academic interests who wish to take an active role in developing their own programs. Qualified students are encouraged to substitute advanced-level for introductory courses in meeting the distribution requirements.

In keeping with its goal of "program flexibility" and "student independence," Muir has fewer requirements than Revelle. These include the completion of a three-quarter sequence in the social sci-

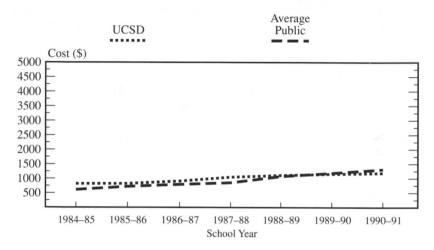

TUITION AND FEES INCREASE
Average Increase/Year: Public = 8.30%, UCSD = 4.56%

Source: The College Entrance Examination Board

ences; another in math or natural sciences; and a two-quarter sequence in the humanities, fine arts, or foreign languages. Students must also complete a two-quarter composition course in their freshman year. True to its namesake, the college is also known for its "green" classes, "Wilderness and Human Values" being one example.

Third College was founded in 1970, and beats the drum for ethnic, comparative, and Third World studies. It enrolls the fewest students and requires a two-quarter writing sequence; a quarter each of biology, chemistry and physics; a three-quarter sequence in the humanities, a foreign language or the fine arts; one quarter in computing and one in math or statistics; and three quarters in "societal analysis." This last entails taking a one-quarter course each in communication, Third World studies, and urban studies and planning. Later, students must choose an upper-division course focusing on a culture or society not their own. Obviously, Third College lays great stress on "multicultural education," and is home to a number of UCSD's politically correct. Many of them major in communications or the visual arts, launching pads for later opinion-molding careers in the media.

Warren College was founded in 1974 and was named after the former Chief Justice of the U.S. Supreme Court. The school was conceived to help students "make a close connection between their undergraduate education and their personal and professional goals for their post-baccalaureate years." Accordingly, the college requires students to obtain part-time jobs with businesses in the area, for which they earn credit. Warren also encourages students to undertake internships and other career-oriented programs. Students are also asked to complete a two-quarter writing course; a one-quarter "Ethics and Society" course; and two quarters of "Formal Skills." This involves two courses in calculus, or two in symbolic logic, or two in computer science, or one in computer science and one in symbolic logic. In addition, the future professionals must later complete two programs of concentration (minors) in areas "noncontiguous" with the major. For example, a history major (humanities) could minor in biology (natural science) or anthropology (social science), but not in literature (a humanity).

Fifth College, established in 1988, concentrates on a "global curriculum" and international relations. The centerpiece of Fifth's

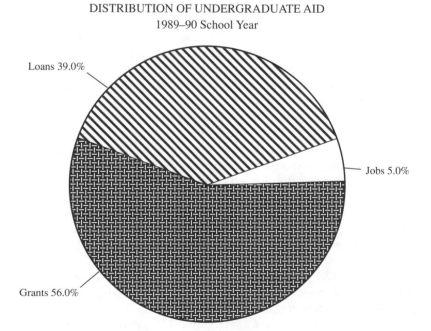

DISTRIBUTION OF UNDERGRADUATE AID
1989–90 School Year

Loans 39.0%

Jobs 5.0%

Grants 56.0%

Source: The College Entrance Examination Board, 1990

distribution requirements is a three-quarter sequence, "The Making of the Modern World," which also involves intensive writing practice. Students must also study the fine arts of both Western and non-Western cultures for two quarters, as well as meet a minimal foreign language requirement (two or three quarters). In addition, they must take two quarters of mathematics and computer science, and two in the natural sciences. Finally, Fifth collegians study a regional specialization for three quarters, one of which must be at upper-division level. Supplementing the curriculum, most of the undergraduates spend a year abroad. The degree of radicalism at Fifth depends primarily upon the professors teaching the Modern World sequence; a different group of three professors teaches it each year, and some are reportedly more political than others.

For all this, UCSD is one of the finest research facilities in the country, the beneficiary of many government-sponsored projects. The faculty boasts several Nobel laureates and 52 members of the National Academy of Sciences, an outstanding record for so young an institution. Predictably, all the hard sciences are very strong. Currently, the School of Medicine is the only professional graduate school on the La Jolla campus, though a School of Architecture is expected to open shortly.

Class sizes vary. Most lower-division lecture courses consist of 100 to 300 students. The classes are then broken down into recitation sections of about 25 students. Upper-division courses are usually smaller, though these are becoming increasingly crowded. They can range from 10 to 75 students. Because it is research-oriented, UCSD depends on teaching assistants, who do tend to be knowledgeable in their fields and accessible to students. Faculty stars, concentrating on their research, teach classes "sometimes." Relations between professors and students are what you would expect—cordial but distant.

The crowded classes are a consequence of a rapidly expanding university; construction never stops on the 1,200-acre campus overlooking the Pacific Ocean. Buildings are contemporary in style, and won't win any awards from the new architectural school, because many of them look like large lumps of dingy concrete. To liven things up, the campus sports what is billed as the largest neon sculpture in the world, a psychedelic contraption that almost shouts, "Made in California." Attached to one of the buildings, it spells out in enormous letters the seven virtues and the seven vices.

By contrast, campus life is relatively calm and laid-back. Each college runs its own coed residential facilities, including dorms and apartments, the latter being in great demand for their extra space and kitchen facilities. Fewer than half the undergraduates can be accommodated in campus housing, however, and preference is given to out-of-town residents; most freshmen and sophomores do live on campus. The rest live at home or rent apartments nearby, preferably on the beach.

The university specializes in outdoor athletic facilities to take advantage of the weather, and the beach is only about five minutes away. The Olympic-size swimming pool is even closer. Much of the student body is involved in the 26 intercollegiate and many coed intramurals teams, some of them very competitive, though water sports predominate. There is a nearby aquatic center which offers classes in scuba diving, windsurfing, and sailing.

A large percentage of the student body commutes; consequently, UCSD is quiet on the weekends. Most on-campus students take off for La Jolla, San Diego, Los Angeles, or even Mexico, all tourist meccas geared up for serious entertainment. What campus socializing there is generally centers around the 16 fraternities and 7 sororities to which about 20 percent of students belong.

UCSD is a relatively quiet campus. Students are generally more concerned with studies than with listening to the latest leftist litany. There are a variety of organizations ranging from a homosexual group to the Young Republicans. Newspapers abound on campus—leftist, black, feminist, conservative, and literary, as well as the regular daily. Though no one group dominates, those of a leftist and liberal bent are larger and more vocal, while those of a more conservative persuasion may find themselves unpopular, even though many students probably quietly agree with them. No one wants to be labeled a "right-wing fascist," so most conservatives remain silent for the sake of their grades and professor recommendations.

Alcohol and drug use are not serious problems. With campus police constantly patrolling the university, there are few disturbances. Most of the campus is relatively well lit, and an escort service is available to walk students to and from their destinations. The low crime rate in the affluent neighborhood adds to campus safety.

UCSD is a solid academic school set in one of the most beautiful environments in the country—if you can ignore the world's largest neon sculpture. The innovative five college system enables students to find their own academic and philosophical niche. There is a group for every political persuasion, ethnic background, or interest. Campus life is generally open and friendly, though you may not want to wear a Ronald Reagan T-shirt to class. Like the weather, most students at UCSD are moderate and temperate, so despite some loud leftist groups, the campus political climate is generally tolerable for traditionalists who are serious about their studies, as well as their surfing.

University of Chicago

Dean of Admissions, University of Chicago
1116 East 59th Street, Chicago, IL 60637 (312) 702-8650

Type: Private and Secular

Students:
3,383 undergraduates
  1,989 men
  1,394 women
5,647 graduate students

Applications:
Closing date: January 15
45% of applicants accepted

	Applied	Accepted	Enrolled
men	3,299	1,454	496
women	2,303	1,079	379

SAT or ACT required
  Score reported by: February 15
  Mid 50% of freshman scores:
    SAT-Math   610–710
    SAT-Verbal 580–680

Costs and Aid:

Tuition and fees	$15,140
Room and Board	5,390

Scholarships:
Academic	Yes
Athletic	Yes
Minority	No

Financial Aid:
Freshmen	73%
Upperclassmen	82%

Library:	5,000,000 titles
ROTC:	Yes
Study Abroad:	Yes

**Percentage of courses that can
be used to fulfill core
requirements:** 9.7

A relative latecomer among the great universities of the world, the University of Chicago, located a few blocks from Lake Michigan on the south side of Chicago, was founded in 1891 with the explicit intention of becoming one of the nation's premier research institutions. The priorities of the new university bankrolled by John D. Rockefeller were never in doubt. Chicago's first president, William Rainey Harper, declared that faculty promotions depended "more upon the results of their work than upon the efficiency of their teaching." While this mentality left the undergraduate college out in the cold during the early years, it did lay the foundation for Chicago's 60 Nobel laureates.

It was not until Robert Maynard Hutchins was named president in 1927 at the remarkably young age of 30 that the college began to acquire the definitive liberal arts bent which has made its reputation since. Hutchins prescribed a four-year undergraduate program devoted entirely to liberal education with no allowances for specialization or electives. While Hutchins's plan was never fully implemented, its general philosophy still influences the undergraduate curriculum.

Indeed, with its history of strong research and teaching, Chicago

77

can boast a powerful academic tradition that equals if not surpasses virtually every elite Eastern school. The names of those who have been (or are still) associated with the school testify to this. In the 1940s Enrico Fermi and others created the first sustained nuclear reaction. At that same time, Hans Morganthau was instrumental in developing the field of international relations. More recently, Milton Friedman and George Stigler have brought even greater luster to the already esteemed economics department.

Courses and Programs of Study, 1990–91:
English 119—Feminist Theory, Feminist Practice.
Professor Lauren Berlant

"In this course we will engage various approaches to the question of woman, focusing on Marxist, psychoanalytic, and mythical perspectives within feminist theory. Literary texts will be used not as mere testing grounds for the theoretical positions we examine, but as grounds for other ways of seeing women as well. The syllabus will include selections from Mary Shelly, George Eliot, Sigmund Freud, Helen Cixous, Alice Walker, Christa Wolf, Adrienne Rich, and Marguerite Duras."

Every undergraduate is enrolled in the college; there are no other undergraduate schools at the university. The college operates on the quarter system. All must select a three-quarter sequence of courses in the humanities, social sciences, biological sciences, physical sciences, civilization studies, languages, and mathematics. The sequences, known as the common core, are integrated and intensive studies designed to impart a certain body of knowledge and a scholarly outlook—as well as to improve writing ability. For example, the Western civilization sequence, which almost 90 percent of Chicago students elect to fulfill their civilization requirement, consists of small classes structured around the 10-volume *Chicago Readings in Western Civilization,* a collection of primary sources. The common core is designed to steep the student in the great thinkers—Plato, Aristotle, Augustine, Descartes, Hume, and Kant, among others.

Half of a student's remaining time in the college is taken up with liberal arts electives, leaving only a quarter of his course load to be devoted to his chosen area of "concentration," as majors are known. Most concentrations require between 9 and 16 courses. There are, however, some concentrations that require 16 to 18 courses, including

TUITION AND FEES INCREASE
Average Increase/Year: Private = 11.15%, Chicago = 9.23%

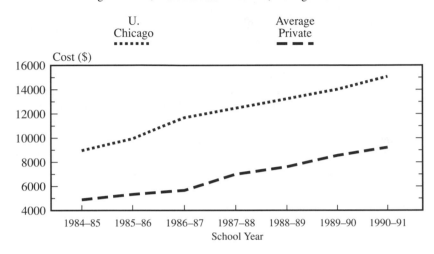

Source: The College Entrance Examination Board

many interdisciplinary majors. Indeed, of 41 concentrations, 11 are interdisciplinary.

Chicago's continuous emphasis on the systematic acquisition of knowledge, reflected in the university's motto *Crescat Scientia Vita Excolatur* (Let Knowledge Increase So Life May be Enriched), has had positive results. Twenty-three percent of College graduates have gone on to receive a doctorate, a percentage unmatched by any American institution during the past 30 years.

Central to the university's academic reputation is the strength of its graduate departments. Any evaluation of the very best graduate schools in the country would have to include Chicago, as it has many departments that would rank in the top 10, if not higher. This strength transfers down to the undergraduate departments, as most of the graduate faculty also hold college appointments, and the "core" is largely taught by professors and not by teaching assistants. Students report that faculty members hold regular office hours, and that they are generally helpful when asked. Undergraduates are outnumbered by graduate students 5,700 to 3,400. They come from all 50 states and dozens of foreign countries. Twenty-two percent are minorities, with a large proportion being Asians or Asian-Americans.

There is some tension between the Chicago's original mission of research and its acquired one of general education. Even though most of the graduate faculty do hold college appointments, a number of the school's approximately 1,500 faculty members never see the inside of a classroom, while some others have not opened a new book in years. Moreover, many are medical nonteaching faculty, so that the real number of faculty is closer to 1,000 than 1,500. Nevertheless, classes—with introductory sciences and economics being notable exceptions—are kept rather small, usually under 30. Furthermore, the discriminating student can easily enroll in a considerable number of courses under one or another distinguished professor.

In any case, the preponderant influence of the graduate divisions and their research mentality can be a godsend to the enterprising student. Many college students take advantage of the opportunity to conduct independent research for credit, some of which is rather advanced. (For example, one student solved a 300-year-old anomaly in Newton's *Principia* as part of his undergraduate thesis.)

DISTRIBUTION OF UNDERGRADUATE AID
1989–90 School Year

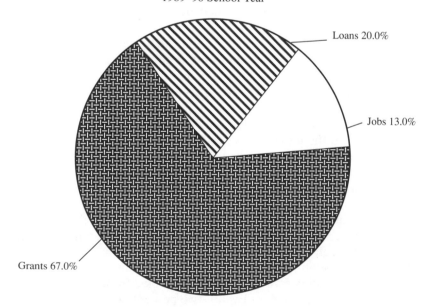

Loans 20.0%

Jobs 13.0%

Grants 67.0%

Source: The College Entrance Examination Board, 1990

Economics, the home of several Nobel laureates, is an extremely strong and popular undergraduate concentration, as are political science (tending more towards political philosophy due to the influence of Leo Strauss's heirs), history, classics, and the natural sciences. While segments of English and the humanities have been co-opted by "tenured radicals," the knowledgeable student can, with some effort, get an excellent education even in these departments. For the particularly dedicated student, Chicago also has very good specialized departments in some rather unusual fields, such as Assyriology.

The University of Chicago has not been immune to the radical attack upon the humanities which seems endemic to American higher education, but students feel that the assault has been less intensive than at Stanford or Dartmouth, for example. While certain books of questionable educational value have crept into parts of the Chicago canon, the incidents are relatively few. In any case, the curriculum is too baked in the humanistic tradition to crumble easily.

When Chicago professor and best-selling author Allan Bloom recalled how, as a youngster, he "saw the University of Chicago for the first time and somehow sensed" that he had "discovered" his life, he should have specified his *academic* life, since the rest of the Chicago undergraduate experience is rather meager. As a relatively young school, the University of Chicago has yet to develop some of the grand traditions characteristic of older institutions of the same caliber. When President Hutchins abolished intercollegiate athletics, Chicago was in the Big 10 in football, Amos Alonzo Stagg had coached there, and the first Heisman Trophy winner had played there. And by banning fraternities, he also eliminated the other major pillar of the college's extracurricular life.

Today, the University of Chicago is back into intercollegiate athletics, but as a NCAA Division-III competitor. However, the Maroons inspire such apathy among the scholastically bent student body that one poll of recent alumni found that an absolute majority had never attended *one* athletic event during their entire undergraduate careers. The advantage of this general indifference is that more students have the opportunity to participate in competitive sports than is common at other schools. There are 20 intercollegiate teams. Additionally, intramurals in 17 sports ranging from football to archery involve most undergraduates at some point in their careers.

The Greek system at the University of Chicago, just recently revived, is currently undergoing the typical criticism for "elitism." Unfortunately, the administration's displeasure carries much more weight at Chicago than elsewhere, since the university is the neighbor-hood's principal landowner. Recently, the largest fraternity, Alpha Tau Omega, and one of the campus's two sororities, Alpha Omicron Omega, lost their leases to university-owned premises and have been reduced to communal apartment living, arrangements hardly condu-cive to traditional Greek life. While apathy towards sports and the Greek system are a source of worry to many devoted alumni, most students seem not to share that concern; the most popular campus hangout for the serious-minded student body remains the Joseph Regenstein Library.

Campus politics are no more exciting than the rest of student life. The radicals' agenda was largely shaped by the rather vocal umbrella group, the Alternative List, and consisted of the usual demands, such as married quarters for homosexual couples, and the introduction of sensitivity speech codes. The group recently controlled the student government for two years during which it achieved few of its objectives and neither of the above. However, the Alternative List has quietly retired from political life as most of its articulate leaders have moved on to comfortable graduate fellowships. The only remaining effective radical group is the Gay and Lesbian Alliance which, although rather large, is subdued except for an occasional outburst. Campus conser-vatives, unlike their counterparts at schools like Vassar or Dartmouth, are a pensive lot. (The founder of the coordinating Conservative Council was a scholar of the historiography of Thomas Masaryk, and his successor recently entered a Catholic seminary.) They prefer to host lectures and publish philosophical tracts rather than stir their colleagues to action.

Two aspects of the Chicago experience help compensate for the deficient social scene. Students entering Chicago are assigned to live in one of about 40 college houses, where most choose to stay for their entire undergraduate careers. Many of those who have moved off campus also elect to remain affiliated with their former associates in a particular house. The houses, many of which date from the university's founding, are small dorms housing from 30 to 100 students, often with their own libraries, dining halls, and recreational facilities. They are led by Resident Heads, junior faculty, or married graduate students who live with their families in the dorms, lending houses a family air while coordinating a diverse calendar of social events. Some dorms have a number of houses within them. Each dorm is in turn led by one Resident Master, usually a senior faculty member.

Helping the individual college houses to break the social monotony is a fairly extensive, albeit underfunded, system of activities and interest groups which number more than 100 and run the gamut of traditional activities, from debate and music to less conventional diversions like rock climbing. The University of Chicago, in addition to having its own nondenominational Divinity School, shares a neighborhood with more than a dozen major theological seminaries, representing such mainline denominations as Roman Catholicism, Lutheranism, Methodism, the United Church of Christ, and others. These are clustered within blocks of the main quadrangle. Working closely with the university, these institutions provide interested students with a wide variety of intellectual, social, and religious services.

When viewed within the context of the overall state of contemporary American higher education, the University of Chicago has not only earned its outstanding reputation, but deserves to retain it. Chicago's ongoing commitment to liberal education, backed by its strong specialized departments, continues to make it an outstanding choice for the student committed to—and capable of—attaining perhaps the best education available today.

Clark University

Dean of Admissions and Records, Clark University
950 Main Street, Worcester, MA 01610 (508) 793-7431

Type: Private and Secular

Students:
2,220 undergraduates
 1,012 men
 1,208 women
 659 graduate students

Applications:
Closing date: February 15
71% of applicants accepted

	Applied	Accepted	Enrolled
men	1,506	987	259
women	1,743	1,320	289

SAT or ACT required (SAT preferred)
 Score reported by: March 1
 Mid 50% of freshman scores:
   SAT-Math   520–640
   SAT-Verbal 470–580

Costs and Aid:

Tuition and fees	$14,380
Room and Board	4,500

Scholarships:

Academic	No
Athletic	No
Minority	No

Financial Aid:

Freshmen	40%
Upperclassmen	42%

Library:	475,000 titles
ROTC:	Yes
Study Abroad:	Yes

Clark University's informal symbol is a pea pod containing peas of different colors with a caption that reads "Categorizing people isn't something you can do here." Kooky though its symbol may be, Clark takes its liberal arts mission seriously and attacks it vigorously, not always with wisdom but certainly with verve.

Although not a big name as universities go, Clark, which was founded in 1887 as a graduate institution, has won international recognition for its scientific contributions to applied and social sciences, particularly for research and teaching in areas where the natural and social sciences intersect. Among them is research that led to the development of the birth control pill, and to the definition and measurement of the windchill factor. Also, Clark was the academic base of Robert Goddard, "Father of the Space Age," and Albert Michelson, the first American to win a Nobel Prize in physics. More recently, the university has won recognition in the fields of nuclear chemistry, technical risk and hazards research, and brain tissue regeneration. These achievements are notable for an institution with fewer than 3,000 students and only 170 faculty members.

Since by far the largest number of students at Clark are undergraduates (2,200) and since most classes are taught by professors, the university seems to be successfully walking the tightrope between teaching and research, a major accomplishment in academia these days. The secret may lie in cross-pollination, which has traditionally involved students in some of the research projects. As the *Academic Catalog* says, "Interaction—among fields of study, between faculty and students and between graduate and undergraduate programs—is a virtue of Clark's university-college environment. The university's hallmark: people and programs that cross academic and cultural boundaries and that blend and integrate the arts, sciences, social sciences, and humanities."

Clark Academic Catalog, 1990–92:
International Development and Social Change 127—Political Economy of Underdevelopment (also Geography 127)
Professor Richard Peet

"Do conventional explanations of underdevelopment strike you as false and unconvincing? A powerful and refreshing alternative perspective exists in Marxist and neo-Marxist theories of social change. This course reviews the main currents within this rich stream including theories of dependency, imperialism, accumulation world systems, unequal exchange, and mode of production. Marxist concepts are used to examine the international role of capital, multinational corporations, and regional decline. Finally, the course presents alternative models of socialist development."

To this end the undergraduate college, which mandates 32 courses for graduation, has developed a program of distribution requirements called "Perspectives." Students must take one semester-long course in each of the six perspectives, choosing from a list of 15 to 20 in each. The perspectives are: Aesthetic (fine arts); Comparative (social sciences); Historical; Language/Culture; Natural Scientific (including a laboratory component); and Value, which is defined as courses that "study the dimensions of value in all domains of life and learning, asking the moral question, 'What should we do?' "

The second part of the required program involves taking two courses in "verbal expression" and two in "formal analysis." Both categories cover courses offered in several departments. Those that

TUITION AND FEES INCREASE
Average Increase/Year: Private = 11.15%, Clark = 8.85%

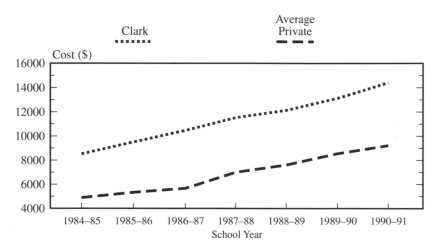

Source: The College Entrance Examination Board

qualify for the first category place special emphasis on the relationship between writing and critical thinking; the second category calls for courses that highlight logical and algebraic modes of thinking.

The interplay between faculty and students is generally excellent, with professors holding regular and well-attended office hours. Most seem genuinely interested in students and encourage discussion both in and out of the classroom. There is an academic advising office, but students also consult professors to whom they are assigned as freshmen and major advisors whom they later choose. While generally satisfied with the level of faculty attention, students often complain that popular courses are hard to get into and that the small size of the faculty limits variety.

The format of most classes is lecture/discussion, and 70 percent of all classes have fewer than 20 students. A few large introductory courses do meet with teaching assistants in small groups. TAs at Clark receive good marks from students. The strongest departments, it is generally agreed, are geography and psychology. Clark claims distinction in both fields: in geography, because so few colleges and universities offer the subject today; and in psychology, because the university presented Sigmund Freud with the only honorary degree he received during his lifetime. Philosophy and chemistry also win kudos.

The English and sociology departments rate raspberries because of their ideological biases, with the former reported to be infested with radical feminists and the latter with rabid multiculturalists. The history department currently seems split between traditionalists and the politically correct. Clark offers programs, but not majors, in peace and women's studies.

Although leftist elements in the administration (supported by a few militant students) are pushing for the addition and revision of courses to comply with the new orthodoxy, a coterie of faculty with more backbone than most is resisting what its members see as invasions of their turf, if not their convictions. So far, professors have beaten back efforts to: link faculty salaries and promotions to how well they integrate pluralism and diversity into their classes; require faculty to explain in writing how they plan to incorporate pluralistic views into

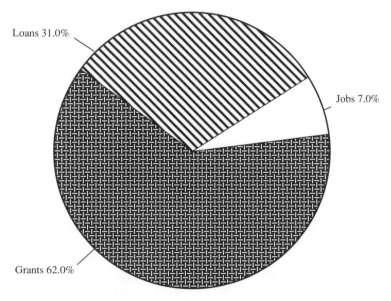

DISTRIBUTION OF UNDERGRADUATE AID
1989–90 School Year

Loans 31.0%

Jobs 7.0%

Grants 62.0%

Source: The College Entrance Examination Board, 1990

their courses; have students formally evaluate professors in terms of how successfully they address race, class and gender issues.

The battle, however, is far from over. In her "Agenda for Enhancing Academic Excellence," the provost has declared that "the high priority for enhancing pluralism must inform every important decision we make about our academic programs, the faculty, administration and staff, and services for students." The same document also boldly declares:

> We should consider strategies for increasing the presence of educators and scholars of color among our tenure-line faculty. . . . It is also important to think of affirmative action as a primary and not an added component of every faculty search. We should all be willing to continue a search when we have not identified qualified candidates of color, just as we continue a search when the right combination of academic qualities does not emerge.

The administration's fixation on pluralism and diversity at the expense, if necessary, of merit is also beginning to infect the student body, about a third of whom come from Massachusetts with the rest from more than 40 states and 50 foreign countries. Nine percent are minorities. "Clarkies" have always prided themselves on their heterogeneity and strong devotion to the rights of the individual. Now, however, some militant students seem to be transferring their loyalties from individual to group rights and adding their voices to the diversity sing-song. Political activism is growing, and is usually dominated by various degrees of leftist thinking. The university's divestment of its South African holdings was applauded, for example, not only by activists but also by normally apathetic students.

When not involved in politicking (which, to be fair, means most of the time), students engage in a variety of "egalitarian" extracurricular activities, since fraternities and sororities are currently not permitted at Clark. (In spite of this restriction, however, three underground fraternities do exist.) There are 80 student organizations and groups; in addition many students make a point of performing community service in working-class Worcester, helping in soup kitchens, tutoring disadvantaged children, and so forth. All this charity work has not greatly improved relations with the natives, however, who still tend to view Clarkies as spoiled rich kids.

Sports don't loom large in the lives of most students, and the university has never sought to compete in big-time athletics, many think because they encourage elitism and discourage a sense of community. Nevertheless, a new student athletic center has given sports on campus a shot in the arm, especially aerobics and scuba diving. The university fields 11 intercollegiate teams for men and 10 for women, as well as 15 coed intramural sports. Men's and women's basketball and soccer are excellent, as are men's tennis and women's volleyball and field hockey. In winter, skiing is not far away.

Facilities on the small 45-acre campus have been greatly enhanced with the recent opening of the new Higgins University Center. The center provides a focal point, long lacking, where students may meet, eat, and do their own things. It includes a dining facility, gamesroom, mailroom, snack bar, general store, and space for assorted offices and conference rooms. It also features a large living room with fireplace that doubles as a dance floor and auditorium.

When venturing off campus, which is dry, Clarkies drink and socialize with students from other colleges around Worcester, a small city that lacks some amenities, but certainly not bars. Although stuck with a blue-collar image, Worcester does sponsor a resident symphony, theater companies and a couple of museums (including the Worcester Museum, one of the finest small art museums in the country). Boston and Providence are both less than an hour's drive for those who want more of everything. In spite of Worcester's watering holes, neither drinking nor drugs seem to be a serious problem at Clark, and students feel relatively safe on campus, though they fear neighborhood crime. Escort services are available.

Housing on the not-very-pretty campus (a mix of red brick and gray granite with a bit of green in between) accommodates more than 1,500 students, and is guaranteed for freshmen and available by lottery for upperclassmen. Dorms are coed and vary in comfort level. A new residence hall, which houses more than 200, is quite luxurious, containing suites with living rooms and kitchens. There are language and special-interest houses, a nonsmoking house, and a "quiet house." Housing is guaranteed for four years and about 70 percent of undergraduates choose to live on campus; the rest make do with unattractive, if cheap, multistoried apartments nearby.

Like its students, Clark University is interesting and lively, but it has also become a contradictory place to live and learn—for the school is beginning to offer mixed signals to its student body. On the one hand, the university takes great care to develop an imaginative and integrated general education that grapples with the great concepts of Western civilization, including its principal hallmark: the evolution of the importance of the individual. On the other hand, a once progressive university is now regressing to the dark ages by endorsing blind loyalty to groups, currently defined mainly by color and gender. So, the jury is still out on Clark. Right now the verdict could go either way.

Columbia University

Director of College Admissions
Columbia College
212 Hamilton Hall, Columbia University, New York, NY 10027
(212) 854-2521

Type: Private and Secular

Students: (Columbia College)
3,200 undergraduates
  1,715 men
  1,485 women

Applications:
Closing date: January 15
29% of applicants accepted

	Applied	Accepted	Enrolled
men	3,770	1,036	439
women	2,935	907	386

SAT required
  Score reported by: March 1
  Mid 50% of freshman scores:
    SAT-Math   620–720
    SAT-Verbal 590–680

Costs and Aid:

Tuition and fees	$14,800
Room and Board	5,770

Scholarships:
Academic	No
Athletic	No
Minority	No

Financial Aid:
Freshmen	41%
Upperclassmen	41%

Library: 6,100,000 titles

ROTC: Yes
Study Abroad: Yes

Percentage of courses that can be used to fulfill core requirements: 11.5

Its football team is a national joke and its campus politics often list to the left, but Columbia College, located in the Big Apple, is definitely not rotten to the core. In fact, its core curriculum, still centered around Western thought, furnishes a rich banquet that tempts many of the best and the brightest to a four-year mindfest at one of the nation's vintage, premier, intellectual institutions.

Columbia College, which long ago broadened into Columbia University, has a long and distinguished history, having started out as King's College, established by royal charter in 1754. The fifth institution of higher learning founded in the American colonies, Columbia remains the smallest undergraduate college in the prestigious Ivy League. Despite its present leftist political reputation, several of America's more conservative founding fathers, notably John Jay and Alexander Hamilton, were among its first students.

Columbia began in the Wall Street area, but kept moving uptown as it expanded. In the mid-19th century, it relocated in mid-Manhattan to accommodate the Schools of Law and Medicine. With the founding of Teachers College and Barnard, an affiliated college for women, Columbia University, still upwardly mobile, moved at the turn of the century to its present location in upper Manhattan. Although the trustees intended to evacuate the university from its urban setting to what was then a rural neighborhood, Morningside Heights, the city quickly encircled the tiny, 36-acre campus, and throughout this century the district has been home to teeming throngs of New York's most recent immigrants and diverse ethnic groups.

Columbia's unusual position as one of the oldest private institutions on Manhattan Island has allowed the university over the years to accumulate vast and valuable real-estate holdings. Columbia is New York City's third largest land owner, and from sales and holdings of valuable property (Columbia owned the land upon which Rockefeller Center was built), it has developed one of the largest university endowments in the nation.

Columbia University Bulletin, Columbia College, 1990–91:
Sociology V3213x—Culture in contemporary America: a sociological
perspective
Professor Jonathan Rieder

"The values and meanings that form American pluralism, the communities that create and consume culture, and the organizations that produce and distribute culture. Examples come from popular and elite culture: American individualism, rhythm and blues, Christian fundamentalism, advertising, abstract art, Orthodox Judaism, abortion politics, Reaganism, television comedy."

Columbia College, then, is a relatively small liberal arts institution (3,200 men and women, mostly from the Northeast), affiliated with a wealthy university of 19,000 possessing a long, proud history. Although administrators are sometimes criticized for subordinating the needs of the college to those of the larger institution, many of them believe that the undergraduate school has a unique mission in today's academic world. Unlike many colleges swallowed up by bloated universities, Columbia has managed to preserve a distinct identity and high academic standards, no mean feat anywhere, particularly in New York, a city dominated by egalitarian politics.

Columbia's academic mission centers around its core curriculum,

TUITION AND FEES INCREASE
Average Increase/Year: Private = 11.15%, Columbia College = 7.38%

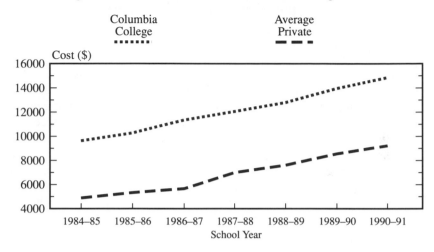

Source: The College Entrance Examination Board

---

or Great Books course, which was first established as a mandatory sequence for all students in 1919 and which, with revisions, has served as a model for other schools ever since. Despite many students' avant-garde politics and their "diversity"—Columbia's minority enrollment is a high 30 percent—most Columbia students will single out the core as their primary reason for choosing the college.

The heart of the hallowed program consists of two year-long courses, each meeting four hours a week, called Contemporary Civilization, and Literature and Humanities. The first covers social and political history and theory, while the second delves into Western literature, history and philosophy, often using original texts. Students are encouraged to complete these courses during their first two years. Two further required courses (one semester each, three hours a week) are in music and art appreciation; other requirements include two years of a foreign language, one of writing, one of science (laboratory not mandated), and a year of physical education.

As the result of pressure from minorities, an "extended core" requirement has recently been instituted, consisting of two semester-long "cultures and issues" courses, which may be selected from a number of options designed to expose students to non-Western civilizations. These, it is important to note, are additions to, not substitutes for, the two-year immersion in Western civilization, and their introduction seems to have defused much minority resentment over the Eurocentrism issue.

The college requires all its professors in the humanities and social sciences to teach "Lit Hum" and "CC" at some time, so even the most prominent faculty share with the lowly undergraduate a thorough familiarity with Columbia's Great Books courses, which are taught in seminars through Socratic dialogues. Students are sometimes initially disappointed with this teaching method, complaining that professors generally give little background information or critical interpretations of the works; instead they solicit student reactions. Another frequently heard grumble concerns the quick pace at which the works are covered—usually, one Great Book a week. This leaves little time for deep analysis, students say. By the conclusion of the sequence, however, most students have become true believers, and express appreciation for having been made to think for themselves about the enduring values

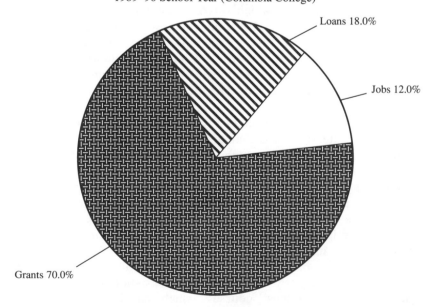

DISTRIBUTION OF UNDERGRADUATE AID
1989–90 School Year (Columbia College)

Loans 18.0%

Jobs 12.0%

Grants 70.0%

Source: The College Entrance Examination Board, 1990

of Western civilization. They also commend the faculty's friendliness and willingness to talk with students outside classrooms and offices. Teaching assistants also come in for a rare share of praise; students say they are so competent (and speak English so well) that it is often hard to tell them from professors.

Since most of the first two years at Columbia is occupied by the core curriculum—which consumes 56 of the usual 62 credit hours for those years—many students find it difficult to sample other subjects before selecting a major. This may be one reason why the most popular majors are overwhelmingly political science, history, and English, with the natural sciences claiming less than 10 percent of students. Outstanding departments are, not surprisingly, English, history, and political science, as well as chemistry and physics. East Asian studies are also top of the line. Math, biology, and some of the 35 foreign languages offered are weaker.

The Columbia academic program, although rigid in terms of basic requirements, is nevertheless accommodating to students who later wish to design their own programs of study. During the past several years, majors in Afro-American studies, regional studies, and women's studies have also been instituted by the college, largely in reaction to demands from the influential minority population, of whom approximately 12 percent are Asian with the rest about equally divided between blacks and Hispanics.

Columbia College has an unusual relationship with its sister institution, Barnard. Although the Columbia trustees tried to manipulate a merger when they decided the college should go coed, which it finally did in 1981, Barnard's administration rejected the take-over attempt and insisted upon remaining a single-sex institution. Many Barnard students seem less committed than their elders to single-sex education, however, and eagerly register for classes at Columbia, join in coed fraternities, and live in Columbia housing as seniors. While this arrangement suits male students very well, Columbia College women, who make up almost half of the undergraduate enrollment, are less enthusiastic about the Columbia-Barnard relationship of extensive cross-registration, merged women's sports teams, and extracurricular activities.

Social life at Columbia is heavily influenced by two factors—the Greek system and New York City. For those who are members of Columbia's numerous male fraternities, coed fraternities, and sororities, life revolves around the Greek system. Only 20 percent of undergraduates are involved, however, and the system does not control the campus because the neighborhood bars, one of which is actually named the "Cathedral," become second homes to most non-Greeks, at least to those with passable IDs. Younger students may have to travel downtown in order to find a bar scene which caters to their needs. Since New York also offers a wealth of other diversions, much of the social life consists of small groups venturing forth to sample its delights. Columbia's Urban New York program introduces students to the city's opportunities free of charge through tours by faculty members.

Security on the attractive, compact campus is surprisingly effective, and the New York City police presence is strong in the surrounding neighborhood. Students say they feel safe in or near the Columbia enclave, but worry, like everybody else, about the dangers of the city subway system, which is the only economical way to travel to and from midtown Manhattan.

On-campus housing is by no means palatial but is guaranteed for all four years. Ninety-five percent of students go for it, largely because of the city's high rents. Housing is overwhelmingly coeducational, and is more comfortable than it was a few years ago, due to extensive renovation and new construction, which has upgraded 50 percent of all housing in the last three years.

With the exception of the football team, renowned for a recent 44-game losing streak, sports at Columbia are generally up to the mark, with men's and women's fencing and swimming being very strong. Also good are men's soccer, wrestling, and tennis. Facilities include stadiums for basketball and soccer, a track, a baseball field, and a recreational gymnasium with swimming pool. Although student enthusiasm for sports is increasing and there are 25 intramurals for each sex, Columbia still lacks teams in men's and women's lacrosse, women's field hockey and men's ice hockey. These sports presently have club status, however, and can be expected to field varsity teams within several years.

Extracurricular groups and organizations at Columbia number 120. Many of the college's most popular campus groups are concerned with community service and helping in various ways the many disadvantaged persons in Columbia's neighborhood. There are also well-subscribed religious and ethnic organizations, including a very militant black student organization and a strong Jewish group, which are often at odds these days. Other groups are more overtly political—from the Young Spartacus League (communist-oriented) to the College Republicans. Campus media reflect this wide spectrum.

In previous years, the Columbia campus has been unpleasantly politicized, but students now appear more moderate. While it is still important to be politically correct, a recent poll of incoming students revealed that more than 60 percent confidently expect to march into well-paying jobs when they graduate, or to go on to law or medical school, hardly a profile of fire-eating radicals.

All in all, Columbia College continues to earn high marks for a challenging academic program rich in the accumulated wisdom of the West, a first-rate faculty which still emphasizes teaching, and the excitement and uniqueness of New York City. But the student who sets his sights on Columbia had better want a capital A for academics, and a capital C for city living. A capital T for toughness wouldn't hurt either, for both Columbia College and New York City are very taxing.

Cornell University

Dean of Admissions and Financial Aid, Cornell University
410 Thurston Avenue, Ithaca, NY, 14850 (607) 255-5241

Type: Private and Secular, Public

Students:
12,734 undergraduates
    7,112 men
    5,622 women
5,555 graduate students

Applications:
Closing date: January 1
30% of applicants accepted

	Applied	Accepted	Enrolled
men	11,687	3,502	1,666
women	8,401	2,531	1,270

SAT or ACT required
    Score reported by: February 1
    Mid 50% of freshman scores:
        SAT-Math   N/A
        SAT-Verbal   N/A

Costs and Aid:
Tuition and fees:

Private	$15,164
Public—in state	5,944
Public—out of state	10,884
Room and Board	4,990

Scholarships:

Academic	No
Athletic	No
Minority	No

Financial Aid:

Freshmen	70%
Upperclassmen	74%

Library:	2,783,529 titles
ROTC:	Yes
Study Abroad:	Yes

**Percentage of courses that can
be used to fulfill distribution
requirements:** 71.8

During the spring of 1990, a popular singing group at Cornell drew appreciative applause for its version of Billy Joel's song, "We Didn't Start the Fire." Their song was titled "We Didn't Go to Harvard." Cornell's undergraduates are, by and large, a fairly distinguished group—smart, talented, athletic, artistic, political, as well as musical— a well-rounded, well-qualified bunch. It is a campus cliché, however, that a lot of them wanted to go to Harvard, didn't get in, and chose Cornell as a very good second best. This rankles, and kindles a robust school spirit among those who cheer the Big Red over the Crimson. Speak the name "Harvard" on campus and expect hisses in response, unless you happen to quote another Cornell platitude which says that while it may be hard to get into Harvard, it is harder to get through Cornell.

Cornell University is larger than most of its Ivy League peers and younger than all. Not founded to train clergymen or Christianize

Indians like two of its Ivy-clad rivals, Cornell was secular from the start. The university was established in 1865 as New York State's land grant college by Ezra Cornell and Andrew Dickson White. The two men wished to create a school to train students in both classical liberal arts and in practical studies, such as agriculture and engineering.

Cornell's eclectic ambition yielded, in time, a unique amalgam of a university composed of a dozen colleges, some of which are public and some of which are private. The Colleges of Agriculture and Life Sciences, Human Ecology, and Industrial and Labor Relations are public. The Colleges of Arts and Sciences, Art, Architecture and Planning, Engineering, and Hotel Management are private. Also private are the Graduate School, the Law School, the Samuel Curtis Johnson Graduate School of Management, the highly rated Medical College, and the Graduate School of Medical Sciences. The last two are located in New York City, the rest in upstate Ithaca. Altogether they matriculate almost 18,900 students, nearly 13,000 of whom are undergraduates.

Course of Study, 1990–1991:
Government 308—Class, Race, and Interest Groups in U.S. Politics
Professor Michael Goldfield

"The American polity is often characterized as a democracy, sometimes as a representative democracy, sometimes as a pluralist democracy. While most people recognize the existence of a great deal of corruption, unequal benefits, special advantages to the wealthy, and even the political exclusion of the 'poor' and 'minorities,' these phenomena are usually viewed as aberrations or imperfections that do not fundamentally define either the distribution of power or the democratic functioning of the political process. In this course we will entertain the proposition that issues of class and race are central to the shaping of politics in this country. While the course will spend some time examining the dominant paradigms in U.S. politics, the bulk of our attention will be devoted to more critical readings."

Students blur public/private distinctions by taking courses across colleges, but some who pay private tuition resent sharing crowded Cornell facilities and the Cornell name with students there at state school prices to study, for example, vegetable crops. Unless a prospective student is committed to a specialized field offered only by an endowed private college, he would do well to consider applying to one

TUITION AND FEES INCREASE
Average Increase/Year: Private = 11.15%, Cornell = 7.92%

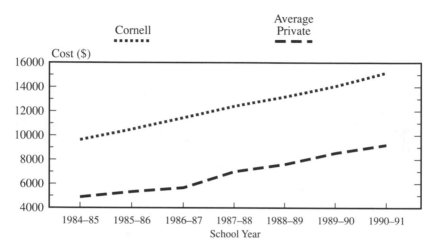

Source: The College Entrance Examination Board

of the state schools. The tuition differential offers compelling reason to do so: The state schools often offer similar programs for much less money. For instance, applicants who think they might major in history or government or sociology, and expect to go to law school, might apply to Industrial and Labor Relations rather than Arts and Sciences. Similarly, a prospective engineer might take the agricultural engineering major in the College of Agriculture and Life Sciences, instead of in the private, pricier Engineering School.

Although some courses are restricted to students enrolled in that college, traditionally it has been possible to take interesting electives in all the different colleges. Due to budget constraints, which are reflected in faculty hires, this is now becoming more difficult, particularly in Arts and Sciences, which enrolls just over 4,000 undergraduates. Popular courses include Psychology 101, which is a frequent freshman elective, and the Hotel School's "Wines and Spirits," a senior-year staple. Probably much more appealing to the politically correct, however, is a brand-new course called "The Body as a Social Text," whatever that may mean.

Class sizes vary. Freshmen commonly find themselves in large lectures with several hundred students. Numbers shrink in most upper-level courses. Language courses and seminars are much smaller, with fewer than 20 students. Much of the teaching at Cornell is done by teaching assistants, and students get individual attention in small sections led by the graduate students. Undergraduates complain a lot about their TAs, especially about those who don't speak intelligible English. (This is a very common gripe in economics courses.) Most professors are accessible to those taking their courses, however, and many repeatedly encourage students to come to them with questions or problems.

On the whole, academics are taken very seriously. Graduation requirements are set by each school. Students in the College of Arts and Sciences must fulfill a set of distribution requirements by taking course sequences in the humanities, the social sciences, and the natural and physical sciences. Cornell operates on the semester system, and Arts and Sciences requires a minimum of 34 courses and 120 credit hours, of which 100 must be taken in A&S.

The general education requirements are: two freshman writing

DISTRIBUTION OF UNDERGRADUATE AID
1989–90 School Year

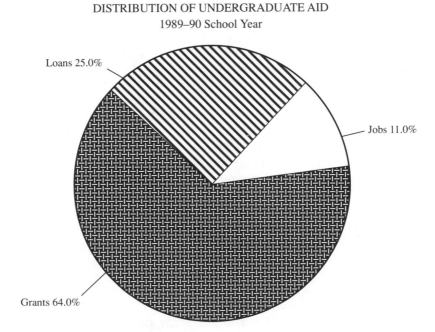

Loans 25.0%

Jobs 11.0%

Grants 64.0%

Source: The College Entrance Examination Board, 1990

seminars; four semester courses to obtain a qualification in two foreign languages or proficiency in one; a sequence of two courses in one physical or biological science; a sequence of two courses in history, or in one of the social sciences (Africana studies, anthropology, archaeology, Asian studies, economics, government, linguistics, Near Eastern studies, psychology, sociology, women's studies, and city and regional planning); a sequence of two courses in the humanities or expressive arts (the humanities category repeats Africana, Asian and Near Eastern studies, as well as women's studies and archaeology, and adds classics, literature, and philosophy); six credits in mathematics or computer science; and finally a sequence of two courses in any subject not already selected.

Although they may sound daunting, these requirements are not very burdensome in practice because of the many (and often bewildering) choices available. Faculty may or may not be helpful in giving guidance, so it is easy to graduate with a half-dozen academic hobbies and very little real learning except in the major. Strong departments include the physical sciences (because so many students are pre-med), history, and government. Economics is considered weak, and foreign languages need beefing up.

In the freshman writing program, most instruction is done by graduate students, and the program suffers because of this. The program's intention is to train new students in basic writing skills, offering courses in a broad range of subjects to teach students that good writing is important in any field. Graduate students use the opportunity to teach obscure topics that are their specialty—or their ideology. Many of these classes are politically charged, and unsuspecting freshmen emerge having learned less about syntax and structure than about sexism and socialism. (In their writing seminars, most also learn how to operate a Macintosh computer. Macs predominate, the university supports their use, and IBM users are not encouraged to exercise their preference.)

Beyond academic pursuits, Cornell students partake of cultural events, an active social life and a full athletic calendar. About 80 percent of students live on campus; housing is guaranteed for freshmen and awarded by lottery for upperclassmen. Dorm life can be crazy or cloistered. West campus is populated primarily by freshmen, and consequently the place is busier and more boisterous than the North Campus residential area. The six West Campus "University Halls," commonly called U-Halls (it can be a challenge to persuade parents that these are not moving trucks) tend to be noisy round-the-clock.

West Campus students have to trudge up a breath-taking hill ("The Slope") on their way to classes each day. North Campus dorms are quieter, with more upperclassmen mingled with freshmen, and the walk to classes is much easier. Balch Hall, the only remaining single-sex dorm on campus, provides beautifully maintained rooms for women; feminism thrives in this dorm. Risley, a residence hall near the center of campus, is reserved for the artistic and dramatic. It is not unusual to find students dressed in medieval clothing jousting on Risley's front lawn, and occasionally there will be a nude modeling session (not on the front lawn) for those who need sketching practice.

The 760-acre campus is a mix of stone buildings, gardens, fields, streams, woods, and open spaces. Towering 173 feet above it all is McGraw Tower, an 1891 landmark containing a set of chimes which were first played on the university's opening day in 1868. Willard Hall, a stately Gothic edifice with cathedral ceilings, marble staircases, and oak paneling is a center of campus life with dining facilities, a small theater, an art gallery, and offices for more than 40 of the 500 student groups and organizations. Close to the campus and open to the public, the Cornell Plantations provide nature lovers with 3,000 acres of woodlands, streams, ponds, gorges and trails, as well as botanical and flower and herb gardens. There is even an arboretum, not to mention a garden of poisonous plants.

Although some students limit their athletic activity to frisbee, more active athletes have a choice of 20 intercollegiate sports for men and 16 for women, plus 26 intramurals for men and 23 for women. Yes, Ed Marinaro played football there once, but Cornell normally fields an undistinguished team. Cornell brags about its hockey, however. The team (mostly Canadian) usually does well, and fans are faithful, loud, and cheerfully obnoxious. The Harvard animus finds an outlet in the biggest game of the season. The rivalry is bitter at the Cornell-Harvard hockey game; Cornell fans throw fish and other debris onto the ice, and tie a live chicken to one goalpost to express the prevailing opinion of their rival. Lacrosse is popular in the spring, and Cornell's squad is typically first-rate. Facilities include a 25,000-seat stadium, a 5,000-seat gymnasium, three swimming pools, a boathouse, as well as plenty of playing fields and courts of various sorts.

Approximately 40 percent of the men, and 30 percent of the women at Cornell join 60 national fraternities and sororities. Generally there is not much hostility between Greeks and non-Greeks. Greek events like Fun-in-the-Sun, and Rallye-Round-the-Lake attract many nonbelongers. The university administration, disapproving of the drinking done at these events, has canceled or downplayed them in recent years.

The same kill-joy impulse has caused the university administration to eliminate other Cornell traditions. In 1990, the university called off the "Dragon Day" celebration, a St. Patrick's day event in which freshman architects parade an enormous dragon around campus, because the affair annually produced drunkenness and disorder. Similarly, Springfest, the last-day-of-classes bash which transformed the Slope into a beery carnival, was canceled due to excessive inebriation. Though revived by popular demand, the new, university-sanctioned Springfest of recent years has lost much of its zest.

Politically, Cornell leans left. In classes, lecturers habitually recite liberal pieties. Quite often, this is good-humored bad-mouthing of capitalism, religion, and Republican presidents. The pervasive leftist slant is more annoying than oppressive, however, and the student who retains the ability to snicker at politically correct talk likely will get through Cornell unindoctrinated. Resident advisors patrol dorms to remove posters or decorations that seem sexist or homophobic or otherwise offensive. Teaching assistants vigilantly correct students who mistakenly refer to female teenagers as "girls," or persist in using masculine pronouns. Though the left can get mean, it takes itself so seriously that it is often too funny to be frightening.

Popular political causes include divestment rallies where students often run into their government, philosophy, or English professors. The Cornell left demonstrates about South Africa and Latin America again and again. They are less interested in other areas of the globe. A small number of hardened activists will turn out regularly to praise "legal and guilt-free" abortion, Cornell's unionized service workers, as well as socialists and Marxists everywhere. In April 1991, about 200 black and Hispanic students blocked entrances to the administration building in a protest against the university's failure to find a director for the Hispanic-American studies program. They also demanded that no black or Hispanic student be denied admission because of lack of financial aid.

It's not that Cornell doesn't care about having the politically correct racial balance. About 20 percent of students are minorities including approximately 12 percent of Asian descent. And the administration does love to praise the place for its diversity. But "diversity" often means having classicists eat lunch with budding horticulturalists, or having one student cram for a physics exam while another burns

midnight oil in a design studio and a third anxiously presides at the
birthing of a heifer. "Diversity," at Cornell does not yet mean only
differences of class or race or gender. And that is good news for
traditionalists.

Dartmouth College

Dean of Admissions and Financial Aid, Dartmouth College
McNutt Hall, Hanover, NH 03775 (603) 646-2875

Type: Private and Secular

Students:
4,275 undergraduates
  1,834 men
  2,441 women
1,024 graduate students

Applications:
Closing date: January 1
25% of applicants accepted

	Applied	Accepted	Enrolled
men	5,229	1,166	589
women	3,087	903	450

SAT or ACT required
  Score reported by: March 1
  Mid 50% of freshman scores:
    SAT-Math   650–730
    SAT-Verbal   570–680

Costs and Aid:

Tuition and fees	$15,370
Room and Board	5,120

Scholarships:

Academic	No
Athletic	No
Minority	No

Financial Aid:

Freshmen	37%
Upperclassmen	50%

Library:	1,700,000 titles
ROTC:	Yes
Study Abroad:	Yes
Percentage of courses that can be used to fulfill distribution requirements:	91

In a landmark case before the U.S. Supreme Court in 1819, Dartmouth alumnus Daniel Webster argued passionately that the State of New Hampshire be prohibited from taking his beloved alma mater and turning it into a public institution. He concluded with this moving appeal: "It is, sir, as I have said, a small college. And yet, there are those who love it." Webster won his case, so that today Dartmouth remains small, private, and fiercely loved by many of its students and most of its devoted alumni. But Dartmouth also continues to provoke political controversy. This time it focuses not on public versus private rights but on the merits of traditional educational values versus the demands of the new multiculturalism.

Founded in 1769 by missionaries in order to educate Indians in Christianity and the benefits of Western civilization, Dartmouth matriculates around 4,300 undergraduates. One of the college maxims has always been that "university" is a dirty word. Dartmouth's loyal alumni and friends have refused to allow that bigger is better, at least as far as their alma mater is concerned. So Dartmouth still proudly calls itself a college, despite the presence of the Dartmouth Medical

School, the Amos Tuck School of Business, and the Thayer School of Engineering, all of them respected in their fields and all important parts of the institution as a whole.

How long this will remain the case, however, is now open to question. In 1988, a year after he took office, President James Freedman (late of the University of Iowa) took pains to declare that Dartmouth was a liberal arts *university*. This shift in emphasis was partly in response to a faculty report stating that Dartmouth had already passed the point of decision and could not return to being a liberal arts college of the traditional kind. Faculty opinion supports more future emphasis on research and less on teaching, and an architectural study has been commissioned to see how the physical plant might accommodate new research facilities.

Dartmouth College Bulletin, September 1990:
Education 24.—The Hidden Curriculum: Socialization and the Schools
Professor Thomas A. Callister

"Children and youth learn far more in school than what is purposely or consciously taught. This course will explore the experience of students in American schools outside the formal, public curriculum. The development of assumptions about learning and ability, sex-roles, ethnic identity, social class consciousness, as well as political indoctrination in both elementary and secondary schools will be considered. Regular field observations (in real-life schools) will be informed by readings in socialization theory. Some consideration of other cultural models will also be included."

Currently, however, the college still maintains a concern for the undergraduate that is uncommon for a modern university, even within the Ivy League. The result is a body of alumni who regard their time at Dartmouth with deep nostalgia, and are passionately opposed to any move that would destroy the singular chemistry of the place. In their rate of giving and their continued involvement with the college, the alumni try to perpetuate the cohesiveness that, together with its high rank in the academic pecking order, has set it apart from other top schools.

Dartmouth's faith in small-college virtue is more than just history, however; in spite of changing priorities, it is still manifested in the classroom by the way professors teach. The battle between the claims

TUITION AND FEES INCREASE
Average Increase/Year: Private = 11.15%, Dartmouth = 7.78%

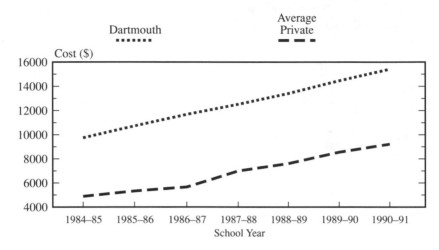

Source: The College Entrance Examination Board

of research and teaching on faculty time has long raged on college campuses, but at Dartmouth teaching has traditionally been victorious. You will not find graduate students leading courses (math and science courses sometimes use grading and lab assistants), and there are few large, anonymous lecture classes. Most seminars enroll 10 or fewer. Moreover, professors are available to and interested in their students.

Strong departments are the rule rather than the exception, with English, history, Romance languages, political science, and computer science drawing special kudos. Special academic facilities include a learning resource center, an art museum, an observatory, and a center for the performing arts.

One of the dominant aspects of Dartmouth academic life is the so-called "Dartmouth Plan," instituted to allow a modest increase in enrollment when the school went coed in the early 1970s. Under this schedule, the academic year is divided into four 10-week terms, one of which takes place in the summer. A student will typically take 11 or 12 terms to graduate, one of which must be a summer session at the end of the sophomore year, colloquially known as "Camp Dartmouth." Thus, students can custom-design their enrollment patterns in order to take advantage of opportunities for employment and foreign study, which might not otherwise be available. On the downside, the D-Plan permits students to spend a large part of the conventional school year away from campus, which can lead to strained friendships and irregular involvement in campus activities. To avoid this, students may decide to elect a very conventional schedule, save for the one required summer term.

Dartmouth's general education requirements are presently geared to give students a very wide range of choice, and there is no compulsion to include the history or intellectual development of Western civilization. For the last decade, however, it has been mandatory to study non-Western cultures. There are programs of women's, Afro-American, Native American, and environmental studies.

To graduate, candidates for the Bachelor of Arts degree need a minimum of 35 term courses. One course must be in English and emphasizes writing. Another is a first-year seminar in one of 25 departments that also emphasizes writing and, additionally, independent study. Students also must take three terms of a foreign language,

DISTRIBUTION OF UNDERGRADUATE AID
1989–90 School Year

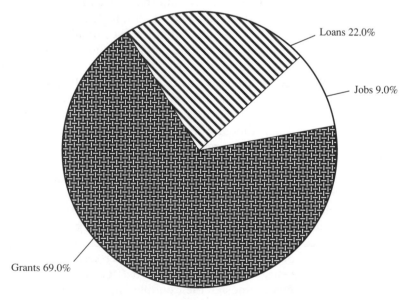

Loans 22.0%

Jobs 9.0%

Grants 69.0%

Source: The College Entrance Examination Board, 1990

unless they pass a proficiency test. In addition, they must enroll in four introductory courses in each of three divisions, the humanities, the sciences, and the social sciences, as well as in one course in non-Western cultures. Finally, students must participate in three terms of physical activities (sports of their choice) and pass a swim test.

The physical education requirements reflect the college's long sporting and athletic tradition. Dartmouth has always had a reputation for attracting outdoor types, no doubt due to its isolated location in a wilderness area. Today, the Dartmouth Outing Club is one of the most active and important organizations on campus. The club maintains part of the Appalachian Trail, as well as many cabins on huge tracts of land owned by the college in the White Mountains. One of these is the beautiful lodge at Mt. Moosilauke, which every freshman gets to know during a five-day hiking trip before the start of the fall term. Almost all first-year students participate, and some form friendships that last a lifetime. The trips, led by upperclass guides, also serve to introduce newcomers to college ways.

Having survived the rigors of mountain living, most students go on to participate in some form of college athletics. Even after recent budget cuts, Dartmouth still fields more intramural teams than any other Ivy League school. Thanks to its location, winter sports are easily available, and many students from warmer climes are happily introduced to the excellent skiing in the area. From the rowers, who train intensively year-round, to the rugby players, who seem to practice mostly by drinking beer, to the ultimate frisbee team, who are out on the green when the sun shines, most students find a sport they enjoy. The school sponsors more than 30 intercollegiate varsity teams and around 35 intramural sports. Although the football team isn't what it used to be, students enthusiastically cheer it on when it confronts ancient Ivy League rivals. Women's sports are very successful, and often win more matches than the men's teams.

As you would expect, facilities are magnificent. The college boasts a new sports complex, a 21,000-seat stadium, several arenas, a fitness center, swimming pools, a golf course, riding stables, and, of course, an ice rink and ski runs. The 265-acre campus is picture perfect, both winter and summer. Built around a green (often white with snow), the buildings are eclectic in architectural style, but dominated by white brick colonials.

On-campus housing is guaranteed freshman year, and allotted on a first-come, first-served basis thereafter. Ninety-five percent of students do live on campus. Freshmen are distributed throughout all the dorms. Accommodation is mostly coed, but some students live in fraternity and sorority houses; there are also special-interest houses. Dorms are divided into "clusters," which organize social activities and other events in order to foster a feeling of community. The college has recently renovated the older dorms, which are spacious and comfortable, and is building new ones. More remarkably, the school has hard-wired the rooms into its master computer system, as it has the classrooms. All students bring their own personal computers to college, or purchase them as freshmen; virtually everyone at Dartmouth takes computer literacy for granted—a legacy of the school's farsighted former President Kemeny, the inventor of DOS.

Extracurricular and social life, largely self-contained on campus, has always revolved around the Greek system to which more than half the students now belong. In 1978, the faculty opened a Pandora's box by voting to abolish fraternities and sororities, which it considered obsolete and elitist. The alumni did not agree, however, and their howls of outrage (plus threats to cut off donations) saved the Greeks, at least for the moment. The system persists in popularity partly because it binds students together despite their different enrollment patterns. With almost 30 fraternities and sororities, there is one to suit almost every interest. Some are dominated by stereotypes (liberals, conservatives, computer hackers, lacrosse players, etc.) and others aren't.

In any case, although the system does provide opportunities to meet people from other classes, backgrounds, and interests, its most important function, students say, is to host large, open parties in an otherwise socially barren area. (Boston, the nearest big city, is almost 150 miles away.) Gone, however, are the days of cruel hazing, though drinking is still a popular pastime. The Greek houses, once all-male and rowdy, now tend to be miniature student centers, making up for Dartmouth's lack of a central gathering place.

Despite the reprieve for the Greek system, tradition is a sensitive topic at Dartmouth. Because the college was founded with the education of local Indians in mind, it was natural to adopt the American Indian as a symbol, particularly in sports. Just as naturally, modern racial chic dictated that the Indian symbol be abolished, since it was "racist" and might offend Dartmouth's minority population of slightly more than 20 percent (9 percent are Asian). It was replaced by the rather less charismatic "Big Green."

Other traditions continued to fall one by one to the onslaught of political correctness—no longer can students sing the rousing alma mater, "Men of Dartmouth," since it has been neutered to the sexless "We of Dartmouth." Freshmen no longer rush across the field during halftime at the Homecoming game to sing the song on the opposing team's stands, since the stampede is regarded as too dangerous. Winter Carnival, once the major regional festival, still draws crowds, but the snow sculptures are not so spectacular, the parties not so big, the winter sporting events not so competitive. In the fall, a huge bonfire is still built and lit the night before Homecoming. But even this widely appreciated event may be done away with soon, due to the protests of environmentalists about the waste of wood.

Contesting this erosion of campus tradition is one voice, that of *The Dartmouth Review*. Also arguing against the college's affirmative action policies and for a return to a Western-oriented curriculum, the newspaper is largely supported by its alumni subscribers, who number in the thousands. The off-campus conservative journal has been publishing since 1980, and has had many confrontations with the Dartmouth administration. In 1988, for example, it took up the case of William Cole, a black music professor who the paper alleged was incompetent. This attack and the furor it created resulted in the college's suspending the editors. Although they were later reinstated by a state court, the controversy wracked the school and drew unfavorable national media attention. Professor Cole has since resigned.

The paper has continued to publish weekly, despite efforts to discredit it. The audacity of *The Dartmouth Review* is more than matched by that of the administration and faculty. Professor Cole's wife, a French professor, assigned her class essays on the *Review,* and then gave the one hapless student who dared support it a D for writing a racist essay. In another incident, a liberal professor tried to have a *Review* staffer suspended on an unsubstantiated plagiarism charge, and succeeded until the uproar forced his readmission. The paper has opposed a minorities-first policy, which called for hiring minority faculty, regardless of the college's vacancies in their fields or their qualifications.

The latest brouhaha, in 1990, involved an anti-Semitic remark published in the *Review*. The staff, some of whom are Jewish, some black, claimed it was introduced by "sabotage" (the offices are open to all, and the remark—a quotation from Adolph Hitler—replaced the standard masthead quotation, which is seldom checked by proofreaders). The editor apologized profusely, initiated an investigation (which later supported the view of sabotage), and recalled as many issues of the paper as he could. Dartmouth President James Freedman refused to accept the *Review*'s explanation, denounced the paper as racist, and in a letter to the *New York Times* called it "an instrument of intimidation." He also attacked well-known, non-alumni backers of the paper. The war continues.

Another controversy revolves around the unpalatable practice of distributing at meals both condoms and brochures detailing how to have safe homosexual sex. Heterosexual sex is also an issue, and as the feminists become increasingly hysterical, charges of rape and sexual assault abound. One Dartmouth female student succeeded in having a male student suspended after waiting months and months to charge him. (She admitted that at the time she had no objections when he pawed her one evening while they were both intoxicated.) The same young man was also accused of causing a hickey on a woman's neck. Soon posters with the offender's picture appeared on campus with the caption, "A warning to all dartmouth womyn: beware this man."

But despite all the turmoil and publicity caused by recent campus disputes, most Dartmouth students are not extremists. By and large, they are middle-class moderates who are trying to preserve a sense of belonging to a tightly knit community, which sometimes seems to be unravelling before their eyes. Whether a student favors "diversity" or "tradition," he cannot avoid confronting the issue at Dartmouth, where it continues to disturb the college's domestic tranquillity both in and out of the classroom.

Davidson College

Dean of Admissions and Financial Aid, Davidson College
P.O. Box 1737, Davidson, NC 28036 (704) 892-2230

Type: Private and Protestant

Students:
1,406 undergraduates
   784 men
   622 women

Applications:
Closing date: February 1
34% of applicants accepted

	Applied	Accepted	Enrolled
men	1,189	374	199
women	890	330	179

SAT or ACT required
  Score reported by: February 1
  Mid 50% of freshman scores:
    SAT-Math   600–690
    SAT-Verbal 540–650

Costs and Aid:

Tuition and fees	$12,440
Room and Board	3,850

Scholarships:
Academic	Yes
Athletic	Yes
Minority	Yes

Financial Aid:
Freshmen	61%
Upperclassmen	62%

Library:	340,000 titles
ROTC:	Yes
Study Abroad:	Yes
Percentage of courses that can be used to fulfill distribution requirements:	44.4

Although Davidson College has been recognized by the *cognoscenti* for years as one of the premier, small liberal arts colleges in the country, recently it has won a wider, national reputation for excellence, especially in pre-professional training. Well over half the alumni go on to graduate school, with nearly a quarter choosing the law, and 15 percent medicine. Davidson can also claim the distinction of having produced the third highest number of Rhodes Scholars among liberal arts colleges, surpassed only by Swarthmore and Williams.

Established in 1837 by ministers of the Presbyterian Church, the school began with 65 students on land donated by the son of a Revolutionary War general, from whom Davidson takes its name. Just before the Civil War, the infant college received a bequest of $250,000, which made it the richest college south of Princeton. The war dimmed that short-lived glory, however, and by 1866 had reduced the student body to a minuscule 24. The college, like so many in the South, struggled to survive. Much later, the Rockefeller family and the Duke Endowment provided badly needed financial buttressing, so that Davidson's young men might continue to pursue "the quest for truth, setting no limits to the adventures of the mind." Since then, generous donations by successful alumni have left Davidson with a comfortable cushion.

While nondenominational, the college is avowedly Christian and its statement of purpose declares emphatically that "Davidson recognizes God as the source of all truth. . . . it sees Jesus Christ as the central fact of history, giving purpose, order and value to the whole of life." Not surprisingly, a large majority of students is Protestant (an estimated 80 percent), but there is a small Roman Catholic minority (an estimated 14 percent). In 1972, the school started to admit women, who now make up almost half the student body.

Although Davidson maintains its dedication to turning out well-rounded graduates through emphasis on teaching (no teaching assistants are employed), its growing national prominence has in the last few years raised questions about the importance of increasing faculty research and publication. The current president is said to encourage this trend out of his ambition for the college, and perhaps for himself. As a result, some alumni and students are concerned that teaching quality will begin to suffer.

Davidson does not have a core curriculum, but it does have the following distribution requirements: one course each in English composition, history, literature, a foreign language, and the fine arts; two in religion and philosophy, one of which must be in religion; two in the social sciences, and three in mathematics and the natural sciences. In 1988, the faculty stiffened the rules so that students can't get by with three general science courses, but must at least take one math course and one lab course. Exemption from the English composition, math, and foreign language requirements, however, is often given through advanced placement test credits. The best departments are reputed to be English, economics, history, and the physical sciences. Economics and history are the most popular majors.

The faculty has also instituted a "cultural diversity" requirement, which it describes as "an approved course exploring societies or cultures which differ from those of the United States or Europe." The initiative for this innovation does not seem to have come from minority students, who are not militants. Less than 10 percent are minorities, about equally divided between blacks and Asians, with a tiny representation of Hispanics (1 percent).

Classes at Davidson are small, even in most introductory courses. Seminars and honors programs are usually limited to 15, while most lecture courses attract between 25 and 30. The small classes, as well

TUITION AND FEES INCREASE
Average Increase/Year: Private = 11.15%, Davidson = 11.56%

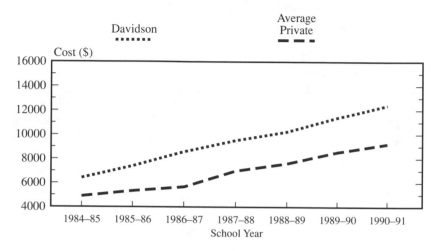

Source: The College Entrance Examination Board

---

as the relatively easy availability of one-on-one independent study courses, help to develop and maintain a close student-professor relationship. Professors are generally available for help and advice, or just a pleasant chat.

Davidson is governed by an honor code based on trust. Examinations are self-scheduled; students are given one week, with two exam periods a day, to take their tests free of faculty supervision and at their own convenience. The honor code is immensely popular among the students who administer, guard, and uphold it zealously.

The college tries to expand the horizons of its students, most of whom come from the South, by offering a variety of study-abroad programs and summer internships, as well as a semester at the Duke University Marine Laboratory in Beaufort, N.C., and an abnormal psychology program at Broughton Hospital in Morganton, N.C. Campus life, despite the college's small size and rural location about 20 miles from Charlotte, is far from dull. The college sponsors a series of concerts and plays annually, and the Grey Student Union hosts a variety of bands, ranging from the Indigo Girls to Sweet Honey in the Rock. The Union also shows popular films and cinema classics, and conducts "study breaks" regularly. The Cunningham Fine Arts building provides galleries for studio art majors to hold their senior exhibits. Patterson Court offers a release for those primal urges to party, as it is home to six fraternities and three women's eating houses. The most popular campuswide activities have been Habitat for Humanity and Amnesty International.

Although Davidson is the smallest college to participate in Division I, sports are not very important to most students and the stadium isn't always packed at home football games. Basketball is the school's showcase sport, but students seem to enjoy participating more than watching. There are 10 intercollegiate teams for men and 7 for women plus 9 intramurals each. A new athletic complex was completed two years ago, and contains a state-of-the-art swimming pool, which has spurred the school to form teams that started competing in the autumn of 1991.

The Student Government Association affords an opportunity to take an active role in campus life. Students elect representatives of the fraternities, women's eating houses, independent students, and the

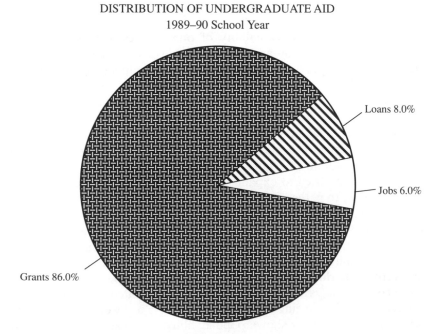

DISTRIBUTION OF UNDERGRADUATE AID
1989–90 School Year

Loans 8.0%

Jobs 6.0%

Grants 86.0%

Source: The College Entrance Examination Board, 1990

four classes. Many pay little attention to the SGA and some consider it a paper tiger when it comes to taking a stand on issues. When students want to organize, which isn't often, they do it through groups like Amnesty International, which sponsored an anti-apartheid march two years ago, or they take their complaints to the school newspaper, which publishes all editorial pieces it receives, unedited. On the whole, students tend to take their own initiative in addressing their grievances, rather than referring them to an organization for group action. There is a Black Student Coalition, but it is small, and generally acts as a beneficial force through its sponsorship of cultural and social events. The only real partisan groups on campus are the College Republicans and College Democrats, with the College Republicans dominant. Yet both lie largely dormant except during election years.

Davidson has not had the extensive problems with crime that plague many large colleges and universities. Although Charlotte, the state's largest city, is only a 20-minute drive, drugs have remained in the background. Alcohol consumption is sometimes a problem. Davidson's police force acts in conjunction with the local town police and sheriff's departments to counteract and contain law violations. Late-night escorts are available but seldom utilized. The bulk of the campus police files consists of parking violations and false fire-alarm reports, the latter the result of an excess of exuberance (and alcohol) by partying pranksters.

Housing is provided in dormitories, coed by floor, as well as in apartments. Most of the dorms were built in the early part of this century but now offer modern conveniences such as air conditioning, lounges with television sets, and soft-drink and ice machines. The apartments are attractively furnished, with single rooms for each of the four suite mates, a kitchenette, and a bathroom. Housing is guaranteed for freshmen, with upperclassmen taking their chances by lottery; however, 92 percent of students do live on campus.

Davidson College still offers an excellent, old-fashioned liberal arts education, and is still geared to success-oriented students who plan postgraduate study. The atmosphere is conservative but tolerant. Yet, as an aspiring institution, it seeks greater prominence at a time when national standards of acceptability press colleges to conform to the new orthodoxy of the politically correct. As an old Presbyterian institution, Davidson now faces the struggle between faith and vanity, with the outcome no longer certain.

Duke University

Director of Undergraduate Admissions, Duke University
2138 Campus Drive, Durham, NC 27706 (919) 684-3214

Type: Private and Protestant

Students:
5,690 undergraduates
  3,421 men
  2,269 women
4,413 graduate students

Applications:
Closing date: January 1
25% of applicants accepted

	Applied	Accepted	Enrolled
men	7,480	1,817	785
women	5,940	1,529	698

SAT or ACT required (SAT preferred)
  Score reported by: March 1
  Mid 50% of freshman scores:
    SAT-Math   640–730
    SAT-Verbal 580–670

Costs and Aid:

Tuition and fees	$14,130
Room and Board	4,680

Scholarships:
Academic	Yes
Athletic	Yes
Minority	Yes

Financial Aid:
Freshmen	39%
Upperclassmen	40%

Library: 3,550,000 titles

ROTC: Yes
Study Abroad: Yes

Percentage of courses that can be used to fulfill distribution requirements: 84

Much like the South which surrounds it, Duke University is a place of conflict, where old and new, tradition and diversity struggle for supremacy. The battle at Duke is more genteel but less in doubt than the battle between the "old" and the "new" elsewhere in the South. The forces of tradition in the rest of the South still contest with new and changing ways; at Duke, the "old" has been largely routed, the "new" has been institutionalized. The fashionable, the strange, and the immediate are definitely in. Tradition, in all its forms, is definitely out.

Most of the talk about tradition at today's Duke is negative—the American tradition means a society built on racial oppression, Western tradition means cultural imperialism, and religious tradition means inherited intolerance. As for Southern pride and hospitality, they have become oxymorons at Duke. It is now possible to say that the only thing "Southern" about Duke University is the North Carolina climate.

Academically, flexibility has replaced tradition as the basis for present-day liberal arts instruction at Duke. Trinity College, Duke's

123

school of arts and sciences, sponsors a "variety of approaches," rather than a consistent one. The college offers two plans called, simply enough, Program I and Program II. The difference is that the latter is a bit more focused on the individual who has an "unusual interest or talent in a special field." Program I recognizes six areas of knowledge—arts and civilization, social sciences, and so forth. The student must take courses in five of the six areas, and many different courses

---

Bulletin, 1990–1991:
Selected course offerings in the Cultural Anthropology Department:

152S. Food in Cross-Cultural Perspectives. (cross-listed with Comparative Area Studies)
Professor Apte

"The behavioral, institutional, linguistic, religious, and ideological aspects in relation to the production, distribution, and consumption of food within and across cultures."

272S. Marxism and Feminism. (cross-listed with Women's Studies)
Professor Smith

"Introduction to the theoretical literature and debates linking Marxism and feminism."

---

will suffice. The Program I student can opt for a conventional departmental major, a less specific program major, or an even more vague interdepartmental concentration. A Program II student is presumed to have special interests which justify an individually designed plan of study, but he must be formally admitted to this status, and his courses must be approved by a special advisor or committee. It is also possible for some better focused students to take advantage of Duke's famous graduate and professional schools by combining the senior undergraduate year with the first graduate one. This is a benefit to those who have resisted the temptation to meander through undergraduate studies; the reward is a more rapid garnering of professional status.

Within individual departments Duke has also done its best to keep up with the latest trends. The English department is now a famous example. Its reconstruction was a major institutional priority and funds from the endowment were committed to it. Duke hired Johns Hopkins University professor Stanley Fish as the department's new chair. Fish

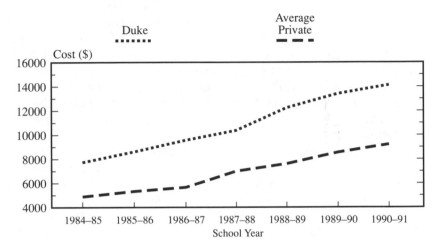

TUITION AND FEES INCREASE
Average Increase/Year: Private = 11.15%, Duke = 10.77%

Source: The College Entrance Examination Board

then hired Marxist literary scholars like Frederic Jameson, members of the "materialist criticism" sect like Annabel Patterson and her husband Lee, and others of similar outlook like Barbara Herrnstein Smith and Frank Lentricchia. Reportedly, some of these professors received six-figure salaries. Thus, Duke has, unquestionably, assembled the best-paid group of nihilists in America.

But Duke's quest for new-fangled academic respectability has become something of an embarrassment. The expensively bought English department is now a nationally known, near-ludicrous symbol for politically correct academic excess. Chairperson Fish did not help much when, in speaking of students and faculty, he said:

> I want them . . . to do what I tell them to . . . I want to be able to walk into any first-rate faculty anywhere and dominate it, shape it to my will . . . I'm fascinated by my own will.

Fish further humiliated the university when he sought to intimidate faculty colleagues interested in starting a Duke chapter of the traditionalist National Association of Scholars by denouncing some fellow professors as fascists and racists.

The English department is but the tip of an iceberg, for other liberal arts departments are also now highly politicized. Race and gender issues have become a central part of sociology courses; jazz classes have become a place for diatribes on racism and affirmative action; freshmen in university writing courses are learning more about sexual choice than they are about sentence structure. New fields of study are also emerging to fit the growing politicization of the academy, including a well-funded women's studies program and an African-American studies program. Some are also actively trying to establish a homosexual studies program similar to those now appearing at other institutions.

The once proud religious heritage of Duke—witness the school's motto *Eruditio et Religio*—has also been subjected to similar treatment. The Duke bulletin notes that "*Eruditio et Religio* reflects a fundamental faith in the union of knowledge and religion, the advancement of learning, the defense of scholarship, the love of freedom and truth, a spirit of tolerance, and a rendering of the greatest service to

DISTRIBUTION OF UNDERGRADUATE AID
1989–90 School Year

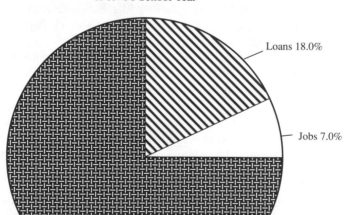

Loans 18.0%

Jobs 7.0%

Grants 75.0%

Source: The College Entrance Examination Board, 1990

the individual, the state, the nation, and the church." Unfortunately, the only remains of the spirit upon which Duke University was founded lie in archival documents and promotional bulletins.

Instead, religion at the university has become consumed with politicized services and gatherings, dominated by support of Marxist guerrillas in El Salvador or condemnation of American military activity in the Persian Gulf. Ministers and professors in the departments of religion and theology spend most of their time "deconstructing" ancient religious documents and restructuring them to be more "inclusive," rather than promoting traditional values for the greater community.

Inevitably, undergraduate life is also affected when the supposedly ethical component, instead of promoting strong values, preaches indiscriminate "tolerance." Officially chartered student organizations have promoted "safe sex" weeks and "coming out" weeks for students of different sexual interests, whereas conventional college organizations such as fraternities and sororities are seemingly always called on to justify their existence. Meanwhile, new organizations that isolate themselves on the grounds of race or sex, or promote new and anti-traditional lifestyles are continually praised.

However much the current regime seeks to impose new ways of thought, it can do little to alter the physical surroundings and the structures reminiscent of the school's original ethos. Duke is properly famous for its transplanted Gothic splendor and for its natural setting. It is a very agreeable place for students to live, and thus the university attracts them from across the country. The reputation of the institution is very important to those who run it. Duke is now a "world renowned" university even though it was founded in its present configuration only in 1924. This conspicuous success is proof that the administration can be relentless in the pursuit of institutional advancement even at the cost of intellectual integrity.

One such conspicuous success is the marriage between sports and academics, difficult to find elsewhere in an age of NCAA violations and double standards for scholarship athletes. The university is properly proud of its sports programs; they are leaders in their respective NCAA divisions, and can boast of high graduation rates and strong academic performances for scholar-athletes. Duke's strong sports program is highlighted by its varsity men's basketball team (1991 NCAA Division I champions), which heads a field of 24 varsity teams, including men's and women's tennis, soccer, and lacrosse (which regularly rank in the top 25 of their respective NCAA divisions), baseball, football, fencing, field hockey, and wrestling. Duke also boasts more than 30 club sports, which interest active sports enthusiasts who wish for a strong and competitive program without the burdens associated with being an active member of a varsity sport. The program includes tennis (men's and women's), water polo, and such diverse sports as skydiving and sailing. The athletic department also organizes intramural events.

Beyond academics and athletics is the university's vivacious social life. Campus parties are usually sponsored by one of the more than 30 fraternities and sororities. Together, the Greek system includes around 40 percent of Duke's women and 35 percent of its men. Campuswide blowouts like Springfest and Oktoberfest offer welcome relief to the demands of academic life. As Durham itself lacks the vitality that college students look for, many make the short trip—about 15 miles—to Chapel Hill on the weekends for bigger and better entertainment of various sorts.

Duke's leadership has tried to gain a new following by creating a university in the academic and social avant-garde while at the same time hoping to retain the loyalty and financial support of its older, more traditionally minded constituency. But the Duke administration is finding it harder to keep these two very different groups from discovering each other. And especially as the latter comes to know more about the former, the balancing act and its pretenses will be more difficult to maintain. In the meantime, the tightrope at Duke appears evermore dangerous to walk.

Emory University

Dean of Admission, Emory University
Boisfeuillet Jones Center
Atlanta, GA 30322 (404) 727-6036

Type: Private and Protestant

Students:
5,259 undergraduates
  2,410 men
  2,849 women
4,131 graduate students

Applications:
Closing date: February 15
55% of applicants accepted

	Applied	Accepted	Enrolled
men	2,873	1,679	530
women	3,389	1,771	503

SAT or ACT required
  Score reported by: March 1
  Mid 50% of freshman scores:
    SAT-Math   550–670
    SAT-Verbal 500-620

Costs and Aid:

Tuition and fees	$13,700
Room and Board	4,300

Scholarships:
  Academic   Yes
  Athletic   No
  Minority   Yes

Financial Aid:
  Freshmen   53%
  Upperclassmen 53%

Library: 2,062,888 titles

ROTC: No
Study Abroad: Yes

**Percentage of courses that can
be used to fulfill distribution
requirements:**   15.4

If you happen to prefer Pepsi to Coca-Cola, you won't be very popular at Emory University, which owes some of its fame and a big boost in its fortunes to the world's long-time love affair with Coke. In 1979, Emory alumnus Robert Woodruff—now deceased but then CEO of the Atlanta-based Coca-Cola Corporation—paused, and refreshed his alma mater with a cool $100 million. This constituted the largest gift to a single educational institution in the history of American philanthropy, and helped raise Emory into the big leagues of nationally prominent universities. One of the things Emory now has in common with many of them is a fixation on multiculturalism and controversial proposals to promote it.

Founded in 1836 as a small Methodist liberal arts college, the school struggled for many years to remain afloat while fighting insufficient funding and small enrollment. Like other Southern colleges, Emory was forced to close during the Civil War, because its young men dashed off in droves to fight the Yankees. During Reconstruction, however, Emory's size and reputation began to grow and, in 1919, the

129

college moved from the small town of Oxford, Georgia, to its present Atlanta campus. Emory continued to evolve academically and socially, allowing women undergraduates in 1953 and black undergraduates in 1962, but it remained a regionally respected school until the big bonanza.

When added to its already substantial endowment, the Woodruff gift enabled Emory to compete on more equal terms with nationally known private institutions. The university rapidly boosted its Schools of Law, Medicine, and Theology, and formed close affiliations with the U.S. Centers for Disease Control, the Jimmy Carter Center, and the Yerkes Regional Primate Research Center. It also continued to develop its undergraduate program.

Emory College 1988–1990:
Women's Studies 102—Women, Power, Property, and Identity (required course for the major)

"Introduction to the study of women and gender from the perspective of the Social Sciences, with special attention to gender as a system of social classification in work, communities, and politics, and to women's identities and roles within and among states, classes, races."

Emory College is the liberal arts nucleus of the university and enrolls just under 4,300 of the almost 9,000 students at the university, most of whom are from the South, although nearly all the states and several dozen foreign countries are represented. There is a sizable contingent from the Northeastern and Middle Atlantic states. About 11 percent of all students are minorities. The college has no core curriculum, but relies instead on a system of stringent distribution requirements, although some exemptions may be earned through advanced placement credits or proficiency tests.

One hundred and thirty-two semester hours of credit are needed for graduation. The distribution requirements fall into six categories. Under "Tools of Learning," every freshman must complete the following: either Rhetoric and Composition or Introduction to Literature. Beyond that, in each of the following three years students must write a major research paper, and "evaluation of the papers shall include attention to spelling, grammar, style and documentation." These may be written in any course with consent of the instructor. Students must also take a year of a foreign language. In addition, still under Tools of

TUITION AND FEES INCREASE
Average Increase/Year: Private = 11.15%, Emory = 10.25%

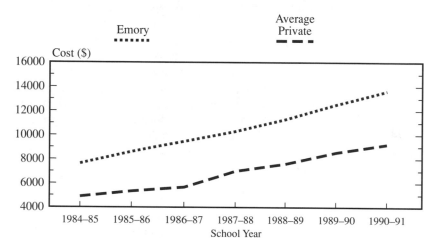

Source: The College Entrance Examination Board

Learning, they must complete one of three listed math courses, or two courses from a short list in math, computer science, philosophy, economics, educational studies, political science, psychology, and sociology.

In the category of natural science and mathematics, students are obliged to take three courses from a specified list in those disciplines. In the third category, "Historical Perspectives of the Western World," they must choose any two courses from a limited list in the following departments: history, art history, music, philosophy, religion, political science, English/theater, and women's studies. Under "The Individual and Society," students must complete two courses, again from a specified list which includes but is not limited to anthropology and African-American and African studies. Under "Aesthetics and Values," they have a choice of two courses from a longer list, which includes but again is not limited to film studies, classics, and several foreign languages—among them Hebrew, Latin, and Greek. The sixth category is health and physical education, which mandates four courses, two of which are health education and swimming.

The luster of this impressive list of distribution requirements is about to be tarnished, however, by the addition, planned for the autumn of 1991, of a required freshman seminar on racial and gender differences. "Sensitivity" sessions are being designed for staff as well. Fraternity and sorority members are also being singled out for the indoctrination program. These attempts at thought control are part of a series of proposals by President James Laney, who announced in the spring of 1990 that, "I am personally taking charge of this challenge to make Emory a model of multicultural diversity." Another of his declared aims is to create a "Center for Teaching and Curricular Enrichment" in order to emphasize black and feminist political viewpoints in the curriculum. He also plans to hire more minority faculty in key departments as well as to start a visiting fellows program for black business and political leaders. In addition, the Laney agenda includes giving scholarships and grants, not repayable loans, to more black freshmen.

In a letter to the *New York Times,* in April 1990, Laney said that in 1988 he had banned "discriminatory harassment," which he defines as "conduct (oral, written, graphic or physical) directed against any

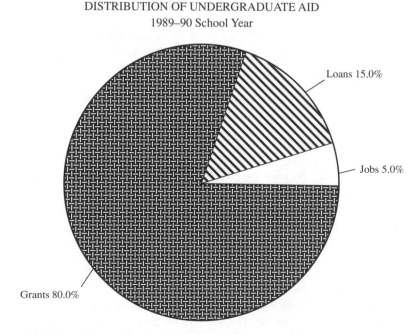

DISTRIBUTION OF UNDERGRADUATE AID
1989–90 School Year

Loans 15.0%

Jobs 5.0%

Grants 80.0%

Source: The College Entrance Examination Board, 1990

person or group . . . that has the purpose or reasonably foreseeable effect of creating an offensive, demeaning, intimidating or hostile environment." He later went on to deny that this policy is a threat to freedom of speech on campus. Indeed, Laney said, it "make[s] it more probable."

Although the anti-harassment policy was two years old at the time of Laney's letter, the spate of new policies he had announced just prior to writing it (see above) was in response to student protests against written and verbal racial attacks on a black female student. That incident had just occurred. According to Captain Jan Freund of the university's security department, it was the first time in his 16 years on the campus that such an occurrence had taken place. But apparently once was enough to risk freedom of speech for the sake of "multicultural diversity."

Although Laney's infatuation with the radical left poses a future threat to freedom in and out of the classroom, at the moment Emory's academic reputation is linked to some famous faculty members, a number of whom have been lured to Emory by the Coca-Cola money. For example, in 1989, three of the five senior members in the French department at Johns Hopkins left Baltimore together for sunnier and richer Atlanta. The faculty included (until his death) Dr. Marshall Hall of the mathematics and computer science department, who worked on the breaking of the German Enigma code during World War II. Other stars are Ulric Neisser, the father of cognitive psychology, and Merle Black, whom many consider to be the foremost scholar in the country on the puzzling subject of Southern politics. Southern politician Jimmy Carter is a frequent and popular guest lecturer. In general, the departments associated with the study of medicine (such as biology and chemistry), and those associated with the study of law (such as political science and philosophy) are the strongest academically. English and psychology are also said to be excellent.

The work ethic at Emory is probably more developed than at many universities. There are no athletic scholarships, and sports stars are not idolized on campus. The academic climate is serious, because many students are aiming at prestigious graduate schools; but it is also underplayed in relaxed Southern style. Most students are very helpful to one another and the campus atmosphere is generally warm and friendly. Class sizes are relatively small and professors are almost always available for private chats. Discussion in class is as important as written work in many courses, and guided independent research and directed reading programs further encourage professor-student relationships.

Naturally, campus life is not all work and no play. Although Emory does not sponsor varsity teams in football and basketball, students enthusiastically support 9 intercollegiate and no fewer than 40 intramural teams for men, as well as 8 intercollegiates and 40 intramurals for women. Tennis and swimming, in an Olympic-size pool, are especially popular. Nature lovers enjoy Lullwater Park, which adjoins the campus and features walking trails, fields, and a small lake.

The 630-acre campus itself is an attraction with its gentle hills, spreading trees, and generous green space. Buildings are colorful and rather grand with marble facades and red roofs. The Woodruff money has generated a rush of new construction, including a library, new residential halls, and a spiffy physical education center. Other impressive facilities have also sprouted up recently, most notably a big research/science center, a student center, and an art and archaeology museum.

All this expansion has enabled Emory to inject new vitality into campus life. There are 200 groups and organizations, including 25 fraternities and sororities to which about half the students belong. The Greeks lead the social scene but don't dominate it, because there are so many attractive alternatives. When students want a break from campus life, they can hurry to downtown Atlanta, five miles away. There they find myriad cultural attractions, as well a multitude of cinemas, malls, gardens, bars and restaurants. The Metropolitan Atlanta Rapid Transportation System (MARTA) goes to all parts of the city. Students can also find many of the above amenities within walking distance of the university (as well as a pawn shop for emergencies). Crime is not a problem at Emory, and the campus security system is excellent. Drug use stays in the closet; alcohol use doesn't.

Housing at Emory has been in short supply recently because of the increased size of incoming freshman classes. Many students prefer to live in apartments or fraternities, however, and almost all students who desire university housing receive it. Freshmen must live on campus; upperclassmen's housing is determined by lottery. All dormitories are coed except for one allotted to women. Comfort levels range from doubles with no sink to small apartments with kitchens.

If it were not for the president's efforts to radicalize the university, Emory's prospects would not seem particularly unpromising. Its academics are strong and extracurricular opportunities abound in pleasant surroundings. However, the university's new obsession with diversity-at-any-cost is already not only curtailing the basic academic traditions, but also provoking the very discord and division it seeks to prevent.

Georgetown University

Dean of Undergraduate Admissions, 37th & O Streets, N.W.
Washington, D.C. 20057 (202) 687-3600

Type: Private and Catholic				

Type: Private and Catholic

Students:
5,725 undergraduates
  2,735 men
  2,990 women
5,611 graduate students

Applications:
Closing date: January 10
23% of applicants accepted

	Applied	Accepted	Enrolled
men	4,957	1,226	653
women	5,701	1,258	674

SAT or ACT required
  Score reported by: early February
  Mid 50% of freshman scores:

Sat-Math	N/A
SAT-Verbal	N/A

Costs and Aid:

Tuition and fees	$14,570
Room and Board	5,900

Scholarships:

Academic	No
Athletic	Yes
Minority	No

Financial Aid:

Freshmen	65%
Upperclassmen	65%
Library:	1,450,991 titles
ROTC:	Yes
Study Abroad:	Yes

**Percentage of courses that can
be used to fulfill distribution
requirements:** 24.9

Not only is Georgetown the oldest Catholic university in the United States, it is also the most prestigious and selective. Located in the nation's capital, the school attracts a highly motivated, cosmopolitan student body from all 50 states and more than 100 foreign countries. Whatever they study, most are drawn to Washington because they "want to be where the action is"; many are also eager to build an understanding of contemporary events on the solid ground of the Western liberal arts, a tradition Georgetown still cherishes.

The school was founded in 1789 by John Carroll, the first Catholic bishop in this country and a member of a prominent Maryland family. His brother, Charles Carroll, was a signatory to the Constitution. Bishop Carroll, who had taught in European Jesuit institutions, yearned to create a system of education in this country that would unite the best of Catholic and republican cultures. "On this academy," he wrote, "is built all my hope of permanency, and success to our Holy Religion in the United States." His academy, which formally became a Jesuit college in 1805, changed little from its founding through the early 1960s. On a trip to America in 1842, Charles Dickens observed, "At George Town, in the suburbs, there is a Jesuit College: delightfully situated, and, so far as I had an opportunity of seeing, well managed. . . . The heights in this neighborhood, above the Potomac River, are very picturesque; and are free, I should conceive, from some of the insalubrities of Washington."

Long past Dickens's time, the college remained a small, liberal arts school for men. (It did not become coeducational until 1979). Georgetown maintained a strong sense of its Catholic identity, insisting upon a well-defined curriculum that followed the lines of the *ratio studiorum* in the Jesuit educational tradition. The emphasis was on the classics, philosophy, theology, the sciences, and literature. All undergraduates must still take two semesters of theology and English and all, except nursing students, must take two semesters of philosophy as well.

Undergraduate Bulletin 1990–1991:
English 112—White Male Writers
Professor Valerie Babb

"When courses are termed Women Writers, Black Women Writers, or Native American Writers to name a few, implicit in their titling is a distinction from a group of writers that have traditionally dominated the American literary canon, white males. It will be the aim of this course to examine white male American writers of the nineteenth and twentieth centuries and explore their treatment of the American identity. By looking at works by Herman Melville, James Fenimore Cooper, Nathaniel Hawthorne, Henry James, and William Faulkner among others, the course will investigate the meaning of 'canon,' and probe why the canon of a pluralistic society remained so uniform."

While professing Roman Catholicism, Georgetown from its inception has always been open to students of all faiths. And, because of its considerable reputation, a significant part of the student body has been non-Catholic (now slightly less than half). Because the university has traditionally attracted many non-Catholics, it did not consider its profession of faith to be incompatible with respect for freedom of conscience and the freedom necessary for academic discourse.

During approximately the last 15 years, however, Georgetown has made a concerted effort to compete with the secular Ivy League schools in regard to alumni giving, admissions selectivity, and endow-

TUITION AND FEES INCREASE
Average Increase/Year: Private = 11.15%, Georgetown = 9.23%

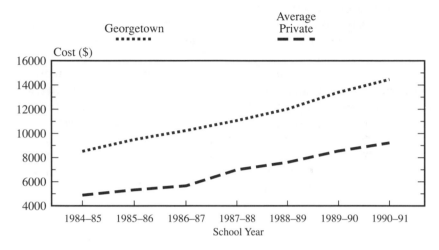

Source: The College Entrance Examination Board

---

ment size. This new goal led to several policy decisions that met with vigorous resistance from many alumni who were concerned about maintaining the university's Catholic character.

The case which attracted nationwide attention in the late 1980s was a lawsuit by a small homosexual group on campus, Gay People of Georgetown University (GPGU). Unlike many student organizations, it was not officially recognized by the administration, because the Catholic Church holds that homosexuality is a sin. So, the group initiated legal action, accusing the university of violating a District of Columbia human rights law that prohibits discrimination on the basis of "sexual orientation." After a protracted battle, Georgetown lost the lawsuit but had the option of appealing the decision to the Supreme Court. It decided not to do so, despite encouragement from other private, religious colleges and universities, who wished to make Georgetown their standard bearer in defense of constitutional freedom of religion. Georgetown then recognized the homosexual group.

Nevertheless, the U.S. Congress subsequently passed a bill exempting local, educational institutions of a religious nature from the D.C. human rights law. Georgetown chose not to take advantage of the bill and continued to recognize the homosexual group, leading many to suspect that the university is now less interested in preserving its religious freedom than in joining the mainstream of elite, secular educational institutions. This suspicion has since been heightened by the university's recognition, in 1990, of a pro-abortion student group.

The years of litigation have not, however, prevented Georgetown from greatly expanding its financial base. Endowment has increased substantially and construction has proceeded apace. The competitiveness of its student admissions has also sharpened considerably, with acceptance ratios now rivaling those of many Ivy League institutions.

The university is composed of five undergraduate schools: the College of Arts and Sciences (approximately 2,300 students); the Edmund A. Walsh School of Foreign Service (1,200); the School of Business Administration (1,100); the School of Language and Linguistics (750); and the School of Nursing (250). High school seniors must choose which of these they wish to apply to, as the schools have their own admission standards and committees. It is possible, though not easy, to transfer later on. The School of Foreign Service, generally

DISTRIBUTION OF UNDERGRADUATE AID
1989–90 School Year

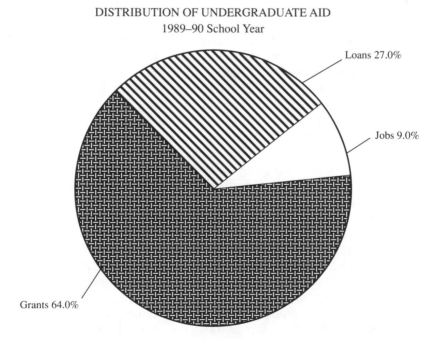

Loans 27.0%

Jobs 9.0%

Grants 64.0%

Source: The College Entrance Examination Board, 1990

reckoned to be the best undergraduate program of its kind in the country, is the hardest to get into, closely followed by the College of Arts and Sciences. Georgetown offers graduate degrees through its Graduate School, and professional training in the highly regarded Schools of Law and Medicine. It has also established the Georgetown University Hospital, a premier medical facility adjoining the campus.

Although all students must acquire some acquaintance with the liberal arts (see above), each school sets its own graduation standards to accord with its declared special purpose. The business and nursing schools are, as you would expect, the least involved with the liberal arts.

Students in the School of Languages and Linguistics ("Ling-Lang") spend much of their time acquiring proficiency in two foreign languages, and distinction in one of them. They must also take courses in linguistic theory, as well as a broad range of liberal arts foundation courses.

The School of Foreign Service (SFS) necessarily devotes much of its highly structured and demanding curriculum to international relations, economics, diplomacy, and issues of foreign and public policy. It also emphasizes the philosophical and historical contexts of all these topics. SFS further demands both oral and written proficiency in at least one foreign language. SFS students benefit especially from Georgetown's location in the nation's capital because of the many internships and part-time jobs available in government-related circles, and because well-known government experts and public figures gravitate to the university to teach, either as full or part-time faculty members. (Former Ambassador Jeane Kirkpatrick is one.)

The College of Arts and Sciences requires 120 semester hours for graduation and general education requirements totalling 12 courses: two each in literature ("normally fulfilled by English literature"); math/science (not necessarily with laboratory); social science; history; theology; philosophy. All students must also demonstrate "mastery of a foreign language [ancient or modern] through the intermediate level." Biology, chemistry and physics majors are exempted from the social science requirement. There is no non-Western multicultural requirement as yet, though a few voices, both faculty and student, have been raised in support of one. Strong departments at Georgetown are philosophy, theology, government, history, English, and foreign languages. The natural sciences and the fine arts are weaker.

Students in Arts and Sciences report that they are generally very well satisfied with the quality of teaching, which is mostly done by faculty members, not by teaching assistants. Some do complain, however, that introductory course sizes are too large (especially in government and economics), though the situation greatly improves at the intermediate and advanced levels when the "stars" take over. The advising system is adequate, with each freshman assigned a faculty advisor. Generally speaking, student-faculty relations are cordial, though not especially close on a personal level.

On the whole, students praise faculty members for their dedication to teaching the subject at hand; few interject their personal politics into classroom discussion, although many of the younger faculty are reputed to stand left of center. This could prove to be a problem in a few years when the older, more conservative professors, who are now a moderating influence, reach retirement age.

Georgetown is one school, however, where "politics" usually refers to national and international policies and events, not to the agendas and activities of the politically correct on campus, and the reactions of their opponents. The large number of international students—who represent a variety of races, cultures, and religions—and the cosmopolitan backdrop of Washington contribute to an atmosphere of tolerance for those who are "different." When foreign nationals are included, almost a quarter of Georgetown students are non-white; but these are less interested in identifying with American minorities than they are in absorbing the total American experience. The university has no "sensitivity" programs, nor speech codes. Its anti-harrassment policy confines itself to addressing discrimination in academic matters.

At Georgetown, when students find they have too little in common, which they sometimes do, they tend quietly to self-segregate, not demonstrate. The serious intellectual atmosphere also adds to the general campus air of peace and good will; most students don't have enough free time to stir things up even if they wanted to.

This is not to say that Hoyas (the odd nickname for Georgetown's students and athletic teams) don't know how to have fun. But fun is often discovering the cultural resources of Washington, or participating in sports or extracurricular activities, not necessarily in drinking until dawn. Although the campus is officially dry due to the legal drinking age of 21, the rule is not strictly enforced. Parties tend to be more or less intimate occasions among small groups of friends, perhaps because fraternities and sororities are not permitted. The new Leavey Student Center provides a central gathering place.

There are more than 100 student groups and organizations to choose from on Georgetown's attractive 110-acre campus—which is

surrounded by a fashionable, residential neighborhood full of picturesque 18th- and 19th-century homes on narrow, sometimes cobbled
streets. Serious campus crime is not a problem. A few blocks away, in
the commercial section of Georgetown, small shops, pubs, restaurants
and movie theaters cater to those looking for less cloistered entertainment. Downtown Washington with its museums, monuments and government buildings is less than two miles away, and reachable by bus.

Although Georgetown's nationally famous basketball team whips
up plenty of enthusiasm, other varsity sports (of which there are 13 for
men and 11 for women) do not generate a lot of excitement. By
contrast, the 23 intramural teams each for men and women are very
popular. Facilities include the magnificent underground Yates Athletic
Center with its Olympic-size pool and diving complex, as well as an
outdoor track, baseball diamond, football field, and the usual courts.

Campus housing is only guaranteed for three years, including the
first two. Freshmen must live on campus; juniors and seniors decide
which year to move off campus, but many upperclassmen prefer to
live for two or even three years in attractive Georgetown—if they can
afford the high rents—and often take a townhouse with several friends.
On-campus dorms are comfortable and both single-sex and coed; there
are some apartments, as well as language and special-interest houses.
Students from all the undergraduate schools are mixed in every dorm.

Georgetown University's international, sophisticated flavor and its
location in the nation's capital attract ambitious, academically minded
students interested in who and what makes the world go round. It is
also a bull's-eye for those who want to learn about the thinkers and
thoughts which helped to form that world; for at Jesuit Georgetown,
open house to so many cultures, Western civilization is still king of the
hill.

George Washington University

Director of Admissions, George Washington University
2121 I Street, NW, Washington, D.C. 20052 (202) 994-6040

Type: Private and Secular

Students:
6,615 undergraduates
　3,179 men
　3,436 women
8,474 graduate students

Applications:
Closing date: February 1
79% of applicants accepted

	Applied	Accepted	Enrolled
men	2,974	2,343	660
women	3,414	2,711	740

SAT or ACT required
　Score reported by: February 1
　Mid 50% of freshman scores:
　　SAT-Math　　530–640
　　SAT-Verbal　490–590

Costs and Aid:

Tuition and fees	$13,950
Room and Board	6,040

Scholarships:
Academic	Yes
Athletic	No
Minority	No

Financial Aid:
Freshmen	51%
Upperclassmen	30%

Library:	1,500,000 titles
ROTC:	Yes
Study Abroad:	Yes

The George Washington University, named after the first and only American president to rise above politics, now caters to throngs of undergraduates who want nothing more than to dive straight into them. From every state of the Union and more than 100 foreign countries, ambitious young men and women flock to GW, many of them hoping to acquire the know-how and the contacts that will one day propel them into public office.

The university's traditional preoccupation with governance harks back to George Washington himself, whose dream it was to establish in the federal city a national university, which would teach the practice and theory of representative government. To that noble end, the president allotted in his will 50 shares of stock which, alas, soon proved to be quite worthless. Twenty years passed before a group of Baptist clergy resurrected his vision if not his bequest, and it was yet another president, James Monroe, who in 1821 signed the act of Congress that gave birth to Columbian College, a private, nonsectarian establishment.

In 1873, the college matured into a university and, in 1904, the

145

institution was renamed in honor of its first benefactor. GW now shepherds through its halls more than 6,500 undergraduates and about 8,500 graduate students. Over the years, the university has moved several times, from a quiet knoll called College Hill to its present location in Foggy Bottom, not far from the State Department, to which some of its graduates have happily repaired. With a campus of 20 city blocks, including high-rise residence halls, GW currently sacrifices bucolic beauty to the sophisticated attractions of the nation's capital, which include cultural vistas, coveted opportunities for useful internships, and acquaintance with the high and mighty, who often speak and teach at GW.

The George Washington University Bulletin, Undergraduate and Graduate Programs, 1990–91:
Women's Studies 125—Varieties of Feminist Theory.
Taught by staff

"A review, through both classical and contemporary texts, of the variety of feminist explanations of women's status. Relationships within the sex/ gender system and arrangements based on class and race. Evaluation, through the lens of feminist theory, of several of the established academic disciplines in the sciences, social sciences, and humanities."

The exclusively urban nature of the university will soon undergo an important metamorphosis, however, when it opens a new 576-acre campus about 10 miles out of the city in Loudoun County, Virginia. The University Center, which may take 20 or more years to complete, will include a mix of school and private buildings, including retail, research, and residential facilities. The first classes for about 450 graduate students are scheduled for the fall of 1991.

Back in Washington, GW now houses the National Law Center and the School of Medicine and Health Science, which is closely affiliated with the George Washington Hospital, as well as the following colleges and schools that offer undergraduate degrees—the Columbian College of Arts and Sciences, the Schools of Education and Human Development, Engineering and Applied Sciences, Government and Business Administration, and the Elliott School of International Affairs. (Medicine and Health Science also offers several undergraduate degrees.) By far the largest of these is Columbian College, with about 3,300 students. Government and Business draws around 1,500, while

TUITION AND FEES INCREASE
Average Increase/Year: Private = 11.15%, G.W. = 12.53%

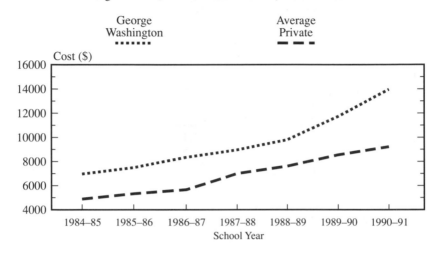

George
Washington
▪▪▪▪▪▪▪

Average
Private
▬ ▬ ▪

Source: The College Entrance Examination Board

the Elliott School attracts 750, and Engineering 600. Education and Medicine and Health Science matriculate the fewest, with approximately 160 and 115 respectively. A large percentage of all students goes on to graduate school.

Although many undergraduate introductory classes are large, they do break down into discussion groups of about 20 students once a week. Upper-level classes are small enough for the most part (often under 20) to stimulate discussion and interaction between students and professors. Professors are generally helpful when asked, but seldom volunteer advice or friendship. Teaching assistants are employed, but have the advantage of a special university training program.

In the dominant Columbian College, students must complete a demanding set of course distribution requirements to insure more than a nodding acquaintance with liberal learning. With 120 semester hours needed for graduation, the mandated general requirements consume 46 to 48. The list of courses and sequences that satisfy the requirement is strictly limited, so that students cannot "escape" through the sieve of broad selection. The categories are as follows: Literacy (six hours of English composition); Quantitative and Logical Reasoning (six hours); Conceptual Foundations and Development of Science (nine hours); Social and Behaviorial Sciences (six hours); Creative and Performing Arts (three hours); Literature (six hours); Western Society and Civilization (six hours); and Foreign Language (for which requirements vary) or Foreign Culture (six hours).

The social sciences are generally conceded to dominate the academic scene at Columbian, especially political science which normally graduates 200 majors annually, and economics which graduates 100. The other schools also attempt to ensure proficiency in such subjects as English composition, mathematics, and the sciences, as well as in their own special disciplines. For example, in addition to a requirement in Western civilization, the Elliott School of International Affairs mandates that students take at least two courses in non-Western culture, one of which must be an interdisciplinary course called, "East Asia: Past and Present."

This commitment to introducing undergraduates to other cultures is fostered by the international flavor of the student body, which draws more than 10 percent of its membership from foreign lands. Approxi-

DISTRIBUTION OF UNDERGRADUATE AID
1989–90 School Year

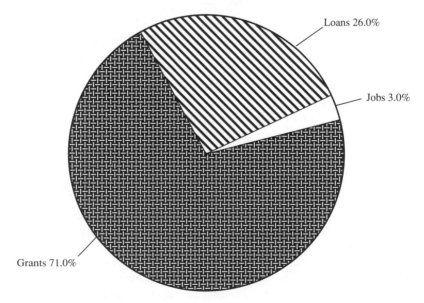

Loans 26.0%

Jobs 3.0%

Grants 71.0%

Source: The College Entrance Examination Board, 1990

mately 15 percent of the entire student body are minorities, mostly black and Asian. Reflecting this heterogeneity, a new multicultural center has been established, as well as a Black Student Union, which is active but not especially militant. The same is true of the Lesbian and Gay People's Alliance, which tries to use sympathy for AIDS victims as a means of promoting the homosexual lifestyle through lectures, films, and social functions. Different ethnic and national groups also sponsor events to highlight and explain their own cultures, such as a "Japanese Night," in which students learn origami and sample Japanese cuisine.

In addition to the attractions of Washington, both social and cultural, the university offers more than 200 extracurricular clubs and activities, and fields intercollegiate teams in 9 sports for men, not including football, and 8 for women. Less high-powered exercise lovers may participate in 14 intramural sports for men and the same number for women. By far the most popular spectator sport is basketball, which usually fills the 5,000-seat gymnasium to overflowing with cheering supporters.

During other free time, about a quarter of the men socialize at 15 national fraternities, while less than 15 percent of the women join the nine available national sororities. The Greeks often host parties, which are usually open to all, and they also sponsor a number of worthwhile service activities. Relations between members and the rest of the GW community are normally cordial.

Living facilities at the university are comfortable, and range from the fraternity and sorority houses to multistoried residence halls and on-campus apartments. Housing, which is both coed and single-sex, is guaranteed to freshmen, and available to upperclassmen on a lottery basis. About 50 percent of all undergraduates live on campus. For the most part, accommodation is rather spacious and very well maintained, with weekly maid service and frequent security patrols. Refrigerators and microwaves are standard equipment, and the apartments have full kitchens.

The residences are friendly places, where the hall councils like to sponsor programs that create a sense of community, such as barbecues, movie nights, and pizza parties. However, the degree of support can vary widely between dormitories. This seems to be characteristic of most student groups on campus, which often have trouble recruiting turnouts for their programs. Undaunted, self-starters don't hesitate to initiate new activities to satisfy their own special needs and interests. One example is "The Breakfast Club," a monthly brunch for transfer students, formed to enable them not only to make friends but also to speak with other students with similar problems adjusting to a new school.

On the downside, many complain of a lack of campus unity, because there are hundreds of different and not always compatible student groups that run the gamut politically, socially, and culturally. Politically, Democrats and Republicans are nearly equal in number with the former having the edge; both are much larger than their more extreme and more vocal counterparts, the Progressive Student Union and Young Americans for Freedom. Dissenting opinions are rarely stifled, as it is difficult to muster a large consensus on any issue, much less politics.

The faculty is regarded as more left-wing than the majority of students, but most faculty are not militantly radical, and so far the administration has kept those who are in line. To wit: In 1988, one male professor was accused of verbal harassment by a feminist colleague; she then wrote a letter of complaint to the president, demanding that the offending male chauvinist be ordered to undergo sensitivity training. The administration replied succinctly that GW did not do that sort of thing, and there was an end of the matter.

No matter what their politics, many students spend a fair amount of time off campus. They not only see the sights, but also work part-time, often at internships on Capitol Hill and in other government offices, or in private, public-policy organizations and law firms. Their career goals do not inhibit students, however, from exploring the byways of the nation's capital as well as its main boulevards. Picturesque Georgetown with its bars and shops is a popular playground, along with the Adams Morgan district, which is home to a variety of ethnic eateries.

"To each his own" could almost be the motto of the entire GW student community, not only because it is so pluralistic in composition, but also because it must largely fend for itself. The administration definitely does not believe in coddling its students, and makes them personally responsible for searching out what they, as individuals, need to know both on and off campus. Students must work to investigate information about scholarships, internships, and job opportunities; they must also keep track of their own course requirements, as advisors no longer need approve schedules.

The George Washington University is no place for shrinking violets, team players, or those bored by the latest political scandal; but it has not yet been taken over by the politically correct and still offers a sound liberal arts education to those who know where they're headed in college and in life, and have conventional ambitions.

Grove City College

Director of Admissions, Grove City College
Grove City, PA 16127-2197 (412) 458-2100

Type: Private and Protestant		**Costs and Aid:**	
		Tuition and fees	$4,390
Students:		Room and Board	2,390
2,163 undergraduates		Scholarships:	
1,083 men		Academic	Yes
1,080 women		Athletic	No
Applications:		Minority	No
Priority date: November 15		Financial Aid:	
44% of applicants accepted		Freshmen	52%
		Upperclassmen	46%

	Applied	Accepted	Enrolled
men	1,020	471	255
women	1,085	462	286

SAT or ACT required
Score reported by: March 31
Mid 50% of freshman scores:
 SAT-Math 530–630
 SAT-Verbal 470–570

Library: 148,000 titles

ROTC: No

Study Abroad: Yes

Grove City College—which is located not in a city but in a small town about 60 miles from Pittsburgh—is no ordinary, little religious school, though it is both little and religious. Founded in 1876 as a coeducational institution affiliated with the Presbyterian Church, the college now matriculates approximately 2,100 young men and women. Its mission was then and is now "to inculcate in the minds and hearts of youth those Christian moral and ethical principles without which our country cannot long endure." To accomplish this, as well as to provide its students with a sound liberal arts education, Grove City is bravely bucking most of the major trends in higher education today. Here's a short list:

1. In order to remain truly independent, the college accepts no funding from the federal government, nor does it allow its students to take federal grants, though they may incur federal loans.

2. Unlike the vast majority of American colleges and universities where fees rise yearly and sharply, Grove City manages to keep costs right down on the ground: For the academic year 1990–91, tuition and room and board came to a very modest $6,780, a figure almost unheard of in private higher education today.

151

3. The college, which maintains a modern physical plant in spite of low fees and a small endowment, raises money for each facility in advance, so that by the time a building is completed it is also paid for. No debt, no interest.

4. On a less pecuniary note, professors are not granted tenure and are employed by annual contract in order to engender greater accountability to the college. They must be Christians.

5. Unlike so many of its sister schools, Grove City has not begun to shy away from "Eurocentrism" and the traditional core curriculum. Instead, the college has just revised its course of study to include a more rigorous Western civilization core, and now exacts of all students 18 credit hours over three years in its "Civilization Series," which focuses on the "origin, development and implications of civilization's seminal ideas."

Although unabashedly Christian and Western in orientation, the school does touch upon other civilizations in this series, which is divided into six semester courses: "The Genesis of Civilization"; "Athens and Jerusalem"; "The Middle Ages, Renaissance, Reformation and the Emergence of Modernity"; "The Birth of Modernity (Europe and America in the 17th and 18th Centuries)"; "Culture in the 19th Century"; and "Culture in the 20th Century." The last two courses consider, among other aspects, developments in Africa and Asia and the "advancement of freedom in the Third World."

In addition to the above, students must meet distribution requirements as follows: six hours in the social sciences; eight hours in the natural sciences (with labs); and six hours of quantitative and logical reasoning, which includes mathematics, logic (no more than three hours), and statistics or quantitative analysis. From 1992, students will also be required to demonstrate proficiency in a foreign language at the second-year level.

Taken together, the core and distribution requirements presently absorb 56 credit hours of a total of 128 needed for the Bachelor of Arts degree. The college, which is exclusively undergraduate, also confers the Bachelor of Science degree, as well as degrees in business, education, and engineering. Honors programs, the requirements for which vary by department, are offered. Students usually take 16 credit hours per semester, and they have classes on Saturday mornings.

About 55 percent of students major in business, education, or engineering, the rest in the liberal arts. The college is proud of giving its professionally oriented young men and women a sound liberal arts base. Among the liberal arts, the strongest departments are psychol-

TUITION AND FEES INCREASE
Average Increase/Year: Private = 11.15%, Grove City = 6.21%

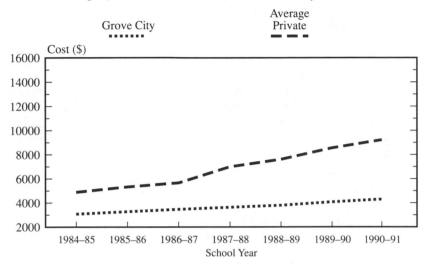

Source: The College Entrance Examination Board

ogy, biology, chemistry, history, and economics. Mathematics tends to be weak. The most popular majors are psychology, chemistry, and biology.

About three-quarters of the student body come from Pennsylvania, but 15 to 20 states are presently represented, as well as a number of foreign countries. International students are often cited as the school's largest minority group, as traditional minorities comprise only about 1 percent of whole. The college does not practice affirmative action, but declares in its Bulletin that, "for over 100 years Grove City College has been committed to a policy of non-discrimination and welcomes folk to its campus regardless of their race, creed, color or sex."

The religious and political atmosphere on campus, as you would expect, is Christian and conservative, both among students and faculty, who often think of themselves as part of an extended family. There seems to be no unrest in either group, nor agitation for substantial change in any meaningful area of campus life. The Young Republicans are the most influential group on campus; the pro-life movement also has a strong following; the homosexual presence is negligible and inconspicuous.

Chapel attendance at Grove City is compulsory 16 times a semester, though services are frequent and varied, and students may choose which suit them best. Although there is no honor code, behavioral rules are sensible and clearly stated; infractions are punished on an individual basis and can include expulsion. Cheating usually results in failure of the course.

Campus housing, needless to say, is single-sex, and it's comfortable. Only students who live at home with their families are permitted to live off campus. First-semester freshmen are required to observe residence hall closing hours; others may regulate their own comings and goings with parental approval. Visiting hours between houses are also limited.

The 150-acre campus itself is a Thoreauean idyll, immaculately maintained, with colorful flowers, spreading trees, and even a babbling brook. Rabbits and squirrels scamper everywhere. A notable landmark is Harbison Chapel, fashioned of stone, with brilliant stained-glass windows that sparkle on a sunny day. More recent buildings include

DISTRIBUTION OF UNDERGRADUATE AID
1989–90 School Year

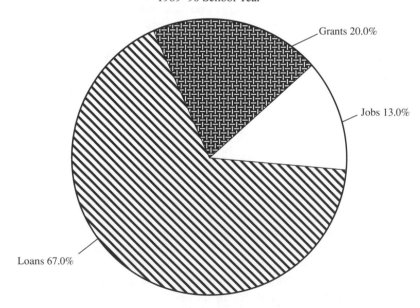

Grants 20.0%

Jobs 13.0%

Loans 67.0%

Source: The College Entrance Examination Board, 1990

two new dormitories and the Technological Learning Center, which contains audio-visual equipment and up-to-date computers. The Physical Learning Center was renovated in 1989 at a cost of $7 million, and accommodates a large arena, two swimming pools, a conditioning track, eight racquetball courts, and a fully-equipped fitness room, as well as a multipurpose area large enough for four basketball or several tennis courts. Another building houses eight bowling alleys. There are 10 intercollegiate sports for men and 7 for women, with 11 intramural teams for each sex.

Student social life centers around campus organizations, because the town of Grove City has a population of only 8,000 and offers few recreational alternatives. The Student Government Association sponsors dances, movies, and other events. Fraternities and sororities, which are local, prove popular with about 40 percent of the students. There are 90 clubs and organizations available. Drugs and alcohol are strictly forbidden on campus, as Grove City is "dry"—which makes for tinkling cash registers at bars and restaurants outside the city limits. (The students may be Christians, but they are not yet saints.)

In comparison with many of today's colleges and universities, where literally anything goes, Grove City is a maverick—an anachronistic throwback to the 1950s and earlier, when administrations acted *in loco parentis* and professors often taught universal principles instead of political polemics. Many young moderns would find it too restrictive, too homogenous, and perhaps a bit claustrophobic. But, for the few who do not expect their college to be all things to all people all of the time, Grove City's lonely beacon continues to illuminate the values of Western civilization and the free enterprise system it created.

Harvard University

Dean of Admissions and Financial Aid
Harvard and Radcliffe Colleges
Byerly Hall, 8 Garden Street, Cambridge, MA 02138
(617) 495-1551

Type: Private and Secular	**Costs and Aid:**	
	Tuition and fees	$15,530
Students: (Harvard College)	Room and Board	5,130
6,587 undergraduates		
3,853 men	Scholarships:	
2,734 women	Academic	No
4,736 graduate students	Athletic	No
	Minority	No
Applications:		
Closing date: January 1	Financial Aid:	
18% of applicants accepted	Freshmen	60%
	Upperclassmen	60%

	Applied	Accepted	Enrolled
men	7,493	1,317	939
women	5,350	939	666

SAT or ACT required (SAT preferred)
Score reported by: February 15
Mid 50% of freshman scores:
SAT-Math 650–750
SAT-Verbal 620–720

Library: 11,781,270 volumes

ROTC: Yes
Study Abroad: Yes

**Percentage of courses that can
be used to fulfill core
requirements:** 8

As the flagship institution of American higher education, Harvard receives close scrutiny and much commentary. What would be a routine event at almost any other university becomes, at Harvard, a proper subject for national examination. Thus it is with its choice of a new president. Derek Bok has retired after 20 years, and Neil Rudenstine is his successor. Bok was a lawyer chosen, it was once thought, because his skills as mediator were needed to maintain internal peace in the turbulent early 1970s. Rudenstine, on the other hand, is an eminent scholar of sixteenth century English literature. Does this fact portend anything for the curricular debates of the early 1990s? Moreover, Dr. Rudenstine's ascent to the pinnacle of the university world is truly remarkable. His father, an immigrant, worked as a prison guard; his mother was a waitress. Here is a triumph of the meritocratic ethic, a brilliant vindication of the traditional American way. What does it augur for a university which is pushed to offer pre-emptive rewards for "historical" injuries? The questions tantalize, and the

157

answers will be years in the coming. To ask them at all is to understand why Harvard College, the undergraduate constituent of the university, is the nation's premiere college address.

Courses of Instruction, 1990–91:
Selected courses from the **English and American Literature and Language Department:**

90vv.—Topics in Gay Male Representation
Professor D.A. Miller

"In addition to those initiated by members of the seminar, topics are foreseen to include: AIDS commentary, ACT UP, *All About Eve,* Baldwin, Capote, Forster, Foucault, Gide, Genet, *GQ,* Hitchcock, Mapplethorpe, muscle magazines, Sartre, *Tongues Untied,* Wilde."

90w.—Feminist Theory
Professor Laura A. Doyle

"Focuses on issues of feminist literary theory but also includes key texts from other disciplines such as anthropology, history, philosophy, and Science." (offered in 1991–92, not in 1990–91)

Indeed, the prestige of the 350-year-old school is so enormous that the actual conditions of undergraduate life almost never enter into a decision to apply and hardly ever into a decision of whether to attend if accepted. Thus, in a way, this makes Harvard the least seriously weighed of undergraduate experiences, even if it may be the most talked about. Its competitors, ever motivated to pull even, must think about themselves in discreet, practical ways which do not burden the leader. But if one is in any sense the "best," what should the word mean?

The school, founded in 1636, consists of the Harvard College, with all of the 6,600 undergraduates, as well as the Graduate School of Arts and Sciences and numerous professional schools—Business Administration; Dentistry; Design; Divinity; Education; Law; Medicine; Public Administration; and Public Health. Enrollment at the university totals more than 18,000. Harvard College sits within this complex of departments and graduate and professional schools, where each professor is recruited with the assumption that he is the best in the world for his particular post. In fact, the presumption is not always wrong; a

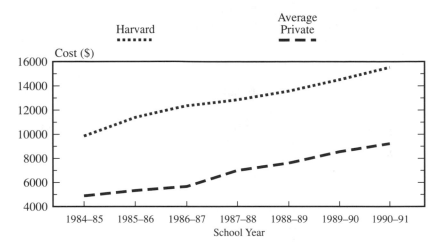

TUITION AND FEES INCREASE
Average Increase/Year: Private = 11.15%, Harvard = 8.03%

Source: The College Entrance Examination Board

goodly number of the Harvard faculty really are the best in the world and the undergraduate's knowledge that they are present in Cambridge—sometimes—can be edifying in its own right. And, moreover, the great academic stars do show up just often enough in the undergraduate classrooms to perpetuate the myth that they are there to work for the students. But, in fact, undergraduate instruction at Harvard has many of the drawbacks associated with great research institutions of far less eminence—classes that are oftentimes unmanageably large and instruction by graduate students, who are "teaching fellows," not "teaching assistants," to be sure, although the arrangement is quite the same.

And beyond the methods is the subject matter itself, Harvard's sense of what an educated person needs to know. Once again, the question has been addressed with extraordinary self-consciousness, for Harvard is aware that it prepares leaders in society and influences how other institutions will try to do the same. Thus, we know more about the evolution of the Harvard undergraduate curriculum than we know about almost any other. It has been *studied*; books have been written about it.

Harvard's own pronouncements on the subject tend to be solemn and lengthy. Back in 1945, the school spelled out its definition of "general education" in a document more than 250 pages long. This represented a view of core learning, if not of a rigid core curriculum itself. Since then, the definitions have become broader, in tandem with the feeling that students needed to be exposed to evermore things. By the 1970s, it was back to the drawing boards, for requirements had become so loose as to be virtually meaningless. The current arrangement dates from 1978. The so-called "core" today is now divided into 10 subgroups—one in Foreign Cultures, two in Historical Studies, three in Literature and Arts, one in Moral Reasoning, two in Science, and one in Social Analysis. Undergraduates must take at least one course from any eight of these areas.

This recodification, in fact, carries the decentralization even further. Nothing in particular is required; the responsibility is sloughed off on the student himself to decide what ought to be studied. Moreover, as one close analyst of the Harvard curriculum has noticed,

DISTRIBUTION OF UNDERGRADUATE AID
1989–90 School Year

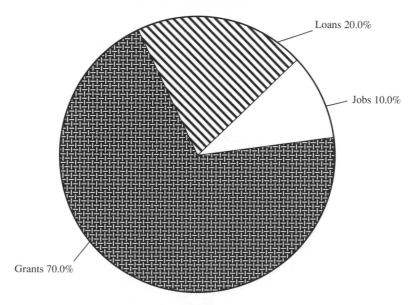

Loans 20.0%

Jobs 10.0%

Grants 70.0%

Source: The College Entrance Examination Board, 1990

no core Literature and Arts course lists any of the great nineteenth-century British novelists among the authors studied, nor does any list such writers as Virgil, Milton, and Dostoevsky. In the core's history areas even students who did the impossible and took every single course would not focus on any Western history before the Middle Ages, nor would they study the history of the Enlightenment, the Renaissance, the American Civil War, or a host of other topics.

Many individual courses and even whole departments may be excellent in themselves, and yet they may add up to a woefully deficient undergraduate education.

Changes may soon be in the offing, however, as the university has appointed not only a new president, but also a new dean of the Faculty of Arts and Sciences—Harvard's second most important academic post. He is British-born, Oxford-educated Jeremy Knowles, a Harvard biochemistry professor. Dr. Knowles will be in charge of the undergraduate program.

As both he and President Rudenstine took up their posts on July 1, 1991, it is obviously far too early to tell which way the academic winds will blow. So far, Dr. Knowles's appointment is seen as signalling increased attention to the sciences—and possibly greater emphasis on teaching. He has already publicly expressed wistful nostalgia for the Oxford system, where students and professors enjoy intimate, intense, individual tutorials.

Even under the present system, however, the academic demands are real and the level of performance can be strikingly high. But a Harvard student is supposed to be smart and is expected, therefore, to master the academic side of things one way or another. Accordingly, students label one another by the extracurricular activities they all participate in. At each semester's registration, students are assailed with extracurricular activities. Publications, environmental groups, political groups, community services, tutoring, ethnic clubs—they all are present, and virtually all Harvard students become intensely involved in at least one extracurricular activity. Their extracurriculars come to be their virtual identification. One never says, "That's the brilliant German scholar." Instead, he would refer to another Harvard student as "a *Crimson* writer" or "the one who runs a homeless shelter."

The social/political climate at Harvard is not much different from that of other prominent institutions. The regnant ethos is smug leftism; sometimes it can become coarse. Older traditions of tolerance and civility are now shaded toward the proper political categories. Thus, it is possible—indeed, routine—to offend racial minorities, which make up almost 35 percent of the undergraduate student body (more than half of these are Asian-Americans), by even the most innocently intended word or deed; but, almost by definition, people with traditional social or religious convictions are fair game. Similarly, it is important to show deference to the left-leaning political leaders of many foreign countries, but certainly not to the president of one's own—if he happens to be of the "wrong" persuasion.

Indeed, the Harvard community, institutionally speaking, seems permanently estranged from the main trends in national politics, and the resentment continues to smolder. As the liberalism associated with Harvard in the popular mind is now routinely repudiated in presidential elections, for example, its Cambridge adherents stress all the more their own natural right to rule. This cannot help but introduce sour notes into the campus's consideration of most public questions. And the resident conservatives end up all the more resented because, despite their seeming impotence on the campus scene, they are somehow connected to a powerful cause at-large. The dislike and ridicule directed toward them now has a real edge to it; it is no longer merely amused disdain toward those once easily dismissed as harmless cranks.

Everyday student life at Harvard is, of course, nowhere near as grave as this Harvard-like analysis of the school might suggest. It is lively and interesting and revolves around the house system, which replaces the usual dormitory or fraternity-house style of living. Freshmen do live together in the dorms surrounding Harvard Yard, but they spend their upperclass years in one of 13 houses—Adams, Cabot, Currier, Dudley, Dumster, Eliot, Kirkland, Leverett, Lowell, Mather, North, Quincy, and Winthrop. These houses, which like the colleges at Yale descend from the venerable arrangements at Oxford and Cambridge, tend to have their own personalities and even idiosyncracies. The system is designed to reduce undergraduate life to a more human scale, and it almost always works. The range of interests within the student body is enormous, and the university-sponsored events to satisfy them seem inexhaustible.

There is also a traditional social scene that still endures, not quite underground but, it seems, destined for that region sooner or later. For example, the exclusive Hasty Pudding Club and the all-male "finals clubs" (there are no fraternities on campus) are some of the oldest social gathering places in the United States. There have been attempts to reform these traditional institutions by some of the more progressive elements on campus—the Hasty Pudding Club began to admit women during the 1970s. Though Harvard's exclusive groups have remained largely unchanged over the years, their importance has diminished. There is just too much competition. There are 175 extracurricular organizations, while the surrounding city of Cambridge and neighboring Boston are full of interesting cultural events, sights, restaurants, theaters, and other activities which are readily accessible to all Harvard students.

One underappreciated aspect of Harvard today is the school's athletic achievement. There are 21 men's and 19 women's intercollegiate sports; the men's hockey team and the varsity crew team are of national championship calibre. Squash, tennis, field hockey, and lacrosse follow closely behind. There is wide participation in intramurals, with 20 sports for men and 14 for women, as well as a degree of school spirit surprising for an institution so long thought to be blasé.

Overall, there is no quarreling with Harvard's success in producing graduates who go on to wealth, power, prominence, and leadership. Indeed, what seems most important to the institution is that its alumni and faculty be *prominent,* and that the university train the leading cadre for all contestants in all struggles, the most articulate advocates of all sides of all arguments. There is more than a little institutional self-protection and self-advancement in this; after all, no matter who or what wins, Harvard will never lose. But, by the same token, the university has long seemed incapable of taking firm stands, or running risks in behalf of any set of real beliefs and convictions. Thus, whether by intention or accident, leadership in the effort to save at least some of our civilization's intellectual heritage for the undergraduate curriculum has passed to Harvard's traditional rival in New Haven, Connecticut—where the administration has been surprisingly and unexpectedly firm in support of educational quality.

Harvard's new president comes to Cambridge after having sat out the last half-decade helping to run one of the nation's most influential foundations. Indeed, he was probably chosen precisely *because* he spent the last years away from involvement in campus controversies which would otherwise have been disqualifying. But now he has a rare opportunity to offend somebody, and it will be interesting to see whether he makes good use of it.

Hillsdale College

Director of Admissions, Hillsdale College
33 East College Street, Hillsdale, MI 49242
(517) 437-7341 ext.327

Type: Private and Secular			

Students:
1,100 undergraduates
   528 men
   572 women

Applications:
Closing date: June 1
84% of applicants accepted

	Applied	Accepted	Enrolled
men	377	301	152
women	422	369	183

SAT or ACT required
  Score reported by: March 15
  Mid 50% of freshman scores:
    SAT-Math   480–570
    SAT-Verbal 460–540

Costs and Aid:

Tuition and fees	$9,030
Room and Board	3,780

Scholarships:

Academic	Yes
Athletic	Yes
Minority	No

Financial Aid:

Freshmen	70%
Upperclassmen	80%

Library:	150,000 titles
ROTC:	No
Study Abroad:	Yes

    Hillsdale might be just another small, private, Midwestern college if it were not for a fierce sense of independence that makes it one of the very few colleges in the country to reject federal funding of any kind. Students are not permitted to accept federal grants or even the GI Bill, and the institution takes no monies for research. Instead, Hillsdale raises scholarship funds privately for the 76 percent of its students who need financial aid.

    Ever wary of encroachments on the freedom it values, Hillsdale fears creeping regulation by government of any institution that becomes dependent upon political funding. Specifically, the college worries about quotas in both faculty and students, which it feels are inimical to academic excellence, and also about increasing pressure to offer courses, or "sensitivity sessions" concerning gender, race, ethnicity, and sexual orientation. The college is very proud of having maintained for nearly 150 years what it calls its "own color and gender-blind" nondiscrimination policies.

    Another reason Hillsdale rejects federal funding is to avoid the proliferation of administrative personnel, who have been hired at other institutions partly to cope with the mountains of paperwork and red tape that customarily accompany federal aid in any form. Hillsdale emphatically declares that it wishes to use its funds to educate its students, not to create more jobs for bureaucrats. To prove its point, the college admits 22 percent of the freshman class on merit scholarships.

Hillsdale, founded by Freewill Baptist clergy in 1844, is quite clear about what "educate" means, and adheres closely to its mission statement, which proclaims Hillsdale "a trustee of modern man's intellectual and spiritual inheritance." In midwestern America, this translates into strong support for the Judeo-Christian tradition generally, and the free enterprise system particularly. The college, however, is not content to promulgate these virtues at home, but actively seeks to extend its mission beyond the confines of the 200-acre campus in southcentral Michigan.

Hillsdale has attracted to its lecture program such internationally famous figures as Ronald Reagan, Warren Burger, William F. Buckley, Jr., and Jeane Kirkpatrick. Programs include the Shavano Institute for National Leadership, which presents annual off-campus lectures on public policy issues; the Ludwig von Mises Lecture Series, which brings free market economists to Hillsdale's campus; and the Center for Constructive Alternatives, which conducts four week-long campus seminars on various topics every year. In 1988–90, these ranged from "The Morality of Defense" to "Popular Entertainment and its Impact on Society." Selections from speakers are printed in *Imprimis,* a monthly publication that reaches 300,000 subscribers and is free upon request.

Hillsdale's cultural evangelism is also reflected in the outreach efforts of its president, George Roche. The author of nine books and numerous articles promoting conservative values, Roche speaks regularly before non-Hillsdale audiences, gathering financial and political support for the college. Consequently, the college maintains an endowment from private supporters and alumni of the college, and continues to draw into its student body the sons and daughters of conservative families across the country, at all socioeconomic levels.

Tiny Hillsdale has thus earned its reputation as a feisty, politically conservative institution. Thus the college, whose student body numbers slightly more than 1,000, 40 percent from out of state, generally appeals to a certain type—the traditional, Christian, free market advocate (or the sons and daughters of such). Hillsdale is, however, quick to point out that it welcomes students of all religious, racial, and ethnic

TUITION AND FEES INCREASE
Average Increase/Year: Private = 11.15%, Hillsdale = 7.14%

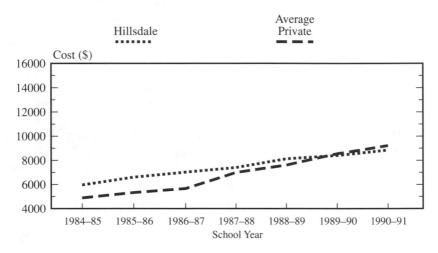

Source: The College Entrance Examination Board

origins who can meet the standards of admission and who feel they can benefit from a Hillsdale education. Currently, minority students constitute about 5 percent of undergraduates.

As a liberal arts college, Hillsdale places great emphasis on a broad, well-rounded education rather than specialized study. There is a modified core curriculum, as well as strictly observed distribution requirements. Freshmen and sophomores must take three English courses, a year of laboratory science, an American Heritage course, and, for Bachelor of Arts candidates, a year and a half of a foreign language, which may be Latin or Greek as well as a modern language. These form part of a larger requirement, which is divided between the humanities and the social sciences. There is an honors program, for selected students, which includes advanced courses in English and the Western intellectual tradition. Majors may be in single or double subjects, or in an interdisciplinary field, such as Christian studies.

The departments graduating the most majors, however, are usually accounting, business administration (both marketing and finance), and education (elementary and early childhood). So, while Hillsdale's mission statement and curriculum reflect a firm belief in the importance of liberal studies as a preparation for life, most graduates go on to pursue careers in the business world.

Most upper-level classes contain 15 or fewer. Teaching assistants are not employed. Professors are accessible, often holding daily office hours, and they frequently offer advice and help with problems outside the classroom. In such a small college, this close association can be comforting or cloying, depending upon the individual student's temperament, but anonymity at Hillsdale is out of the question. The campus operates by a strict honor code, which most take very seriously. Cheating is rare.

Because Hillsdale is small and not a research institution, its library holdings and other research facilities are rather inadequate. The library does have a number of special collections, including the personal library of Ludwig von Mises, the famous Austrian economist. Russell Kirk, the "Intellectual Father of Modern American Conservatism," has promised his papers.

On the social side, Hillsdale supports a flourishing Greek system,

DISTRIBUTION OF UNDERGRADUATE AID
1989–90 School Year

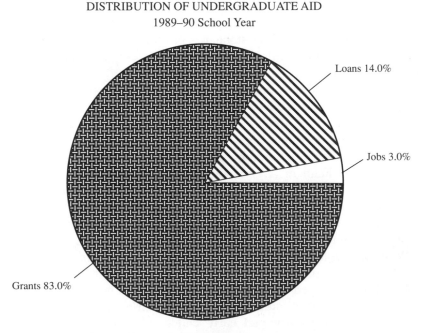

Source: The College Entrance Examination Board, 1990

with five fraternities and four sororities to which half the students belong. Some students live and eat in the Greek houses; the rest live in dormitories, which are all single-sex. Because the town of Hillsdale is quite small, much of the social life of the college revolves around the fraternities and sororities, which provide informal and formal dances, parties, hayrides, and other group activities.

The college endures its fair share of disruptions due to the Greek system (complaints from neighbors, an occasional rumor of hazing), but the most persistent problem is a moderate level of tension between those students who are members and those who are not. This is closely linked to the predominant Christian presence on campus, as some students with strong religious beliefs feel that the Greek system encourages drinking, sexual activity, and social exclusivity on campus.

Compared to most colleges and universities, Hillsdale's social policy is stringent and strictly enforced. No alcohol, for example, is allowed in any of the fraternities or sororities, or in any of the student residence halls. Room searches to enforce this rule occasionally occur, and alcohol confiscation by campus security is not unknown. There are no midweek parties allowed in any campus residence, and all weekend parties must be registered. The punishment for violations is usually a monetary fine and/or suspension of social privileges. These rules would cause student revolt on most campuses, but Hillsdale students merely grumble.

There are visiting hours in the residences for the opposite sex, with lobby times allotted every day and room times during certain hours of the weekend. Of course, some students gripe about all these restrictions, especially by a school that proclaims its dedication to freedom and denounces government interference in private affairs. They also complain that they are being treated like children and that college is merely an extension of boarding school. Nevertheless, many students—even some of those who complain—appreciate guidance and the privacy and moral behavior which such restrictions encourage. Sexual promiscuity, alcohol consumption, and drug use still occur at Hillsdale, but the prevailing social policy and conservative attitude of the majority of students make such behavior the exception rather than the rule it so often is at other colleges.

The small community which surrounds Hillsdale consists mostly of factory workers, farmers, local businessmen and businesswomen, and college employees. The town boasts a movie theater, a bowling alley, a roller skating rink, a few specialty shops, and an array of fast food eateries. Relations between the college and the community are generally cordial, although it is not uncommon to hear students refer to the "townies" in a condescending manner, nor is it unheard of to encounter townspeople with vocal animosity toward "those spoiled college kids." The nearest cities are Toledo (about one and a half hours), Detroit (two hours), and Chicago (four hours). Restless students often take "road trips" to these metropolises or the larger state universities.

Extracurricular activities and sports are popular on campus. Varsity sports such as football, track, baseball, basketball, volleyball, and in recent years women's swimming, continue to attract large numbers. There are 8 intercollegiate and 7 intramural sports each for men and women. With the completion two years ago of a new $11 million sports facility, the college boasts one of the finest athletic complexes of any small college in the country. There are also an 8,000-seat stadium, an Astroturf football field, a pool, bowling alley, a 200-meter track, and indoor tennis courts.

The same cannot be said of Hillsdale's music facilities, which are outdated and inadequate. The college has, however, nearly completed a drive to fund a new fine arts complex, and a friendly foundation has recently donated more than $3 million to construct this center. Other activities range from a drill team to a literary magazine; there are 30 groups and organizations.

Hillsdale often projects the reputation of being a stuffy, snobby private school, because its students are homogeneous, well-behaved, and conservatively dressed. Indeed, most students dress rather formally for class (skirts for the women and dress slacks for the men); sweatpants or jeans are usually in the fashion minority. And because of the relative affluence of some Hillsdale families, it is not unknown to see neatly dressed students tooling down the streets of this rural community in expensive cars. The scene is almost reminiscent of the carefree 1950s, which will be reassuring to many in this era of tense campus polarization. But Hillsdale is definitely not carefree about its primary mission. It works hard to teach and promote the venerable absolutes of truth, beauty, and goodness.

University of Illinois at Urbana-Champaign

Director of Admissions and Records
University of Illinois at Urbana-Champaign
10 Administration Building, Urbana, IL 61801 (217) 333-0302

Type: Public

Students:
26,084 undergraduates
14,633 men
11,451 women
8,173 graduate students

Applications:
Priority date: November 15
Closing date: January 1
65% of applicants accepted

	Applied	Accepted	Enrolled
men	8,500	5,320	2,936
women	6,581	4,484	2,366

SAT or ACT required
  Score reported by: January 1
  Mid 50% of freshman scores:
    SAT-Math   550–680
    SAT-Verbal 460–580

Costs and Aid:
Tuition & fees:

In state	$2,850
Out of state	6,390
Room and Board	3,650

Scholarships:

Academic	Yes
Athletic	Yes
Minority	Yes

Financial Aid:

Freshmen	80%
Upperclassmen	85%

Library: 3,200,000 titles

ROTC: Yes

Study Abroad: Yes

The University of Illinois at Urbana-Champaign is a huge academic powerhouse and ranks as one of the country's major research institutions. For the lowly liberal arts undergraduate, however, it can be an impersonal and confusing marketplace of ideas increasingly dominated by the orthodoxies of the left.

Illinois was one of 37 public land grant institutions created within a decade of President Abraham Lincoln's signing the Morrill Act in 1862; it was chartered by the state in 1867 (as the Illinois Industrial University), and opened its doors to students in 1868. The university now serves a student population of more than 34,000—of whom approximately 26,000 are undergraduates. Although state law does not mandate preference in admission for in-state students, 94 percent do come from Illinois. The rest arrive from all the other states and more than 100 foreign countries. The university claims to possess the nation's largest alumni association (117,000 members), including eight Nobel laureates and 16 Pulitzer Prize winners.

171

It also boasts numerous national centers—the Materials Research Laboratory; the Plant and Animal Biotechnology Laboratory (scheduled to open in 1992); the Prokaryotic Genome Analysis Center; and the famous dynamic duo—the National Center for Supercomputing Applications and the Center for Supercomputing Research and Development—as well as several major interdisciplinary units, including the recently completed Beckman Institute for Advanced Science and Technology, as well as Centers for African Studies, East Asian and Pacific Studies, and Russian and East European Studies.

Undergraduate education at Illinois is represented by the Institute of Aviation, the School of Social Work and eight colleges—Agriculture; Applied Life Studies; Commerce and Business Administration; Communications; Education; Engineering; Fine and Applied Arts; and Liberal Arts and Sciences—which altogether offer more than 4,000 courses and 150 programs of study. Graduate and professional programs are under the auspices of the Graduate College and the Colleges of Law, Medicine, and Veterinary Medicine. Of all these, the College of Liberal Arts and Sciences is considered the "heart" of the University while the College of Communications is deemed the school's "soul" (according to Chancellor Morton W. Weir).

Liberal Arts and Sciences is the largest and most diversified college, matriculating about 40 percent of all undergraduates. Candidates for the Bachelor of Arts or the Bachelor of Science degree must complete 120 semester hours, 21 of which must be in advanced courses. No more than 24 hours may be taken outside the College of Liberal Arts and Sciences.

Other requirements for graduation include English and a foreign language. Students must complete: either a one-semester, four-hour a week writing course, or a two-semester, three-hour a week writing course; and four semesters of a single foreign language (unless four years of a single language have been passed in high school).

The general education requirements include five semester courses (three hours each a week) from an approved list in literature, the arts, and the social sciences. The university recently adopted a mandated course in non-Western cultures as well as one in Western cultures. In addition, one course must be selected from each of these categories: Literature and the Arts; Historical and Philosophical Perspectives; and Social Perspectives. Another course may be chosen from any of the three categories. Further, five three-hour courses must be completed in the mathematics and the sciences. One must be taken in "Science and Society," and one each in physical science, biological science,

TUITION AND FEES INCREASE
Average Increase/Year: Public = 8.30%, Illinois = 9.08%

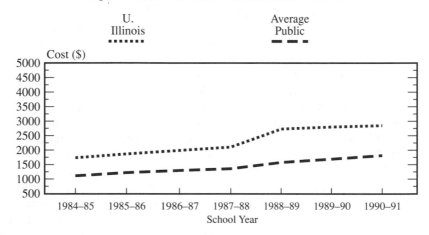

Source: The College Entrance Examination Board

---

behavioral science, and mathematics. The fifth may be selected from any of the last four categories.

Illinois offers an honors program for 100 freshmen each year, who may be enrolled in any undergraduate curriculum (sophomores may apply as well). The administration invites the cream of the incoming freshman crop to participate on the basis of standardized test scores and exceptionally strong high school records; however, any incoming freshman may ask to be considered for the program. These students, known as Chancellor's Scholars, take small (15 students), enriched versions of the general education courses during their first two years. As juniors and seniors, they may supplement course work in their majors with interdisciplinary honors seminars. They also take one capstone seminar "that best fits the student's personal interests as well as his or her college and departmental curricular requirements." The scholars receive grants of $1,000 for summer projects or travel, priority registration for classes, graduate student access to the university library, free computer workshops, and use of the Honors House, where they may study or relax with other honors students. The program does not replace specialized departmental honors programs.

The Edward J. James Undergraduate Honors Program is similar

in nature, but carries no financial stipend. James Scholars may "self-nominate" into the program provided that the decision is based on prior achievement and on high school or college faculty advice. They also are privy to special honors courses, seminars, and interdisciplinary colloquia, and are encouraged to pursue independent research projects. In the College of Liberal Arts and Sciences, entering freshmen with "higher than a predetermined college selection index" are automatically admitted as James Scholar Designates.

While the university boasts one of the nation's largest collegiate libraries (after Harvard and Yale), extensive research facilities, and prestigious academic programs, the average liberal arts student can feel like a very small cog in a very big wheel. Many introductory classes are offered in large lecture halls, with sections often taught by teaching assistants, whose command of English is sometimes marginal. Although 79 percent of class sections have fewer than 30 students, the introductory courses contain many more. Several typically gear up for nearly 1,000 students at a time. Due to overcrowding, students report

DISTRIBUTION OF UNDERGRADUATE AID
1989–90 School Year

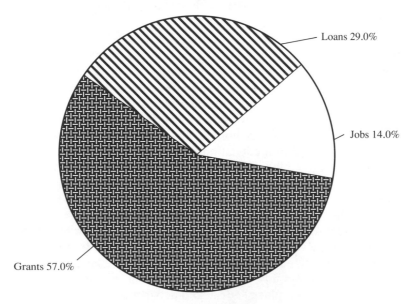

Loans 29.0%

Jobs 14.0%

Grants 57.0%

Source: The College Entrance Examination Board, 1990

they often have trouble getting into the courses they need or want to take. Cheating, while generally no worse at Illinois than at most universities, is often a problem in these classes, where the examinations are usually multiple-choice.

Because the faculty is large, it is difficult to generalize about teaching quality, which varies; but as the university is research-centered, research takes precedence over teaching. Most of the star professors teach only one or two upper-level classes if they teach at all. Professors have office hours, but students seldom take advantage of them. Every undergraduate is assigned an advisor, but for freshmen and sophomores these are often graduate students, who usually try to be helpful but often lack knowledge and information about courses outside their own fields.

Politically speaking, students complain of left-wing bias on the part of certain faculty members in the College of Liberal Arts and Sciences, particularly but not exclusively in the humanities and social sciences. For example, one student reported that a political science professor delivered a stunning denunciation of former president Reagan and former secretary of state George Schultz. According to the professor, the United States was mistaken in liberating Grenada and supporting the Nicaraguan freedom fighters—"failed policies which shall haunt the nation for years to come." Another political science professor pretended to a sense of humor: "While we all realize that eight years of Reagan will effectively put this country in decline for more than a century," he railed, "I just somehow can't bring myself to dislike the man. He's too much of a happy cowboy." Less humorously, perhaps, a political science advisor posted "Vietnam Veterans Against the [Gulf] War" propaganda all over his office door.

Still knocking the Republicans during one of his lectures, a philosophy professor declared, "I don't understand how Republicans can be so hypocritical with respect to their policies on issues . . . I mean, they're against abortion but for the death penalty." Later, he admitted that he approved of abortion and opposed capital punishment. All this during a lecture that was supposed to be about René Descartes. Not to be outdone, a physics professor wore his politics on his back, with a T-shirt advertising the "People's Alliance on Central America," a campus organization that openly supported the Sandinistas and other communist groups.

Unlike many faculty members, the vast majority of students tends to be indifferent to politics and more irritated than persuaded by left-wing rhetoric. However, black groups complain of discrimination. In

March 1991, the Student Government Association, long a mouthpiece for white liberals, was taken over by the Vision Slate, dominated by black and Hispanics who are demanding the hiring of more minority faculty, greater efforts for minority student retention, and "sensitivity awareness" programs. There are even calls for "affirmative funding" of student organizations, although the university already provides special programs for minority students, including an Office of Minority Student Affairs. About 23 percent of undergraduates are members of minority groups.

Also enjoying official university recognition are the People for Lesbian, Gay and Bisexual Concerns. The Illini Union Board sponsors an annual "Alternative Prom" for homosexual and bisexual students, although there is no prom for heterosexuals.

Radical groups are also agitating to abolish the university's traditional American Indian symbol, Chief Illiniwek, which they say is an insult to Native Americans. Feminists also have their agenda: In 1990, they hurled well-publicized charges of sexism at the female aerobic-dance squad, the Illinettes, whose athletic displays and brief costumes they felt demeaned women as sex objects. This campus sensation earned the popular team still more recognition in the form of an appearance on the Oprah Winfrey Show, and so far they—and the Chief—are winning their battles, although the Illinettes will be covering up in future.

Social life at Illinois produces few killjoys. Almost everybody enjoys partying, a way of life in the big and powerful Greek system, which claims about 20 percent of all undergraduates in 50 fraternities and 25 sororities. Alcohol flows freely in spite of the legal drinking age of 21. Non-Greeks make do with smaller parties and forays into Campustown, a bar-studded district near the university, where 19-year-olds are admitted but not allowed to drink—a law, needless to say, more honored in the breach than in the observance. The nearest big cities, Chicago, Indianapolis, and St. Louis, are all two hours away by car.

The variety of sports and extracurricular activities more than makes up for the university's location in the monotonous flatlands. The football season furnishes a thrill a minute for Fighting Illini fans during home games, when partying becomes frenetic. In quieter seasons, jocks play on 11 varsity teams for men and 8 for women (in the Big 10), or plunge into intramural sports—33 for men and 32 for women. Facilities are abundant, including a sports and recreation center, a stadium, golf courses, an ice rink, and even an armory.

Housing on the 700-acre campus accommodates about 8,800 students and is available on a first-come, first-served basis to upperclassmen. Unless granted special permission to do otherwise, all first-year students must live in university housing, which includes 23 residence halls, numerous private facilities, as well as fraternity and sorority houses. Residences are both coed and single-sex and arranged in neighborhood clusters with their own facilities, including libraries, and dining and study halls. About a third of all students live in university housing, and the rest have no trouble finding convenient, sometimes inexpensive housing off campus.

Like its megalithic peers throughout the country, the University of Illinois tries to be all things to all students, a Herculean if not impossible task. Unfortunately, education in the traditional liberal arts, for undergraduates of average ability and motivation, is falling through the cracks—as students are subjected to increasingly intensive bombardment by the proponents of the politically correct.

University of Iowa

Director of Admissions, University of Iowa
Calvin Hall, Iowa City, IA 52242
(319) 335-3847, (800) 553-IOWA

Type: Public				**Costs and Aid:**	
Students:				Tuition & fees:	
19,110 undergraduates				In state	$1,880
9,199 men				Out of state	6,220
9,911 women				Room and Board	2,770
8,935 graduate students				Scholarships:	
				Academic	Yes
Applications:				Athletic	Yes
Closing date: May 15				Minority	Yes
84% of applicants accepted				Financial Aid:	
	Applied	*Accepted*	*Enrolled*	Freshmen	N/A
men	4,457	3,660	1,702	Upperclassmen	N/A
women	4,627	3,972	1,812	**Library:**	3,018,599 titles
SAT or ACT required					
Score reported by: May 15				**ROTC:**	Yes
Mid 50% of freshman scores:				**Study Abroad:**	Yes
ACT composite 22–27					

Because two-thirds of its undergraduates are from Iowa and many of the rest hail from contiguous states, the University of Iowa's light is hidden from most of the country under all those bushels of corn; but it shines brightly for students in many of its excellent pre-professional and graduate programs. In the undergraduate College of Liberal Arts, alas, the glow dims. This is partly a reflection of preoccupation with career-directed studies, as well as the faculty's focus on research, but mostly it results from a lackluster approach to the life of the mind on the part of undergraduates. Sadly, many often appear to be scratching the surface to obtain a degree, instead of digging in to achieve an education.

Founded in 1847, Iowa now has 28,000 students, more than 19,000 of whom are undergraduates. Six percent are minorities. All 50 states are represented, as well as approximately 90 foreign countries, albeit in small numbers. In addition to the College of Liberal Arts, freshmen may enter the School of Engineering. As juniors, liberal arts students may transfer to the Colleges of Business, Education, Nursing, or Pharmacy to obtain undergraduate degrees in those fields. Graduate

179

schools include the College of Law, the College of Medicine, which boasts the nation's largest university-owned teaching hospital, and the Colleges of Dentistry, Engineering, and Business. Each of these is nationally respected and continues to gain prestige. A graduate program that deserves special mention is Iowa's famous creative Writer's Workshop, once attended by Tennessee Williams and other literary luminaries, and still a scribbler's dream.

General Catalog, 1990–1992:

"In 1949, the University of Iowa became the first institution of higher learning in Iowa to offer courses in leisure studies and in 1960, the first to offer a program in leisure studies. The mission of the Department of Leisure Studies has three major components: liberal education through leisure studies, professional preparation for the leisure service profession, and the research of leisure as a behavioral and cultural phenomenon.

By studying the value and function of leisure in a modern society that is at once blessed and burdened with more free time, the department serves the cause of the liberal arts ideal, a fuller and more humane life."

Leisure Studies 104:60—Leisure in Contemporary Society

"Basic philosophical, historical, and scientific foundations and developments in leisure and recreation, function and settings of organized recreation."

Leisure Studies 104:101—Leisure Research

"Research methods presented and applied to leisure research topics, emphasis on processes of research proposal assembly."

The College of Liberal Arts operates on the semester system and, since it enrolls more than four-fifths of Iowa's undergraduates, is a pivotal point of the university. Its general education requirements for the bachelor's degree are numerous if not strenuous: one or two courses in rhetoric; two in "historical perspectives"; a course called the "Interpretation of Literature" and two others in the humanities; two in the natural sciences (one of which must have a laboratory component); two in the social sciences; one in quantitative or formal reasoning; one in a foreign civilization and culture; and four semester hours in physical education. In addition, students must demonstrate

TUITION AND FEES INCREASE
Average Increase/Year: Public = 8.30%, Iowa = 7.20%

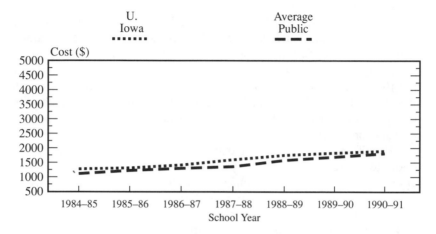

Source: The College Entrance Examination Board

proficiency in a foreign language through the second-year college level or the fourth-year high school level.

The college's greatest fault, academically speaking, is an almost obsessive concern with producing "well-rounded" students. This pre-occupation means that graduates run the risk of being jacks-of-all-trades and masters of none. In the College of Liberal Arts, general education requirements total more credit hours than those demanded by most majors. While students may elect extra hours in the major fields, few do; many opt for a double major instead, and learn neither of them well, often losing interest in both.

Another problem with Iowa's general education requirements is that they defeat their stated purpose of providing a general education and producing that elusive, well-rounded graduate. Students are not required to study classic works of literature, nor the history and cultural roots of their own country. Rather, they may fulfill require-ments with narrow-interest courses like "Social Anthropology of the Caribbean," or "German Heroic and Erotic Literature of the Middle Ages." Additionally, many courses that meet general education re-quirements seem to have a leftist slant. Professors often teach social criticism instead of social studies, though this problem is not endemic to all departments nor all professors. Most departments are solid, if unspectacular. English, psychology, the fine arts, and astronomy are particularly strong.

A further difficulty for students is big-institution bureaucracy, which has run amok at Iowa and today rivals the federal government in nuisance value. Besides wasting great chunks of time waiting in lines and filling out forms, many students become so entangled in red tape that they have problems graduating in four years. This is often due to serious administrative errors in course scheduling, for which the student pays the price. Catastrophes also occur if courses are taken out of order, or if forms are incorrectly completed.

Faculty members are not particularly helpful to bewildered undergraduates, and the advisory system is weak. Classes are generally large, though for an elite group of freshmen a Unified Program does exist, which lasts four semesters and satisfies the general education requirements through small seminars. Of a freshman class of almost 2,800, only approximately 160 join the Unified Program. Interested

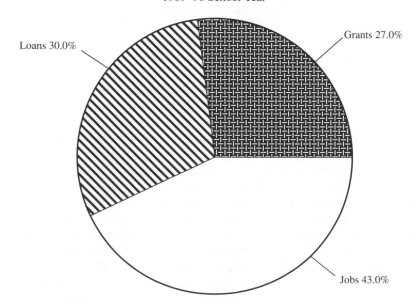

DISTRIBUTION OF UNDERGRADUATE AID
1989–90 School Year

Loans 30.0%

Grants 27.0%

Jobs 43.0%

Source: The College Entrance Examination Board, 1990

students apply before matriculation; the college selects the winners on the basis of ACT scores and individual essays.

Politically, the university community tends to lean leftward. The central commons is often overrun by protesters, who demonstrate against everything from the CIA to U.S. involvement in the Mideast. Marijuana legislation rallies are an annual event, as is the Gay and Lesbian Pride March. However, Iowa also has a fair amount of activism from the right. An independent conservative newspaper is written entirely by students. Conservative student groups are growing in number and membership.

The 900-acre campus and the surrounding community represent one of the university's greatest assets. The administration has preserved much of what everyone there calls "green space," and more is on the way. Off campus, Iowa City is a town of about 60,000 which discourages heavy industry and is also environmentally sensitive, maintaining several pleasant parks. Just a few miles away there is a reservoir which students use for boating, swimming, or just sunning.

On-campus housing is limited, accommodating only 5,800 students. This does not prove to be a problem, however, as only freshmen are required to live on campus. Most upperclassmen live in or near the town in reasonably priced rooms and apartments. On campus, housing is coeducational except for one female dorm, and is allotted on a first-come, first-served basis. The residential environment is totally permissive; the only regulations seem to be the fire laws. Alcohol flows in the dorms and drug use is not uncommon, with marijuana and psychedelics generally the mindblowers of choice. The former is more popular, perhaps because it seems to suit the relaxed lifestyle of the average Iowa student.

Social life centers around fraternities and sororities (although less than 20 percent of students belong) and around the bars that have sprung up like mushrooms within a few hundred yards of the campus. There are 12 of these, closely clustered, which can and often do cater to 4,000 students at once. Others, a short walk or drive away, take the overflow. Competing with the bar scene, 29 fraternities and 20 sororities provide living quarters for members and parties for the multitudes. More soberly, Greeks at Iowa as elsewhere devote considerable time to philanthropic activities.

On the cultural side, Hancher Auditorium is the site of many fine orchestral and ballet presentations from around the nation, as well as excellent plays, which benefit from the Writer's Workshop. There are

300 campus organizations, which run the gamut from homosexual support groups to the bagpipe band.

Sports are a big deal at Iowa with 11 intercollegiate men's teams and 10 women's. There are 20 intramural sports, with men's, women's, and coed teams. The stadium seats 70,000 rabid football fans of the hard-driving Hawkeyes, and the wrestling team wins national championships with predictable regularity. Other popular and well-played sports are basketball, men's swimming, and women's field hockey. The extensive athletic facilities have been recently renovated and include a golf course.

As with so many of America's giant universities endeavoring to educate the masses, Iowa's masses often don't get educated, at least on the undergraduate level. They obtain degrees instead. But most students probably don't care about the difference, and they do have a good time in the process, on the playing fields and in the bars—where they doubtless celebrate surviving Iowa's bureaucratic battles. And, after all, who is to say that such an achievement isn't a very important part of a modern education?

The Johns Hopkins University

Director of Admissions
The Johns Hopkins University, 140 Garland Hall
34th and Charles Streets, Baltimore, MD 21218 (301) 338-8171

Type: Private and Secular

Students:
2,898 undergraduates
  1,867 men
  1,031 women
1,214 graduate students

Applications:
Closing date: January 1
49% of applicants accepted

	Applied	Accepted	Enrolled
men	3,313	1,746	558
women	2,272	1,008	278

SAT or ACT required (SAT preferred)
  Score reported by: February 15
  Mid 50% of freshman scores:
    SAT-Math   640–730
    SAT-Verbal 580–680

Costs and Aid:

Tuition and fees	$15,380
Room and board	5,570

Scholarships:
Academic	Yes
Athletic	Yes
Minority	No

Financial Aid:
Freshmen	60%
Upperclassmen	66%

Library: 2,000,000 titles

ROTC: Yes

Study Abroad: Yes

Percentage of courses that can be used to fulfill distribution requirements: 75

The prestigious Johns Hopkins University, now home to 4,000 students, was founded in 1876 as the first institution of higher learning in the United States deliberately based upon the German model, which holds that high-quality university education depends more upon preeminence in research than it does upon excellence in teaching. The expansion of knowledge through cutting-edge research is supposed to permeate the entire academic community and raise the general standard, including that of undergraduate education. Therefore, there has never been a separate undergraduate school of the liberal arts at Hopkins.

According to the course catalog, in the School of Arts and Sciences, which enrolls slightly more than 2,000 undergraduates as well as a number of graduate students, "undergraduate education, graduate education, and the conduct of primary research are integrated in an organic way." According to some observers, however, this organic unity is now breaking down, and the undergraduate component is in danger of being overwhelmed by the other two.

What most people think of as "the university" are the School of Arts and Sciences and the smaller G.W.C. Whiting School of Engineering, both of which are located on the 140-acre Homewood campus not far from Baltimore's waterfront. But these two schools are, in fact, only the tip of the iceberg of a greater conglomeration known as the Johns Hopkins Institutions. These consist of the world-renowned Johns Hopkins Hospital, the highly ranked School of Medicine, the School of Public Health, and the School of Nursing—all in East Baltimore; the Peabody Institute—a professional school of music—in the Mt. Vernon area of Baltimore; the Paul Nitze School of Advanced International Studies (SAIS) in Washington, D.C.; the Applied Physics Laboratory located between Baltimore and Washington and operated for the federal government; and various other small, semi-autonomous divisions in Maryland, Italy, and China.

Undergraduate and Graduate Programs, 1990–91:
Anthropology 070.342—Political Economy of Health.
Professor Emily Martin

"Health in relationship to economic, social and political organization in pre-capitalist societies; the history of the development of scientific medicine, women's health, health in relation to imperialism; nationalized health care; socialized health care."

So far as the undergraduate liberal arts are concerned in the School of Arts and Sciences, specific course requirements outside the major do not exist. The course guide explains the underlying philosophy. "Like graduate students, undergradutes are largely free of university-wide curricular requirements, so that every scholar . . . can go forward rapidly or go forward slowly according to the fleetness of his foot and his freedom from impediment."

Students must acquire 120 credit hours and take 30 of these outside their major area. For a major in the social or behavioral sciences or the humanities, 12 of these credits must be in math or science; if majoring in math or the natural sciences, 18 credits must be accrued in the humanities, or the social and behavioral sciences. Students may choose interdisciplinary majors, or help design their own programs. One major of particular interest is in creative writing where students study with well-known authors and playwrights.

Upperclassmen may take courses at other local schools—Goucher

TUITION AND FEES INCREASE
Average Increase/Year: Private = 11.15%, Johns Hopkins = 9.67%

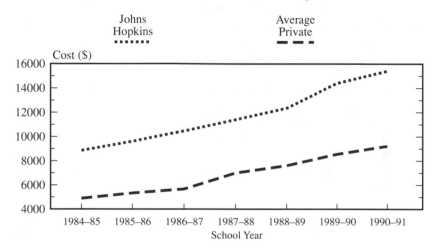

Source: The College Entrance Examination Board

College, Loyola College, Morgan State University, the College of Nôtre Dame, and Towson State University—if they are "substantially different from those offered at Johns Hopkins." The Maryland Institute College of Art and the Baltimore Hebrew College also enroll a few Hopkins students. On the home campus, undergraduates report that in small and moderate-size classes there is much interaction between professors and students, in spite of the faculty's propensity to research. Graduate students often serve as teaching assistants, however, particularly in lower-level classes. Typical of major research institutions, many of these teaching assistants are foreigners with a limited mastery of the English language.

In the School of Arts and Sciences, the most popular majors are biology and international studies, probably because of the university's renown in these fields at the graduate level. Other strong departments are history, art history, and English. First-semester freshman courses are offered pass-fail. Transcripts only list the courses passed during that term. While this is done to "alleviate some of the pressures of adjustment for freshmen," students note that this method can be more of a curse than a blessing. Some succumb to the temptation to do what they think is just enough work to pass, only to discover they have miscalculated, failed, and ended with no credit for the course—a real handicap in Hopkins' intellectually competitive atmosphere.

To avoid pitfalls like this, Hopkins runs an orientation program for incoming freshmen. About a half-dozen students are assigned to each student advisor, a sophomore who helps them with course selection and class registration. Freshmen also have a chance to meet professors. Although there is a substantial minority enrollment at the university, with Asian-Americans predominating, students report that there is no attempt by the administration to reorient freshmen beliefs to correspond with what is seen on other campuses as politically correct.

Although finances are a problem at many American colleges, both private and public, money is central to an understanding of the current situation at Johns Hopkins. The university finds itself in straitened circumstances, largely due to cutbacks in grants by the federal government (particularly NASA), as well as to overextension in financing the Beijing Center, the radio station WJHU, and the Peabody Institute. The School of Arts and Sciences, which tends to receive very little of

DISTRIBUTION OF UNDERGRADUATE AID
1989–90 School Year

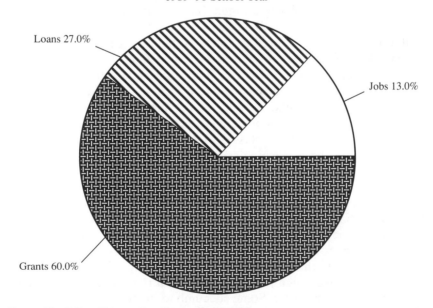

Loans 27.0%

Jobs 13.0%

Grants 60.0%

Source: The College Entrance Examination Board, 1990

the government funding for research and is traditionally not self-supporting, has borne the brunt of these difficulties. It had expected to be in the black based on NASA support, but the Challenger disaster put much of the expected funding on hold. As a result, the school has run substantial annual deficits since 1987.

Consequently, Arts and Sciences has had to take money from wealthier divisions of the university, which were reluctant to relinquish funds only partly from fear of losing their autonomy. (William C. Richardson, the new president of the university, notes that Hopkins is "one of the most decentralized universities in the United States.") The financial transfers were made in the end, but in return the school was required to come up with a scheme to enable it to operate in the black. A five-year plan was developed, mandating by 1992 a 10 percent increase in undergraduate numbers coupled with a 10 percent reduction in faculty members. In addition, some cuts in departmental budgets have been implemented.

The classics and French departments were among those affected by the cuts. In 1987, two of four senior members left the classics department in response to more appealing offers. Similarly, last year, three senior French professors, out of the total of five in the department, made tracks for Emory University and took some of their graduate students with them. However, Lloyd Armstrong, the dean of the School of Arts and Sciences, argued that these defections were typical of current bidding wars, and said, "I doubt that we would have tried to match them [the offers] in any case."

At other schools, this sort of restructuring might have resulted in noisy student protest. At Hopkins the plan was effected with scarcely a murmur of dissent. It's simple: very few care. Most students seem primarily interested in gaining one of the nation's better degrees before they go on to graduate schools, often in law or medicine. Students interested in taking French only to fulfill a language requirement have little interest in the internal problems of the French department.

Desperately earnest and exceptionally competitive, Hoppies work constantly. One undergraduate noted that the students were "cutthroat to the nth degree." The Eisenhower Reference Library, open 24-hours a day, seven days a week, always has at least a handful of students in it. Pop in during midterm week and it will be full to capacity even at three in the morning. This devotion to academics, while admirable, also reflects a lack of undergraduate college spirit. Created as a graduate institution, Hopkins added undergraduates as something of an afterthought, so they did not appear in any numbers until the

1920s. The emphasis placed on the graduates precluded the growth of undergraduate social institutions, and the shortage of campus accommodation meant that many students commuted from the surrounding Baltimore suburbs. Lack of campus housing and social life are still problems.

Freshmen are guaranteed on-campus housing, which is both single-sex and coed, but after that 40 percent of students must find living quarters elsewhere. The others, who receive their places by lottery, live in campus dorms, or university-owned apartments nearby. The neighborhood is seedy. Student harassment by area residents late at night is growing, but instances of physical harm have been few so far. An escort service is available.

Many students complain of a dull social life, though they don't do much to enliven it. About a quarter of the undergraduates belong to 13 fraternities and 3 sororities. However, the Greeks do not maintain a particularly high profile and generally shy away from the large-scale flings common at other schools. Part of this is due to the location of the fraternity houses, many a mile or so from campus; consequently, their visibility in terms of the party scene is far lower than at other universities. Other extracurricular activities revolve around 80 groups and organizations, as well as intercollegiate and intramural sports. There are 13 intercollegiates and 18 intramurals for men and 11 intercollegiates and 16 intramurals for women. Nobody works up much of a lather about any of them, except for lacrosse.

Perhaps the only thing that does excite young Hoppies outside the classroom is the lacrosse team. This is Hopkins's only Division I team; football, baseball, and basketball are Division III. A lacrosse home game will see the stands full of cheering students and loud bands. These athletes are viewed with a certain reverence, unlike other sportsmen on campus. This said, the team's performance has been less than exemplary of late. Beaten by Maryland in the finals in 1989, the team didn't even make it that far in 1990. But however badly the team plays, it always seems to be forgiven; so far as sports go, Hopkins *is* lacrosse.

Politically, as well as socially, Hopkins is relatively quiet. This is a conservative school in the sense that most students are more or less content with the status quo. The College Republicans are almost moribund, while the Young Democrats, whose newspaper went out of business three years ago, are only marginally more energetic. Again, undergraduates are just too busy at the computer terminals to give more than a passing thought to current issues and events.

In January 1990, there was a minor eruption when the feminists protested against an allegedly sexist cartoon that appeared in the conservative campus paper, the *Hopkins Spectator*. But the incident faded. Even the debate over ROTC has been mild. The *Spectator* supported keeping ROTC on campus; another college newspaper and the homosexual organization opposed it. The President noted that he saw no future change in ROTC's position on campus. No one else seemed particularly interested, even the ROTC cadets.

Naturally, Johns Hopkins has its share of "tenured radicals." The Chaplain's Office is still more concerned with contras than Christ, Sandinistas than sacraments. The sociology department offers the usual selection of ideology-dominated courses: "Class, Gender and Ethnicity in Contemporary America" and "Race and Ethnic Relations." Political science has a couple of professors whose favorite means of communications revolves around "otherness," "intertextual analyses," "problematics," and "constructs." And what English Department would be complete without "Women's Consciousness in Fiction," not to mention a homosexual interpretation of Shakespeare? The Humanities Center contributes with "Colonization, Sexuality, Resistance." Still, it's been a while since anyone openly defended Mao or Stalin at Hopkins. Nor does anyone seem much interested in removing the history department's "Occidental Civilization, 1640– Present" (two semesters) from the curriculum.

All in all, the School of Arts and Sciences at Johns Hopkins is still traditionally oriented and academically more rigorous than most, if less exciting than some. In other respects, life there seems tedious. The future of undergraduate education at Johns Hopkins will depend, in large measure, upon the resources the university allots to it, both financial and intellectual.

Kenyon College

Dean of Admissions, Kenyon College
Gambier, OH 43022-9623 (614) 427-5000, (800) 848-2468

Type: Private and Protestant		**Costs and Aid:**	
		Tuition and fees	$14,870
Students:		Room and Board	3,260
1,525 undergraduates		Scholarships:	
732 men		Academic	Yes
793 women		Athletic	No
Applications:		Minority	No
Closing date: February 15		Financial Aid:	
SAT or ACT required		Freshmen	N/A
Score reported by: February 15		Upperclassmen	N/A
Mid 50% of freshman scores:			
SAT-Math N/A		**Library:**	350,000 titles
SAT-Verbal N/A		**ROTC:**	No
		Study Abroad:	Yes

At first impression, Kenyon College appears to be a miniature Oxbridge transplanted to Ohio. Founded in 1824 under the auspices of the Episcopal Church with which it is still loosely affiliated, the liberal arts school looks as if it has been in a time warp ever since. Its stately Gothic architecture and village atmosphere perpetuate this changeless image. Resting on a hill in central Ohio (grandly dubbed the "Magic Mountain") and virtually engulfing tiny Gambier, the smallest college town in the U.S., the campus exudes old English charm, its serenity seemingly undisturbed by the sharp shocks of modern life. A visitor can almost glimpse the gleam of ivory towers winking in the distance. Looks, however, as everyone knows, can be deceiving.

Kenyon has at last been touched, if not jolted, by the turbulent world outside. Recent attempts by some students, faculty, and administrators to update the Kenyon "experience" have resulted in numerous skirmishes between the old guard and the new breed. These revolve around the usual subjects—de-Westernizing the curriculum, feminizing it, diversifying the student body, and de-emphasizing the Greek system. Thus far neither side has won a decisive victory, so, at this point in its history, the future of Kenyon College hangs in the balance. What will it become?

Right now the traditional liberal arts still shine brightly for the college's 1,500 students. Perhaps the most luminous among them is the English Department, which is more popular than ever and has recently celebrated the 50th anniversary of its famous literary journal, the *Kenyon Review*. The department initially gained national prominence in mid-century under the leadership of John Crowe Ransom. Through the years, it has not succumbed to the modern theories of deconstructionism and has also expanded at a great rate, which has proved a mixed blessing. While retaining star professors, the department has to some extent compromised traditional quality for the sake of quantity. It is increasingly difficult for students, including English majors, to get into desired or required courses. The numbers crunch has become such a problem, in fact, that special early registration has been set up for majors, who represent fully a third of the student body, to ensure that they receive priority.

Courses, 1990–91:
Interdisciplinary Course 3—Introduction to Women's
and Gender Studies.
Visiting Professor Harry Bond and Professor Linda Smolak

"This interdisciplinary course is designed to help develop a critical framework for thinking about questions relating to gender and sex roles, including some of the most important issues that arise in the contemporary world. The course will introduce students to the fields of women's and men's studies, out of which some of the most innovative and challenging developments in modern scholarship are arising. Topics to be covered will include basic concepts in the study of gender; female and male socialization; families; feminist theory; political ideologies and movements; ethical issues; work; the media; race and ethnicity; violence; and sexuality and homosexuality. Everyone's opinions and points of view will be respected in lectures and class discussions, but we will be challenging each other to analyze critically the process by which opinions are reached. Texts may include Arthur Miller, *Death of a Salesman;* Tavris and Wade, *The Longest War;* Jane English, *Sex Equality;* Alice Walker, *The Color Purple;* Richardson and Taylor, *Feminist Frontiers;* and Sophocles, *Antigone.*"

Increasingly prominent and now beginning to acquire some national standing is the political science department, which has grown much stronger during the last 25 years. Its accent on the philosophy, as contrasted with the practice, of politics makes it unusual among

TUITION AND FEES INCREASE
Average Increase/Year: Private = 11.15%, Kenyon = 9.62%

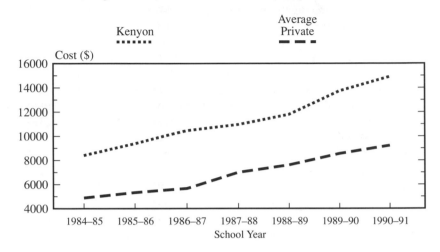

Source: The College Entrance Examination Board

undergraduate political science departments. Regrettably, however, it has lost its conference center, which once attracted many celebrities of political academia (including Allan Bloom, Irving Kristol, Harvey Mansfield, Jr., and George Will) for lively discussions on hot topics such as civil rights, censorship, and democratic capitalism. Still, the quality of the department's faculty is now probably the best at the college and the number of students in the discipline has grown to make it the second most popular major at Kenyon.

The history department, on the other hand, has shed rays of darkness across the campus by becoming a breeding ground for a politicized curriculum and trendy courses—"American Women in the Trans-Mississippi West" or "History of the Sixties." Needless to say, it has managed to make icons of women's and Afro-American studies. History, however, is not the only discipline to be infiltrated by political agendas.

Sociology and even religion are notable offenders. Some faculty in these classes have been known to intimidate into silence those with opposing viewpoints. What makes this situation even more discouraging is the fact that the professors are extremely erudite in their fields but nevertheless permit their political ideology to alienate students.

For instance, several apolitical students have praised a certain professor of religion for valuable instruction in the subject, yet complain
about his annoying digressions into the sins of American foreign policy.

When a community the size of Kenyon contains factions as polar
and political as those of some of its faculty, sparks are bound to fly.
Little disputes erupt everywhere from the public pages of the campus
newspapers to the closed meetings of the faculty. The major irritant is
the curriculum question. The campus left presses to diversify everywhere, while about 40 stalwart professors resist sweeping changes
designed to weaken the canon. In one memorable fit of pique, a leader
of the left accused the traditionalists of no less a crime than "academic
sabotage."

At the moment, Kenyon has no core curriculum, but there are
distribution requirements—although you can graduate without taking
a foreign language or mathematics. Students do have to complete two
semester courses in one department of each of the four divisions:
humanities; fine arts; social sciences; natural sciences. In addition,

---

DISTRIBUTION OF UNDERGRADUATE AID
1989–90 School Year

Loans 15.0%

Jobs 5.0%

Grants 80.0%

Source: The College Entrance Examination Board, 1990

comprehensive examinations are *de rigueur* in the major field, a big plus for Kenyon and a rarity in modern American academia. Also a standout, the Integrated Program of Humane Studies is a three-year sequence, drawing on several disciplines. Warning signals are beginning to flash, however, as reports circulate about infiltration by the deconstructionists.

In spite of certain troubling signs, something wonderful remains unchanged at Kenyon—the warm intimacy between faculty and students and the small classes, where discussion is encouraged and everyone can have his say. In many ways, life at Kenyon is like life in an extended family, where people feel free to argue and bicker because they feel secure and safe.

One of the issues the Gambier community argues about is campus housing. Contrary to the system at many other colleges, Kenyon's fraternities share housing with independents, and eat in one of the two common dining halls. Due to the fact that campus fraternities are nearly as old as the college, they are housed in the most historic—and therefore at Kenyon the most desirable—residence halls. A controversy arose when an administration-appointed task force deemed it "inequitable" housing practice to favor fraternities with the "traditional" housing. This issue moved to the forefront of college affairs when the administration attempted to pull the rug out from under the Greeks over the summer vacation.

During the long break in 1989, the College published the *Report of the Commission on Student Life,* a one-sided document based on a questionnaire to which only 38 percent of the campus had responded. The report recommended the removal of fraternities from their accustomed housing. Greeks and non-Greeks alike objected to the way they felt the administration was railroading them. Greeks were especially hostile, recognizing that their proposed ejection was based on nothing more solid than the administration's desire to imitate other "progressive" schools.

What the college also failed to consider at the time was Kenyon's unusually modest endowment. The potential loss that the school might incur should it alienate Kenyon's most active alumni constituency, fraternity members, could be considerable. Now that they recognize this, the powers-that-be have applied the brakes, and the ultimate outcome is uncertain.

With or without their accustomed housing, fraternities form the nucleus around which Kenyon's social life revolves, as 55 percent of the men belong. (Only 2 percent of women belong to the single sorority.) There is, however, no pressure for men to join one of the seven national fraternities. Most weekend parties are sponsored by Greek organizations and dispense free beer and hospitality to all students. When they are not boozing and schmoozing, students may select from almost 100 clubs and organizations, with singing groups the strongest attractions, along with the very fine Bolton Theater for the Performing Arts. Those who venture off the Magic Mountain into the real world for culture and entertainment drive to Columbus, an hour away, or as far afield as Cincinnati or Cleveland, each three hours distant.

Yet the Kenyon *ambience* can be constricting rather than expansive, and at times due to its limited size, isolation, and homogeneous population (93 percent of students are white and most are upper middle-class Midwesterners), the atmosphere can become claustrophobic. It's no wonder then that many turn to sports for a breath of air and a break from boredom. The 800-acre campus represents a vast playground for its small population, with ample playing fields, a 2,000-seat gymnasium, a stadium, and numerous tennis courts. Swimming and soccer are particularly popular with both sexes. Both the men's and women's swim teams are record-breaking, perennial NCAA Division III champions. Intercollegiate sports have historically drawn most participation, but intramurals are now catching on. There are 11 each for men and 10 each for women.

Politically, most students in Gambier are apathetic, but they remain dormant only so long as they are left alone. (If they hadn't wanted to be left alone, they wouldn't have gone to Kenyon in the first place.) As soon as they perceive that their "rights" are threatened, however, they awaken with a shake, and begin barking to protect them. It remains to be seen whether the administration, ambitious for national prominence, and a sizeable segment of the faculty, eager to break out of Gambier's conservatism, can bind their students with the chains of academia's New Left. Right now the students and the liberal arts still have more than a fighting chance to stay free on top of the Magic Mountain.

University of Massachusetts at Amherst

Director of Undergraduate Admissions
University of Massachusetts at Amherst
University Admissions Center, Amherst, MA 01003
(413) 545-0222

Type: Public	**Costs and Aid:**	
Students:	Tuition & fees:	
19,188 undergraduates	In state	$3,480
9,347 men	Out of state	8,330
9,841 women	Room and Board	3,690
6,631 graduate students	Scholarships:	
	Academic	Yes
Applicants:	Athletic	Yes
Closing date: February 15	Minority	Yes
52% of applicants accepted	Financial Aid:	
SAT or ACT required (SAT preferred)	Freshmen	65%
Score reported by: February 15	Upperclassmen	70%
Mid 50% of freshman scores:		
SAT-Math 500–620	**Library:**	2,345,974 titles
SAT-Verbal 440–560	**ROTC:**	Yes
	Study Abroad:	Yes

As New England's largest public university serving more than 40,000 students on three campuses, UMass is now a force to be reckoned with in American higher education. Although the university has only recently emerged from relative obscurity, the main campus at Amherst currently attracts national media attention for its politically correct postures, which rival those of bigger and better known institutions, such as Berkeley and Wisconsin. The setting for this "modern" academic climate is 1,200 acres located in a rural valley of lush green fields, formerly the site of an agricultural school. (The university was founded as a land grant college in 1863.) However, the landscape is UMass's only remaining connection with small-town, traditional values.

UMass matriculates approximately 25,000 students on the Amherst campus. About 80 percent of all students are from Massachusetts with the rest from almost every state in the Union as well as 20 foreign countries. About 8 percent are minorities. Nearly 10,000 students matriculate in the College of Arts and Sciences. The other schools and

199

colleges, offering both undergraduate and advanced degrees, are: Education; Engineering; Food and Natural Resources; Management; Nursing; Physical Education; and Public Health. Two-year associate degrees are offered on the Stockbridge campus, and there is a School of Medicine located in Worcester.

1990/91 Undergraduate Catalog:

Selected course offerings in the **Economics** Department:

308—Political Economy: Theory and Application

"Application of the theory of political economy to selected economic problems and issues. Topics vary; list usually available at pre-registration. Past topics: economic crises; race and gender; military spending; class structure; imperialism."

348—The Political Economy of Women

"A critical review of neoclassical, Marxist, and feminist economic theories pertaining to inequality between men and women in both the family and the firm."

The proponents of political correctness at Amherst support the idea that social engineering is a legitimate function of the university, and this creed affects both extracurricular and academic life. For example, the College of Arts and Sciences' program of Afro-American studies offers a course called "Theater with a Conscience," which "encourages students to use theater as a tool to effect social change." The same department also sponsors for academic credit a seminar called "Student Leadership and Student Groups: The Process of Managing by Objectives," which is billed as "an introduction to useful group development and management techniques for student leaders in undergraduate groups." The radical economics department deserves special mention, however, for several of its polemics, including Political Economy 308, whose "past topics include economic crises; race and gender; military spending; class structure; imperialism." Then, there is "The Political Economy of Women—A critical review of neoclassical, Marxist, and feminist economic theories pertaining to inequality between men and women in both the family and the firm."

But the radical left is perhaps most proud of its *pièce de résistance,* an interdisciplinary program of Social Thought and Political

TUITION AND FEES INCREASE
Average Increase/Year: Public = 8.30%, U. Mass.-Amherst = 12.65%

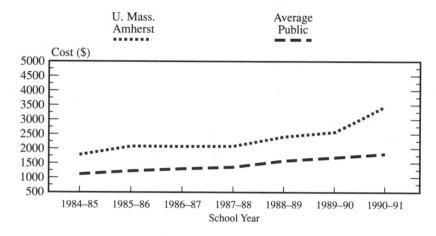

Source: The College Entrance Examination Board

Economy (STPEC), which the course catalog defines as the study of "the interrelationship of racism, sexism, and class oppression . . . the relationship of Western to non-Western countries . . . the structural inequality in the economy." Examples of course offerings are: "Anarchism"; "Economics of Minorities"; "Economics of Cuba"; "Feminist and Womanist Theory"; and "Women and Social Democratization in Latin America."

As part of its general education requirements, UMass lists two writing courses, one to be taken as a freshman and the other as a junior in the major department. The instructors use the courses to indoctrinate students with "correct" attitudes toward racial and social diversity. This is done by requiring students to read and talk about the literature of "victimology" in which the characters experience discrimination and oppression. Students also work with materials from print and broadcast media dealing with issues of diversity.

According to Anne J. Herrington, the program's director, "The purpose of the program is not to bring in specific content but to provide 'prompts' that encourage students to reflect on their own experiences and deal with their own prejudices." She also obliges the faculty members and teaching assistants who conduct the course to participate in a three-day "sensitivity" workshop.

UMass, which operates on the semester system, requires 120 credits for graduation. In addition to the writing courses, university-wide general education requirements compel students to take courses in four areas: the Social World; the Biological and Physical World; Basic Math Skills; Analytic Reasoning. In the Social World category, two of the eight courses mandated must be in "social and cultural diversity." The others must be in literature (one); the arts/liberal arts (one); historical studies (one); social and behavioral sciences (two); and one more in any of the Social World subjects. In the Biological and Physical World category, students must take one course in a biological science, one in a physical science, and a third in either. One course each is required in basic mathematical skills and analytic reasoning, although students may be exempted from the math course if they pass an examination. In addition to the university requirements, the College of Arts and Sciences obliges candidates for both the B.A.

DISTRIBUTION OF UNDERGRADUATE AID
1989–90 School Year

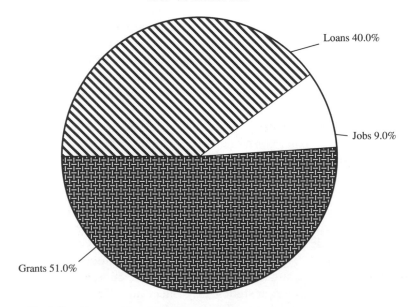

Loans 40.0%

Jobs 9.0%

Grants 51.0%

Source: The College Entrance Examination Board, 1990

and B.S. degrees to complete a foreign language course at the intermediate level (exemption by advanced placement credit or examination).

The honors program, in which approximately 700 undergraduates participate, requires students to take at least one honors course a semester, with a minimum of six completed with a grade of B or higher. These courses may be taken in any department. Successful candidates, who are designated Commonwealth Scholars, must complete requirements for departmental or interdisciplinary-track honors, both of which require a research project, such as a thesis or portfolio.

The strongest departments at UMass are not generally reckoned to be in the liberal arts, although the hard sciences, especially chemistry, are better than most. Students say that economics and communications are among the worst. The most politicized are generally named as economics, anthropology, English, and sociology. Regardless of their political agendas, most professors are helpful when approached, though students report that the advising system is too big and bureaucratic to be very useful.

A special feature of both social and academic life is the Five College Consortium, which also includes Amherst, Mount Holyoke, Smith, and Hampshire Colleges, all of which are within a few miles. Students at any of these schools may take courses at the others at no extra cost. A free bus service links all the campuses.

Housing on the UMass campus can accommodate about half the student population, but is guaranteed for all four years, because so many elect to live off campus. On campus, there are four residential areas containing a variety of low- and high-rise accommodation, some with suites. Each area is encouraged to provide a range of academic and cultural programs to establish its own identity and small-community spirit. Residences are both single-sex and coed, and include honors houses, language and special-interest houses, fraternity and sorority houses, as well as "social awareness corridors." Minority students often choose to live in "theme" houses. All residence hall counselors must undergo race relations training.

Sports are low-profile but offer a lot of variety. There are 13 intercollegiate teams each for men and women and 26 intramurals each for men and women. Soccer and lacrosse are very good; softball and volleyball are very popular. Facilities include: 120 acres of playing fields; 24 tennis courts; 3 pools; 5 handball/squash courts; weight rooms; universals; courts for basketball, volleyball, and badminton; indoor/outdoor tracks; as well as gyms and weight equipment in many of the dormitories. The Mullins Convocation Center is scheduled to open in 1993, and will have a multi-use arena available for, among other things, basketball and skating. The campus's location in the beautiful Berkshire hills also provides easy access to skiing, hiking and canoeing.

The Amherst area is generally considered quite safe, and campus crime is not a problem. Perhaps because the university has banned keg parties, social life does not revolve around the 15 fraternities and nine sororities to which less than 10 percent of the student body now belong. It does revolve around the Five College Consortium, the bars of Amherst, the nightlife of Boston (90 miles distant), and the 250 student organizations which sponsor concerts, dances, and films, as well as the usual special-interest activities, including an operatic society, an orchestra, jazz and marching bands, and of course many politically oriented groups.

One of these, Queer Nation, attracted notoriety in the autumn of 1990 by invading a Republican Club office to stage a "kiss-in" for homosexuals. Homosexuals are high-profile at UMass, and hold an annual "gay awareness" week, funded by compulsory student contributions. In the same vein, for a number of years, homosexuals, blacks, and other minority groups have been awarded non-elective seats in the student governing body, but this policy is now changing due to a recent election that installed a moderate majority. Students other than minority members have always been subject to elections.

Not only is preferential treatment given to minorities, but the expression of conservative and moderate opinion is stifled. For instance, during a pro-life rally, the microphone being used by the pro-lifers was set to a volume level that made the speakers' voices completely inaudible. The person who turned the volume down was from the Student Activities Office.

In another incident, several fraternity pledges disrupted a class as a prank. The professor happened to be showing a film about homosexuals and, angered at the interruption, automatically blamed conservative student organizations for instigating the disturbance.

Racial confrontations also occur with regularity. In 1986, several black students were injured in a fight with white students when feelings ran high after a World Series baseball game, which they had all watched on television; in 1988, two black male students and a white woman were assaulted near a dormitory.

In addition to multicultural course requirements, race relations training, and special privileges for minorities on the student governing body, the university has attempted to defuse the explosive atmosphere on campus by conducting an annual Civility Week, which so far seems to have produced little civility and less good will. (The administration has now abolished Civility Week.) A case in point: In April 1990, a group called the Third World Caucus invited faculty and students of the economics department to a forum on Eurocentrism. In an 11-page paper, the caucus castigated the department for failing to "confront the imperialism of Western (Euro-U.S.) thought." The paper then attacked Eurocentric education "as a weapon to colonize Third World peoples, 'pacify' them and quash any resistance." While stipulating that the economics department "considers itself radical," the paper nevertheless criticized the content of many courses for not being radical *enough,* and accused the department of ignoring the issue of "imperialism and colonial plunder." It also complained that "the possibility of recasting the notion of exploitation in the light of unequal international relationships remains beyond the pale of our courses."

Finally, the paper addressed what it called the "problem" of the retention of students in the department and the hiring of "Third World" faculty. The caucus rejected the argument that there were not enough qualified minority candidates, and accused the department of "being too short-sighted to accept them," or of not being "attractive enough for them to accept us." It also stated:

> [There is a] lack of commitment to helping students get through the program once they are admitted . . . Attention must be given to the different needs and interests of students of diverse backgrounds. . . . Failure to do so leads to the Eurocentric conclusion that when Third World students have problems it is because they are not qualified, whereas white students' difficulties are attributed to other factors.

This chip-on-the-shoulder mentality has permeated not only the economics department at UMass, but also the general atmosphere campus wide. Therefore, it is becoming increasingly difficult for individuals to engage in dispassionate discussion of issues inside or outside the classroom. The campus is becoming polarized between groups of "victims" and "oppressors." Dissenters who dare to reject these labels and the mental straitjackets they impose often find themselves part of a lonely new minority.

Miami University

Director of Admission, Miami University: Oxford Campus
GLOS Admission Center, Grey Gables, Oxford, OH 45056
(513) 529-2531

				Costs and Aid:	
Type: Public				Tuition and fees	
Students:				In state	$3,390
14,456 undergraduates				Out of state	7,370
6,824 men				Room and Board	3,100
7,632 women				Scholarships:	
1,687 graduate students				Academic	Yes
Applications:				Athletic	Yes
Closing date: January 31				Minority	Yes
65% of applicants accepted				Financial Aid:	
	Applied	*Accepted*	*Enrolled*	Freshmen	50%
men	4,679	2,986	1,472	Upperclassmen	50%
women	5,350	3,492	1,679	**Library:**	950,000 titles
SAT or ACT required					
Score reported by: February 28				**ROTC:**	Yes
Mid 50% of freshman scores:				**Study Abroad:**	Yes
SAT-Math	560–660				
SAT-Verbal	490–590				

Founded in 1809, Miami University, after a long period of struggle and obscurity, has now developed into one of the nation's better state-assisted universities. Combining a strong sense of tradition with an energetic faculty, varied course offerings, and a wide array of extra-curricular activities, Miami proffers a well-rounded undergraduate experience at a state school price.

The university traces its origins back to 1792 when George Washington signed a land grant act that provided for the creation of a college in the Ohio territory. By 1809, the state of Ohio had officially established Miami University, but classroom instruction didn't begin until 1824 on a pretty campus near the tiny town of Oxford. Though Miami's early growth was sporadic, and in fact non-existent when the university closed for 10 years after the Civil War, the school now thrives with approximately 18,000 students on four campuses on two continents. (Besides Oxford, two of these are two-year commuter campuses at Hamilton and Middletown; the third hosts Miami's study abroad program in Luxembourg.)

207

Miami counts among its accolades the titles of "Mother of Fraternities" (three nationals were started there), "Public Ivy" (partly because of its classically beautiful campus), and the distinction of having one of its graduates, Benjamin Harrison, become president of the United States. Now, three-quarters of its students come from Ohio, with the rest from the other 49 states and 50 foreign countries.

Miami has six undergraduate schools: the College of Arts and Sciences; the School of Business; the School of Education and Allied Professions; the School of Applied Science; the School of Fine Arts; and the School of Interdisciplinary Studies. Each division has its own prerequisites for graduation, but, starting with the freshman class in the autumn of 1992, all students will be required to complete recently revised general education requirements known as the Miami Plan.

While Miami's liberal arts division, the College of Arts and Sciences, has always been the university's largest component, its strength has been increasing in recent years. Fifty-five percent of Miami students now major in this division. The Miami Plan, which took four years to develop, builds upon previous distribution requirements and seeks to provide the student with an integrated, overall academic design. With 128 credit hours needed for graduation, the Plan is divided into three parts: 30 to 36 hours in "Foundation—Intellectual Concepts"; 80 to 86 hours in "Field—Specialization"; and 12 hours in "Focus: Advanced Liberal Learning."

The Foundation component calls for zero to six hours in English composition (depending on waiver); three hours in the fine arts and six in the humanities; nine hours in social science and world cultures; nine hours in the natural sciences, including one laboratory course; and three hours in mathematics, formal reasoning, or technology. Field (or major) requirements are set by the relevant departments. The Advanced Liberal Learning requirement involves nine hours in sequence of related courses in a field outside the major.

The last three hours of the Miami Plan's requirements are called the "Senior Capstone Experience" and aim to "bring together liberal learning and specialized knowledge toward the close of baccalaureate work, to promote integration and provide for intellectual accountability." Ideally, the capstone would combine field and focus (major and minor) subjects, but need not, and might take the form of colloquia or workshops, research seminars, creative work in studios or laboratories, or individual or group projects.

It is important to note that the Miami Plan insists that the student select, from among his Foundation courses, one from a group that

TUITION AND FEES INCREASE
Average Increase/Year: Public = 8.30%, Miami University = 6.04%

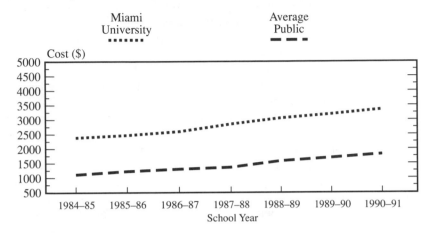

Source: The College Entrance Examination Board

---

introduces him to "a perspective different from the dominant cultural heritage of the United States," and which might involve "non-Western civilizations, black or women's studies, or studies of developing nations." Another Foundation course must be chosen from a group that provides "historical perspective."

Strong departments at Miami include political science, which is the most popular major, the natural sciences, particularly microbiology, chemistry, and botany, as well as the international studies program, which takes a perverse pride in the fact that its students are heavily recruited by both the Peace Corps and the CIA.

In the last decade, Miami's reputation and atmosphere have been steadily, if slowly, changing. The university has been concentrating on more selective admissions and has become better at publicizing itself to the professional world and to alumni. A massive, private fund-raising drive is now underway, which aims to fill the coffers with more than $100 million to increase endowment, faculty, scholarships, and to add certain physical facilities. Much of this will come from alumni, who are loyal and generous, having already donated large sums to build an art museum, a conference center, and an admirable scholarship program, which is unusual today in that its awards are based on academic merit. Need-based financial aid is also available.

The honors program coordinates much of the activity for these scholarship students, as well as for others. Begun in the early 1980s, the program invites selected freshmen to participate in two first-year seminars taught by senior faculty to groups of no more than 20. Upperclassmen must take two more seminars and write a senior thesis to earn the designation "University Honors." Additionally, the Honors Program drives a number of student-directed committees that bring speakers to campus and organize forums about social concerns, especially minorities and women.

Miami operates on the semester system. Most classes in the College of Arts and Sciences are lectures and their size averages between 30 and 40, though upper-level classes can be significantly smaller. Scheduling is a problem, because popular courses often have too few sections, compelling students to search for alternatives or plead for admission. Miami is taking steps to correct this by seeking

DISTRIBUTION OF UNDERGRADUATE AID
1989–90 School Year

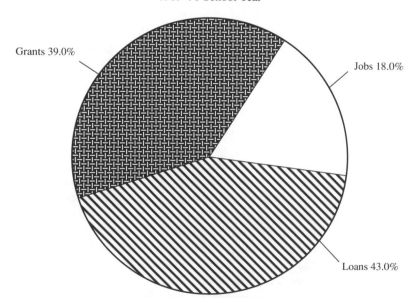

Grants 39.0%

Jobs 18.0%

Loans 43.0%

Source: The College Entrance Examination Board, 1990

more funding for additional faculty, but it will be some time before the process is significantly improved.

On the other hand, although teaching assistants are employed, most classes are taught by full-time faculty in accord with the university's policy of emphasizing teaching over research. Most professors are accessible and accommodating, maintaining regular office hours. Regrettably, however, Miami's growing prestige is causing the administration and department chairs to place more emphasis on research for promotion, and this trend puts pressure on professors to spend less time preparing for classes and advising students.

Miami's 1,000-acre main campus is exceptionally attractive and well-cared for. Redbrick Georgian architecture is the norm for nearly all of the buildings, academic and residential, which frame numerous open areas of green. The ivory cupolas, slate roofs, stone bridges, and the gentle patina of copper domes and spires contribute to the campus's tranquil atmosphere. Half the student body lives in the residence halls (Miami does *not* have "dorms") and the other half either commutes or lives off campus. They walk or bike between the four residential quads, each located near the academic area. Two are given over exclusively to freshmen. Both upperclass and freshman halls offer single-sex and coed options. The halls have resident assistants for each corridor, and each freshman hall also has a resident academic advisor. Residences have their own governments, which run a number of philanthropies and social events, as well as the houses themselves. This includes setting the hours for "vis," or visitation privileges, for the single-sex dorms or areas. "Vis" has come under fire in the past for being overly restrictive, but a satisfactory system balancing student freedom with campus security remains to be achieved.

Associated Student Government (ASG) is the campus-wide body politic. ASG is an all-consuming passion for some and a continual source of irritation for others. It has made great efforts to be an activist government, jumping into nearly every dispute on campus. ASG not only registers students to vote, but also orchestrates protests, and regularly applies pressure to the administration. ASG does not confine its energies to the campus, however, and has caused controversy by encouraging the student body to vote on local issues in Oxford, including a proposed school tax levy. Since students outnumber permanent residents two-to-one, this effort to defeat the proposal produced friction between the locals and the university.

Perhaps more memorable was ASG's call for the elimination of the gender-based syntax in university publications. On the credit side, the organization was largely responsible for a campus-wide transportation service beginning in 1990, two student seats on the board of trustees, and the creation of a student-run credit union.

A burning issue is how the university should attempt to attract more minority students. Right now, they comprise 5 percent of the student body, and the state has been after the university to increase representation. So far, the affirmative action program has generated surprisingly little discord. Minority enrollment has increased slightly, though retaining minority students has been difficult.

Another not unrelated stumbling block (for some) is the traditional image of Miami students as upperclass, "preppy," conservative business majors. While this is an exaggeration, the impression probably persists for several reasons. The rural environment, attractive campus, and overwhelmingly white student body contribute to the perception that Miami is a private school with a conservative and Ivy League atmosphere. The strong Greek system also adds to this image, as does the students' propensity to dress up more for class than at other schools. But Miami has the usual mix—Greeks, honors program students, militant feminists, conservative business students, and avant-garde liberals. But the very fact that there is such a cross-section of stereotypical Miamians demonstrates a kind of diversity in the student body.

There is certainly plenty of diversity in the university's social life, as more than 300 student clubs and organizations vie for attention in politics, religion, sports, service and professional endeavors. Much of Miami's education takes place beyond the classroom. "Training for leadership" is an important component of the university. Student organizations are responsible for nearly all campus activities such as lectures, concerts, and publications. New groups sprout up frequently and are often quite creative. Examples include the *Ragamuffin,* a satirical newspaper, the Tower Players Improvisational Comedy Troupe, and the Skyscrapers, a club for tall people.

One major student outlet is the Greek system. The Greeks have a long legacy at Miami going back to 1833, and now claim about a third of the students, who tend to be the men and women most loyal to their alma mater in college and later. Fraternities have off-campus residences, while sororities use suites in the residence halls. Competition to get into them is stiff, and for some rejection can be difficult to deal with. Concerns about this recently led to sorority rush's being moved back a semester so that women, like the men, will spend at least one semester unaffiliated. Fraternities and sororities are closely monitored by the university to prevent hazing and alcohol abuse.

Unlike some campuses with a strong Greek influence, the social life at Miami is not overwhelmed by it, especially since the drinking age was raised to 21. "Uptown" is located next to campus and is the location for most merchants and for all of Oxford's bars, which cater to the college crowd and are the prime site for socializing, inelegantly referred to as "face-time." For those under 21, off-campus house parties and gatherings in students' rooms are popular outlets. Despite the university's repeated efforts to reduce underage consumption and emphasize nonalcoholic activities, drinking is still the norm, though drugs are not.

A wealth of other activities exists at Miami. The theater department is prolific (though rumored to be academically weak), producing seven plays and musicals each school year with a number of other avant-garde productions occurring sporadically. The art museum sponsors four major exhibits annually, and houses an impressive permanent collection for a museum of its size. The performing arts series is the crown jewel of Miami's cultural scene, however, bringing in from around the world artists accomplished in ballet, opera, and music. To augment the series, the university also showcases budding, young instrumental soloists. For the lower brows, pop concerts and films attract large audiences.

Sports enthusiasts at Miami enjoy a respectable athletic program with hockey, football, and basketball ranking as the biggest intercollegiate sports. Of greater interest to most students is the intramural program in which nearly 90 percent of all students participate at least once during their four years. The most popular activities are weightlifting, broomball (a game played on the ice arena without skates and with a ball), basketball, softball, and volleyball. There is also an Outdoor Pursuit Center that provides equipment and organizes a number of outdoor activities from stargazing to rock climbing to bike riding.

On the whole, Miami University succeeds in striking a sound balance between academics, extracurricular activities and social life. The faculty's commitment to accessibility and teaching distinguishes it from many other state-assisted universities, and its lower fees distinguish it from the more renowned institutions it otherwise envies.

University of Michigan

Director of Undergraduate Admissions, University of Michigan
1220 Student Activities Building, Ann Arbor, MI 48109-1316
(313) 764-7433

Type: Public

Students:
23,285 undergraduates
12,268 men
11,017 women
13,189 graduate students

Applications:
Closing date: February 15
60% of applicants accepted
SAT or ACT required
  Score reported by: February 15
  Mid 50% of freshman scores:
    SAT-Math   580–700
    SAT-Verbal 500–610

Costs and Aid:

Tuition & fees:	
In state	$ 3,290
Out of state	11,020
Room and Board	3,860

Scholarships:	
Academic	Yes
Athletic	Yes
Minority	Yes

Financial Aid:	
Freshmen	35%
Upperclassmen	35%

Library:	3,000,000 titles
ROTC:	Yes
Study Abroad:	Yes

Just as Michigan's top-ranked Wolverines roll over weaker teams, so the large university that fields them consistently overwhelms its competition by sheer mass. The university, jealous of its ranking in both scholarship and football, frequently subordinates undergraduate concerns to its goal of winning fame as a premier research institution, and leaves the hapless student to run interference for himself.

Properly speaking, the University of Michigan consists of three campuses at Ann Arbor, Dearborn, and Flint. Founded in 1817 as the university's flagship, Ann Arbor is by far the largest of these with 2,600 acres and no fewer than 12 undergraduate and 17 graduate schools. The campus serves approximately 36,000 students, more than 23,000 of whom are undergraduates from 50 states and more than 100 foreign countries. They study almost everything under the sun, from molecular biology to the musical theater. The most popular school, however, and one that affects every student who attends UM, is the College of Literature, Science, and the Arts (LSA). Almost all undergraduates, regardless of the school they enroll in, take at least one class in LSA, which was founded in 1841 and remains the heart of UM.

215

Recently, Michigan enacted a controversial new requirement for graduation mandating that each student enroll in an approved course in ethnicity, race, and racism. Until then, there had been no core curriculum, except for a two-course writing requirement. Instead, students are asked to meet requisites in a foreign language, and nine semester hours each in the humanities, social sciences, and natural sciences/mathematics. The program need not be rigorous, however, because there is such a multitude of courses on offer that requirements can be met through a series of large-lecture, introductory classes. A lab science is not mandatory; neither is a basic knowledge of Western civilization. This omission is ironic, as well as irresponsible, in light of the university's insistence on student exposure to politically correct ideas about race and ethnicity.

LSA's strongest departments are usually reckoned to be psychology, anthropology, philosophy, classical studies, history, political science, and some foreign languages. Although the faculty boasts some of the brightest stars in the academic firmament, Michigan's obsession with research and the prevalence of large classes mean that many students, in and out of the classroom, rarely have the opportunity to exchange ideas, or even to chat, with their professors. Teaching assistants are widely employed, and students report that one notorious introductory course has even been taught by videotape.

Resourceful and persistent students, however, can find their way to smaller, more personalized courses called recitations, and the prospect is even brighter for the 2,000 enrolled in the Honors College, which conducts small classes and requires a long senior thesis. There are special programs that are of interest, too, including foreign study in many countries, as well as the home-based Residential College (RC). In all courses in the Residential College students receive written evaluations instead of letter grades. Other opportunities include a program for immersion in the study of a foreign language and Interflex, a highly competitive, intense pre-medical program.

Students who are not being cosseted in a special program, however, often complain bitterly about the unsatisfactory advisory system, which they feel should be especially competent in so large and confusing a place as UM. They say the counselors, who at least are readily available, respond mechanically to questions, never volunteering more than they are asked, and that they often recite a long laundry list of courses, leaving the bewildered student to pick and choose among them as best he can.

The university does somewhat better with housing, guaranteeing

TUITION AND FEES INCREASE
Average Increase/Year: Public = 8.30%, Michigan = 8.11%

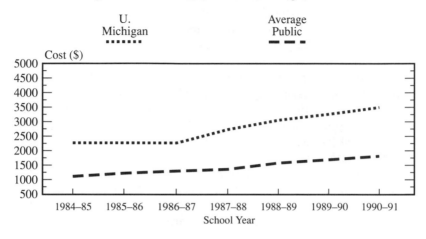

Source: The College Entrance Examination Board

---

it for all freshmen, who get to choose where they want to live on a first-come, first-served basis. Sophomores also often elect to live on campus and there is room for them, but by the junior year they generally wish to move into the abundant, sometimes even reasonably priced off-campus accommodation. Each campus hall has its own personality and reputation. For example, East Quad is the politically active dorm, while South Quad is favored by jocks, and West Quad is the loudest and most rambunctious.

Once at UM, there is something for everybody; in fact, extracurricular and social life, like the academic, can be bewildering. There are a staggering 482 special-interest groups and organizations on the Ann Arbor campus. The town itself is attractive and boasts a popular summer art fair, many small shops and eateries, and is the former home of the infamous $5 pot law. There are always people passing out information about one cause or another, so a stroll can easily provoke hours of heated debate with anyone from "Preacher Mike," a fundamentalist Christian, to students in Spark, a socialist organization.

The U Club, located in the Student Union, plays music every night; there are movies galore, and performances by both professional and student acting and musical companies. Lectures abound, as do poetry readings, and, of course, sporting events (everybody goes to football games, and basketball is popular too, thanks in large part to the UM team's winning the 1989 NCAA Championship). The Greek system is extensive as well, taking in about a quarter of the undergrads, and when bars like Charley's, Rick's, and Dooley's are included, entertainment is available almost around the clock.

There is a dark side, however, to campus life. Many students worry about crime and say they are afraid to venture out alone at night. Larceny is the largest problem on campus, and harassment is allegedly second. Date-rape is reportedly a problem as well, according to the Sexual Assault Prevention and Awareness Center. Lighting is better in some places than in others, but the most traveled parts of campus are equipped with emergency phones connected directly to the Department of Public Safety and Security. There is also an ongoing controversy about whether campus security officers ought to be deputized and equipped with sidearms. Security is being reorganized, but progress is slow.

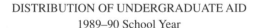

DISTRIBUTION OF UNDERGRADUATE AID
1989–90 School Year

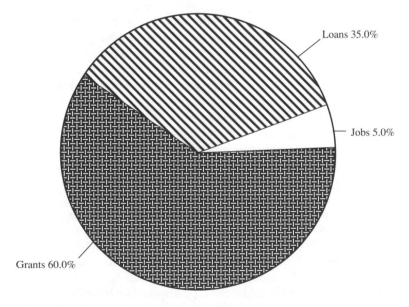

Loans 35.0%

Jobs 5.0%

Grants 60.0%

Source: The College Entrance Examination Board, 1990

Of the substances used on campus, alcohol is by far the most popular. According to one estimate, alcohol is involved in more than 80 percent of the violent crimes (from rape to harassment) on campus. It is a much larger problem than anyone (the administration included) wants to acknowledge. On the positive side, dry rush was just voted into place by the Inter-Fraternity Council. Regulations against alcohol in dorm rooms, however, are seldom applied as long as students are discreet. Marijuana possession used to carry a small $5 fine, but a city referendum recently increased the penalty to $25. Pot is widely available and its use unfortunately carries less of a stigma than it ought to. Crack cocaine is also a factor in Ann Arbor, but it is comparatively uncommon.

While some students are troubled by alcohol and drugs, many more are disturbed and distracted by the growing atmosphere of racial, ethnic and sexual tension, and the social fragmentation it fosters. A very vocal homosexual contingent led by the Lesbian and Gay Male Rights Organizing Committee recently asked for a six-fold increase in its budget and a lounge reserved for homosexuals. Like other minority groups, the homosexuals demand not only acceptance and toleration, but also the privilege of isolation, goals many deem both contradictory and unfair.

Michigan, like so many institutions, operates under the paradoxical policy of both affirmative action and equal opportunity—which leads to clashes between those holding the competing views. Minority enrollment has steadily grown during the past few years to approximately 17 percent and continues to rise. This reflects the goals of the university's 11th president, James Duderstadt, inaugurated in 1988. His strenuous efforts to implement the Michigan Mandate, a project aimed at achieving an ethnically and culturally diverse campus have earned him the nickname, "Mr. Diversity." Duderstadt seems to define diversity vaguely in terms of universal tolerance. Unfortunately, his execution of the Mandate often results in the protection only of those considered politically correct.

In 1987, racial slurs on a student radio program, in combination with several other incidents, sparked a controversy that has not yet subsided. White students have complained of reverse discrimination; they say a presumption exists that they are guilty of racism until proven innocent by supporting affirmative action, and purged of impure thoughts by being forced to attend the mandatory class on racism. They also object to the prevailing campus definition of racism that declares minorities are incapable of racist attitudes.

The preoccupation with racism also affects faculty. Not long ago, Professor Reynolds Farley of the sociology department conducted a course on race relations. He assigned reading material written in the 19th century that defended slavery. A student then accused him of racism because he had not also directed the class to read what she deemed was enough material castigating slavery. Professor Farley, unhappy at being labeled a racist and unwilling to allow students to determine his course content, threw up his hands and stopped giving the course.

Several campus organizations support a "uni-directional" definition of racism, and proselytize loudly at student gatherings, where there is tremendous pressure (both by peers and resident hall assistants) to accept the proposition that only whites can be guilty of racism. Of special concern are efforts, which include demonstrations and sit-ins, to exclude "offensive speech" from the purview of the First Amendment. As a result of these pressures, a yearly fund of $35,000, taken from the general revenues (i.e., student tuition and alumni donations), has been allotted to the Black Student Union, which uses it to bring speakers like Steve Cokely (a Louis Farrakhan protegé) to campus. Another group, the United Coalition Against Racism, built two shanties on the "Diag," the campus's main thoroughfare, which bear the insignia of the Black Action Movement and the Black Panthers.

In 1988, as the Stop Offensive Speech movement grew, the university enacted a policy barring speech and certain actions deemed offensive by minority groups; this code was later struck down by a federal judge as unconstitutional, and the university is trying to reformulate along similar lines a policy that will pass judicial scrutiny.

Racial tensions aside, the political atmosphere is an acid rain of leftist ideology. Despite widespread apathy among individuals, student, faculty and campus organizations are disproportionately radical. The political speakers they invite are usually one-sided, including Cokely and the notorious Angela Davis. When George Bush (then vice president) and Jeane Kirkpatrick spoke, however, they were shouted down. News of the forthcoming appearance of Supreme Court Chief Justice William Rehnquist was greeted with howls of protest during the winter of 1989–90, but since admission was strictly limited to law students, there was no further incident.

Further unpleasantness can almost be guaranteed at Ann Arbor, and this may be welcome to those who crave a diet of political activism and demonstrations along with their beer—or for those who can ignore all the uproar to concentrate, instead, on mining an education out of the rich Michigan ore. But students who believe the learning process requires tranquillity and time for reflection had better look elsewhere for their ivory tower.

SUNY-Binghamton

Assistant Vice President for Enrollment Services and
Management, State University of New York at Binghamton
Vestal Parkway East, Binghamton, NY 13901 (607) 777-2171

Type: Public

Students:
9,310 undergraduates
4,357 men
4,953 women
2,908 graduate students

Applications:
Priority date: January 15
36% of applicants accepted

	Applied	Accepted	Enrolled
men	7,500	2,465	706
women	8,167	3,217	909

SAT or ACT required (SAT preferred)
  Score reported by: February 1
  Mid 50% of freshman scores:
    SAT-Math   560–660
    SAT-Verbal 480–600

Costs and Aid:
Tuition & fees:

In state	$1,550
Out of state	4,900
Room and Board	4,150

Scholarships:

Academic	Yes
Athletic	No
Minority	Yes

Financial Aid:

Freshmen	70%
Upperclassmen	70%

Library: 1,368,368 titles

ROTC: No

Study Abroad: Yes

The State University of New York (SUNY) is one of the world's
largest university systems, and Binghamton is thought by many to be
the supernova in its constellation of 64 campuses serving more than
400,000 students. One of 24 four-year centers, Binghamton educates
9,300 undergraduates and nearly 3,000 graduate students, 95 percent
of whom are from New York State.

Although recently established in 1946, the university's liberal arts
and science unit, Harpur College, has earned high marks for academics
during its relatively short history—a reputation now being called into
serious question by those who believe that the quest for truth should
take precedence over the imposition of leftist groupthink.

Harpur College, named for a colonial patriot and teacher who
settled in the area, matriculates well over half the undergraduates at
Binghamton, and due to its relative prestige exercises considerable
influence on the whole campus. The other undergraduate schools are:
the School of Education and Human Development; the School of
Management; the Decker School of Nursing; and the Thomas J.

223

Watson School of Engineering, Applied Science, and Technology. All of these, save for the newly established engineering school, have built solid reputations in their fields.

Bulletin, 1990–1991:

Afro-American and African Studies 425—20th Century Revolution in the Third World (also Sociology 425)

"Theory and practice of greatest 20th century revolutions, Russian, Chinese, Vietnamese, Cuban, and African. Problems of class formation, imperialism, people's war, socialist transition."

Afro-American and African Studies 445—Comparative Black Political Thought (also Political Science 445)

"Historical and contemporary theories of liberation expounded by theoreticians from an Afrocentric perspective; pan-pigmentationism theories and political movements concerned with the question of slavery, colonialism and racial oppression; pan-proletarianism theories and political movements concerned with the questions of economic justice within the framework of capitalism or socialism in one country and on the global scale; theoreticians ranging from C.R.L. James, W.E.B. Dubois, Marcus Garvey to Martin Luther King, Jr. Malcolm X, Julius Nyerere, Amilcar Cabral and Angela Davis."

To graduate from Harpur College, a student must have accrued 126 academic credits with one semester-long course representing four credits. The school has no core curriculum and a student may fulfill the general education requirements without studying Western civilization, the Great Books, or American or European history. Currently, Harpur imposes these general distribution requirements: two courses each in the three divisions of the humanities, science and mathematics, and the social sciences; four liberal arts courses chosen from the two divisions other than that of the major; and two credits of "physical education activity coursework." In addition, students must elect from any division four or five (depending upon the category) courses that have been designated either "writing" or "writing emphasis." There is a minimal foreign language requirement for those who have not taken in high school either three years of one foreign language or two years each of two foreign languages.

College-wide honors are earned through a fairly complicated grading system. Departmental honors are also awarded. Harpur's most

TUITION AND FEES INCREASE
Average Increase/Year: Public = 8.30%, SUNY-Binghamton = .61%

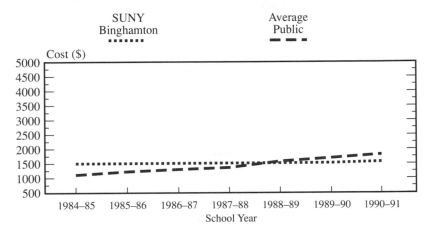

Source: The College Entrance Examination Board

---

popular major is psychology. The political science department has a heavy pre-law emphasis, giving short shrift to other areas. The once-strong history department has been damaged by increasing politicization of its course offerings, which emphasize social issues, labor, and women's history. The English department is popular and offers students a wide choice of course offerings, including an intensive creative writing program. Classics (Latin and Greek), classical civilization, and medieval studies are superb. Among foreign languages, Spanish and Italian are strong and, although there is no Russian department as such, the Russian language program is outstanding. There is also a noteworthy Judaic studies program, now in the process of maturing into a department.

Classes at Harpur are large, especially in such introductory courses as psychology, calculus, and "Introduction to World Politics." Seminars are generally only available to upperclassmen. Most large lecture courses employ teaching assistants in their sections, and in some departments they don't speak comprehensible English. Physical education courses are nearly impossible to get into until junior year, and many other courses are overcrowded. The current New York State budget crunch is exacerbating this situation. While faculty-student relations are generally good, they are usually impersonal, and the advisory system is only average. Cheating is fairly widespread though not rampant; it often goes undetected by faculty and unpunished. There is no university-wide attendance policy, so many students do not show up for classes.

The administration, and much—but not all—of the professorate are politically left-liberal. Predictably, their current campaign is to promote "diversity" and "sensitivity." They do this by attacking dissenting opinions, inviting hackneyed revolutionaries and pseudo-intellectuals to speak on campus, and organizing events such as a Vietnam Retrospective. Nor is it unusual for professors to use their classes as soap boxes for their radical views, students report.

One example of leftist bias occurred in 1988 when a Syracuse, N.Y., printer refused to put out an issue of the homosexual newspaper, *The Other Voice,* because he considered it to be blatantly pornographic (which by any reasonable standard it was). The Student Association, which supported the paper out of mandatory student contributions,

DISTRIBUTION OF UNDERGRADUATE AID
1989–90 School Year

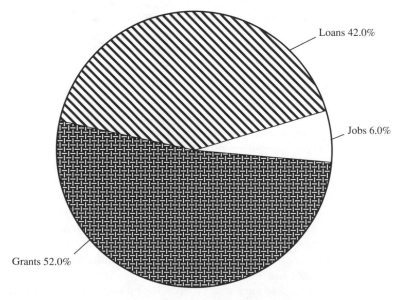

Loans 42.0%

Jobs 6.0%

Grants 52.0%

Source: The College Entrance Examination Board, 1990

then passed a resolution prohibiting all student publications so funded from using that printer on the grounds that he was discriminating against homosexuals.

More recently, the university was not able to provide blood for the soldiers in the Persian Gulf. Earlier, the administration, in response to Student Association demands, had banned the Red Cross from conducting blood drives on campus. The reason given was that the Red Cross was guilty of unfair discrimination because it would not accept blood donations from sub-Saharan Africans due to the high prevalence of the AIDS virus in their blood.

In addition to the leftist Student Association, the most powerful student groups include NYPIRG, a Naderite lobbying organization; the Black Student Union, which has invited such radicals as Kwame Toure (Stokely Carmichael) and Lenora Fulani to speak; the Latin American Student Union, which works closely with the Latin American Solidarity Committee, a campus adjunct of CISPES (Committee in Solidarity with People of El Salvador); and the Gay People's Union. (A Gay and Lesbian interdisciplinary studies program at Harpur is under discussion; interdisciplinary programs already exist in women's studies and African-American and African studies.)

Political organizations of similar stripe include the Democratic Socialists of America and the publications *OFF!* and *Looking Left.* All these groups wield enormous influence and power with the Student Association and the administration. Also flexing its left-wing muscles is the influential Fernand Braudel Center, which was established some years ago to study Marxist thought. It no longer confines itself to cerebration, however, and now actively promotes anti-West and anti-American propaganda. During the 1990–1991 school year, for example, the center sponsored two widely publicized colloquia called "Colonization and Decolonization in the U.S. Today: Some Pedagogical Implications," and "La Malinche and the Conquest: Issues of Gender, Ethnicity, and Nationalism in Mexico."

The major opposition to radical agendas comes from a newspaper, the *Binghamton Review,* which was founded several years ago by a group of moderately conservative student activists. But, "diversity" as a policy only applies to ideas and groups left of center; there is very little tolerance for centrist or conservative positions, although the College Republicans have recently emerged from obscurity and worked successfully to elect several local candidates to office.

Politics aren't confined to extracurricular activities. In the autumn of 1990, a group of militant students took over the dean's office at

Harpur and made a series of demands: the resignation of the acting chair of the Latin American Caribbean Area Studies Program and a restructuring of that and the African-American and African Studies Program; increased numbers of Black, Latino, Caribbean, and African personnel in all university hiring and in student admissions; increased numbers of fellowships and scholarships for the same groups; a restructuring of the affirmative action office; the institution of a multicultural center with its own personnel, programming, services and "cultural kitchen to serve our dietary needs"; the banning of companies that support South Africa ("i.e., Coke and Pepsi"); and the expansion and implementation of "the diversity requirement not only for Harpur College but to [sic] all schools in the university." (About 18 percent of the current student body are minorities.)

The administration promised to address all these demands. In fact, the financially hard-pressed and state-supported university had already managed to find $50,000 to be awarded to faculty to create new courses and "to redesign extant courses to remove any bias—cultural, racial, religious, sexual or other—whether by omission or commission." In the spring of 1991, proposals were on the table to introduce required courses in culture and gender studies. During the winter and spring of 1991, workshops (voluntary but strongly recommended) were held to disabuse students, faculty, and staff of any politically incorrect views they might have had regarding racism, sexism, homophobia, ableism, antisemitism, and classism. Although faculty hiring has been officially reduced due to the budget crunch, the administration announced that of five planned faculty searches, three places will be reserved for underrepresented minorities. Faculty members in all departments were urged to find and propose minority candidates.

The surrender to student demands did nothing to improve race relations on campus, however. They shortly became worse than ever, and in one notorious incident involved physical intimidation of faculty members. On March 14, 1991, during a lecture on the triumph of freedom after the fall of the Berlin Wall, a crowd of students, many of them black, poured in to disrupt the talk, presumably because it was being given under the auspices of the National Association of Scholars, an organization whose declared purpose is to preserve academic freedom in American universities. According to an account in the April 10 issue of the *Wall Street Journal*:

> The lecturer was political science professor Richard I. Hofferbert, who had been on the scene when the Berlin Wall was dismantled and had

taken photographs—large, glass-framed pictures—which he exhibited to the audience. As one of the pictures—of his small grandchild on the shoulders of an East German policeman—was passed around, one of the student demonstrators grabbed it and hurled it across the crowded room. The elderly faculty member nearby chastised the student, who promptly lunged at him. The student blew his nose, sauntered up to the lectern and dropped his used tissue in the speaker's coffee cup. Jeers and verbal assaults were directed at the speaker, as crowds brandishing sticks milled around. . . .

The response of the school's president, Lois Defleur, has been curious to say the least. About the gang that disrupted the meeting she had only exculpatory comments. . . .

Queried about what action the university might take, Professor Defleur explained that the student who hurled the picture had some problems, that the picture had not in any case shattered. She further noted that the elderly professor whom the picture hurler tried to attack had 'spoken very insultingly' to the student. Of the general disruption and intimidation, the president said, this had much to do with national problems, social ills left festering.

Although the university administration is apparently unwilling to take action against the shocking social ills festering under its nose in Binghamton, it is trying to do something about a much less urgent matter, overcrowded campus housing. Construction was recently completed on a 548-bed housing complex. Housing is guaranteed for all four years, because upperclassmen usually elect to live in nearby Binghamton, where students run an excellent bus service to the university. The surrounding countryside of the Susquehanna Valley is scenic and green because it rains a lot. The 600-acre campus itself is attractive, featuring large grassy areas, fountains, and a pond. The buildings, however, are modern and functional, without charm or distinction.

In the main, Binghamton is not a big party school, but there are plenty of extracurricular activities, including 200 organizations for the student willing to seek them out. Fraternities and sororities, which now number 29 (five of them local), have been growing rapidly in the past few years, but they lack houses and only about a quarter of students belong. The university strictly enforces state law prohibiting alcohol for those under 21. The same cannot be said of drug use, which occurs with some frequency but is by no means pervasive. Weekend party-goers usually attend off-campus bashes via SUNY-Binghamton's bus lines; New York City and Buffalo are each about three and a half hours away by car. The campus and surrounding area are safe, and crime is infrequent.

Sports are not stressed at Binghamton, though adequate facilities exist, including two gymnasiums with pools, an indoor track, dance and karate studios, a fitness trail and cross-country course, as well as a 400-meter track and the usual playing fields and courts. Ten intercollegiate sports, not including football, are offered for men and nine for women. Tennis, soccer, and hockey shine in competition. Intramurals, nicknamed "Co-Recs," are popular, with 20 teams for men and 18 for women, including coed football teams of three men and three women each.

It's only in sport that the playing fields are level at SUNY-Binghamton. In political debate and increasingly in the classroom, SUNY-Binghamton tilts the ground to the left, thus encouraging an intolerant intellectual atmosphere, capitulation to special interest groups, and politicized courses. A few traditionalist professors continue their efforts to resist the onslaught, but it appears that they are being overwhelmed by the leftist orthodoxy of militant students, alienated teachers, and the present administration.

North Carolina State University

Director of Admissions, North Carolina State University
P.O. Box 7103, Raleigh, NC 27695-7103 (919) 737-2434

Type: Public

Students:
22,121 undergraduates
  13,427 men
  8,694 women
4,088 graduate students

Applications:
Priority date: January 1
Closing date: February 1
61% of applicants accepted

	Applied	*Accepted*	*Enrolled*
men	6,149	3,675	2,161
women	3,985	2,483	1,288

SAT or ACT required (SAT preferred)
  Score reported by: March 1
  Mid 50% of freshman scores:
    SAT-Math   510–620
    SAT-Verbal 430–530

Costs and Aid:
Tuition & fees:*

In state	$1,050
Out of state	5,550
Room and Board	3,100

Scholarships:

Academic	Yes
Athletic	Yes
Minority	Yes

Financial Aid:

Freshmen	49%
Upperclassmen	36%

Library: 1,200,000 volumes

ROTC: Yes

Study Abroad: Yes

*(For approximate past tuition, see the tuition chart for the University of North Carolina.)

As you drive through Raleigh's business park, the streets are lined with signs from their high-tech residents. IBM, Unisys, Burroughs Welcome, and many others call it home. It's North Carolina's Research Triangle Park, one of the few successful high-technology industrial parks built in the last two decades. The three intellectual anchors of this sprawling complex are Duke University, the University of North Carolina at Chapel Hill, and the lesser-known North Carolina State University. As part of this consortium, North Carolina State shares many of the advantages enjoyed by its more prominent neighbors, but virtually none of the prestige.

NCSU was founded in 1889 as the North Carolina College of Agriculture and Mechanical Arts. It may come as a surprise to most that NCSU is the state's largest institution of higher learning with 26,000 (22,000 undergraduate) students on a 623-acre main campus (a new 1,000-acre "Centennial Campus" is under construction). Eighty-five percent of all students are in-state residents, but the rest represent all the other states, as well as 90 foreign countries.

231

There are 10 colleges and schools within the university: Agriculture and Life Sciences; Education and Psychology; Textiles; Physical and Mathematical Sciences (which includes pre-med, pre-dental, and pre-vet programs); Design; Engineering; Forests Resources; Veterinary Medicine; and Humanities and Social Sciences. Engineering is the largest, with 6,500 students, but Humanities and Social Sciences (CHASS) is a close second, enrolling more than 5,500.

As NCSU began as a scientific and technical college, its reputation rests in those areas. But don't be misled: The liberal arts are very strong at NCSU.

CHASS's "distribution requirements" ensure that students are exposed to a variety of fields—the mark of a traditional liberal arts education. Students must take six hours of English composition (or one honors course) and at least three hours of English literature, plus six hours of history, twelve hours of a foreign language and three hours of philosophy. Students must also take twelve hours of social sciences, and eight of natural sciences, as well as six hours of mathematics. Four hours of physical education are also required. Additionally, an "area elective" covering anything from Greek Literature to Music is mandated.

No ethnic, feminist, or Third World courses are required, though they are available. Credit for Afro-American studies may not be used to fulfill the CHASS requirements. No courses in Western civilization are required, but they are offered and, unlike the non-traditional courses, are heavily subscribed.

English is one of the strongest departments in CHASS, and like others, has a highly structured curriculum. English lit majors, for example, must spend six credit hours surveying English and American literature; three hours on Shakespeare; three hours on literary criticism; twelve hours on elective upper-level English courses (which can include six hours of "Literature of the Western World," a "Great Books" course); three hours each in "blocks" covering early English literature, 18th- or 19th-century English or American literature, and contemporary literature respectively; and three hours in linguistics, modern English, or upper-level composition and rhetoric.

In short, a CHASS student is exposed to all of the basic traditional liberal arts disciplines and cannot take a course such as "Marx on Medieval Literary Theory" in place of Chaucer or Milton. This trend—generally—also runs through the other CHASS departments.

Unlike some large liberal arts universities, the CHASS faculty is not remote from the student body and surrounded by a phalanx of teaching assistants (who protect them from nettlesome undergraduate questions that interfere with book-writing). The faculty members at NCSU are very approachable and are genuinely interested in the welfare of their students. Professors welcome them into their offices for academic advice or conversation. The atmosphere is that of a small liberal arts college that happens to be tucked away in the corner of a huge university.

Some introductory courses are taught by graduate students, but most of the liberal arts classes, and especially the upper-level courses, are taught by professors. Classes usually comprise no more than 25–35 students, and many upper-level courses (especially honors courses) are restricted to 12. A liberal arts student at NCSU is known by name, not by social security number.

Each department has its own honors program, while the university as a whole offers a University Scholars Program for outstanding students and a Scholars of the College Program for entering freshmen and sophomores who demonstrate high potential. Honor is not, however, a word frequently spoken by undergraduates. Although academic dishonesty is expressly forbidden by the Code of Student Conduct, NCSU lacks a formal honor code, academic or otherwise. Cheating in large survey courses is not uncommon; in the dorms, anyone who doesn't lock his room or leaves personal property lying around is inviting theft.

Although students may generally be described as apathetic with conservative leanings, the faculty's politics range from strong conservative to hard-line leftist. The greatest hotbed of the Left is CHASS, particularly the philosophy department (the sciences and engineering tend to be apolitical). With its several Marxist professors, the philosophy department was the headquarters for the campus peace movement during the Persian Gulf war. Several professors wrote a letter to the student newspaper denouncing the war from a Marxist viewpoint. Fortunately their impact on student thought appears to be almost nil.

Less radical but still demonstrably left-wing is the political science department. Many students report clear-cut bias. A course pack for a current U.S. foreign policy course, for example, contains articles arguing against U.S. intervention in Latin America and protesting against American "arrogance" and "illegality"—but contains no articles with dissenting views.

The English department also deserves opprobrium. While curricular conservatives presently dictate department policy, increasing numbers of radical younger faculty are agitating for curricular reform—

abandoning the Great Books approach for multicultural literature, deconstructionism, and Marxist criticism. One recent course on modern literature concentrated on the "literature of colonialism," with works by oppression-studies writers. One professor returned a student's paper with the comment "too white and too male" written in the margin (the paper, to be fair, received an A). Others refuse to allow prolonged discussion of dissenting opinions.

Such incidents, however irritating, are fortunately not common in CHASS and most faculty members seem open-minded and fair. At present, traditionalists are holding their ground, but intra-departmental factionalism is becoming common. It is not clear whose views will ultimately win control. So far, even radical liberals tolerate dissenting views in the classroom, though exceptions exist. For example, one student told of facing outright intimidation from a professor when he attempted to support the Great Books curriculum in her class. The professor is on the University Courses and Curricula Committee,

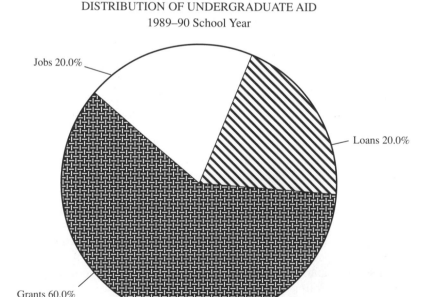

DISTRIBUTION OF UNDERGRADUATE AID
1989–90 School Year

Jobs 20.0%

Loans 20.0%

Grants 60.0%

Source: The College Entrance Examination Board, 1990

which approves all new course proposals and reviews current courses. An ominous sign.

It is from this committee that the most overt, politically correct views have come. Recently, it announced a set of "Perspectives" to be included in all new courses. These were "Interracial" ('define the limits of the Euro-American perspective'), "Gender Issues" ('use gender-neutral terms, identify gender concerns'), "Environmental" ('global responsibility'), and "Special Populations," which urged that students be indoctrinated with concern for "children, the handicapped, substance abusers, the imprisoned, the elderly and the homeless." The conservative student paper, the *State Critic,* exposed this PC blueprint in one of its issues. As the Raleigh *News and Observer* explained, "[The *Critic*] pounced . . . A month later, Associate Provost Murray Down yanked the form and told the committee to come up with something more clear." That many faculty members opposed one or more of the "Perspectives," is encouraging.

By and large, however, the administration ignores the student/ faculty political activity on campus. It does mouth the usual platitudes about racism and sexism, however. The official policy statement says that NCSU "is committed to taking all steps necessary to prevent racial harassment," including racial sensitivity seminars "designed to make individuals aware of the nature of racial bias." There are, however, no records of students being sentenced to the sensitivity gulag.

As a large, urban campus, NCSU security has to be tight. Unfortunately, it sometimes is not. No person can (in theory) gain admission to a dormitory without going through security procedures, but sometimes nonresidents are admitted through propped-open doors. Though Public Safety patrols the campus, their apparent reluctance to get out of their cars and patrol on foot hampers their efficiency. However, the campus is fairly safe for pedestrians even at night, and an escort service is available for those students who feel vulnerable walking alone.

There are several options for students seeking on-campus housing. NCSU offers coed, all-male and all-female dormitories, but housing on campus is assured only for the freshman year. There are some theme residence halls, most notably an "International" dorm (in which American students are paired with foreign roommates) and an athletic dorm. Reasonably priced off-campus housing is available, and many students decide to live in the Raleigh area after their freshman year.

NCSU hosts more than 300 student clubs and organizations.

Approximately 10 percent of the student body belong to a national fraternity or sorority, and pre-professional and honorary fraternities also exist. Social fraternities and sororities are primarily housed on a university-owned "fraternity court," but some have off-campus houses. Most religions sponsor campus social and encounter groups. There is a weekly newspaper, which is at best readable and at worst illiterate, an award-winning conservative magazine, a radio station, various departmental clubs, and an active, if ineffective, student government.

Raleigh is ACC country, so naturally, the most popular sport at NCSU is basketball. In fact, it you have not lived in North Carolina but have heard of N.C. State, it's probably because you have seen the Wolfpack on national television in one of its two NCAA men's basketball championships. After a big basketball victory, thousands of students line the streets around the campus, celebrating and raising hell. While football games are also popular, nothing compares to basketball for student interest.

NCSU competes in 13 Division I varsity sports for men and 11 for women. In addition to the success of the men's basketball team, the women's basketball and soccer teams are national contenders, while the men's soccer team is also very successful. NCSU has a strong intramural and club sports program; the club sports range from rugby to ice hockey to karate. The main gym has an indoor track, many racquetball and squash courts, two swimming pools, weight rooms, and a rock-climbing wall among other facilities. Outdoor facilities are also excellent.

It is impossible to make a general statement about student social life in a university the size of NCSU, but if you had to use a single word it would be "beer." Many students attend fraternity parties, while others imbibe in nearby student bars. Still others attend off-campus parties, or patronize bars in downtown Raleigh. While some drug use undoubtedly occurs, it is minimal and appears to be generally unpopular with the students.

There is a gay-lesbian group (which rejoices in the name GALA), but it is almost totally quiescent. Its only major activity is an annual "Blue Jeans Day" when students are supposed to wear blue jeans in support of "gay rights." Instead, jeans disappear from the campus for a day, the event is ridiculed by the students, and soon ritual letters from GALA appear in the newspaper denouncing their fellows as insensitive philistines. Then all is quiet again. Also relatively quiet is the Black Student Union, which recently moved into a palatial three-story "African-American Cultural Center" and is busily occupied with its own affairs in its brand-new quarters.

North Carolina State University offers a solid education in any of a number of technical fields. Its lesser-known, but worthwhile liberal arts program so far remains largely untainted by the radicalism that now affects so many other institutions. But, lacking the prestige of its more prominent neighbors in Durham and Chapel Hill, NCSU will probably retain its reputation as a fall-back school for North Carolina residents, thus depriving it of the best and brightest who could benefit most from its sound grounding in the liberal arts.

University of North Carolina at Chapel Hill

Director of Undergraduate Admissions
University of North Carolina at Chapel Hill
Country Club Road, Monogram Club, CB #2100
Chapel Hill, NC 27599-2100 (919) 966-3621

Type: Public

Students:
15,463 undergraduates
  6,404 men
  9,059 women
8,129 graduate students

Applications:
Closing date: January 15
33% of applicants accepted

	Applied	Accepted	Enrolled
men	7,433	2,319	1,307
women	8,948	3,117	1,884

SAT
  Score reported by: January 15
  Mid 50% of freshman scores:
    SAT-Math   520–650
    SAT-Verbal 470–590

Costs and Aid:
Tuition & fees:

In state	$1,020
Out of state	5,520
Room and Board	3,280

Scholarships:

Academic	Yes
Athletic	Yes
Minority	Yes

Financial Aid:

Freshmen	35%
Upperclassmen	34%

Library: 1,712,122 titles

ROTC: Yes
Study Abroad: Yes

Percentage of courses that can be used to fulfill distribution requirements: 20.5

In 1776, as the American continent was giving birth to a nation, the citizens of North Carolina were crafting their first Constitution. In addition to creating a system of government, the legislators set forth their vision for a publicly funded system of higher education. Nineteen years later, the University of North Carolina opened its doors in Chapel Hill to 41 students. On the eve of UNC's bicentennial, North Carolinians speak of their university with understandable pride. The rich curriculum, low tuition, and tradition of academic excellence have enabled Carolina to remain largely true to the vision of its founders.

By 1860, enrollment at Chapel Hill had grown sufficiently so that it ranked second only to Yankee Yale University. Unlike many Southern colleges, UNC managed to remain open throughout the Civil War, although it was forced to close for five years during the hard times of Reconstruction. The university has since expanded to 16 campuses, with a total enrollment of more than 144,000.

One of the most appealing aspects of the Chapel Hill campus is its location in one of the prettiest college towns in America. The community has an excellent relationship with the university and often becomes a second home to students. Chapel Hill has retained the best of the small-town Southern tradition while providing residents with the cultural benefits of a much larger urban community. The 1,200-acre campus is a picture in wide green lawns and red brick buildings, with flowers bursting out all over in the spring and fall.

Like most public universities, UNC experienced an enormous growth in enrollment with the institution of the GI Bill following World War II. This growth continued substantially unchecked until 1972, when the General Assembly resolved to limit the university's expansion to approximately 1 percent each year. Currently, Carolina's student body numbers more than 23,000, about one-third of whom are engaged in graduate or professional studies. Additionally, the university boasts over 1,900 full-time faculty, and offers instruction in more than 100 fields including medicine, dentistry, and law. Carolina's impressive list of distinguished alumni include Pulitzer Prize-winning journalists and authors, 31 governors and President James K. Polk.

But despite its considerable accomplishments, the university's expansion has obviously strained the state's budget. With approximately 13,000 graduate and undergraduate students, Chapel Hill remains the flagship of UNC's 16-campus system, but it has not escaped the budget axe. In an effort to keep tuition low, the school has postponed or foregone overdue improvements in a variety of areas. Many buildings desperately need repair, the computer facilities are always on the verge of running out of supplies, professors' salaries are comparatively small, and faculty are being lured to wealthier colleges. Nevertheless, the university manages to maintain sufficient infrastructure to give its students an opportunity to obtain a top-notch education.

But being a publicly funded university has its drawbacks. The number of out-of-state students is limited by law to no more than 16 percent of the undergraduate student body. Thus, the university is required to draw at least 84 percent of its freshmen from the state which in 1989 had the dubious distinction of posting the lowest average SAT scores in the nation. Despite a relatively rigorous admissions policy, UNC harbors many mediocre and unmotivated students.

Evidence of this abounds. The libraries are devoid of undergraduates on Fridays and Saturdays. The computer labs are generally empty until the last three weeks of the semester. Class attendance on

TUITION AND FEES INCREASE
Average Increase/Year: Public = 8.30%, North Carolina = 5.76%

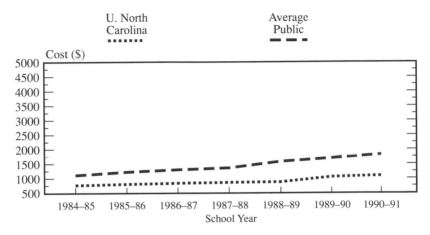

Source: The College Entrance Examination Board

an average day is rarely more than 75 percent. Most students avoid upper-level courses, even within their discipline. Even the most casual observer will be struck by the pervasive academic apathy exhibited by Chapel Hill's students. It is an unfortunate fact that ideas matter very little to the average Tar Heel.

In place of a core curriculum, Carolina has developed a program commonly referred to as the "Perspective System." This program mandates that every freshman and sophomore complete a total of nine semester courses in history, literature, philosophy, fine arts, foreign language, and math. Selecting from the wide array of courses which fulfill these requirements is generally left to the individual. Predictably, many students choose the easiest classes and learn little. The legacy of this "salad bar" approach to basic education is thousands of graduates who have no understanding of Western culture and its academic traditions. It is not uncommon for a political science major to graduate without having read John Locke, Adam Smith, or Thomas Jefferson, and most students don't seem to mind.

Not surprisingly, professors usually ask little of their students. The typical requirements for an undergraduate humanities or social science course are limited to two five-page essays, a mid-term, and a final exam. The university does not require graduating seniors to complete a thesis. It is a sad commentary that an average student can do little or none of the assigned readings and still maintain something close to a B average. As one political science professor complained, "It is possible to graduate from Carolina without ever writing anything longer than a five-page paper." Not only is it possible, it is commonplace.

Yet in spite of, or perhaps because of, the prevailing anti-intellectual attitude among students, it is equally possible to receive a first-rate education at Chapel Hill. A serious and motivated student will find ample opportunities to explore the limits of his interests and abilities. If he chooses his classes carefully, he can avoid the large and impersonal lower-level courses. There are many small seminars available to undergraduate students. Those who wish can create as strong, challenging, and enlightening a curriculum as can be found at any university in America. Particularly if they are honors students.

Chapel Hill's honors program is outstanding and may begin in the

DISTRIBUTION OF UNDERGRADUATE AID
1989–90 School Year

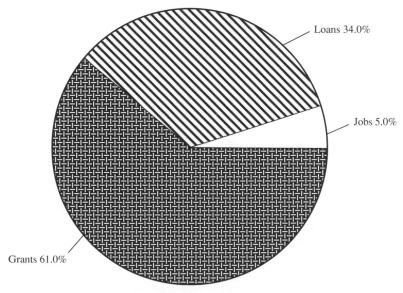

Loans 34.0%

Jobs 5.0%

Grants 61.0%

Source: The College Entrance Examination Board, 1990

freshman year by invitation to top-ranked high school students. These fortunates are treated to small, work-intensive seminars led by high-powered professors. Qualified sophomores and juniors may also join the program, which culminates in the senior year with a thesis in the major department that usually runs between 80 and 100 typed pages. Between 550 and 600 students participate in the program out of a total of 11,500 liberal arts undergraduates. Strongest departments are chemistry, classics, history, political science, and classics. English and foreign languages are weaker.

Another clear benefit of Carolina's academic approach is that nearly all professors personally teach undergraduate courses. Research continues to have a high priority, but the faculty remains accessible and usually willing to work individually with undergraduates. With so few interested and engaged students competing for faculty time, Chapel Hill's best minds find it easy to command individual attention. At UNC, however, the burden of attaining a good education clearly falls upon the student.

Ironically, UNC's student body continues to be one of its greatest strengths. Among the 5 to 10 percent of undergraduates who take their education seriously academic competition is keen and the student community is active. This small and elite group, which is often referred to as the "intelligentsia," is the driving force behind the university's multitude of first-class student organizations. Chapel Hill is home to a new and growing credit union, a nationally syndicated television station, and one of America's most innovative radio stations. The UNC debating team consistently ranks among the best in the nation, there are several active political groups, and the Campus YMCA hosts the largest student environmental action group in the United States. Carolina's student publications are outstanding as well. The daily newspaper has won several awards and is recognized as one of the best in the region. Tar Heel students also publish a monthly historical magazine, a quarterly literary magazine, and an award-winning conservative journal.

As is evident from the preceding list of student groups, Chapel Hill's best and brightest vigorously debate the political issues of the day. And while many students tend to adhere to the leftist orthodoxy prevalent on most campuses these days, a vocal and well-organized conservative coalition often steers the debate. More importantly, the tacit repression of certain "unenlightened" opinions that one finds at many other universities is notably absent at Carolina. Although there is in place a policy forbidding and punishing "insensitive" and "offensive" speech, UNC's administration allows much more latitude in this regard than its counterparts on many other campuses.

Race relations are generally less hostile than at a number of other big schools, but there is considerable underlying tension that bursts to the surface from time to time. In 1990, the university erected a sculpture featuring images of several students, both black and white, in different garb and poses. Black students were angered by two—one a black basketball player and the other a black woman with a book on her head. Protesters said both replicas were racist stereotypes, implying that blacks are good only at sports or at carrying burdens on their heads as they had in their slave days.

The political climate within the faculty is generally politically correct. The teaching corps is full of left-of-center ideologues. A professor in the history department offered this succinct indictment of his colleagues: "Every professor I know is either radical or liberal." This is probably an exaggeration. While left-wing professors abound, there is a notable absence of "tenured radicals" and, as students will quickly discover, even they are willing to discuss opposing views in class.

Social life at Chapel Hill is active, especially on Thursdays which is the big bar night as distinguished from Fridays and Saturdays, which are party nights. About a fifth of undergraduates go Greek in 30 national fraternities and 15 national sororities, but they do not dominate the social scene, which is exciting enough to attract regular weekend crowds of Duke students who find Chapel Hill much more fun than Durham.

Housing at Chapel Hill is guaranteed for the first two years and available to upperclassmen by lottery. It is both single-sex and coed, but nothing to rave about—ranging from fairly Spartan old dorms to cramped modern highrises. About 50 percent of students live on campus, the rest finding comfortable and affordable accommodation nearby.

Sports play a prominent role at UNC, though—except for football (poor team) and basketball (good team)—they are not as big as you might expect. There are 13 intercollegiate sports each for men and women, and 18 intramurals for men and 15 for women. Students love to cheer and jeer the Tar Heels and their rivals in the new "Dean Dome," which seats 21,000 and is named after basketball coach Dean Smith. Besides basketball, soccer and baseball are strong.

Clearly UNC is not the ideal school for every prospective under-graduate. For the motivated, ambitious, and independent, Chapel Hill can provide a first-class education, but many well-intentioned students find the effortless path to graduation simply too enticing to eschew.

University of North Texas

Director of Admissions, University of North Texas
P.O. Box 13797, Denton, TX 76203-3797 (817) 565-2681

Type: Public

Students:
20,583 undergraduates
9,959 men
10,624 women
6,577 graduate students

Applications:
Closing date: June 15
73% of applicants accepted

Applied	Accepted	Enrolled
4,846	3,515	2,228

SAT or ACT required
  Score reported by: June 15
  Mean freshman scores:
    SAT-Math   507
    SAT-Verbal 462

Costs and Aid:
Tuition & fees:

In state	$1,020
Out of state	4,140
Room and Board	3,150

Scholarships:

Academic	Yes
Athletic	Yes
Minority	No

Financial Aid:

Freshmen	27%
Upperclassmen	25%

Library:	1,407,445 titles
ROTC:	Yes
Study Abroad:	Yes

As one of its history professors recently pointed out with some pride, North Texas is a "fairly large state university struggling to get better. And frankly we are doing a not bad job of it." His confidence is well founded. Relatively unknown outside the Lone Star State, North Texas goes quietly about its business of educating approximately 27,000 students, more than 20,000 of whom are candidates for bachelor's degrees. Most who graduate in arts and sciences leave with a solid foundation in the principles and practices of Western civilization. No less a critic than former Secretary of Education William Bennett has praised the school for its program in the liberal arts.

Established in 1890 as the Texas Normal College and Teacher Training Institute, it began by instructing on a high school level, and strived for years to build a program that qualified for higher education. In 1919, the teachers college awarded its first five baccalaureate degrees. In 1937, it became possible to graduate without having to take courses in education, or qualify for a teacher's certificate. In 1964, North Texas was finally rewarded when it achieved recognition as one of Texas's five public universities.

The university now contains Colleges of the Arts and Sciences,

247

Business Administration, Community Services (social work), Education, Human Resources and Management, Music, and Library and Information Sciences. The College of Arts and Sciences, which matriculates 9,500 undergraduates (most of them Texans), is distinguished by two unusual programs based on the traditional study of Western civilization. They are both optional and fulfill part of the general education requirements. In 1989, the "Classic Learning Core" (CLC) was cited by Lynne Cheney, Chairman of the National Endowment for the Humanities, as a model program providing coherence in college studies. It is designed, according to the Undergraduate Catalog, "to emphasize the underlying unities of knowledge, the study of classical books and documents, critical and creative thinking, and a thorough mastery of reading, writing and speaking."

Students who elect the CLC must demonstrate proficiency in the "basic literacies," defined as mathematical and computer and written skills. (In 1990–91, 375 students of an entering class of 4,000 matriculated in the program.) They do this by taking three hours each of specified math and computer courses, and six hours in English, again in two specified courses. In math and computer science (but not in English) they may fulfill the requirement by passing an examination. Next, students must take six hours in a foreign language at the intermediate level; they are encouraged but not required to choose Latin (about 50 usually do). In the humanities, they take six hours in "World Literature," three hours in ethics, and three in the social sciences. All these courses are especially developed for and open only to CLC students.

In addition, they must select two three-hour courses in art appreciation, non-Western societies, or oral communication. Only one course each is offered in art and oral communication, but students have a choice among three in non-Western societies. Finally, CLC students must take 16 hours (four four-hour courses) in the physical and life sciences, all with laboratory. Two must be in the natural and life sciences (biology, geology, and/or anthropology), and two in the physical sciences (physics and/or chemistry.) At the end of the CLC program, students participate in a "Capstone" seminar where they synthesize what they have learned in a thesis.

Another option, the Great Books Program, is interdisciplinary and entails participation by faculty members from the departments of English, history, and philosophy. It lasts for one year; students take one three-hour course in each of the three subjects for two semesters. The weekly lectures are offered by a literary scholar, an historian, and

TUITION AND FEES INCREASE
Average Increase/Year: Public = 8.30%, North Texas = 13.72%

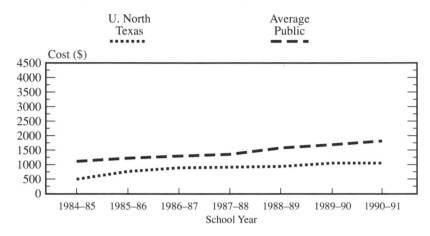

Source: The College Entrance Examination Board

a philosopher. One class period is set aside for discussion in each subject. Students study the themes, issues and arguments of 80 works and are encouraged to apply them to their own lives and experiences.

All candidates for the Bachelor of Arts or Science degree, must satisfy the same general distribution requirements as those following the CLC program, but they have a somewhat wider choice of courses. Additionally, by state law, all students must complete two three-hour courses on the U.S. and Texas Constitutions, as well as two three-hour courses in U.S. history (although proud Texans may substitute the history of the Lone Star State). Candidates for both the Bachelor of Arts and Bachelor of Science degrees must complete 128 semester hours to graduate.

North Texas offers an honors program that cuts across all undergraduate schools and is built on special sections of the general education courses in the College of Arts and Sciences. Courses are taught in seminars with a maximum of 25 students and from one to three professors. Admission to the honors program is limited to 50 incoming freshmen, and applicants are selected on the basis of their SAT scores, an essay and an interview.

The best departments are mathematics, chemistry, political science, and history. Weaker are communications and anthropology. Foreign languages also need strengthening and more variety. Currently, majors are offered only in Spanish, German, French, and Latin.

One of the biggest problems at the university is overcrowding. Students complain that it is often difficult to complete all requirements because they can't get into the courses they need or want to take. Teaching assistants are used in about 30 percent of classes, and there are mixed reviews about their competency. Faculty-student relations are generally good, but the usefulness of the advising system seems to depend upon the persistence of the student.

Overcrowding is also a problem outside the classroom. Although 40 percent of students live at home and commute, only 15 percent can be accommodated on the 425-acre campus, which leaves almost half to find quarters elsewhere. Campus housing is overwhelmingly coed. A few students live in the 17 fraternity and 10 sorority houses, but since only approximately 5 percent are Greek affiliates that doesn't

DISTRIBUTION OF UNDERGRADUATE AID
1989–90 School Year

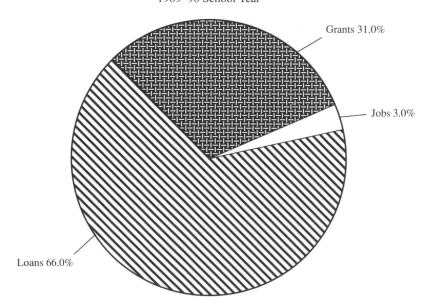

Grants 31.0%

Jobs 3.0%

Loans 66.0%

Source: The College Entrance Examination Board, 1990

ease the housing crunch. Fortunately, local accommodation is reasonably priced and not difficult to find.

There are almost 200 extracurricular organizations, none of them militantly political, although there are special-interest groups for homosexuals and minorities. Approximately 16 percent of North Texas students are minorities; a substantial number are Asians. Since most students juggle part-time jobs with classes and studying, few have much time left for campus politics.

The university is known for the excellence of its music school, and musical activities are popular. Sports are limited, with only 8 intercollegiate teams for men and 7 for women. The 11 intramural sports are coed, including football. Facilities include a 20,000-seat stadium, swimming pools and an 18-hole golf course.

Social life is enlivened by a highly visible group of foreign students (mostly in graduate programs), who relieve regional parochialism. Denton is a small but culturally alive city with a community theater and a light opera company and a community orchestra. Dallas and Fort Worth, each only about 30 minutes away, provide big-city distractions.

But it's not the rather humdrum social or sporting life—and it certainly isn't an academically elite student body—that distinguishes North Texas from dozens of similar institutions. Like so many, it is not highly competitive in admissions, though it is becoming more so, and it is refreshingly unambitious about ascending to the peak of national prominence or becoming another "great research university." What does make this unsung university remarkable when compared to more famous and prestigious colleges is its dogged devotion to excellence in teaching and to the fundamentals of liberal learning. These qualities, which are eroding all across the country, deserve a wider audience and a round of applause from traditionalists everywhere.

Pennsylvania State University

Director of Admissions and Assistant Vice President for
Academic Services, Penn State University Park Campus
201 Shields Building, Box 3000
University Park, PA 16802 (814) 865-5471

Type: Public

Students:
31,621 undergraduates
  17,630 men
  13,991 women
6,097 graduate students

Applications:
Priority date: November 30
44% of applicants accepted

	Applied	Accepted	Enrolled
men	13,369	5,520	2,230
women	10,942	5,063	2,054

SAT or ACT required (SAT preferred)
  Score reported by: November 30
  Mid 50% of freshman scores:
    SAT-Math   520–660
    SAT-Verbal   450–570

Costs and Aid:
Tuition & fees:
  In state $3,750
  Out of state   7,900
Room and Board 3,330

Scholarships:
  Academic   Yes
  Athletic   Yes
  Minority   Yes

Financial Aid:
  Freshmen   61%
  Upperclassmen 73%

Library: 2,168,072 titles

ROTC: Yes

Study Abroad: Yes

The Pennsylvania State University, or Penn State, leans so far left that, like the famous tower at Pisa, it looks as though it may lose its balance any minute. In a no doubt well-intentioned but surely misguided effort to motivate minority students, the university has been paying black students (and only black students) for academic achievement—with sums ranging from $250 to at least $580 per semester depending on the student's average grade. The sums thus "earned" are deducted from their tuition bills.

This policy, known as the Blacks Incentive Program, does little to promote either genuine learning or increased self-esteem among its recipients, and it fosters understandable resentment on campus among students who are not so rewarded. In fact, it has created so much controversy that at least one university official has denied that it exists. Another admits it, but says that the program will shortly be abolished, to be replaced by a "diversity" grant to all "underrepresented" groups. This new grant will be based not on specific grades, but on normal academic good standing.

In the same politically correct vein, some Penn State professors are notorious for marking down those who express politically incorrect opinions, a practice which may spread now that the school has instituted course requirements in ethnic diversity for graduation. More generally, like other megalithic institutions Penn State tends to sweep its undergraduates under a green carpet of research dollars, subordinating student education to the pursuit of money and status.

Originally chartered by the state legislature in 1855 as the Farmers High School, Penn State opened its doors in 1859 with four faculty and 69 male students. Designated four years later as the Commonwealth's land grant college, the school began to admit women in 1871 and it achieved official university status in 1953. Today, its 69 students have multiplied into a mammoth 71,000 and the university's tentacles now stretch across the state to 22 campuses, the oldest and largest being at University Park in the imaginatively named town of State College. The other campuses are much smaller and more specialized in their services, accommodating, for example, only commuters or junior college and graduate students in certain fields.

1990–91 Baccalaureate Degree Programs Bulletin:
Comparative Literature 101—The Theme of Identity in World Literature:
Race, Gender, and Other Issues of Diversity

"Themes of gender and heritage, centrality and marginality, self and other, as expressed in literary works from around the world."

University Park, Penn State's flagship, contains more than 9,000 acres and is about a four-hour drive from either Philadelphia or Pittsburgh. The campus is a bucolic beehive, occupied by 11 academic units and approximately 32,000 undergraduates, as well as more than 6,000 graduate students. Eighty-eight percent of the former are Pennsylvanians, many of them from rural areas. Most of the remaining undergraduates are from adjoining states. Approximately 12 percent are minorities.

Baccalaureate degrees are offered by the School of Communications and the Colleges of Agriculture, Arts and Architecture, Business Administration, Earth and Mineral Sciences, Education, Engineering, Health and Human Development, Liberal Arts, and Science. Strongest

TUITION AND FEES INCREASE
Average Increase/Year: Public = 8.30%, Penn State = 7.94%

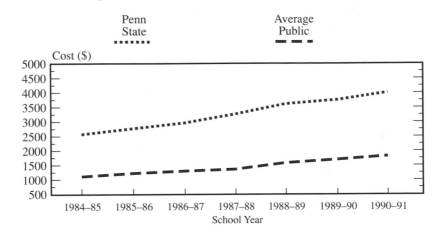

Source: The College Entrance Examination Board

among these are Agriculture, Business, Engineering, and Communications. The arts and humanities are the neglected stepchildren of a university hell-bent on raising its technical and material standards rather than its spiritual and aesthetic ones.

Nevertheless, the College of Liberal Arts and the College of Science, which are separate at Penn State, together matriculate about 12,000 students, with Liberal Arts enrolling approximately 8,000. They operate on the semester system with three credits given to most courses and 120 needed for graduation. Both colleges have in common a 46-credit general education program whose requirements are: nine credits in writing/speaking courses; three in mathematics and three additional credits in math, statistics, computer science, or symbolic logic; three in physical education and one in health science; nine in the natural sciences; and six each in the arts, the humanities, and the social and behavioral sciences. Further, Penn State stipulates that these credits must be divided between "breadth and depth" courses.

In addition, in March 1990, the university's faculty senate passed a "diversity" requirement for graduation. All students must now take one "diversity-focused" course that concentrates entirely upon race, religion, sexual orientation, feminism, and/or "global perspectives."

As an alternative to this massive dose of politics, students may take their medicine more gradually by enrolling instead in 12 credits of "diversity-enhanced" courses that devote 25 percent of class time each to the views of the approved interest groups.

A typical example is "Sociology and Sex Roles," known to students as "Feminism 101" because its professor, who is also the director of the women's center, requires readings by various radicals. (One of them is Angela Davis, vice-presidential candidate of the Communist Party of America.) As part of the course curriculum, students have also been required to attend events sponsored by or featuring presentations from the Lesbian and Gay Student Alliance, abortion advocates, and supporters of left-wing causes. One such supplementary program instructed students in the arcane mysteries of feminist witchcraft rituals.

At Penn State you can't always tell by the title of the course what you are likely to encounter in terms of content and instructor bias. For example, in 1990, a Christian student reported in detail in a college

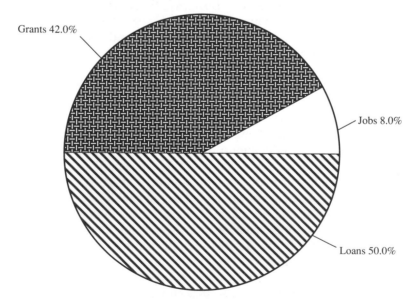

DISTRIBUTION OF UNDERGRADUATE AID
1989–90 School Year

Grants 42.0%

Jobs 8.0%

Loans 50.0%

Source: The College Entrance Examination Board, 1990

publication how he was downgraded in an English class for written work that expressed a Christian perspective. In two assigned papers, one on the 19th-century black intellectual, Frederick Douglass, and another about the Georgia sodomy law, the student commented from a Christian viewpoint. Leaving aside the interesting question of why such topics were being addressed in an English class in the first place, the student reported that—despite thorough research and hard work— he received a D on the first paper and a C minus on the second. When he protested against the second low mark, his professor told him he had better stop writing about Christianity. The student said he then "sold out" and wrote his last two papers about television, and women in engineering. He received As on both.

Many courses at Penn State are taught by graduate students, some of whom are foreigners with a questionable command of English. The better courses are in the earth sciences and astronomy and meteorology. Class sizes, especially for first- and second-year students, can run up to 400. Cheating, students say, is endemic and frequently goes undetected and unpunished. The advisory system is weak due to faculty preoccupation with graduate students and research, though it improves slightly for juniors and seniors. Much of the advising, such as it is, is done by bureaucratic types in the administration who, students say, are often almost as unintelligible as the foreign teaching assistants. Things do look up, however, for the very bright—with combined SAT scores of 1,300 or more—who are invited into the University Scholars Program (other high achievers may apply). These privileged few (about 1,400 of them) have opportunities for independent study, as well as to take honors in regular courses.

About 35 percent of University Park students live on campus, the rest in the surrounding area. All freshmen are guaranteed residence on campus. Accommodation is both single-sex and coed and includes dormitories, apartments, honors and language houses, as well as special-interest houses, such as the one named for Martin Luther King, Jr. and the luxurious Nittany Halls, home to the pampered varsity athletic teams. Most students living off campus find rooms and apartments in State College, a pleasant town that owes its existence primarily to the university, and where rents are generally quite high. Others settle in fraternity houses, most of which are located close to the campus, although sororities are allotted space in dorms.

Penn State's reputation as a great party school may be a blessing in disguise, considering the uneven quality of its liberal arts education; or perhaps it's the academic shortcomings that drive Penn Staters to drink. Whatever the reason, the university is known for its conviviality, and although alcohol is not permitted on campus for those under 21, this cruel deprivation doesn't cramp many styles and does fill to the brim the numerous bars as well the parties thrown by more than 50 national fraternities and approximately 20 sororities. Drug use is also said to be fairly widespread. Violent crime is not a problem, however, as Penn State lies in the heart of a rural, low-crime district.

Although only about 15 percent of undergraduates belong to the Greek system, everyone agrees that the Greeks outplay and outparty the rest of the campus. In their more temperate moments, members also raise funds for worthy causes and perform charity work. Fraternities and sororities tend to break down by mutual interest; some are known for jocks, some for "farm types," others for their ethnic and racial make-up.

The university claims almost 400 extracurricular groups and organizations, including 26 religious groups, which range from evangelical Christians to evangelical Muslims. The most prominent special-interest groups, however, are those involved in political issues or movements. College Democrats and Republicans sponsor many events and actively participate in local political campaigns. Liberal, left-wing, and especially anti-establishment groups frequently win in the no-holds-barred bouts of campus activism. The most energetic left-of-center groups include the Lesbian and Gay Student Alliance, various segments of the Undergraduate Student Government, and Students and Youth Against Racism. An informal coalition of members and leaders of these groups frequently pools its resources in programs and demonstrations.

The *Daily Collegian*, Penn State's only school-wide newspaper, almost always supports the efforts of this coalition. A lower-profile, but more mainstream, unofficial coalition of conservative students is beginning to step up its own activism. Penn State Students for Life, Christian organizations, and alternative student publications focus attention on more traditional viewpoints.

Big-time sports have always engaged the rapt attention of Penn Staters, particularly the prowling, growling, nationally-ranked Nittany Lions, perennially coached by the legendary Joe Paterno and now a Big 10 team. This football colossus takes pride of place in University Park, jamming the 84,000-seat stadium during home games and providing excuses for still more student and alumni partying before, during, and after the spectacle. Also strong is the men's basketball team—the

1990–91 Atlantic 10 champs—and the women's basketball team, a top 10 powerhouse.

Women's basketball is currently at the center of a controversy sparked by the coach's refusal to allow lesbians to play on her team. As the result of pressure from homosexual rights activists, the university, in May 1991, added sexual orientation to its list of personal characteristics (such as racial and ethnic origin) that may not be used to discriminate against an individual.

Of the 13 additional intercollegiate sports for men and 12 for women, championship teams include men's soccer, wrestling, golf, indoor and outdoor track, swimming, and softball. Women have won titles in tennis, volleyball, and gymnastics. There are 21 intramurals each for men and women and dozens of club sports. The facilities, even at huge Penn State, are wondrous to behold: six gymnasiums; five swimming pools; indoor and outdoor tracks; two golf courses; a skating rink; two rifle ranges; a jogging course; bowling alleys; 32 acres of practice fields; and almost countless courts of one sort or another.

Overall, while Penn State is a happy hunting ground for pre-professional and graduate students, jocks and partygoers, it is definitely not the college of choice for undergraduates serious about either the liberal arts, or the spirit of open and free enquiry. At Penn State, the social engineers may preach diversity, but what they seem to demand is conformity.

University of Pennsylvania

Dean of Admissions, University of Pennsylvania
1 College Hall, Philadelphia, PA 19104-6376 (215) 898-7507

Type: Private and Secular

Students:
9,949 undergraduates
  5,736 men
  4,213 women
10,356 graduate students

Applications:
Closing date: January 1
41% of applicants accepted

	Applied	*Accepted*	*Enrolled*
men	6,886	2,674	1,332
women	4,320	1,906	949

SAT or ACT required (SAT preferred)
  Score reported by: February 1
  Mid 50% of freshman scores:
    SAT-Math   N/A
    SAT-Verbal N/A

Costs and Aid:

Tuition & fees	$14,890
Room and Board	5,700

Scholarships:
Academic	No
Athletic	No
Minority	No

Financial Aid:
Freshmen	53%
Upperclassmen	53%

Library: 3,576,227 volumes

ROTC: Yes
Study Abroad: Yes

Percentage of courses that can be used to fulfill distribution requirements: 10.6

The University of Pennsylvania was chartered in 1755 by Benjamin Franklin as the College of Philadelphia. True to Dr. Franklin's penchant for useful rather than theoretical knowledge, Penn soon established itself as a leader in pre-professional studies and practical arts, with less emphasis on the liberal arts. Today, Ivy League Penn remains one of the pre-eminent, pre-professional institutions in the United States, with a total enrollment of more than 20,000. However, its liberal arts component, which the university has moved to strengthen in recent years, is now losing ground as radical elements fight for control.

The University of Pennsylvania hosts almost 10,000 undergraduates and four undergraduate schools—the College of Arts and Sciences, the Wharton School of Business, the School of Engineering and Applied Science, and the School of Nursing. The School of Arts and Sciences, commonly known as the college, is home to 5,700 of the university's undergraduates, and serves as the liberal arts base of the university. The humanities and sciences are centered in the college, as well as a varied assortment of special programs and departments, including women's and Afro-American studies.

Despite the aggressive liberalization of the curriculum in recent years, the college still pays lip service to foreign language proficiency and a solid grounding in the humanities. The best departments are archaeology, anthropology, and psychology, which is reputed to be rigorous; the worst is English, which has been thoroughly infiltrated by the political militants and literary anarchists (i.e., deconstructionists). Other strong departments are history, the natural sciences, and the romance languages. Economics is the most popular major.

Undergraduate Academic Bulletin and Course Description 1989–1991: Sociology 465—Sociology of Language (also Education 465/507)

"This course will be concerned with language contact and with the relationship between linguistic diversity and social inequality. Three major topics will be considered: (1) Linguistic imperialism: linguistic imposition as the result of military, political, and/or economic dominance, and the educational implications for developing nations. (2) The United States as a multilingual nation: the status of immigrant languages, bilingual education, nonstandard dialects and the teaching of standard English, Native American languages and their maintenance. (3) Language and sex: The differences between men's and women's speech, the reflection of sexist attitudes in language, and problems related to sexism in dictionaries and textbooks."

A recent and persistent controversy has centered on a proposed non-Western studies requirement advanced by an assortment of campus radicals and faculty members. Good sense has prevailed for the present and it has been rejected, but future assaults on the traditional curriculum are certainly in the offing and may not be so easily repulsed. A proposed speech code prohibiting remarks that might be considered offensive to minorities has also fallen by the wayside, at least temporarily.

At the moment, the college mandates for graduation a "General Requirement," which consists of 10 semester courses from among six cross-disciplinary "sectors"—Society; History and Tradition; Arts and Letters; Formal Reasoning and Analysis; the Living World, and the Physical World. Two courses each must be chosen from the first three sectors and four from the last three. To complete a foreign

TUITION AND FEES INCREASE
Average Increase/Year: Private = 11.15%, Penn = 7.59%

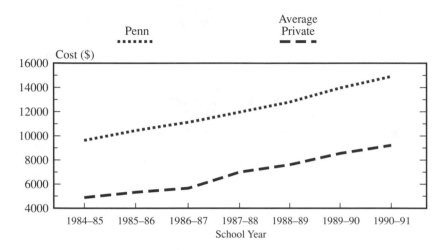

Source: The College Entrance Examination Board

language requirement, a student must take three courses in the language, or else be exempted through a proficiency test or advanced placement credits. According to students, none of these requirements is onerous, the courses for the most part being considerably "watered-down." No laboratory science is compulsory.

Although lectures are often huge at Penn, the school does offer a freshman seminar program within the six sectors, with 15 to 18 students in each class; students are advised to take at least one such seminar in order to gain the experience of working closely with a professor and exchanging views with a small number of classmates. Opportunities for small-group learning also exist for 125 very bright and motivated freshmen who are selected to become Benjamin Franklin Scholars; these come from all the undergraduate schools and are automatic candidates for general honors. They may also participate in faculty research projects. General honors courses are small and highly intense, covering a few issues in depth.

While college students have sometimes been labeled "liberal" and "unmotivated," students at Wharton are called "conservative" and "driven." And justifiably so. Wharton remains the top undergraduate business school in the country and the tough competition for admission reflects that fact. However, the prospective student should not consider the option of applying to Arts and Sciences and planning a later transfer to Wharton. To discourage such ploys during the admissions process, the administration has implemented a stringent transfer requirement of a 3.4 grade point average. Only rarely are exemptions made.

The two other undergraduate schools in the university are Engineering and Nursing. The Engineering School boasts a distinguished faculty as well as an illustrious history since the first computer, ENIAC, was developed there. The Nursing School prepares students not only for nursing careers, but also for those in health care management.

One of the most distinctive features of the University of Pennsylvania is the cohesiveness of its member schools. Even though a candidate applies to a pre-professional school, once enrolled a student is required to take a varied course load, and is encouraged to broaden his intellectual horizons through the use of elective courses. A number

DISTRIBUTION OF UNDERGRADUATE AID
1989–90 School Year

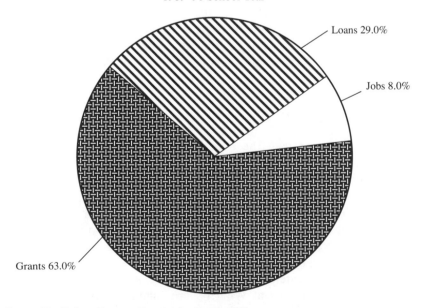

Loans 29.0%

Jobs 8.0%

Grants 63.0%

Source: The College Entrance Examination Board, 1990

of formal programs are available to unite fields of study, most notably
the Management and Technology Program operated jointly by the
Wharton and Engineering Schools. Dual degrees in the Wharton
School and College are easily attained by completing the relevant
requirements of the various departments.

Certainly no undergraduate experience would be complete without offering a great deal more than academic pursuits. At Penn,
frequently described as the most social of the Ivy League institutions,
the party scene remains alive and well despite some administration
efforts to discourage it. Fraternities and sororities play a prominent
role, as approximately a quarter of the campus is Greek. In recent
years, the system has suffered some set-backs as administrators and
allied radicals attempt to "diversify" the campus. The fraternities have
created hostility by committing regrettable acts of rudeness towards
minorities and women. As a result, some fraternities have been moved
off campus, and open parties and "wet rush" are now firmly a thing of
the past, with alcohol officially prohibited on campus for those under
21. Many observers expect an alumni revolt, however, which could
slow anti-Greek sentiment, particularly in light of the recently announced $1 billion capital campaign.

While the university sponsors a minimal number of non-Greek
social events, this shortcoming is being reversed through student
efforts. Plans for a variety of open parties, cultural events, Homecoming parties, and an Ivy Ball are impressive and should be implemented
soon. Due to the dearth of open parties at the fraternities, much social
life now centers around private events, both on and off campus.

Philadelphia offers a number of options with bars, clubs, and
sporting events available to even the mildly adventurous. South Street,
Philadelphia's scaled-down answer to Greenwich Village, is frequented
by a large number of Penn students. Since Penn does not offer weekend
dining services, students are forced off campus to eat, and tend to stay
in the city afterwards to socialize.

On-campus housing is guaranteed for freshmen and available to
upperclassmen by lottery. About 80 percent of all students live on
campus, which is roughly the same percentage as students who come
from out of state. All 50 states and 100 foreign countries are represented. Housing is coed and includes dormitories, apartments, and
married housing. Dorms in the three highrises, filled mostly by upperclassmen, may look like big-city boxes, but do offer kitchens. The
pleasant 250-acre campus is next door to downtown Philadelphia and
contains a mix of old and new buildings.

In addition to academics and social life, extracurricular activities are central to the Penn experience, which also encompasses a tradition of athletic excellence. Football games are noted for their festive atmosphere as well as rousing, if alcohol-induced, support of the team. The university offers 16 intercollegiate sports for men, 14 for women, and 16 intramurals for each. Men's basketball and lacrosse and women's field hockey are strong, but facilities are mediocre and often overcrowded.

Around 250 campus student organizations present a rich choice of activities. From the Armenian Club, the Comic Collectors Club, and Amnesty International to the College Democrats, the Students of Objectivism, and the Philomathean Society, Penn offers something for everyone. The student activities are also the springboard for campus political debate, which is characterized by intense polemic and divisive rhetoric. On the left, the Progressive Student Alliance, the Black Students League, the Women's Alliance, and the Lesbian/Gay/Bisexual Alliance are often united and, with the support of the administration, have achieved significant success in attaining university financial support for their activities and political agendas.

As a result of the left's efforts, certain fraternities have been removed from the campus, a women's studies program has been developed, Louis Farrakhan has spoken, the DuBois House (for blacks and others who wish to immerse themselves in African-American culture and history) has been established, and a Gay and Lesbian Awareness Week has been celebrated. Of late, a campus publication, *The Red and Blue,* working with the College Republicans, has opposed the radicalization of the campus, and consequently was removed from the list of official university activities. After several applications, the paper was finally restored; but such discrimination tends to mute conservative voices for fear of charges of "racism," "sexism," and "homophobia."

In spite of—or perhaps because of—these actions by the university, racial strife continues to divide the Penn community. Minority representation is growing (it now comprises more than a quarter of the student body), and although the Hispanic and Asian populations seem to be integrating nicely, blacks remain largely isolated both from the other minorities and from the white student community. This is partly due to the paternalism of the administration, which encourages blacks to think of themselves as victims, and partly due to the attitudes of their leaders, who advocate diversity in principle, but often encourage separatism in practice.

The minority community scored a recent coup by persuading the administration to make compulsory a "Diversity Education" program for incoming freshmen, during which, among other things, they act out possible scenarios involving racial, religious, and sexual discrimination (against homosexuals and women). The sessions provide enlightenment or indoctrination, depending upon your point of view. Regardless, the program has done little to form a sense of community on this racially polarized campus in the City of Brotherly Love.

Although a Wharton student was arrested not long ago for dealing crack in New York City, drugs are not a large problem at Penn, though marijuana use is widespread. Alcohol, however, is consumed in large quantities by many students. Security is a primary campus issue. Penn students are regularly confronted with crime and violence. It should be noted, however, that the students themselves have contributed to these incidents through either foolhardiness (walking alone off campus at all hours or leaving doors unlocked), or drunkenness. Although the Penn community has yet to realize that the campus does not provide a safe haven from the dangers of life in a modern metropolis, the administration has recently attempted to shore up relations with the Philadelphia police and to strengthen the campus police force. Penn has also established a motorized escort service to provide transportation to off-campus apartments. On-campus housing is well-equipped with 24-hour electronic and human security services, but crime is a rising tide.

Despite the rough spots, four years at the University of Pennsylvania can still make for a rich educational (and even adventuresome) experience for bright students who can ignore or surmount the growing radical tensions and the campus's traditional preoccupation with the professions rather than the liberal arts.

Pomona College

Dean of Admissions, Pomona College
333 North College Way, Claremont, CA 91711-6312
(714) 621-8134

Type: Private and Secular

Students:
1,394 undergraduates
   733 men
   661 women

Applications:
Closing date: January 15
34% of applicants accepted

	Applied	Accepted	Enrolled
men	1,532	567	198
women	1,644	511	171

SAT or ACT required
  Score reported by: February 1
  Mid 50% of freshman scores:
    SAT-Math   640–730
    SAT-Verbal 580–670

Costs and Aid:

Tuition & fees	$14,030
Room and Board	5,700

Scholarships:
Academic	No
Athletic	No
Minority	No

Financial Aid:
Freshmen	52%
Upperclassmen	52%

Library: 1,600,000 titles

ROTC: Yes

Study Abroad: Yes

Percentage of courses that can be used to fulfill distribution requirements: 64.8

Back in 1887 when the 35-mile ride to Los Angeles still took a day by horse and carriage, a group of pioneering Congregationalists decided that what southern California needed was a "Christian college of the New England type" to provide quality higher education for the area's burgeoning population. A century later, Pomona College manages to blend California's sunny, laid-back lifestyle with some of the academic rigors often attributed to colder climes. During its long journey toward eminence, Pomona has severed its ties with the Congregationalist Church and relinquished its Christian character. It now reveres the new god of relativism.

Pomona is one of the Claremont Colleges, a group of six adjoining schools originally modeled after England's Oxford. The colleges jointly support a number of central facilities and open their courses and libraries to each other's students. This unique arrangement combines the advantages of a small college with those of a large university. The other five institutions in the system are Claremont McKenna, Harvey

Mudd, Scripps, Pitzer, and the Claremont Graduate School. Each has its own particular personality, as well as academic specialties.

Pomona, ranked highest academically, is also the largest, even though it limits enrollment to around 1,400. Sixty percent of its students come from out of state, mostly from the Northwest, but all states are usually represented as well a number of foreign countries. Almost 30 percent are non-white, with Asians and Hispanics predominating.

Pomona is recognized for its strong English, foreign language, mathematics, anthropology, biology, chemistry, philosophy, and history departments; Claremont McKenna for its government, economics, and accounting; Pitzer for psychology; Harvey Mudd for its engineering and physics; and Scripps for its humanities.

1990–91 Catalog:
Women's Studies, Interdisciplinary Course ID 186—The Politics of Gender. The Humanities.
Professors Houchins and Pohl

"One of a series of three courses each with a different interdisciplinary approach. The ways in which gender is culturally constructed through visual, performing, and written texts, drawing upon the methodologies of art history, literature, and the theatre. The interaction of gender with class, race and ethnicity, sexuality, and third world conditions in establishing and maintaining hierarchies of power. Films and field trips required."

Instead of a core curriculum, Pomona offers a "Breadth of Study" program. The college does not work on the system of credit hours, but counts instead the number of courses taken. The standard load is four per semester; each course generally meets four hours per week, although foreign language classes may involve six hours. Students are required to take three courses of their choice in each of three divisions (the humanities, the natural and the social sciences), and the courses must divide between the two or three sub-categories within each field. Students must also pass three semesters of a foreign language and take two writing-intensive courses, one of which is the freshman seminar.

Introduced in the fall of 1986, the freshman seminar, usually given in sections of 15 students or fewer, offers a choice of writing-intensive, interdisciplinary courses on a kaleidoscope of subjects that may in-

TUITION AND FEES INCREASE
Average Increase/Year: Private = 11.15%, Pomona = 8.14%

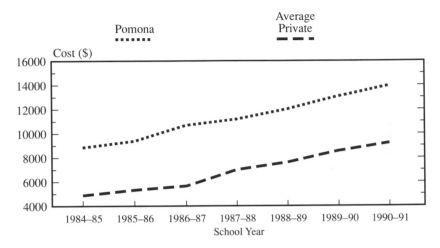

Source: The College Entrance Examination Board

clude: environmental issues; biological determinism; the historical roots of apartheid; epidemics and society; postmodernism; and (more romantically) a course entitled, "California and the West in the American Imagination." Professors are given—and take—great liberty in tailoring these courses to their own personal tastes and agendas.

The number of courses that qualify for the breadth-of-study list is large and growing; English literature and Western civilization may fall through the cracks, however, as neither is mandated. Watered-down versions of harder, introductory science classes (like biology for non-majors) are offered as the most painless ways to meet the requirement, and are also popular with students who want to dabble in another field without risking bad grades.

Pomona offers considerable flexibility in choosing a major. Students can have double and triple majors, interdisciplinary majors like the popular PPE (philosophy, politics, and economics), as well as individually designed majors. The most common major among 1990 graduates was economics, followed by English.

For those restless souls who want to explore the rest of the world, the college offers an unusually eclectic study-abroad program. Among the many locations available are the remote reaches of Nepal and

Africa, as well as urban centers like Tokyo and Edinburgh. Pomona also has exchange programs with Smith, Colby, and Swarthmore Colleges for those who prefer to remain in the United States. A remarkable three-fourths of the total student body participate in off-campus study programs sometime during the four years.

On campus, although Pomona's academic departments are considered solid, there are few well-known scholars within the ranks, and the faculty generally is left of center. Economics and government instruction is to be taken with several large pinches of salt. Pomona's government department is reputed not to have had a Republican in its ranks since 1974, and the economics department consistently idolizes the superannuated John Maynard Keynes. For relief, students may cross-register in some of Claremont McKenna's more conservative courses.

Because Pomona is a small college, its professors do not have to rely on teaching assistants to teach their classes, most of which have fewer than 20 students. Faculty members also have flexible office

DISTRIBUTION OF UNDERGRADUATE AID
1989–90 School Year

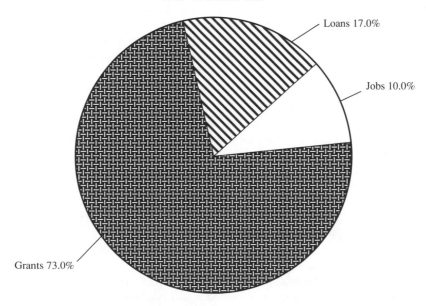

Source: The College Entrance Examination Board, 1990

hours, and are quite generous in helping students with their course-work and other questions. In fact, some professors host small get-togethers at their homes nearby, and many students reciprocate by inviting their mentors to lunch at the dining hall or the campus grill.

Another of Pomona's assets is its sponsor-group program. All freshmen are placed in groups of about eight with one sophomore or junior sponsor. These associations ensure a small circle of friends for the first nervous weeks of freshman year and many remain close for four years. Unfortunately, the sponsor-group program is spoiled by freshman orientation, during which the groups are forcefed the politi-cally correct positions on sexism and racism.

Campus housing is coed, guaranteed for all four years, and con-sists of comfortable and sometimes luxurious dorms and apartments, often with patios opening onto a lawn. About 99 percent of students live on campus. All of the dorms are designed differently, from the old Spanish adobe style of Clark I to the modern Oldenborg. Housing is determined by an annual lottery at which students draw random numbers according to their class. The most sought-after rooms are spacious singles with fireplaces (not often lit, needless to say). Most dorms have lounges with TVs, and many have complete kitchens.

One dorm on campus, the Oldenborg Center for Modern Lan-guages, is popular both with foreign students and with Americans learning a new language. Students in "The Borg" sign up for a particular language hall and live among fellow speakers of that lan-guage. Lunch at Oldenborg is unique; tables are marked with small flags of foreign countries and students and professors are asked to speak only in that country's language. Oldenborg is the only dorm on campus with air conditioning, which is useful in September, and Borgers are fond of flaunting their luxury.

There is a running debate about whether the North Campus is better than South Campus. The difference is really in the dorms. Traditionally, most seniors and juniors reside on the north side, and most freshmen and sophomores live on the south side. Because of their design, South Campus dorms are better suited for personal interaction, and "hall life" is more vibrant. North Campus, however, is closer to the library, and the fraternities, which host the best parties, are located in the basements of North Campus houses.

In spite of all its amenities, campus life has been criticized lately as dull, because state drinking laws have tightened up, impelling the administration to crack down on fraternities. Thirty years ago, the seven fraternities (all local and four of them coed; there are no sororities) maintained houses off campus in the mountains where they held their parties. Alcohol-related accidents moved the college to relocate them on campus so students would not have to drink and drive. This worked well until a number of events involving alcohol and vandalism led to a growing anti-fraternity mood, primarily within the administration but also among feminists, who constantly agitate for the abolition of all-male fraternities, although they support the nearby all-female Scripps College. Some say that it's only a matter of time until the all-male clubs relocate off campus again to avoid persecution.

While the administration's war on alcohol has met with some success, the college turns a blind eye to drug use, which is quite common. The administration is disgracefully lax in dealing with the problem, so much so that on a routine walk through a dorm, campus security found a potted marijuana plant sitting in the public hallway. In another incident, a student senator caught possessing illegal drugs, scales, and other paraphernalia who admitted he intended to sell the drugs was merely fined and put on probation for a year. Further, a fraternity newsletter that drew campus-wide censure for its allegedly sexist contents was virtually ignored when it pointed out Pomona's pervasive drug use.

On the whole, the administration, faculty, and student body of Pomona are very permissive and proud of it. The Gay Lesbian Student Union, the Office of Black Student Affairs, the Women's Union, and a number of smaller clubs are all very active in rallying for quirky, or leftist causes. As at other colleges across the country, sexism, racism, and homophobia are the watchwords of the student-faculty thought police, who literally try to suppress other views. Their intolerance was exemplified not long ago when Pomona's admissions office repeatedly removed from circulation stacks of a student publication that criticized the office's affirmative action policies.

In spite of Big Brother's watchful eye, campus security at Pomona and all the Claremont Colleges is best described as unpredictable and many students criticize it roundly. One Claremont McKenna student, who was forced to lie on the ground near his car as an armed assailant stole it, called both campus security and the Claremont city police. The police arrived quickly and told the student not to bother calling campus security again since it was so unreliable. On the plus side, not since 1986 has there been an attempted rape reported on campus, due in part to the installation of better lighting and emergency telephones.

Larger physical improvements on campus are also underway. Pomona now sports several new or renovated buildings: a huge, multimillion dollar gym with everything from racquetball courts to jacuzzis; a new dorm; a $10 million center for the performing arts; and a refurbishment of a hallowed hall reckoned to be the oldest-dorm-west-of-the-Mississippi-that-was-previously-not-earthquake-proof. In addition, the school is constructing a new administration building and has beefed up its already powerful computer labs. A massive expansion of the central library of the Claremont Colleges was completed in 1987.

Pomona teams up with Pitzer for all of its sports. Pomona athletics can be either enjoyable or miserable, depending on whether you play or just watch. As a fan, you join an apathetic student body in rooting for often unsuccessful teams. Interest in sports at any level is probably lower at Pomona than at most schools. On the other hand, for athletes interested in playing intercollegiate athletics but unable to compete at larger schools, Pomona is ideal. The competition, coaching, and conditioning are quite good even if, so far, the level of play isn't.

Men's basketball is the biggest spectator draw, with interest especially high for the two games against rival Claremont McKenna. Soccer, tennis, and women's volleyball are all tough, attracting good crowds. Other strong teams include water polo, swimming, and women's basketball. In addition to football, baseball and track tend to be weak. Pomona offers 11 intercollegiate sports for men and 7 for women, with 3 intramurals for each. There are also 11 coed sports. Facilities include an all-weather track, a couple of swimming pools, and the usual playing fields and courts for tennis, racquetball, and squash.

Pomona is situated in the quiet L.A. suburb of Claremont, about 45 minutes from both the beach and the nearest ski resort. Shopping is within walking and biking distance. In the Village, a collection of high-priced shops, stores, and restaurants adjacent to the campus, strollers will encounter a curious clutter of aging hippies and senior citizens walking the sidewalks and window shopping. Restaurants, bars, pubs, and malls abound within five miles of campus, and students with a love of Mexican, Chinese, or Thai food will delight in the many convenient ethnic restaurants.

Pomona College definitely is a mixed bag. It, like the great State of California, has come a long way in 105 years; but the college, at least, may have traveled too far too fast. Although the quality of its student body continues to improve, the school's unwavering commitment to diversity—and all that implies today—undermines its liberal arts mission, and is in danger of turning pretty Pomona into a propaganda machine for the politically correct.

Princeton University

Dean of Admission, Princeton University
Box 430, Princeton, NJ 08544-0430 (609) 258-3060

Type: Private and Secular		

Students:
4,524 undergraduates
  2,725 men
  1,799 women
1,770 graduate students

Applications:
Closing date: January 2
25% of applicants accepted

	Applied	Accepted	Enrolled
men	3,367	1,185	639
women	5,242	928	505

SAT or ACT required (SAT preferred)
  Score reported by: March 1
  Mid 50% of freshman scores:
    SAT-Math   660–750
    SAT-Verbal 600–710

Costs and Aid:

Tuition & fees	$15,440
Room and Board	5,060

Scholarships:

Academic	No
Athletic	No
Minority	No

Financial Aid:

Freshmen	70%
Upperclassmen	70%
Library:	4,292,000 titles
ROTC:	Yes
Study Abroad:	Yes
Percentage of courses that can be used to fulfill distribution requirements:	60

As a consummate institution of higher learning, Princeton has it all—small classes, a superb faculty whose energies are not constantly siphoned off by a huge graduate school presence, a thriving sports program, and most importantly, a bright and enthusiastic student body which brings the school's academic mission to life. Set against the background of a majestically beautiful Gothic campus, the Princeton experience affords constant opportunities for both aesthetic and intellectual stimulation.

Yet Princeton is, in many ways, a confused giant. As the recently coeducational school (1970) grapples with its historic identity as a bastion of jovial old-boy networking and fraternal camaraderie, it appears to be alternately proud of and defensive about its semi-sacred mantra—Tradition. From the annual freshman race to steal the bell clapper signaling the beginning of classes to the dent in Nassau Hall caused by a cannonball fired during the Revolutionary War, Princeton, founded in 1746 as the College of New Jersey, has always worn its cultural history like a badge of honor.

Today, however, references to tradition often come tinged with sarcasm and bitterness. There is concern that Princeton's rich heritage is actually nothing more than a series of glorified male-bonding rituals that cannot accommodate an increasingly diverse student body, which now embraces not only women, but also blacks, Asians, and Hispanics. Nearly 22 percent are minorities, with Asian-Americans making up almost 10 percent of the total. Many students, arguing that traditions serve to perpetuate the school's questionable legacy as a romping ground for the "white male elite," have demanded that a number of the university's most time-honored institutions and practices either modernize to fit changing times, or disappear. Yet, others cherish old-fashioned structures and customs, insisting that the preservation of tradition has intrinsic importance and that the practice in question may serve an important purpose.

Course Offerings Spring 1990–91:
Afro-American Studies 374—Civil Rights, Vietnam, and Central America: The Changing Locus of Social Movements.
Professor R. Sobel

"Seminar discusses the origins, goals, results, and interrelationships of recent social movements: Civil Rights, anti-Vietnam War, and Central America movements using race, class, and gender as analytical focuses, examines relationships between the movements, including contributions of Civil Rights to New Left, King's opposition to the Vietnam War, and lessons of anti-Vietnam for Central America movement."

Afro-American Studies 262—Rap Music 1990. (also Music 262)
Professor R. Sadin

"Rap Music 1990 is a study of the place of Rap in Afro-American musical life. The conflicting tendencies and directions, the diverse ideologies, and the custom threads, which link the entire rap community will be investigated. The historical genesis of these trends will also be studied. (Guests from the world of rap will participate in weekly meetings.)"

Occasionally, as in the case of two remaining all-male eating clubs, the polemics reach a fever pitch. In response to a lawsuit from a female undergraduate who was denied membership in several eating clubs because of her sex, the New Jersey Supreme Court recently ruled that the Ivy Club and the Tiger Inn must admit women. Fortunately,

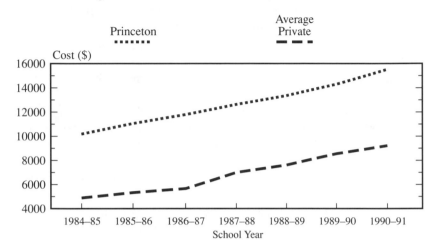

TUITION AND FEES INCREASE
Average Increase/Year: Private = 11.15%, Princeton = 7.15%

Source: The College Entrance Examination Board

however, traditions are often good-naturedly modified without resort to the courts.

A few years ago, the first bold contingent of women participated in Princeton's favorite rite of winter—the Nude Olympics. This drunken round of outdoor calisthenics, always held at midnight on the day of the first snow fall, has been all-male for years—because of the event's physical exigencies more than anything else. Now, however, more and more females join in, proving that they too can shiver and shake through the chilly revelries. A coed Nude Olympics definitely gives a new look to an old tradition, yet the raucous spirit of the event is clearly undiminished.

The constant tension between the school's diehard "tradition" lobbyists and those "diversity" advocates who wish to disrupt or deconstruct all that has gone before makes for a sometimes polarized political climate. For example, the campaign for "inclusionary" language—language that is purportedly free of racist, sexist, heterocentric or classist biases—quickly gathered steam, as the term "freshman" was replaced by "first-year student" and college "master"—a term that to some evoked 19th-century plantation owners—will soon be replaced by the more egalitarian "mentor."

The agenda of Princeton's radical element is largely shaped by one especially vocal group—Students for Social Responsibility. SSR has grabbed headlines and monopolized debate over such emotional issues as flag-burning and the chanting of obscenities at hated public figures. Perhaps due to the graduation of several charismatic leaders, SSR seems to have lost focus as of late; their waning influence in campus politics may pave the way for more measured and rational discussion of the relevant issues.

On the other hand, things may get much worse, if a recent incident involving death threats to a student is any indication. The victim, reported the *Philadelphia Inquirer* on May 29, 1991, "is not what students call 'politically correct'," because he opposed a "Take Back the Night" march, organized annually to marshal campus opinion against sexual harassment and rape.

He objected to the event because, he said, its organizers excluded men from the initial planning and issued their demands directly to the

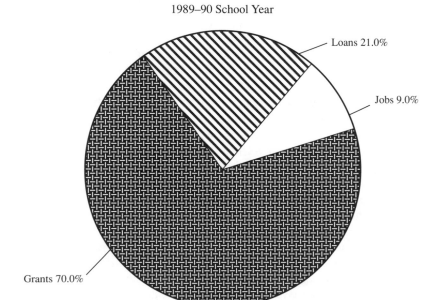

DISTRIBUTION OF UNDERGRADUATE AID
1989–90 School Year

Loans 21.0%

Jobs 9.0%

Grants 70.0%

Source: The College Entrance Examination Board, 1990

administration, thus violating the freedom of speech of men and those who held differing opinions.

The student reported receiving two telephoned death threats after the student newspaper published his objections to the march. He also claimed he had been socially ostracized and verbally threatened on campus. As a result, he said he would no longer publicly express his political views either at Princeton or at New York University, where he planned to begin graduate work in the fall of 1991.

In spite of such horror stories, the Princeton experience can be a gratifying one, because its academic life is so stimulating. Particularly important is the "precept" format—introduced by Woodrow Wilson when he was president of the university—around which most courses are organized. Nearly all large lecture courses break into these small discussion sections, where lecture material is further explained, questions are asked, and alternative interpretations are presented. Although precept sections are sometimes led by the professor, many students actually prefer to have teaching assistants for their preceptors, as undergraduates tend to feel more comfortable asking graduate students the "stupid questions" too embarrassing to bother professors with. At any rate, students seem to find precepts both helpful and enjoyable; while it's not unusual for students to cut an occasional lecture, most attend the precepts regularly.

The honor code, adopted in 1893, is another time-honored Princeton tradition that still receives almost universal student support. Students must sign the code as a condition of admission. It stipulates that students write on each examination paper, "I pledge my honor that I have not violated the honor code during this examination." Exams are unproctored and cheating is beyond the pale. Violations are the province of the Undergraduate Honor Committee, which recommends penalties to Princeton's president. These involve suspension, which lasts between one and three years, depending upon individual circumstances.

Unlike all its Ivy League brethren save Dartmouth, Princeton is primarily an undergraduate institution, hosting a total student population of slightly more than 6,000, of whom 4,500 are undergraduates. They come from all over the U.S. and more than 50 foreign countries. There are no professional graduate schools at Princeton, though many of the university's alumni go on to the best in the country.

Princeton operates on the semester system and requires 30 courses in eight semesters for graduation with a Bachelor of Arts degree. A Bachelor of Science degree is not awarded, even for science majors, though there is a Bachelor of Science degree in engineering. Princeton lacks a core curriculum and substitutes a relaxed system of distribution requirements in writing, a foreign language, and four "general areas." These are easy to fulfill, as students have all four years in which to complete requirements in the general areas. The writing requirement, however, must be accomplished before the end of the sophomore year by choosing one of nine writing-intensive courses in English, literature, classics, and the literatures of the Romance languages, Germanic languages, and the Near East. The foreign language requirement, which must be completed by the end of the junior year, may be met through a proficiency examination or by taking whichever number of courses the university deems necessary to reach proficiency. (For the study of a new language, this is usually a not very demanding three or four semesters.)

The four general areas are science (laboratory courses); the social sciences; arts and letters; and history, philosophy, and religion. Students must take two courses in each, which may or may not be from the same department within the area. Almost every department at Princeton is strong; history, math, economics and philosophy are considered among the best in the country while psychology and sociology are not. The newer departments—anthropology, for example—are still accumulating staff and resources and should become stronger as they continue to grow. One of Princeton's most prestigious programs is the Woodrow Wilson School of Public and International Affairs, which admits about 80 juniors selected on the basis of their backgrounds, interest in public affairs, and their academic records.

Unfortunately, English and, to a lesser degree, political science have largely been co-opted by the "tenured radicals." Elaine Showalter, outspoken champion of feminist literary criticism, has recently assumed the chairmanship of the English department. As one student commented about the politicized modes of textual interpretation now favored by the department: "It's hard to tell what came first—the literary theory or the chip on the shoulder."

The radical bias of academia is a problem everywhere, and Princeton is no exception. Slanted presentation of material is pervasive, and ranges from the mildly offensive to the outright intolerable. Self-righteous young graduate students in hammer-and-sickle earrings and chukka boots are to blame for the most egregious assaults on objectivity; professors tend to be more subtle in their insinuation of a left-of-center point of view into course material.

Anecdotes to this effect abound. In 1987, a European history professor struck Milan Kundera's *The Unbearable Lightness of Being*—a masterful novel about lovers in occupied Prague during the Soviet invasion of Czechoslovakia—off the course's reading list. When asked for a reason, the professor replied, "I just thought it was so . . . knee-jerk anti-Soviet. It seemed to me as if every other page was, like, the Russian tanks rolling in." Another teacher, apparently not able to dispense with Orwell's *1984* quite so conveniently, nevertheless conducted the entire discussion of the novel without one reference to Stalinism. Her interpretation of *1984* was to present the book as a critique of "information societies," and she matter-of-factly compared nightmarish Oceania to Reagan's America.

Orwellian echoes also reverberate in Princeton's anti-harrassment code, which provides for disciplinary action against student offenders. The code stipulates sanctions for "abusive or harassing behavior, *verbal* (emphasis added) or physical, which demeans, intimidates, threatens or injures another because of his or her personal characteristics or beliefs." If minority students feel they have been discriminated against, they may file a complaint, which is dealt with by a hierarchy of individuals and panels.

In the spring of 1991, the university held its first Diversity Workshop, designed to promote better understanding of minority problems; it was voluntary, and as of then there were no plans to make future workshops mandatory. On the whole, the campus is relatively free from racial and ethnic tensions. Most students are too involved with academics to become seriously entangled in campus politics, the province of a few zealous activists.

In general, the social scene at Princeton is not so lively as life in the classroom. In spite of a healthy relationship between university and community, quiet, upscale Princeton is not your average college town. There is no dancing, no campy all-night cafés, little live entertainment, and no bar scene. As many traditional college activities are thus eliminated, Princeton students have to make their own fun. Since New York and Philadelphia are each an hour away by train, going out often means hitting the 12 eating clubs—beautiful mansions lining Prospect Street that are comparable to fraternities and sororities. This can get tiresome after a while; moreover, the clubs themselves are a divisive element. As there are few social outlets besides the clubs, nearly every sophomore wants to join one. The tortuous "bicker" interviewing process necessary to become a member of one of the selective eating clubs is dreaded by everyone, as competitive allegiances are formed, strategies are manufactured, connections are milked, and groups of friends are eventually split up as some are chosen and others are not. Even the non-selective clubs are difficult, as memberships are determined by participation in a highly competitive lottery.

By contrast, the five underclass residential colleges are a relatively new Princeton tradition, and seem to be working out very nicely. Freshmen and sophomores live and eat meals in their residential colleges, each a cluster of dorms with library, café, and calendar of social events. Critics do say, however, that the system discourages cross-class mingling and creates a gulf between lower- and upper-classmen.

The sporting life at Princeton goes some way toward closing this gap for students who participate; there are 45 intramural sports, 18 intercollegiate teams for men, and 15 intercollegiate teams for women. Facilities on the spacious 600-acre campus are excellent and include a golf course, ice rink, Olympic-level water course for crew and sailing races, a 6,500-seat gymnasium, and a 45,000-seat football stadium— which overflows when old rivals Yale and Harvard come to hunt the Princeton Tiger. Princeton also offers 200 extracurricular organizations, including the Triangle Club, famous for its musical productions— and for Jimmy Stewart who, among other theatrical luminaries, once trod its well-worn boards.

Its drawbacks notwithstanding, Princeton University is an academic powerhouse whose reality *almost* equals its reputation. The school's commitment to providing a top-quality undergraduate education, combined with the resources necessary to achieve this goal, continue to make a Princeton degree a valuable asset and a source of lifelong pride.

University of Puget Sound

Dean of Admissions, University of Puget Sound
1500 North Warner Street, Tacoma, WA 98416 (206) 756-3211

Type: Private and Protestant			**Costs and Aid:**	
			Tuition & fees	$11,420
Students:			Room and Board	3,800
3,214 undergraduates			Scholarships:	
1,354 men			Academic	Yes
1,860 women			Athletic	Yes
200 graduate students			Minority	No
Applications:			Financial Aid:	
Closing date: March 1			Freshmen	70%
67% of applicants accepted			Upperclassmen	70%
	Applied	*Accepted*	*Enrolled*	
men	1,286	834	266	**Library:** 310,000 titles
women	1,769	1,224	365	
SAT or ACT required			**ROTC:** Yes	
Score reported by: March 1			**Study Abroad:** Yes	
Mid 50% of freshman scores:				
SAT-Math	500–620			
SAT-Verbal	450–570			

In 1991, the University of Puget Sound celebrated the centennial of its founding by a group of Tacoma Methodists. Despite its religious origins, this prodigal school was once referred to as the "University of Parties and Sex," but in the last 15 years it has gained national notice for academic excellence. In the early 1980s, UPS admitted 80 percent of its applicants, but the pool of interested students has become so large that this figure is rapidly decreasing. Well over half the student body now comes from outside the state of Washington, and this selective group regularly contains many National Merit Scholars and others who opted against more "prestigious" schools for the relaxed atmosphere of UPS.

The person most responsible for this turnaround is President Phillip Phibbs. Phibbs, a political scientist who was the first male administrator at Wellesley College before coming to Puget Sound in 1973, has made the academic atmosphere of the university his primary concern, a concern shaped by his own education at the University of Chicago. This influence—informed by the teaching of thinkers like Leo Strauss—has made Phibbs suspect among some faculty members and

285

administrators who see in his desire for a more classical curriculum at UPS a hidden ideological agenda.

Phibbs would like to institute a Great Books approach to learning at Puget Sound. Unfortunately, he has met opposition from faculty members who, usually using the language of relativism and occasionally the slogans of racism and sexism, decry efforts to elevate Western culture and values above "openness" and "multiculturalism." Ironically, Phibbs himself has a scholarly interest in India and he is also a strong proponent of cross-cultural studies. Indeed, the Asian studies program at Puget Sound is a very fine one. Moreover, the university's honors program stresses the "canon" of Western civilization. Here, the faculty endorses the "elitism" involved in closing the honors courses to the majority of the student body.

Bulletin 1990–1991:
English 435—Literature and Gender

"This course explores the dynamics of gender in literature. Students will analyze literary texts to raise questions about the intellectual, social, cultural, political, and philosophical contexts from which they emerge. Issues discussed will include sexual politics and power; the relation of imperialism and racism to questions of gender; and the influence of gender on writing as an act of self-determination. Students will read works by Gordimer, Walker, Hong Kingston, and others."

UPS's self-styled "core curriculum" is more on the order of distribution requirements designed to expose students to many fields of study. The "core" is divided into nine areas: Written Communication (all but a select few are required to take English 101); Oral Communication; Quantification; Historical Perspective; Humanistic Perspective; Natural World; Society; Fine Arts; and Comparative Values. Students are required to take courses in each. Though many different courses can be used to satisfy the requirements, some are pushovers. There are ways for English majors to avoid taking calculus, and "real science" can be avoided with courses like "The Historical Development of the Physical Sciences" and "Chemistry in the Community."

One effect of the honors program, the four-year course of study that stresses "the Western intellectual tradition," is to almost isolate the Great Books from the rest of the curriculum. It is as if the program

TUITION AND FEES INCREASE
Average Increase/Year: Private = 11.15%, Puget Sound = 10.34%

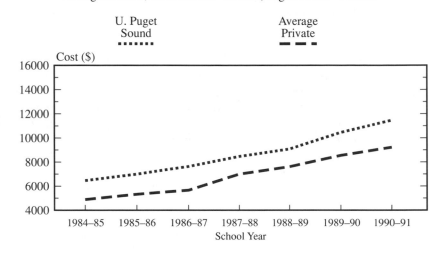

Source: The College Entrance Examination Board

---

represents a modus vivendi between the traditionally minded Phibbs, and a more trendy group of professors. Many students think that there is a need for the classics to be diffused into the mainstream curriculum. At the moment, only the most highly motivated and aware undergraduates are able to select courses which reflect the full breadth of Western learning. For others, the rigors of real liberal education are still too easily dodged.

The university has engaged a faculty with excellent scholarly credentials, and a strong commitment to teaching. Most faculty members teach freshman courses. As there are primarily undergraduates on the main campus (the Law School is in downtown Tacoma), teaching is given top priority. Even in large introductory classes, professors are available outside of class for consultation. Many students and professors become friends, and it is not unusual to see them sharing a pint of Washington ale at the pub several blocks from campus or (for those under 21) a cup of coffee in the Student Union Building. All professors serve as advisors, though the quality of advising varies. Students report that some have long sessions with their mentors every semester but that other professors sign uncompleted registration forms and leave them outside the door.

Among the best departments are economics, politics and government, English, art history, Asian studies, astronomy, computer science, and biology. Puget Sound has science facilities which are the envy of larger research-oriented universities. Undergraduates (even non-science majors) have access to an electron microscope and Apollo computer with about 20 terminals. Students are encouraged to aid professors in their research and are sometimes published with their teachers. There are two microcomputer labs on campus that are free to all students, and feature Macintosh and IBM computers, most of which are connected to laser printers. These labs are popular with younger students who use them to write papers and older students who use them to write resumés.

The major political voice on campus, predictably, is left-liberal in orientation. The campus newspaper and student activists give the intellectual cause of the day, be it disinvestment in South Africa (big a few years ago) or unconditional funding of the arts (popular now), passionate and informed advocacy. Occasionally, activists will over-

DISTRIBUTION OF UNDERGRADUATE AID
1989–90 School Year

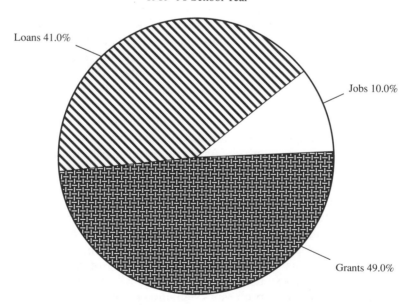

Loans 41.0%

Jobs 10.0%

Grants 49.0%

Source: The College Entrance Examination Board, 1990

step the bounds of reasoned debate. (In 1989, vandals plastered "CIA KILLS" on many campus buildings.) The student paper, on those rare occasions when it allows a "conservative" access to its pages, will then turn around and resume the chant of racism, sexism, or even fascism.

Even so, there is nonetheless a conservatism among the students, but it is more temperamental than ideological. For the predominant student interest at Puget Sound is still to get a "practical" education and to prepare for the "real world." Although 68 percent of students are liberal arts majors, many are business majors, and their education consists of such popular courses as "Money and Banking" and "Financial Accounting." Learning for its own sake, they believe, is a waste of time.

The city of Tacoma (population 200,000) boasts a fine symphony, a professional theater, a large shopping mall, a minor league baseball franchise, and a professional soccer team. The Tacoma Dome regularly hosts the major concerts in the Pacific Northwest featuring such acts as Bill Cosby, Bruce Springsteen, and Billy Joel. Tacoma is only 40 minutes from Seattle (metro-population 2.5 million), and is close to many ski resorts, the Olympic National Park, and the Pacific Ocean. On campus, students can take advantage of a museum of natural history, a fine art gallery, and theaters; shopping is within walking distance. The Student Union (ASUPS) sponsors campus films, as well as dances, lectures, and performances by internationally recognized performers.

Students are required to live on campus during their freshman year, either in dormitories or one of several A-frames and chalets. Following this, they may move into Greek houses, campus-owned houses, "theme" houses, or apartments farther from school. There are always several dormitory rooms left open to upperclassmen, but these are extremely hard to come by. Some dorms are coed by room, some by floor, and there is one all-female dormitory. It is usually wise for a freshman, early in the second semester, to begin thinking about housing for the following year, as it is frequently difficult to qualify (in the lottery system) for a campus-owned house. Theme houses include foreign language houses and an honors house, where some in the program live together.

Fraternities and sororities play an important role on campus. There are six national fraternities and six national sororities which compete for members twice a year (though rush for incoming freshmen is deferred until the spring). These organizations, to which more than a third of the student body belongs, are major forces in campus leadership and philanthropy. All houses are owned by the university, and thus are strictly regulated. Most students get along, and there is no intense rivalry among Greeks (except during rush), nor between Greeks and independents. Fraternity parties are typically open to all students before midnight and there is a congeniality among Greeks and their guests unmatched by many larger Greek systems.

Alcohol can usually be obtained regardless of student age, though state law is generally well enforced in the dormitories. An awareness (made keener by accidents on other campuses) exists of the dangers of drinking and fraternities require automobile keys to be left at the door. In addition, certain members remain sober and alert for instances of harassment. Intoxicated people are frequently escorted home from fraternity houses if they become too obnoxious and females are always escorted home—either by sober fraternity members or by the 24-hour campus security force. Drugs are more a problem off campus than on, and while they are certainly used, they are frowned upon by the majority of students. Indeed, tobacco smoking is not even allowed in most private fraternity and sorority rooms, though it is permitted in private dorm rooms.

Attracting minority students has been a new priority of the UPS office of admissions. Heavy recruiting is only part of the effort. Some students volunteer in the PUSH/EXCEL program in local Tacoma schools. There has been talk of a required course in Afro-American studies and of racial quotas in hiring of faculty. Such proposals are not considered radical at a university with a "Feminist Research Seminar" and a dean of students who proposed, following Berkeley's lead, limiting dialogue by punishing those students *accused* of speech considered "insensitive"—by him, it is supposed. For all this, UPS is not yet in the forefront of such efforts. Because political correctness has come to Tacoma later than to other places, UPS may be able to learn that such "initiatives" promote far more divisiveness than tolerance.

Overall, however, the University of Puget Sound is an institution with considerable potential. It is trying to retain a commitment to traditional educational standards even as it feels it must bend to the powerful corrosive trends now loose in the academic world. Which way UPS goes may depend upon the strength of leadership summoned up by President Phibbs or his successor.

Rhodes College

Dean of Admissions and Financial Aid, Rhodes College
2000 North Parkway, Memphis, TN 38112
(901) 726-3700, (800) 238-6788

Type: Private and Protestant

Students:
1,386 undergraduates
  636 men
  750 women

Applications:
Priority date: February 1
66% of applicants accepted

	Applied	Accepted	Enrolled
men	913	577	166
women	1,064	735	206

SAT or ACT required
  Score reported by: February 1
  Mid 50% of freshman scores:
    SAT-Math   580–670
    SAT-Verbal 530–630

Costs and Aid

Tuition & fees	$11,630
Room and Board	4,280

Scholarships:
Academic	Yes
Athletic	No
Minority	Yes

Financial Aid:
Freshmen	70%
Upperclassmen	67%

Library:	145,044 titles
ROTC:	Yes
Study Abroad:	Yes

If you are not familiar with Rhodes College, perhaps you have heard of Clarksville, Montgomery Masonic, Stewart, or Southwestern. These were all earlier names of present-day Rhodes, which was last renamed in 1984 (in honor of its then most recent president). In its new guise, the college—which was founded in 1848 and is affiliated with the Presbyterian Church—has risen rapidly in the rankings of small, regional schools and appears about to don a national reputation for excellence.

Although the college is small (1,400 students), it has managed to attract a faculty of distinction. Ninety-six percent hold terminal degrees in their field, which is on a par with the most prestigious institutions in the country, and the average class size is 17. All courses are taught by professors, not teaching assistants.

On the student side, about 80 percent of Rhodes freshmen ranked in the top fifth of their high school classes. The college has produced a number of Fulbright Scholars and National Science Fellows in the last decade. In recent years, the acceptance rate of Rhodes applicants to medical schools has consistently topped 90 percent; to schools of law, dentistry, business, and international studies nearly 100 percent. Once graduated, Rhodes alumni remain loyal to their alma mater and have tripled their annual giving during the last 10 years, thus enabling the school to update its plant and increase financial aid.

Sited in a residential section of Memphis and often described as looking just like an English village, the compact, 100-acre campus is dotted with neo-Gothic buildings made of slate and stone, and smothered in ivy. Thirteen of them are listed in the National Register of Historic Places. The original architect also designed the Wellesley campus and a quadrangle at Princeton. Medieval on the outside, these buildings are modern inside, with the latest in scientific and computer equipment. The college also boasts a large telescope, electron microscopes, and an art gallery. Although its library is small, students have access to the Memphis libraries with more than 1.5 million volumes.

Rhodes awards no advanced degrees, concentrating its efforts exclusively on undergraduate education. One hundred and twelve semester hours are mandatory for the bachelor's degree. There are no remedial courses. Distribution requirements in the humanities include one of these two imaginative and unusual alternatives: a four-semester course called "The Search for Values in the Light of Western History and Religion"; or, "Life Then and Now," also consisting of four semester-long courses.

In the first year of the "Search for Values" program, students study ancient history and cultures, including the Mesopotamian, Greek, Roman, Hebrew, and early Christian. In the second year, they concentrate on the influence these peoples had on the institutions and ethical and moral values of later times. The program is interdisciplinary and offers a selection of courses from the departments of religious studies, history, philosophy, and literature.

For students opting for the "Life Then and Now" series, the focus is narrower. The first year zeros in on the Judeo-Christian tradition as developed in the Old and New Testaments; during the second, the lens opens wider to include the subsequent history of that tradition, culminating in contemporary views of its relevance. Both "Search" and "Life" employ many original texts in translation.

Further distribution requirements also include an English writing course to be taken in the freshman year by those not exempted; nine further hours in the humanities; nine hours in the natural sciences, including three in a laboratory course; nine hours in the social sciences; and six in the fine arts. An easily-met foreign language require-

TUITION AND FEES INCREASE
Average Increase/Year: Private = 11.15%, Rhodes = 10.67%

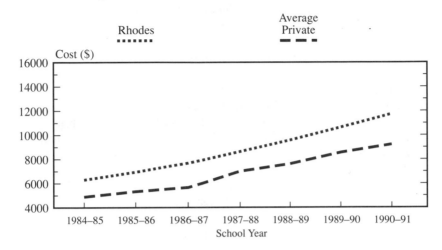

Source: The College Entrance Examination Board

ment and three half-semester courses in physical education must also be achieved. There are honors programs in all departments.

Rhodes draws its students primarily from the South, but 63 percent are from out of state, with a smattering of foreign students from countries all over the world. Less than 10 percent are minorities, and around 70 percent are Protestant. Most have traditional, middle-class attitudes. Students are generally more interested in their own concerns than in national and campus politics or the rights of certain groups.

The college does not have an affirmative action program and maintains the same admissions standards for all. Nor does it maintain departments of women's or ethnic studies. But Rhodes covers these bases with such courses as "Racial and Ethnic Minorities," "Peoples of Africa," "Peoples of South America," "Peoples of the Pacific," "Power and Prestige in Non-Western Societies," "Introduction to Afro-American History," "The Civil Rights Movement," "Native American History," "Women in American History," and "Gender and Society." There is a Black Students Association, which whites are encouraged to join.

Rhodes is governed by an honor code most students take for granted. It is so much a part of campus life that professors regularly leave the classroom when they administer exams. An elected Honor Council maintains the system and disciplines offenders. The Student Assembly represents student concerns and needs to the faculty and administration. A partly elected body, the Social Regulations Council, governs social and moral conduct on campus and, like the Honor Council, is empowered to impose penalties for violations of social legislation, which it initiates.

When they snap the books shut, most Rhodes undergraduates carry them back to comfortable residential halls. There is room for approximately 80 percent to live in campus housing, which is single-sex. New residences have recently been added, including a cluster of townhouses for those with special interests, like foreign languages. Still, accommodation is currently guaranteed for the first two years only and awarded to upperclassmen by lottery. Off-campus housing is reasonably priced but leaves some students feeling left out of the campus scene.

About 65 percent of the student body belong to six national

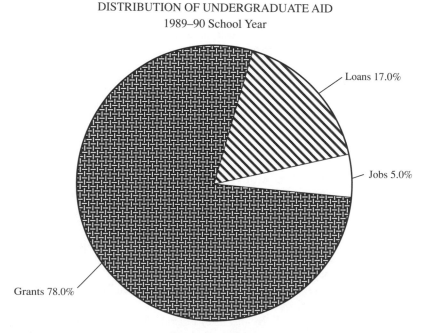

DISTRIBUTION OF UNDERGRADUATE AID
1989–90 School Year

Loans 17.0%

Jobs 5.0%

Grants 78.0%

Source: The College Entrance Examination Board, 1990

fraternities and six national sororities, around which social life revolves—although members do not live in the Greek houses. Drinking
tends to be heavy, though drug use is no problem. Most students seem
to enjoy campus life, so they don't make a mad dash for the exits on
the weekends, except to drop into Memphis watering holes or picnic
on the banks of the Mississippi. On campus, more than 50 organizations vie for student participation, with the Briggs Student Center a
common meeting ground for many. Sports, however, are only average
at Rhodes; the college fields eight men's and five women's intercollegiate teams, plus several intramural leagues, including splashy, coed
water polo.

Underneath its soft Southern way of life, Rhodes seems motivated
by a harder purpose that transcends mere academic excellence. The
college unequivocally declares that "Christian commitment and church
relationship are more than assent to a set of vague or sentimental
emotions. Ours is a view of existence and reality based upon faith in
God as creator, sustainer and redeemer of life. It recognizes that the
fear of God is the beginning of wisdom and that truth is God's self-
revelation." Whether or not he sees the same vision, the questing
student can obtain a superb education at Rhodes College.

Rice University

Director of Admissions, Rice University
P.O. Box 1892, Houston, TX 77251 (800) 527-6957

Type: Private and Secular			**Costs and Aid:**	
			Tuition & fees	$7,150
Students:			Room and Board	4,600
2,741 undergraduates			Scholarships:	
1,652 men			Academic	Yes
1,089 women			Athletic	Yes
1,286 graduate students			Minority	No
Applications:			Financial Aid:	
Closing date: January 2			Freshmen	85%
24% of applicants accepted			Upperclassmen	80%
Applied	*Accepted*	*Enrolled*		
5,219	1,256	615	**Library:**	1,500,000 titles
SAT required				
Score reported by: March 1			**ROTC:**	Yes
Mid 50% of freshman scores:			**Study Abroad:**	Yes
SAT-Math	640–750		**Percentage of courses that can**	
SAT-Verbal	570–690		**be used to fulfill distribution**	
			requirements:	52.3

Although born in 1912—which makes it a relative latecomer to the academic world—Rice University matured so rapidly that it has charged ahead of its more venerable collegiate cousins and marched steadily into the front ranks of American higher education.

Established as the Rice Institute by a bequest from oil tycoon William Marsh Rice, the fledgling college quickly earned a reputation for excellence in science before concentrating on the humanities. Today it has one graduate school, the Jesse Jones Graduate School of Administration, and departments of graduate studies in Engineering, the Natural Sciences, the Social Sciences, Architecture, and the Humanities. Of its 4,000 students 2,700 are undergraduates, who enter Rice in one of five divisions (there is no single undergraduate liberal arts unit): Engineering, Architecture, Music, Natural Sciences, and Academic, which is Rice's catchall for English, the humanities, foreign languages, and the social sciences. About 1,300 students matriculate in the natural sciences and academic divisions.

In accordance with the vision of its founder, Rice was influenced by the three institutions he admired most—New York's progressive,

297

tuition-free Cooper Union for the Advancement of Science and Art, Princeton University, and England's Oxford University. Although no longer tuition-free due to escalating costs, Rice has managed to retain deep in the heart of Texas both the intimate "clubby" atmosphere of Princeton and Oxford's system of residential colleges.

General Announcements, 1990–91:
Sociology 395—Feminist Social Thought
Professor Elizabeth Long

"Feminist Theory as critique and reconstruction—from Wollstonecraft, Mill, and Simone de Beauvoir to contemporary debates and equity, difference, knowledge, sexuality, and power." (fulfills a distribution requirement)

Sociology 463—Power and Culture in Contemporary Social Theory
Professor Long

"Marxist and poststructuralist cultural criticism: elite vs. popular or 'mas', domination and resistance, cultural capital and imperialism, ideology and the construction of subjectivity. We will consider Williams, Hall, Bourdieu, Foucault, Robinson. Not offered 1990–91."

The colleges are eight—Baker (named after Secretary of State James Baker's grandfather), Brown, Hanszen, Jones, Lovett, Richardson, Wiess, and Will Rice. Students are assigned to colleges before they arrive and join a small community which includes faculty members and administrators as well as alumni. The colleges also recruit distinguished business and professional leaders to become "Community Associates." They are invited to dine and talk to students about life in the real world. President George Bush is an associate of Lovett College, but students report that he hasn't been to a dinner in at least a dozen years.

The colleges are self-governing and organize their own parties and cultural events. They are all coed and comfortable, but each has developed its own distinctive character. Although many students choose to live off campus for one of the three upperclass years, they remain loyal to their colleges and participate in their social events.

Academically, Rice has put in place a complicated system of general education requirements, which combine core courses and the more usual distribution requirements. The underlying principle is that

TUITION AND FEES INCREASE
Average Increase/Year: Private = 11.15%, Rice = 9.77%

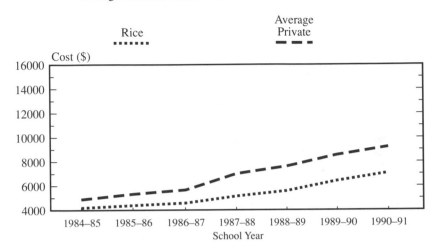

Source: The College Entrance Examination Board

to be broadly educated students need to take courses in fields outside their own areas of specialization. Therefore, natural science and engineering majors must take two semesters of a prescribed "Foundation" course in the humanities and one semester in the social sciences; academic majors, on the other hand, must take a Foundation course only in the natural sciences. (Math may be substituted.) Music and architecture majors must take the Foundations in all three areas.

In total, all students are required to take four courses in each of three areas—the humanities, the arts, and foreign languages; the social sciences; mathematics and the natural sciences. They may subtract the Foundation courses from the total number required in the relevant area. The non-Foundation courses must be chosen from an approved list; students have all four years to complete the general education requirements. Candidates for the Bachelor of Arts degree must pass a minimum of 120 semester hours to graduate, while Bachelor of Science hopefuls need at least 134.

Academic integrity at Rice is governed by an honor system administered by a student council whose members are elected annually. The system has been in place since 1916 and remains essentially unchanged. Generally respected by students, it allows examinations to be taken without faculty supervision; some cheating does occur, but it is not widespread.

Faculty-student relations are warm. Students have two faculty advisors during the freshman and sophomore years, as well as student mentors. Professors regularly dine with students in the colleges and attend social events. Sometimes they also provide serious students with research opportunities. Class sizes range from large lectures to small seminars, and the quality of teaching is considered good. Not many teaching assistants are employed, which is unusual in a research university.

Most departments at Rice are strong, but the natural sciences are outstanding, particularly biochemistry, which benefits from the proximity of the nearby Houston Medical Center. History and philosophy, both taught with due respect for Western civilization, are excellent, as are Russian and the Slavic languages. English is also highly rated, although it is being rapidly infiltrated by doctrinaire feminists.

Examples of politically correct courses at Rice include "Old

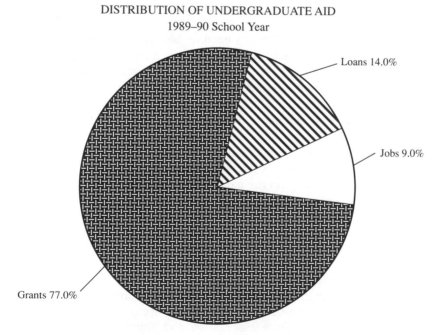

DISTRIBUTION OF UNDERGRADUATE AID
1989–90 School Year

Loans 14.0%

Jobs 9.0%

Grants 77.0%

Source: The College Entrance Examination Board, 1990

English: Gender and Power in Translation" (ancient texts include the epic poem *Beowulf*); "Rethinking Western Tradition," and "Colonial and Postcolonial Discourse," which sounds harmless enough until you read its description which states, accusingly, that the course will cover, "one of the most important theoretical issues in the study of Third World peoples, namely how Europeans and Americans have created definitions of who these people are and how they behave by virtue not of their systems of knowledge but ours."

Although there is no academic mandate to study non-Western cultures, and no required diversity/sensitivity orientation program, Rice says that the humanities and social science Foundation courses are geared to include "a wide variety of views." Outside the classroom, the university has approved a cultural diversity week held for the first time in the spring of 1991 and intended to be an annual event. Feminists and radicals tend to congregate around the Center for Cultural Studies, which was formed in 1987 for interdisciplinary research, and "to provide a cross-cultural vehicle for the intellectual study of foreign cultures." Other special-interest organizations include the Black Student Union, the Hispanic Association for Cultural Education, and the Chinese Student Union. Campus politics are usually moderate, however, and the students apathetic except for a small minority of strident left-wing activists. As one student succinctly said, "This is not a Northeastern school."

Almost half the students hail from Texas, and many of the rest come from the Southwest. Nearly all states are represented along with about 30 foreign countries; approximately 18 percent of students are minorities. Although Rice has always been coeducational, the school matriculates half again as many men as women, perhaps because of its reputation for excellence in science.

Unusual for such a school, Rice's President George Rupp is a theologian. Before he assumed office in 1985, he served as dean of the Harvard Divinity School. An increasingly controversial figure, Rupp caused a flap in 1991 during a search to replace a professor about to retire from the religious studies department. A group of faculty protested against what they saw as the president's effort to recruit a multiculturalist who would minimize the intellectual heritage of the Western tradition. The administration denied the charge. It is interesting to note, however, that in his book, *Existentialism and Zen: Religion in a Pluralistic World,* Rupp declared, "The most fundamental challenge we face is to criticize the pervasive and corrosive individualism of our prevailing culture." In another work, *Commitment and Com-*

munity, he said, "As we move increasingly toward an integrated planetary culture, we must . . . press for policies that protect and further the interests of the Third World."

The Third World is definitely not a burning issue for most Rice students, who are much more interested in life closer to home. When not worrying about grades, graduate school, or jobs, they relax in their colleges with beer, pretzels, and loud music. (Sororities and fraternities are forbidden.) They also go to a lot of movies. Otherwise campus social life is not particularly scintillating, though Houston is so close (four miles) that it is almost an extension of the university. Fortunately, neither drink nor drugs are a problem, and students say they feel safe on campus.

The 300-acre campus is pancake-flat but lovely with its Spanish-style, red-roofed architecture and 4,000 trees. (Somebody counted.) There are 200 extracurricular organizations to choose from, plus seven intercollegiate sports for men and six for women. Intercollegiate intramurals are very popular, as are the Gulf beaches less than an hour away. Facilities include the usual playing fields, courts, and a swimming pool, plus a 72,000-seat football stadium—but the team isn't much to cheer about.

Rice itself rates at least two cheers. Its academics and faculty are first class, and its students reasonably serious about taking advantage of both. If creeping political correctness doesn't spread any farther, Rice is likely to continue to offer a solid foundation in the liberal arts.

Rutgers University

Assistant Vice President for
University Undergraduate Admissions
Rutgers—The State University of New Jersey: Rutgers College
P.O. Box 2101, New Brunswick, NJ 08903-2101 (908) 932-3770

Type: Public

Students: (Rutgers College)
8,366 undergraduates
  4,333 men
  4,033 women

Applications:
Closing date: January 15
43% of applicants accepted

	Applied	Accepted	Enrolled
men	6,875	2,943	841
women	7,461	3,205	826

SAT or ACT required
  Score reported by: January 15
  Mid 50% of freshman scores:
    SAT-Math   540–670
    SAT-Verbal 470–600

Costs and Aid:

Tuition & fees:	
In state	$3,430
Out of state	6,390
Room and Board	3,830

Scholarships:	
Academic	Yes
Athletic	Yes
Minority	Yes

Financial Aid:	
Freshmen	79%
Upperclassmen	51%

Library: 3,129,861 volumes
(Rutgers University)

ROTC: Yes
Study Abroad: Yes

Rutgers, the State University of New Jersey, now ranks as one of the nation's major public systems with 47,000 students on three campuses incorporating 13 undergraduate colleges, 11 graduate schools, and two offering both graduate and undergraduate degrees. It all began in 1766 with the establishment of small, private Queens College, one of only a handful chartered before the Revolutionary War. Queens, a classical liberal arts institution, opened its doors in 1771 with one instructor, one sophomore, and a few freshmen. In 1825, the college was renamed to honor a former trustee and Revolutionary War veteran, Colonel Henry Rutgers.

Throughout the 19th century, Rutgers maintained its strong, classical academic traditions even while other colleges were integrating vocational studies. In 1864, Rutgers became the land grant college of New Jersey. After the Civil War, the college president, Merrill Edwards Gates, stoutly maintained that the American college is "designed to give a liberal education, not to train specialists." However,

303

by 1900 Rutgers had begun to fill the vacuum that existed due to the lack of a state university. Enrollment, state grants, and programs all proliferated. In 1924, the college achieved university status; by 1956, the state legislature had designated it the State University of New Jersey.

In the process of expansion, Rutgers lost much of its identity as a tightly integrated, classical college. Its history since the turn of the century has been one of ongoing tension between that tradition and the college's evolving role as New Jersey's primary institution of higher learning in the practical as well as the liberal arts. More recently and more dangerously, Rutgers has been plagued with tension between the supporters of traditional Western values and the revolutionaries who seek to overturn them.

Undergraduate Catalog, 1989–1991:
Africana Studies 413—Colonialism and Neocolonialism

"Political and economic aspects of colonialism. Colonized mind and behavior as portrayed by such authors as Mannoni, Balandier, Memmi, and Fanon. Neocolonialism as a technique of control."

Today, Rutgers College is one of nine undergraduate schools on the flagship New Brunswick campus. Five of them are professional: Cook College, the land grant institution specializing in agricultural, environmental and life sciences; the Mason Gross School of the Arts (dance, music, theater, visual arts); the highly regarded College of Engineering; the College of Pharmacy; and the two-year, upper-division School of Business.

Besides Rutgers College itself, there are three liberal arts schools: Douglass College, founded in 1918 and now the largest women's college in the United States with 3,400 students; Livingston College, established in 1969 with the motto "Strength through Diversity"; and University College, started in 1934 and offering adult education. In addition, there is a large unit, the Faculty of Arts and Sciences, which is responsible for most of the liberal arts programs offered in all four liberal arts colleges. Students enrolled in one of these may take courses in another, as well as in the professional schools.

Rutgers College, the direct descendant of Queen's College, presently matriculates approximately 8,350 men and women and is the largest residential college in the university. Operating on the semester

TUITION AND FEES INCREASE
Average Increase/Year: Public = 8.30%, Rutgers C. = 10.41%

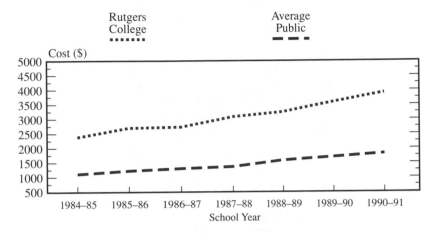

Source: The College Entrance Examination Board

system, the school requires a minimum of 120 credits for graduation. To complete the general education requirement, candidates must take two semester-long expository writing courses from a designated list, as well as one course in mathematics, plus a second in math, computer science, statistics, or logic. They must also complete two courses in any subject in each of three areas: the humanities; the social sciences; the natural sciences. Finally—although there is no Western civilization requirement—students must select one course about the non-Western world from a designated list. Rutgers "recommends" that students establish proficiency in a foreign language but does not demand it. Lab courses are not required to satisfy the natural science requirement. In addition to the general education and major programs, students must declare and complete requirements for a minor.

A General Honors Program is open by invitation only to selected freshmen, who participate thereafter in honors seminars and special lectures and discussions. They go on to complete departmental honors requirements. Some of the topics covered in the program include "The Quest for Peace and the Limitation of War," and "Racism as a Literary and Scientific Phenomenon."

Outstanding seniors may apply for the Henry Rutgers Scholars

Program, which offers opportunities for independent research. Rutgers takes pride in what it calls a "tailor-made education," personalized to suit the interests of the student. To that end, the university offers five-year dual degree programs (e.g., a B.A. in a liberal arts field combined with a B.S. in engineering), and encourages double majors, indepen-dent study options, and the creation of interdepartmental majors.

An advisory program exists, but does not seem to be much utilized by students; professors are generally amenable to giving advice if asked, but the general attitude is that college students are adults who should be able to assume personal responsibility for sorting out and meeting requirements. Students retort that the administration itself needs to take more responsibility, mainly for simplifying cumbersome registration procedures unaffectionately dubbed the "R.U. Screw."

Outstanding departments are generally reckoned to be archeology, history, religion, math, chemistry, psychology, and political science. The political science department boasts Professor Benjamin Barber, a nationally known academic and leading proponent of a community

DISTRIBUTION OF UNDERGRADUATE AID
1989–90 School Year (Rutgers College)

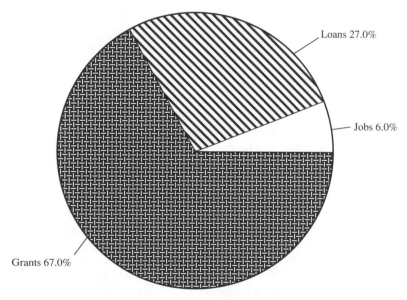

Loans 27.0%

Jobs 6.0%

Grants 67.0%

Source: The College Entrance Examination Board, 1990

service requirement in the university (a program that has attracted the attention of President Bush). The psychology department encourages students to contribute regularly to research projects and credits them with co-authorship in scientific journals. The biology department luxuriates in a 350-acre ecological preserve, also used for birdwatching. On a more political note, the English department is heavily influenced by feminists and deconstructionists. Feminist influence also extends beyond the official curriculum; in 1991, Rutgers students were invited to attend a scintillating program entitled "Feminist Readings in Japanese Comic Books."

Outside the classroom, politics of any kind usually fail to raise the pulse rates of a majority of students; most are just not very interested. The organizations that do get the most attention tend to have the smallest memberships and the most bizarre agendas. For example, the Committee in Solidarity with the People of El Salvador (CISPES)—membership about 12—was investigated by the FBI for sending out counterfeit documents, i.e., fake draft notices, which they hoped would generate anti-government sentiment among the surprised recipients.

Besides CISPES, there are nearly 300 extracurricular groups and organizations supported by students from all the New Brunswick colleges. Rutgers College recognizes more than 100 of these, including a number catering to minority interests. There are several clubs for blacks, at least one for homosexuals, as well as a veritable United Nations of organizations for Armenians, Chinese, Japanese, Pakistanis, Filipinos, Poles, Portuguese and Brazilians, Koreans, Haitians, Indians, West Indians, Muslims, and supporters of a Palestinian homeland. As you would expect, these clubs reflect the disparate nature of the student body, which is about 30 percent minority (10 percent are Asian). While more than 90 percent of students are from New Jersey, they also come from all the other states and many countries.

Although Rutgers proudly embraces all kinds of students, its allegiance to equal opportunity has evolved into a pattern of promoting diversity for its own sake. This has resulted in intolerance of those who value individual rather than group rights, as well as in a punitive attitude toward those deemed "insensitive."

In 1990, a student was convicted of insensitive speech and sentenced to 50 hours of community service for calling another student a homosexual. The "victim" was his best friend, who was not a homosexual, but who didn't object, in this instance, to the label. The two students were in the adolescent habit of showing their affection by regularly trading friendly insults through notes tacked up on the message boards outside their rooms. The accuser was a third-party passerby, who saw and reported the indiscretion. The fact that the person to whom the remark was addressed had no objection was apparently a matter of indifference to the powers-that-be.

Intolerance in the classroom is another manifestation of the importance of toeing the politically correct line, which can include religious convictions. In one class, according to a student report, a professor and a student got into an argument about Christianity. The student objected when the professor said that Christianity is a "myth." The professor then told the student that he "ought not to be in this class" and ordered him not to speak out again for the duration of the course.

On a more secular note, it is perhaps worth mentioning that during the autumn of 1990, a Rutgers group hosted a convention of university students from across the country. They were the Young Communist League, a group not especially well known for its own toleration of diverse opinion.

Housing on the 2,800-acre campus accommodates almost 65 percent of students, is both single-sex and coed, comfortable, and inexpensive. Guaranteed for freshmen and available by lottery to upperclassmen, it includes freshmen dorms, honors and language houses, as well as Hispanic and "black experience" sections. The Rutgers campus is an attractive mix of ivy-colored brick and modern buildings connected to the other New Brunswick campuses by an excellent shuttle bus system.

Sports have had a long and honorable tradition at Rutgers, starting with the Rutgers-Princeton rivalry. The first intercollegiate football game ever played was between Rutgers and Princeton in 1876. As a result of the yearly competition, a vigorous rivalry emerged that lasted for nearly a century. Rutgers then decided to stop playing Ivy League teams in favor of "big-time" (Division I-A) football. Consequently, Rutgers gets trounced on a regular basis by national contenders like Michigan State, Penn State, and Syracuse. A lot of football fans miss the Princeton Tigers.

There are, however, bright spots in Rutgers sports programs. The men's soccer team is consistently ranked in the top five in the country. Further, the men's and women's basketball teams are very competitive, as are lacrosse and crew. There are 16 intercollegiate sports each for men and women, as well as 20 intramurals for men and 19 for women. Facilities include four gymnasiums, a pool, and the usual assortment of courts and playing fields. Most of the time, though, nothing seems to breathe new life into Rutgers's sagging school spirit, deflated by consistent losses since the shift into big-time athletics.

Social life isn't much better. In fact, it is poor and getting worse, but this doesn't affect the many students who go home on weekends. Outside the Greek system, which the administration discourages, there is not much to attract the average upperclassman. (Greeks account for only about 10 percent of the students, who belong to 32 fraternities and 15 sororities, mostly national.) All the local clubs and bars admit only 21-year-olds, and the nearest movie theater is beyond walking distance. Recent administrative guidelines may further curb the social life of upperclassmen. Tailgating parties have been forbidden at Homecoming football games and kegs will soon be banned at Greek events due to insurance policy restrictions as well as the administration's caution in the wake of alcohol-related deaths.

Fortunately, New York and Philadelphia are only as far away as the nearest train station, which is a three-minute walk from College Avenue. The big cities, each about an hour's ride, offer everything both head and heart could desire, although at a price. The San Janero Festival, an annual "happening" in New York's Little Italy, is a particularly popular event with Rutgers students. The major drawback about visiting either metropolis is the cost; students moan that getting there isn't cheap and that finding inexpensive food and entertainment is next to impossible.

Finding a solid liberal arts education at Rutgers College isn't yet as difficult as that, but it is getting harder. On the one hand, the state's much publicized budget problems have increased the university's temptation to go after lucrative research contracts at the expense of undergraduate instruction. On the other hand, multiculturalist dogma is establishing a toehold in the curriculum, while the study of Western civilization is gradually being weakened. Outside the classroom, politically correct attitudes are becoming *de rigueur*. So, there is a real danger that the proud liberal arts tradition of free inquiry at Rutgers College may go the way of the cherished Princeton football games to become just an echo of the past.

St. John's College—Annapolis

Director of Admissions, St. John's College
P.O. Box 1671, Annapolis, MD 21404 (301) 263-2371 ext.222

Type: Private and Secular

Students:
410 undergraduates
  242 men
  168 women
  50 graduates

Applications:
Priority date: March 1
SAT or ACT not required
  Mid 50% of freshman scores:
    SAT-Math   520–650
    SAT-Verbal 550–680

Costs and Aid

Tuition & Fees	$13,020
Room and Board	4,410
Scholarships:	
Academic	No
Athletic	No
Minority	No
Financial Aid:	
Freshmen	43%
Upperclassmen	48%
Library:	85,000 titles
ROTC:	No
Study Abroad:	No

St. John's College—Santa Fe

Director of Admissions, St. John's College
1160 Camino Cruz Blanca, Santa Fe, NM 87501
(505) 982-3691 ext.231, (800) 331-5232

Type: Private and Secular

Students:
409 undergraduates
  224 men full time
  185 women full time
  75 graduates

Applications:
Priority date: March 1
83% of applicants accepted

	Applied	Accepted	Enrolled
men	119	96	57
women	119	102	53

SAT or ACT not required
  Mid 50% of freshman scores:
    SAT-Math   520–650
    SAT-Verbal 550–660

Costs and Aid:

Tuition & fees	$13,020
Room and Board	4,410
Scholarships:	
Academic	No
Athletic	No
Minority	No
Financial Aid:	
Freshmen	78%
Upperclassmen	61%
Library:	52,600 titles
ROTC:	No
Study Abroad:	No

St. John's College—which has two campuses, in Annapolis, Maryland, and Santa Fe, New Mexico—offers an undergraduate education unique in this country today. While many so-called liberal arts colleges are turning away from the traditional canon and toward the academic relativism that assigns equal value to all cultures, St. John's continues to resist the winds of change and to hold aloft the standard of Western civilization.

This tiny college of about 400 students and 50 faculty on each campus stands alone in completely shunning textbook interpretations in favor of contemplating the Great Books themselves, sometimes in their original languages. All courses in these seminal works are mandatory for all four years, so there are no majors permitted and only two electives—a true core curriculum. As a result, after St. John's students earn the right to turn their tassels on graduation day, they walk away into their futures with a profound appreciation of the best of the West, past and present.

The third oldest college in the country, St. John's Annapolis was founded as King William's School in 1696, and was chartered under its present name in 1784. Early ties to the Episcopal Church have long been severed and the college has no religious affiliation despite its name. The Santa Fe campus is a 20th-century offshoot, established in 1964. Because course requirements and content are the same on both campuses, students may transfer freely between east and west—a plus factor for travel buffs.

During its first 150 years, the college functioned as a conventional liberal arts institution of its time, but in 1938 the Great Books program was created and initiated by President Stringfellow Barr and Dean Scott Buchanan, both associates of the University of Chicago's famous Robert Maynard Hutchins. Its theme involves reading and discussing the formational works of Western civilization in roughly chronological order, from the Greeks through the twentieth century.

The "Program," as the St. John's curriculum is known, is comprised entirely of the liberal arts, in the true and ancient sense of that now common and often-abused phrase. The original liberal arts were the *trivium* of grammar, rhetoric and logic, and the *quadrivium* of arithmetic, geometry, astronomy, and music. St. John's Dean Eva Brann writes in an essay on the liberal arts:

> these arts are traditionally called "liberal" for three reasons. First because they are taught to the free children of politically free parents, second because they liberate these youths from their dogmatic opinion, and third because they are done freely, without money-making in mind.

TUITION AND FEES INCREASE
Average Increase/Year: Private = 11.15%, St. John's = 7.87%

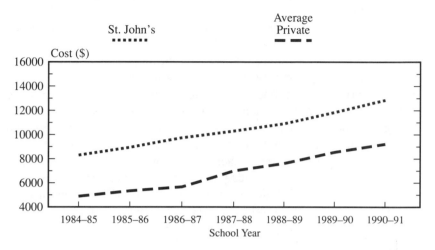

Source: The College Entrance Examination Board

Students at St. John's, or "Johnnies," take four courses each year. The requirements are: seminar (four years); laboratory science (three years); music (one year); language tutorial (two years each of French and ancient Greek); and mathematics tutorial (four years). In the seminar—the heart of the program—roughly 20 students guided by two faculty members read and discuss the philosophy and literature of the Western world. Freshmen engage the Greeks: Plato, Aristotle, Aeschylus, Sophocles, and Herodotus, among others; sophomores read medieval and Renaissance texts, including the Bible, Thomas Aquinas, Augustine, Martin Luther, Dante, and Shakespeare. Juniors grapple with the 17th and 18th centuries, including German, French, and English philosophers; seniors press forward into the 19th and 20th centuries, reading widely and examining Supreme Court cases and other political documents.

Tutorials follow the chronology of the seminar, so that while freshmen read the Greek philosophers in seminar, they study the Greek geometer Euclid in math class and learn to read ancient Greek in language class. In math, the program begins with Euclid and moves on to astronomers Ptolemy and Copernicus, returns to the geometry of conic sections with Apollonius, tackles the immense transition from geometry to algebra in Descartes, teaches calculus directly from Newton's *Principia,* and, in the senior year, concentrates on non-Euclidean geometry.

Lab science works similarly, though many of the original texts read are not finished works but "lab reports" or informal essays by early experimenters. Later, labs dealing with light, heat, and mechanics use the writings of Newton, Galileo, and Einstein. Students also read modern scientific books and journal articles on issues ranging from quantum atomic mechanics to molecular genetics. While undergraduates who might have majored in math or science elsewhere often find that St. John's fails to bring them to the cutting edge of these disciplines, the program does teach them how to read difficult primary sources and thoroughly grounds them in basic principles, as well as in the history of scientific development. In place of lab, sophomores study music in the tutorial—from Gregorian chant and Bach to Webern and Stravinsky—and learn piano and voice in the practicum. In Santa

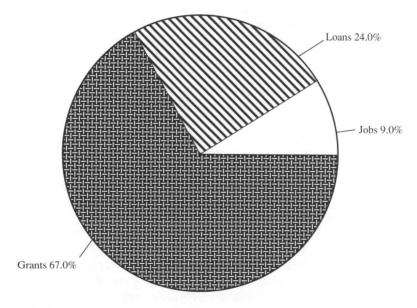

DISTRIBUTION OF UNDERGRADUATE AID
1989–90 School Year

Loans 24.0%

Jobs 9.0%

Grants 67.0%

Source: The College Entrance Examination Board, 1990

Fe, a visual-arts segment in which paintings and architecture are considered was recently added to the senior year program.

Those who at other colleges would be called professors at St. John's are tutors, an indication that they are considered not authorities but simply the most advanced students in the class. Tutors are expected to represent the ideal of Renaissance man by preparing themselves to teach all classes in the program. New tutors usually have all the freshman classes and work their way through the program with the students, sometimes approaching subjects for the first time with their pupils. Though there are obvious disadvantages to this system of non-specialization, it is the only practical way for St. John's, which considers all the disciplines to be closely interrelated and requires their study by all students for all four years. The advantages are also real: Tutors tend to remain excited about learning, communicating this to the students, and they avoid the burnout which often affects those who teach the same subject over and over again year after year.

Many of the faculty do, however, possess expertise in a given field when they arrive at St. John's, as approximately 60 percent on each campus hold doctoral degrees. During their SJC careers, tutors say goodbye to researching for status and promotion, because the college expects them to become full-time teachers (and students), basing tenure and promotion not on the number of publications they chalk up, but instead on their success in the classroom.

This dual role of learner/teacher seems to encourage faculty to become aware of and sympathetic to students' problems, because the intellectual problems, at least, are sometimes mutual. Faculty are almost always available to students and often attend their social functions, where philosophical talk spills over from the classroom. Tutors do give letter grades, but generally these are used for transfer purposes, graduate schools, and job applications. Many students never request to see their grades. Rather than long weeks of midterm and final exams, more relevant and informative work evaluation is done in "don rags," a term borrowed from Oxford University. The pupil and all his tutors gather around a table, where the latter discuss the student's progress in the third person as if he were not present. Following all the reports, the student has a chance to reply, defend himself, or ask for further clarification.

Examinations in the conventional sense don't exist; students are assessed orally (sessions are scheduled for 30 minutes but often last 60 to 90) or by their seminar essays, which they write at the end of each semester. An unusual feature of these efforts is that they involve no research into secondary sources but become, in effect, dialogues between the student and the author of the Great Book under scrutiny.

No transfer students are accepted at St. John's. All students begin as freshmen, and it is a remarkable indication of their dedication that 30 percent of the average freshman class have one, two, occasionally three years at another school, which they are willing to sacrifice to begin again at SJC. As a result, the freshman class has recently ranged in age from 15 to 43. This lends a richness to seminar discussions, which would be lacking with a group of 18-year-olds. Practically, it means that freshmen are allowed cars, off-campus housing, and all personal privileges of the other classes.

The lack of a traditional curriculum with a major field of study has not prevented recent Johnnies from gaining admission into reputable graduate schools and departments, including law, divinity, business, and even medicine—with one post-baccalaureate year of pre-med study. About 65 percent of SJC students undertake advanced degrees at some time in their lives.

Because of St. John's unusual academic program, the college tends to attract unusual students and faculty. They often become so wrapped up in their intellectual cocoons that they tend to pay little attention to what goes on in the outside world and seem immune to the political currents sweeping across so many American campuses.

The college has no racial or ethnic admission quotas, nor any affirmative action "goals," and minority students are, accordingly, the minority among applicants. There are, of course, no ethnic or women's studies, no militant minority caucuses, and no speech codes or "sensitivity" training. Johnnies demonstrate less frequently and spend less energy on outside "causes" than their counterparts at many other universities. As a general rule, the only time the college community shows a mild interest in the nation's affairs is during elections, when those who bother to vote, both faculty and students, tend to favor Democratic candidates.

Although limp-minded about the rest of the world, Johnnies often rev up when it comes to campus matters that directly affect them. In Annapolis, for example, two students recently led the college into the computer age by striking a deal to buy personal computers at large discounts on behalf of both the college and interested individuals. Self-starters also solicited alumni gifts to purchase new racing shells for the crew. In Santa Fe, after one student vandalized a campus fresco painted by a local Hispanic artist, others were stirred to write letters to the editor of the local paper and attend community meetings. The culprit was eventually identified and expelled from the college to almost everyone's satisfaction.

While academic structure, love of learning, and political apathy are common to both campuses, each does have its own distinctive character. After all, Annapolis and Santa Fe can hardly be more dissimilar and these differences affect campus life. In Annapolis, where sailing is a popular recreation, sporting activity centers on the water, and crew and croquet are the college's only intercollegiate sports. Students also enjoy tennis and intramural team sports. In Santa Fe, by contrast, where the 260-acre campus abuts a national forest high in the Sangre de Cristo mountains, hardy souls hike, rock-climb, take camping trips, and ski, as well as paddle their canoes. Fencing and soccer are the only intercollegiate athletic activities in Santa Fe, but many students join the college Search and Rescue unit, which trains regularly and is called out by the state police on emergency rescue missions several times a year. On a more exotic note, one dedicated tutor leads a group of early risers in Tai-chi exercises every morning at 6:30.

Organized social life on both campuses is limited, and fraternities and sororities are nonexistent. A not unexpected St. John's tradition features old-fashioned waltz parties, which everyone, East and West, seems to enjoy. In Annapolis, students sometimes escape to nearby Baltimore or Washington for a taste of city sophistication. In Santa Fe, the high life takes place in the wide open spaces, with many taking off to watch the colorful International Hot Air Balloon Festival in Albuquerque or to celebrate local Indian customs amid dancing and fireworks.

Although for most who choose it, a St. John's education sparks intellectual fireworks that can last a lifetime, for some the pyrotechnics fizzle. Due to the lack of rigorous examinations and formal grading criteria, the lazy and undisciplined can slide through nearly untouched by the Great Minds; due to the small size and homogeneity of the student body, the intellectually unmotivated don't learn outside the classroom, as they often do in other colleges, by rubbing elbows and exchanging ideas with a wide cross-section of Americans.

St. John's may offer the best undergraduate education in the nation, however, to the precious few who love learning with a passion and who believe, in the words of Cicero, that "pygmies placed on the shoulders of giants see more than the giants themselves."

Smith College

Director of Admission, Smith College
Garrison Hall, Northampton, MA 01063 (413) 585-2500

Type: Private and Secular		**Costs and Aid:**	
		Tuition & fees	$14,610
Students:		Room and Board	5,650
2,675 undergraduates			
all women		Scholarships:	
308 graduate students		Academic	No
(some men)		Athletic	No
		Minority	No
Applications:		Financial Aid:	
Closing date: January 15		Freshmen	60%
57% of applicants accepted		Upperclassmen	70%
Applied *Accepted* *Enrolled*			
women 2,453 1,409 615		**Library:**	600,000 titles
SAT or ACT accepted			
Score reported by: February 15		**ROTC:**	Yes
Mid 50% of freshman scores:		**Study Abroad:**	Yes
SAT-Math 560–660			
SAT-Verbal 530–640			

"You've come a long way, baby" might have been written about feminine and feminist Smith College, which was started in 1875 with a legacy from one of the first women's righters, Sophia Smith. Influenced by her clergyman, she envisioned an academic community that not only provided women with a first-class liberal arts education, but also maintained an atmosphere "pervaded by the Spirit of Evangelical Christian religion." More than a century later, many consider the education to be first class, but the evangelism has shifted from Christianity to a new secular religion called "Diversity."

Beginning with a minuscule 14 students, Smith's enrollment has now reached nearly 2,700, making it the largest private women's college in the United States and fiercely proud of that status. Undergraduates come from all 50 states and more than 50 foreign countries; almost 20 percent are minorities, and that percentage is growing.

"The Smith Design for Institutional Diversity," promulgated several years ago, declares the college's war on racism and goes on to explain that "Embracing diversity involves identifying and undoing conscious and unconscious expressions of racism that exist in American society. The clearest steps we are taking to overcome racism are

319

to define, implement and enforce a civil rights policy and to adopt an aggressive affirmative action policy.''

The grand design does not specify how the college plans to tackle ''unconscious'' expressions of racism (a word that also seems to encompass other ''oppressed'' groups like homosexuals and the handicapped, not to mention women in general), but it is certainly going after what it considers the conscious kind. In 1990, the Office of Student Affairs put out a document headed ''Definitions'' that tells students which vocabulary is appropriate to use about different groups. Subheadings are ''Factors of Oppression in General,'' ''Specific Manifestations of Oppression,'' ''Preferred Terms,'' and finally ''Names Self-chosen by Groups with a Mutual Identity.''

In the 1990–1991 College Bulletin:
Government 366a—Seminar: Ideology, Culture, and Politics
Professor Philip Green

''How are hierarchies of class, gender, and race maintained in a democratic society? How does the ruling class maintain its rule? Patterns of domination and resistance in everyday life, with emphasis on the role of the mass media, especially television and films, in the United States.''

Some of the terms under ''Specific Manifestations of Oppression'' include interesting new additions to the English language, all ending, of course, in ''ism.'' Here's a sample: ''*Ableism*—oppression of the differently abled by the temporarily abled; *Classism*—oppression of the working class and non-propertied by the upper and middle class; *Heterosexism*—oppression of those of sexual orientations other than heterosexual, such as gays, lesbians and bisexuals; this can take place by not acknowledging their existence; *Lookism*—the belief that appearance is an indicator of a person's value; the construction of a standard for beauty/attractiveness, and oppression through stereotypes and generalizations of both those who do not fit that standard and those who do.''

If the students are slow studies in learning the politically correct terminology, they may enroll in courses designed to instruct them. These are given not only in women's and Afro-American studies, but also in other departments such as art and philosophy. During the 1989–1990 academic year, the college established its Fund for a More Inclusive Curriculum, which sets aside $30,000 annually to ''encourage

TUITION AND FEES INCREASE
Average Increase/Year: Private = 11.15%, Smith = 7.94%

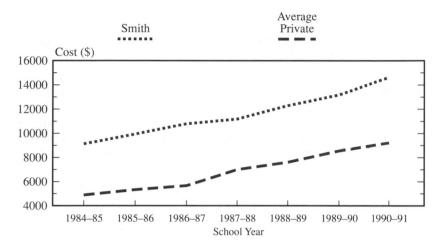

Source: The College Entrance Examination Board

the study of world cultures and American cultures beyond the traditional focus on Western Europe and white America." The money is given to professors to design new courses along these lines, or to expand existing ones. So far, the introductory course in what once was Western art history has been revamped to include African, American Indian, Asian, Islamic, Oceanic, and pre-Columbian art. Other new courses are the philosophy department's "Rights and Race," and the psychology department's *pièce de résistance*, "Psychology Through the Eyes of Minority Women Psychologists."

Diversity is not confined, however, to dogmatic pronouncements issued by the administration and some faculty; it is also encouraged by a plethora of student enclaves, which agitate for inclusion while practicing self-segregation. Some of them are: the Asian Students Association; EKTA (*South* Asian students); Korean Students at Smith; the Black Students Alliance; the Smith African Students Association; NOSOTRAS (Hispanic students), and the International Students Association. Last year they came together (for a change) in a week-long sit-in to demand the establishment of a multicultural center to replace previous space allotted in an administrative building. Protesting students accused the college of ignoring diversity on campus, taking minority students for granted, and failing to provide for their "needs."

When the college is not preoccupied with the demands of these and other groups—notably the very vocal lesbians for whom the college is becoming notorious—students often settle down to serious study. Although Smith has long since abandoned both a core curriculum and required courses of any kind except within the major, most Smithies manage to obtain a decent academic education. In general, they are not pre-professionally oriented in their course planning and tend to select a fairly wide range of electives. Most have a variety of interests outside their career goals and it is not uncommon for pre-med students to be English majors or math majors to complete a number of courses in the humanities.

Smith, which has only one graduate school, in social work, prides itself on being an undergraduate teaching institution. Professors are almost always accessible outside of class and encourage students to attend their office hours. Among the strongest departments are reli-

DISTRIBUTION OF UNDERGRADUATE AID
1989–90 School Year

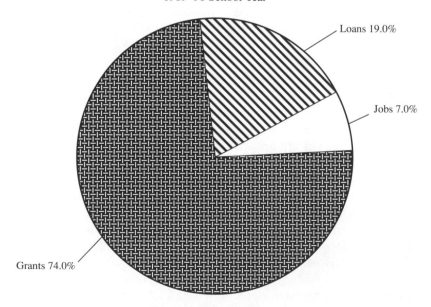

Loans 19.0%

Jobs 7.0%

Grants 74.0%

Source: The College Entrance Examination Board, 1990

gion, math, art, theater, and government. The science departments are solid but small, though this should change with the completion of the Bass Science Center, scheduled for 1991.

Smith is part of the Five College system which includes the University of Massachusetts, and Amherst, Hampshire, and Mount Holyoke Colleges. Students can cross-register for classes at any of these campuses after their first semester. Students cite UMass courses as an easy way to improve their GPA. A free bus service between campuses provides reliable transportation.

The Academic Honor Code looms large in Smith life. Signed by every student in the beginning of the year, it requires integrity in examination behavior, the use of the library and computer facilities, and in the preparation of course work. The code is taken seriously and infractions are weighed by a board of students and faculty. Cheating seems to be relatively rare. Students enjoy the code because it allows Smith to maintain a system of self-scheduled exams during a four-day period. The college is on a four-one-four month schedule. A January Interterm provides time to do research projects, to take "fun and frivolous" courses, or just to have a long Christmas vacation. No credit is granted for work done during that month.

Smith's geographic location on a small (125 acres) but attractive campus in a large town 85 miles from Boston tends to give some students itchy feet by junior year. More than a quarter of the junior class opt to go abroad, joining Smith-sponsored programs in Florence, Geneva, Paris, and Hamburg, or affiliating with those of other institutions elsewhere.

When in Northampton, students live in residence halls accommodating from 16 to 97 women. Each house has its own distinctive personality and contains members of all four classes, a popular system that quickly integrates freshmen. Every house has a living room and/ or study and most have their own dining rooms. Smith provides excellent meals, buffet-style, except on Tuesdays and Thursdays when they are served family-style. Unfortunately, due to recent budget cuts, the traditional Thursday candlelight dinners will no longer have linen napkins and tablecloths.

Despite being a women's college, social life at Smith is active. On weekends, individual houses give parties and provide music, beer, and snacks. Men from UMass, Amherst, and other New England colleges are almost always plentiful. On an average weekend, enough men turn up to make the college look coed. Room parties are common, and usually begin on Thursday nights. Although there is an explicit alcohol policy, it is not strictly enforced. The respect for privacy is greater than respect for the law. Head residents and security personnel will not enter individual rooms, except in unusual cases, so violations of the alcohol policy are usually ignored except for infractions occurring in public areas of the houses.

The Smith social scene is fairly inclusive. Anyone who wishes to take part in it is generally welcome. However, for those who dislike Smith parties, primarily because of their tendency to become meat markets, there are movies, lectures, and concerts sponsored by the Five Colleges, as well as quick trips to Amherst and UMass, less than 10 miles distant.

Sports facilities at Smith are excellent, including both indoor and outdoor tracks, two gyms, an indoor swimming pool and diving pool, tennis courts, weight rooms, and riding rings. In an anachronistic throwback to a gentler time, Smith even boasts a croquet lawn. In addition, scenic Paradise Pond, which is right in the middle of the campus, provides boating opportunities. There are 22 intercollegiate teams and a number of intramurals.

Every student is a part of the Student Government Association, which supports more than 50 clubs, organizations, and special-interest groups. The most influential groups on campus are the Lesbian-Bisexual Alliance, the Black Students Alliance, and the Asian Students Association. The local NOW chapter also is active. These groups often dictate college policy because they are loud and strident. Free speech is not encouraged on campus unless it touts the politically correct set of beliefs, so moderate students sometimes hesitate to express their views. Also, those who enter the college unsure of what they believe are often swept up by the fervor and excitement of the campus activists without understanding the actual issues. In other words, the student body as a whole is not so radical as it appears to outsiders.

The same cannot be said for the Student Government Association, which has taken measures to suppress groups with unpopular views. These measures were implemented after the chartering of the Pro-Life Alliance and a conservative journal, and stated, "Any organization or activity which takes one view or opinion on a multi-sided issue may not receive SGA support." Student response to these attempts at censorship has been largely negative and SGA policies should face strong opposition in the future.

When all is said, Smith still boasts a prestigious, Ivy League reputation, though the quality of its applicant pool has suffered since coeducation conquered the college scene in the 1960s. Nevertheless,

Smithies are regarded as intelligent, ambitious, and determined to succeed. Many of them have; Smith alumnae have made their professional and personal marks in many fields. Some of the most famous include Nancy Reagan, Barbara Bush (who left after freshman year to marry the future president), Gloria Steinem, Betty Friedan, and Julia Child. Graduates, who are scattered throughout the world, are loyal to their alma mater and helpful to other Smith women on both a personal and professional level. Smith's Career Development Office is also top-notch and very active on behalf of alumnae both at the beginning of and throughout their working lives.

Despite radical changes in its curriculum and its current obsession with diversity, Smith is still a college where women feel free to concentrate on academics instead of men, and profit intellectually and spiritually from their labors. So long, that is, as they take with a large grain of salt the advice of their 1990 commencement speaker, Helen Caldicott, a leader of the anti-nuclear movement, who said, "You, this generation of women, were born for one reason—to save the world. That is your task in life, and that is why you graduated from Smith."

University of the South

Director of Admissions, University of the South
Sewanee, TN 37375 (615) 598-1238

				Costs and Aid:	
Type: Private and Protestant				Tuition & fees	$12,720
Students:				Room and Board	3,310
1,075 undergraduates				Scholarships:	
565 men				Academic	Yes
510 women				Athletic	No
75 graduate students				Minority	No
Applications:				Financial Aid:	
Closing date: February 1				Freshmen	71%
71% of applicants accepted				Upperclassmen	65%
	Applied	*Accepted*	*Enrolled*		
men	660	443	173	**Library:**	261,613 titles
women	476	364	144		
SAT or ACT required				**ROTC:**	No
Score reported by: February 1				**Study Abroad:**	Yes
Mid 50% of freshman scores:					
SAT-Math	N/A				
SAT-Verbal	N/A				

Nestled on a quiet mountainside in the scenic high country of Tennessee, the University of the South remains today relatively untouched by the cyclone of change currently kicking up dust on other campuses. So far, Sewanee, which takes its nickname from the Indian word for the area, has succeeded in preserving both its avowed Christian heritage and the traditional tenets of a liberal arts education.

On its huge 10,000-acre campus, Sewanee educates a small coterie of approximately 1,100 men and women, who come from 42 states and 15 foreign countries with a large majority from the southern United States. After Sewanee, many of them go on to graduate school, mostly law, business, and medicine. Technically a university, the institution concentrates its efforts primarily on undergraduate education in the College of Arts and Sciences. Sewanee's only graduate division is the well-respected School of Theology, which awards advanced degrees and is also an accredited seminary of the Episcopal Church.

Although Sewanee encourages applications from students of all races and religions, most who matriculate are white and Christian (minorities, who benefit from affirmative action policies, now compose

327

only 3 percent of the student body). This religious homogeneity is a legacy from the university's founding in 1857 by leaders of the Episcopal Church, which still owns Sewanee. In a statement of purpose, the board of trustees has declared, "The University of the South is an institution of the Episcopal Church, existing for the education of all who come here in such disciplines as will increase knowledge, understanding, and wisdom, pursued in close community and in full freedom of inquiry, and enlightened by Christian faith, to the end that they may be prepared to search for truth, to seek justice for all, to preserve liberty under law, and to love and serve God and man."

Sewanee is proud not only of its clear-eyed educational and religious mission on this side of the Atlantic, but also of its ties with Great Britain, the mother country of both the Anglican tradition and American liberties. Alma mater of 22 Rhodes Scholars, an unusual record for a small liberal arts college, Sewanee began its love affair with England after the Civil War, which destroyed both the endowment and the physical plant of the brand new university. At that time, colleges of both Oxford and Cambridge Universities donated money to rebuild Sewanee as well as 1,800 books to begin a library, which is now housed in spacious new quarters, a section of which is open 24 hours a day.

Academically, Sewanee has always placed heavy emphasis on a broad-based, general education and has just revised its distribution requirements to be "more rigorous" and to "provide for study in greater depth." The new program will begin with the entering class in the fall of 1991. Thirty-two semester courses are required for graduation and the distribution requirements will comprise a third of them. Students will take four courses per semester, each worth four hours of credit.

The new requirements are four courses in the humanities, including one in English literature, one in fine arts, music or theater, one in a foreign language at the 300 level or higher, and one in philosophy or religion; two courses in the social sciences, including one in history and one in anthropology, economics, or political science; three in mathematics and the natural sciences, one being in math and two in the natural sciences (one with a lab); two writing-intensive courses; and two courses in physical education. Still in the planning stage is an additional requirement for a course dealing with the Judeo-Christian tradition, as well as a four-semester humanities program that would integrate the fine arts, history, literature, philosophy, and religion. The

TUITION AND FEES INCREASE
Average Increase/Year: Private = 11.15%, U. of the South = 8.53%

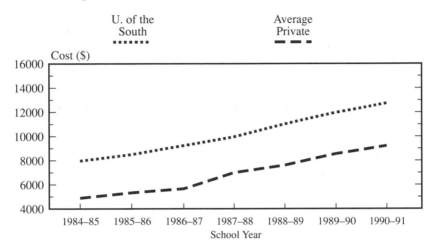

Source: The College Entrance Examination Board

---

latter would provide an alternative to several of the current distribution requirements.

Unlike many universities, Sewanee offers no remedial courses in English or mathematics, nor does it have a special honors program. To qualify for honors degrees in the normal program, students must attain a GPA of 3.25 for *cum laude,* 3.50 for *magna cum laude,* and 3.75 for *summa cum laude.* At last count, 18 percent of undergraduates earned honors.

Degree candidates choose majors from the usual departments, plus Third World studies, an interdepartmental program "designed to allow students to develop an understanding of the traditions, cultures and problems of Third World countries . . . defined as most of Asia, Africa, the Middle East and Latin America." There is also a course on Indians and blacks in America, as well as one on the Old South and another about politics in the South. No department is devoted to women's studies, although courses about women are offered in other departments, for example, the "Anthropology of Gender," and "Women in the U.S. Economy."

Both men and women at Sewanee are expected to abide by the university's century old honor code, which demands that "an honorable person shall not lie or cheat or steal." Going beyond that formulation, the administration admits that, "No code can adequately define honor. Honor is an ideal and an obligation; it subsists in the human spirit, and it lives in the relations between human beings. One can know honor without defining it." Nevertheless, the Honor Council, consisting of elected undergraduates from all four classes, does define honor in terms of the Sewanee community. The council holds trials, renders verdicts, and sometimes allows appeals. Guilty offenders may be put on probation, but the more usual penalty is suspension, or in extreme cases expulsion.

On the student government level, Sewanee's organization is bicameral and only partly elected. It consists of a Student Assembly and a revered group called the Order of the Gownsmen, which is an honorary society based on academic merit. The Gownsmen are privileged to wear flowing, black academic gowns around campus, as do the faculty, but the rest of the students must make do for classes with

DISTRIBUTION OF UNDERGRADUATE AID
1989–90 School Year

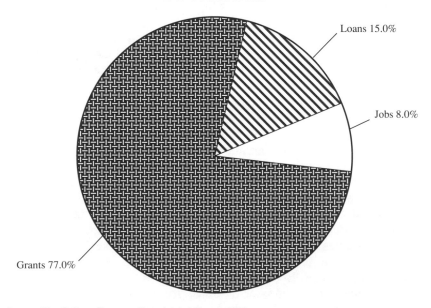

Loans 15.0%

Jobs 8.0%

Grants 77.0%

Source: The College Entrance Examination Board, 1990

dresses and skirts or jackets and ties. The prevailing look is definitely preppy, although there are a few mavericks dubbed "Earthies," who would have looked at home in the Berkeley of the 1960s.

Classes at Sewanee are small and intimate. Fully a third contain fewer than 11 students, and more than 70 percent have 20 or fewer. Student-faculty relations are generally ideal, with professors taking a personal as well as professional interest in their students.

Social life is largely self-contained on the Domain, as the rural campus is colloquially called, and often centers around sororities and fraternities, to which about 70 percent of the men and 74 percent of the women belong. There are 11 national fraternities and several local sororities, as well as a women's center. The Greeks *are* social life at Sewanee, though non-joiners are welcome at their parties, where alcohol flows faster than water. When students tire of each other and the great outdoors, they take off for Chattanooga or Nashville, which are respectively 50 and 100 miles distant.

Back on campus, Sewanee students participate in more than 85 clubs and organizations, which include a radio station and several publications. Many students also perform community service at the Sewanee Youth Center, which organizes educational and recreational programs for the neighboring village's youth.

Sports play a prominent part in college life, although Sewanee awards no athletic scholarships. Academic standards for athletes are the same as for other students. Sixty percent of its varsity players are graduated within four years compared to 68 percent of all undergraduates; 70 percent make it in five years compared to 75 percent of the whole student body. The school fields 17 varsity athletic teams, 9 for men and 8 for women. Intramurals are strong; a high 70 percent of all students participate in one or more of the athletic programs, with track, soccer, and tennis proving especially popular. There is also a lake nearby, as well as terrain suitable for more rugged activities like caving, rock-climbing, and rapelling.

On-campus housing at Sewanee is guaranteed for all four years (there is nowhere else close enough except the neighborhood caves). Coed dorms exist, though most are single-sex. There are language houses and married-student quarters. Honor students get to choose their dream quarters first.

Although Sewanee is working to attract a more varied student body as well as faculty and therefore has made a few adjustments to its curriculum, the school is still unwilling to compromise its Christian ethos and its respect for Western civilization. Due partly to its church affiliation and partly to its rural and rather isolated geographical position, the University of the South remains at the moment a safe and comfortable haven for traditionalists.

Stanford University

Dean of Undergraduate Admissions, Stanford University
Old Union, Second Floor, Stanford, CA 94305 (415) 723-2091

Type: Private and Secular				**Costs and Aid:**	
				Tuition & fees	$14,280
Students:				Room and Board	5,930
6,505 undergraduates					
3,675 men				Scholarships:	
2,830 women				Academic	No
6,849 graduate students				Athletic	Yes
				Minority	No
Applications:				Financial Aid:	
Closing date: December 15				Freshmen	68%
18% of applicants accepted				Upperclassmen	62%
	Applied	*Accepted*	*Enrolled*		
men	8,721	1,470	860	**Library:**	5,700,000 titles
women	6,191	1,156	707		
SAT or ACT required				**ROTC:**	Yes
Score reported by: January 1				**Study Abroad:**	Yes
Mid 50% of freshman scores:				**Percentage of courses that can**	
SAT-Math	660–750			**be used to fulfill distribution**	
SAT-Verbal	600–690			**requirements:**	15

In the years since World War II, Stanford has become a case study in university success. Today, it is rich, prominent, sought after, and, with Rice University of Houston, the only private university west of the Mississippi that can claim parity with its better-pedigreed Eastern rivals. Yet, like all parvenus, Stanford still seems afflicted with a combination of arrogance and defensiveness that betrays a lack of real self-assurance. For example, its strained efforts to be a cultural leader by toppling Western civilization from a modestly preferred place in the college curriculum led mostly to an embarrassing nationwide controversy.

It is now wading into societal ethics, with a ruling that homosexual couples should be permitted to live in married-student housing. And, in yet another humiliating episode, its president spent the spring of 1991 trying to explain how and why Stanford charged the U.S. government "overhead" for research contracts, which included maintenance of a grand piano, a cedar-lined closet, a 72-foot yacht, and fresh flowers for his house—practices which the Stanford community would condemn if they occurred within the hated military-industrial complex.

Still, Stanford understands what really matters; it decided to return about half a million dollars worth of such dubious charges to the federal government and is expected to take an annual cut in federal research payments of about $25 million, as the result of insistence by government auditors who claim that the university pads its expense accounts. Further, the school hired a celebrated Washington public relations firm to help it weather the storm.

But Stanford's real genius is revealed in a master stroke by its President Donald Kennedy, who has solemnly proclaimed that the institution must return to an emphasis on undergraduate teaching and de-emphasize faculty research and its pressure to publish or perish—all for the good of students, of course. However, this sea change will not occur on President Kennedy's watch. In the wake of the over-charge scandal, he has announced his resignation, effective in August 1992.

Stanford University Bulletin, Courses and Degrees, 1990–91:
Anthropology 114A.—The East-West Game
Professor Nabti

"First of a two-quarter sequence studying the relationship between Islam and the Shriners (a Masonic Organization) as expressed at the East-West Game at Stanford Stadium. Background information on Islam and on the Shriners, draft questionnaire, practice interview techniques."

Anthropology 114B.—The East-West Game
Professor Nabti

"Sequel to 114A. Students interview people at the East-West Game, input and analyze the data. Prerequisite: 114A."

Given the havoc the Stanford administration has already wrought—or consented to—with undergraduate instruction, one can only wonder what remains in store for this decade's students. Stanford has a large and growing number of distribution requirements (DRs), including Cultures, Ideas and Values (CIV), one or two quarters of freshman English, and eight other DRs. These include one course under the heading of "American Studies," which "should examine topics pertaining to the history, significance and consequences of racial, ethnic and/or religious diversity in the culture and society of the United States." Since the American requirement is brand new, nobody knows what courses will satisfy the requirement or what their content will be.

TUITION AND FEES INCREASE
Average Increase/Year: Private = 11.15%, Stanford = 6.65%

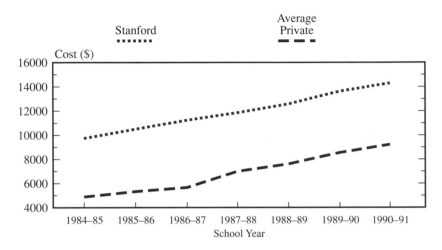

Source: The College Entrance Examination Board

Recently, Stanford replaced its old "Western Culture" require-ment, taken during the freshman year, with CIV in response to political demands that the curriculum be made less "Eurocentric." The change-over was accompanied by an intense and often vituperative debate, but actual alterations in the curriculum have not been as great as the commotion that surrounds them. A "track" called "Europe and the Americas" has been installed; works by "women and people of color" have been added; but the former Western-oriented reading lists have been more denounced than eliminated. The official line of the admin-istration is to have it both ways by reassuring traditionalists that the changes are meaningless while, at the same time, reassuring radicals that the university is committed to "multiculturalism."

In fact, there are eight CIV tracks, which can vary from "Struc-tured Liberal Education"—designed specifically for freshmen and pronounced "slee" in Stanfordspeak—to Values, Technology, Science and Society (VTSS), a program which can lead either to a B.A. or a B.S. and is widely viewed as a "gut." Unlike the others, SLE is selective and residentially based, which means all 82 SLE students live together in East Florence Moore Hall. SLE's intensity means that dorm life tends to revolve around it, yet many students claim that SLE is the best one-year humanities sequence at the university and most veterans of the program are very satisfied with it.

Still, students often complain about the sheer number of distribution requirements. They must take 10 courses drawn from 8 areas, making the curriculum far more eclectic than coherent. During the past decade, so it seems, the administration has decided that there is yet one more thing students should know, thus adding another item, ''non-Western culture'' or ''social progress,'' to the menu. There is a foreign language requirement, but most students with any foreign language exposure in high school easily pass out of it.

Among traditional departments, psychology, history, political science, and economics are of highest repute. There are several interdisciplinary programs. Human Biology, which combines biology, anthropology, and public policy, is very popular. Other interdisciplinaries include International Relations, Modern Thought and Literature, and American Studies (or Am Stud, vide the T-shirts worn by majors reading ''I Am Stud'').

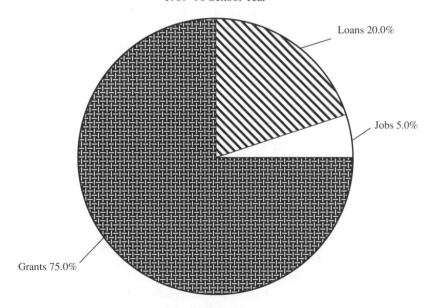

DISTRIBUTION OF UNDERGRADUATE AID
1989–90 School Year

Loans 20.0%

Jobs 5.0%

Grants 75.0%

Source: The College Entrance Examination Board, 1990

Though President Donald Kennedy has indeed announced that the university would place an increased emphasis on undergraduate teaching over research, the implications of this supposed shift will not be known for several years. Meanwhile, Stanford does go to great lengths to encourage *students* to do individual research. As in all larger universities, many, indeed most, faculty members seem remote and unapproachable, but most, too, are willing to help a student if asked. Student-faculty contact generally requires initiative from the student, even if that often proves nowhere near as hard as it seemed at first. If professors are eager for one-on-one contact with students, most appear too busy with their own projects to initiate it themselves.

For some reason, other aspects of life at Stanford have also become disputatious. Students, teachers, and administrators seem unwilling merely to enjoy the idyllic surroundings. For example, the university seems obsessed with the demands of black students on campus, but despite Stanford's best attempts to lure more black students, Asian-Americans are the most prominent among "students of color." Racial tensions, while never terribly strained, may have peaked in 1989, with the administration's predictably ritualistic capitulation to the usual "demands"—after a student occupation of the president's office—but since then, some think that the racial and political situation at Stanford has moderated, especially after the departure of several of the more divisive and radical student leaders.

Stanford's speech/harassment code typifies reigning campus political thought. While students ostensibly have the "right to hold and vigorously defend and promote their opinions," speech that is deemed to be politically incorrect, that is, "harassing" to the currently favored groups, is not protected. This policy, along with others of a leftist bent, has led to a greater willingness by many to confront the dominance of the politically correct at Stanford during the past two years. A new student political party, Students First, sprang up to oppose the coalition of students-of-color organizations and "progressive" whites that dominated student affairs. There was a campus-wide reaction to reports in the student newspaper that some student leaders were linked to off-campus political groups with radical political agendas. These and other reports were something of an embarrassment to the super-politically correct and even emboldened a few moderate and conservative students to become a bit more visible and vocal.

For example, there is now the *Stanford Review,* an independent weekly newspaper that provides a forum for conservative students on its editorial page; its unofficial motto is "politically incorrect and proud of it." The university-supported student paper, the *Stanford Daily*, is known for its leftist stance, but some students detect a movement towards the center in recent years. Then, too, there are hundreds of traditional, nonpolitical extracurricular activities on campus, ranging from theater to publications, and the renowned Leland Stanford Junior University Marching Band. (The band became even more famous when it was officially disciplined for making fun of Oregon's spotted owls; such is the university's fear of easily outraged environmentalists and such are the astonishing lengths to which politically correct administrators can go.)

The campus is beautiful, situated among the foothills at the base of the San Francisco Bay peninsula. It covers 8,200 acres of palm trees and redwoods and even boasts a shopping mall. California's seemingly perpetual drought has browned the lawns and turned Lake Lagunita into Lakebed Lagunita (the lake hasn't been filled since 1988), but the campus as a whole is still breath-taking. The buildings, with a few exceptions, are all built in the traditional mission style with red-tiled roofs and sandstone-colored walls, making the place look like a giant Taco Bell, in the words of one student. The campus is often called "The Farm," since it was originally Leland Stanford's horse farm, and it is quite spread out—a bicycle is a necessity.

Stanford is also lively, especially when compared to surrounding Palo Alto. The Concert Board hosts big-name concerts several times a year, the campus Coffee House hosts bands and stand-up comedians, and something is always going on in White Plaza at midday. Sunday Flicks bring together 2,000 students in a frenzy of yelling, hissing, and throwing paper at the screen and at each other as a way of venting the week's frustrations. The Rodin sculpture garden is a tranquil oasis in the midst of all the uproar.

Housing is extremely varied—dormitories, co-ops, self-ops, apartments, fraternities, and trailer parks. The number of dormitory spaces will increase considerably in 1991 with the opening of Kimball Hall, a new undergraduate facility, and the university hopes soon to guarantee four years of housing and finally close down the "temporary" trailer parks that have stood since the late 1960s. Each co-op at Stanford has its own unique atmosphere; some are more bohemian than others. The university decision, after relocating two co-ops and one fraternity, to demolish and rebuild three old buildings due to earthquake damage has generated some resistance from fanatically loyal co-op residents.

Traditional fraternities remain an important source of Stanford's social life, but are by no means dominant. The dorms also throw parties, some of which, like the Exotic Erotic Ball or Club Ujamaa, have become institutions, in spite of the university's new alcohol policy, which prohibits university employees from buying alcohol with university funds or distributing it, and technically empowers the school to discipline underage student drinkers. (So far no students have had any action taken against them and it is unlikely that any ever will.) Drugs are a definite problem but not prevalent, and the campus is relatively safe at night. The police sometimes appear to be everywhere and the student government offers an escort service. Bicycle theft, in particular, is rampant and many students go through three or four bicycles in the course of their Stanford careers.

Stanford prides itself on its intercollegiate athletic competitiveness, for it is not content to cede even the playing field to less academically rigorous institutions. It produces national championship teams and individual athletes who sometimes are national and international celebrities in their own right. For the ordinary mortal, opportunities are extensive, the facilities superb, and the climate supportive of outdoor sports especially. Indeed, good health and fresh air enjoy cult status.

Overall, Stanford undergraduates see themselves as a practical lot. They value the Stanford name, for it is highly valued by corporations and their recruiters. Many also admit that the workaholic thrives best on the campus, and the elaborate efforts students used to make to disguise the fact that they worked hard or had any real intellectual interests seem to be fading. Like California, the Golden State, Stanford has thrived on an image of golden boys and golden girls in a golden age, immune to the normal vicissitudes of life. But reality, like the California droughts and earthquakes, is starting to encroach on Eden.

Stanford's current situation, in fact, is an example of what can happen when the leadership of a university allows its proper academic and intellectual missions to be shunted aside by its own political proclivities. Thus, it refused to be the site for the Reagan Presidential Library, thereby surrendering the chance to be a center for scholarship on a significant era. It has also carried on a politically motivated feud with the internationally renowned Hoover Institution, an autonomous unit of the university and a world-class center for the study of modern history and politics in its own right. In its day-to-day business, the Stanford leadership strikes stylish political poses on curriculum decisions and hiring practices, inexorably depleting the institutional capital accumulated in the last generation. This, and not its overcharging of the government, may prove to be Stanford's more enduring and consequential deficit.

Swarthmore College

Dean of Admissions, Swarthmore College
500 College Avenue, Swarthmore, PA 19081-1397 (215) 328-8300

Type: Private and Secular	**Costs and Aid:**	
	Tuition and fees	$15,490
Students:	Room and Board	5,220
1,304 undergraduates		
672 men	Scholarships:	
632 women	Academic	Yes
	Athletic	No
Applications:	Minority	No
Closing date: February 1		
24% of applicants accepted	Financial Aid:	
	Freshmen	51%

	Applied	Accepted	Enrolled
men	1,681	420	158
women	1,777	407	158

Upperclassmen 49%

SAT required
  Score reported by: February 15
  Mid 50% of freshman scores:

SAT-Math	630–720	
SAT-Verbal	600–710	

Library:	780,000 titles
ROTC:	Yes
Study Abroad:	Yes
Percentage of courses that can be used to fulfill distribution requirements:	77.5

Swarthmore was founded in 1864 by the Society of Friends as a small, coed, liberal arts college which supported the egalitarian ideals of the Quakers. Known for years as a hotbed of radical political activism, it was dubbed in the early 1970s the "Kremlin on the Crum" after a creek that runs through the campus. More recently, however, Swarthmore has achieved national prominence, and is grappling with the internal conflicts generated by a dual desire to maintain a healthy endowment and attract a "diverse" student body while also remaining committed to its original ideals of preserving peace and harmony on all sides.

One of these ideals would incorporate an egalitarian system of self-government much like the old New England town meetings, where all classes of citizens represented themselves, and sometimes made decisions by voluntary consensus. However, the difficulty of obtaining agreement in this way, even in a small community with only 1,300 students, has caused dissension between students and administration, as well as a general re-examination of the future direction of Swarthmore. Some complain about the "corporate mentality" of the administration and its recent attempts to sidestep student opinion. The administration defends itself by claiming to be grappling with the practical problems facing a wealthy institution that is responding to national and "mainstream" recognition.

The college president, David Fraser, had been at the center of these controversies for the past several years. While Fraser, an epidemiologist, oversaw the rapid growth of the college endowment, new construction on campus, and a leap in number of applicants, he nevertheless encountered many difficulties with both the governing board and the students. In the face of administrative restructuring and the sudden departure of several top administrators, Fraser also left, in August 1991. His successor is Alfred Bloom, formerly dean of the faculty at Pitzer College, Claremont, California. The change in leadership underlines the uncertainty of the future political and economic directions of the college.

College Bulletin 1990–91:
English Literature 91—Feminist Literary Criticism.
Professor Laurie Langbauer

"What is feminism? What is its relation to literary criticism? In this course, we will explore the role of politics in answering those questions, examining the ways that feminism exposes as political those very spheres that have traditionally seemed exempt from, if not opposed to, politics. Readings in current feminist literary criticism and theory."

Academically, Swarthmore is one of the most rigorous and demanding schools in the country. Its students are very bright and intellectually oriented. Most of them come from the Middle Atlantic states, but all states are usually represented, as well as 30 or 40 foreign countries. About 20 percent are minorities. Classroom discussions are held at an extremely high level and the workload is unusually challenging.

Thirty-two semester courses are needed for graduation. There is no core curriculum, but students are required to take three courses in each of three divisions, the humanities, social sciences, and natural sciences. Two courses in each division must be in at least two different departments, and two must also be designated PDCs, or primary distribution courses, which emphasize analytical thinking and writing. Second-year students are required to produce a so-called "sophomore

TUITION AND FEES INCREASE
Average Increase/Year: Private = 11.15%, Swarthmore = 9.39%

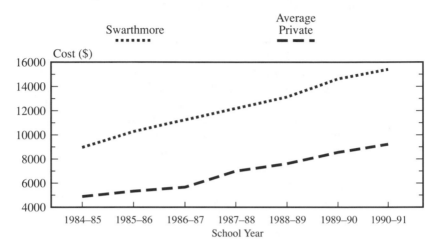

Source: The College Entrance Examination Board

---

paper" outlining their plan of study for the next two years. This effort has been the subject of much dispute and is generally considered a waste of time by the students.

Swarthmore is now shying away from the traditional Western canon and showcasing other cultures, as well as little-known women and minority writers. This trend is not surprising in view of the college's history and the left-leaning tendencies of many of the professors, who often give short shrift to other viewpoints. Samples of feel-good courses include a "Feminist Interpretation of Scripture," "Representations of Women's Identity," and "Black Culture and Black Consciousness."

On the academic plus-side, however, Swarthmore offers a unique honors program, which is roughly modeled on Oxford's tutorial system. During the junior and senior years, about 140 students take only two courses per semester in the major, the aim being depth rather than breadth. During this period no grades or examinations are given, but at the end of the senior year students are tested rigorously, both orally and in writing, by outside examiners (usually professors from other colleges). This system offers an excellent opportunity to experience small, intense discussions and debates. There have been accusations, however, of faculty and examiner bias against students who stray from the leftist orthodoxy.

The best departments at Swarthmore are engineering, biology, psychology, and economics, though none is really weak. The engineering department, unusual in small liberal arts schools, is outstanding. The biology and psychology departments, in particular, boast a distinguished faculty, but the introductory courses are among the largest at Swarthmore (around 100). Other than these few large lectures, however, the small class size is a major attraction of Swarthmore. Regular classes rarely have more than 20 students; seminars do not enroll more than 12. Discussion is lively in both, and professor-student relationships are warm and friendly. If the intimacy thus engendered palls, Swarthmoreans may expand their horizons by cross-registering at nearby Haverford and Bryn Mawr, or taking a semester at schools farther afield, including Brandeis, Mills, Rice, and Tufts.

Campus life is pleasant, and the school offers almost every activity you can imagine. The Swarthmore music and dance department spon-

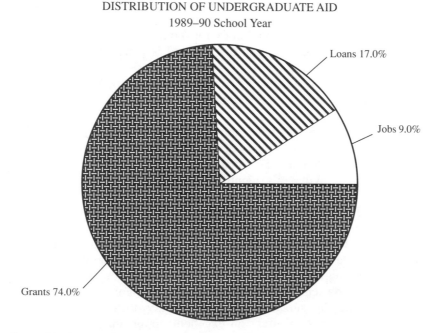

DISTRIBUTION OF UNDERGRADUATE AID
1989–90 School Year

Loans 17.0%

Jobs 9.0%

Grants 74.0%

Source: The College Entrance Examination Board, 1990

sors a series of concerts which are widely attended. The construction of the new Performing Arts Center promises more such events with better facilities. The film series is also popular—movies are shown free on campus on weekends and one week night. At least four lectures or special presentations are held weekly in the afternoons and evenings, and the Drama Board sponsors a variety of productions each semester.

WSRN, the campus radio station, plays progressive, classical and jazz music, and it is possible for nearly anyone to host a radio show. It is also relatively easy to become nominated for an administration-related college committee; these committees are usually small and give students good opportunities to voice concerns to the administration. Other activities include a wide variety of clubs and organizations, including student government and judiciary boards, the internationally recognized Amos J. Peaslee debate society, the environmental society Earthlust, a gospel choir, Amnesty International, an outdoors club, and an extensive volunteer program for groups in nearby Chester.

While there is certainly plenty to do on campus, many upperclass-men feel restricted by the small size of the college and look elsewhere for fun, if not games. Philadelphia is only a stone's throw away, and New York and Washington within weekend reach. Social life on campus is in a transitional period. Following a change in 1990, alcohol is no longer paid for by the student activities fund. In an attempt to preserve the Swarthmore ideal of open dialogue and trust between students and administration, the new alcohol policy is still extremely lenient. Nevertheless, the rules have created a fairly strong separation between drinkers and non-drinkers. The two campus fraternities now hold major parties every weekend, which have little appeal to many non-drinkers. All-campus parties, once a unifying campus event, are now dry and sparsely attended. The student-run club/coffeehouse is alive but struggling since the demise of the enormously popular Thursday night beer/dance party.

Campus groups include the Black Cultural Center (BCC) and the Alice Paul Women's Center. The BCC remains relatively self-contained and sometimes tends to isolate the black community. The women's center, once populated by a more radical group, now maintains a moderate profile and is much more open and part of the mainstream. ASIS, the "sexual minority" support group, is also relatively low-key compared to the past. Swarthmore's sexual minorities have been "out of the closet" for such a long time that they are widely accepted and do not make campus visibility their main agenda.

The ideological tone is very liberal, but the corresponding political implications are quite vague. With the current surge in applicants, the old guard of leftist political activists is a dying breed at Swarthmore. Although students remain overwhelmingly liberal, the political agenda is not so strong or well defined as it was in the 1960s or 1970s, and apathy currently competes with activism. The conservative minority is not well mobilized on campus and has not been articulately represented in any campus publication. Some students feel that conservatives are ignored to such an extent that they can only gain attention if they adopt reactionary positions, and hence are not respected. Nevertheless, there have been a few attempts in the past several years by conservative students to promote their viewpoints as intellectually valid; there are no organized conservative publications or groups on campus.

Freedom-of-speech issues have not been actively addressed in a while. Several years ago, when anti-homosexual graffiti appeared in response to gay and lesbian graffiti, the college quickly reprimanded both groups, but the free speech debate was ultimately left unresolved. There is no "sensitivity" or harassment code for minorities, though sexual harassment is forbidden. Political speakers invited to campus are almost always liberal, although the pro-choice and pro-life groups have worked together on occasion to bring speakers of both viewpoints to campus. The more conservative speakers are not harassed, although they are certainly not enthusiastically received.

Athletics at Swarthmore have traditionally been a weak point; however, in recent years sports have gained more respect and attention. While the physical education department has long suffered from low funding, there is a strong movement among students and some faculty and board members for renewed attention to the importance of sports. Now, there are 11 intercollegiate and several intramural sports each for men and women, but only a few dedicated jocks work up much of a lather. As always, athletes at Swarthmore have to balance their training requirements with the heavy academic demands of the college. Most coaches are sympathetic to the weight of the course load and students' academic priorities. Club sports like rugby are relatively new but growing in popularity. Also extremely popular are intramural softball, basketball, and volleyball. At least half of the student body participates in some form of organized athletics.

Campus facilities are fairly well maintained. Except for a couple of dorms in poor condition, housing arrangements, both coed and single-sex, are spacious, comfortable, and guaranteed for all four years. The housekeeping services are more extensive than those at many other schools. Campus security is also sufficient; "safewalkers" and off-campus shuttles are provided and there have been no major incidents of crime in the past few years.

In spite of its leftist tinge, Swarthmore's strong points can outweigh its shortcomings. In so small a community, relationships are intimate and leap across age and status barriers. Students enjoy close friendships with their peers, their professors and members of the administration, many of whom open their homes to students for dinners, receptions, and parties. On the intellectual level, activity is white-hot inside the classroom and often outside, too. For those who can take the heat and enjoy its intensity, Swarthmore can be the crucible of choice.

University of Texas at Austin

Associate Vice President for Student Affairs and Director of Admissions, University of Texas at Austin
Austin, TX 78712-1159 (512) 471-7601

Type: Public	**Costs and Aid:**	
	Tuition and fees	
Students:	In state	$ 930
38,118 undergraduates	Out of state	3,660
19,933 men	Room and Board	3,300
18,185 women		
12,127 graduate students	Scholarships:	
	Academic	Yes
Applications:	Athletic	Yes
Closing date: March 1	Minority	Yes
62% of applicants accepted		
	Financial Aid:	
	Freshmen	28%
	Upperclassmen	42%

	Applied	Accepted	Enrolled
men	9,703	6,022	3,461
women	8,276	5,049	2,900

SAT or ACT required	**Library:** 2,800,006 titles
Score reported by: March 1	**ROTC:** Yes
Mid 50% of freshman scores:	**Study Abroad:** Yes
SAT-Math 520–650	
SAT-Verbal 450–580	

The University of Texas at Austin, mandated by the Texas constitution, was founded as the state's public institution of higher learning in 1883. The university campus now occupies about 300 acres in Austin, the state capital, and has become a worthy competitor of the political scene for local attention. And with more than 50,000 students, Texas is one of the most populous universities in the nation.

The sheer mass of the University of Texas is boon and bane. The College of Liberal Arts is one of 14 major university divisions and one of these, the Graduate School, is further subdivided into two other large graduate components. (One of these is the famous Lyndon B. Johnson School of Public Affairs.) There are about 10,000 liberal arts undergraduates. But Texans, who think BIG, seem happy to see their flagship college grow even larger. Throughout the 1960s and 1970s, the huge and hugely financed system became famous for recruiting some of the best-known professors in the world. The school still retains an international reputation for its "quality" faculty. Unfortunately, but predictably, most undergraduates never meet them. Many classes,

349

especially lower-division liberal arts courses, are taught by graduate students who seem to function with little or no higher supervision. It is clear that the separation of professors from teaching prevents Texas from affording undergraduate instruction of a quality consistent with the high profile of the faculty.

Large classes. Somehow the sense that students are trapped in them seems greater at Texas than it does at comparable institutions in other states. In any case, the bad feeling on the subject has an edge to it you seldom find elsewhere. In the sciences especially, the lecturers seem uninterested, unenthusiastic, and generally uninspiring to the approximately 600 students who gather for the weekly presentation. Some students report that the characteristic attitude toward undergraduates is disdain. But, inevitably, the undergraduate corps comes to understand that the school aspires to be an excellent graduate research center and that many professors aspire to a kind of academic nirvana— having no teaching to do at all. Some attain it.

Texas is a place where the tradition of educational populism must now compete with ambitions for elitist excellence. The University of Texas has grown as large as it has because it was open to every Texan who wished to attend. "Open Admissions" is a thing of the past, but the need to place even more stringent restrictions on enrollment seems a political impossibility. The university is rich enough in its own right to pursue an independent course; it is famous for owning oil wells and for having an enormous endowment, even though it is a public institution. But the state provides enough of the operating budget to prevent the regents from acting in anti-democratic fashion. So the growth continues and the tuition remains low. As a consequence, the availability of undergraduate classes is becoming a problem, their size notwithstanding, and some students now complain that it takes five years to complete the course requirements. Those requirements, depending upon the major, can indeed be taxing. The common ones add up to 52 credit hours drawn from four different areas. Students must then deal with their major departments, of which there seem to be about 100. And, of course, there is the state law that requires *all* degree recipients to have studied at least *some* Texas history.

One remedy for this bewilderment, also tried elsewhere, is the creation of honors programs in the liberal arts; Texas has three. So-called "Plan II" offers an interdisciplinary liberal arts degree. Once admitted to the program, the student finds that requirements are lax and that the program depends for its success on the simple fact that the students who choose it are of higher quality. Two other honors

TUITION AND FEES INCREASE
Average Increase/Year: Public = 8.30%, Texas = 17.92%

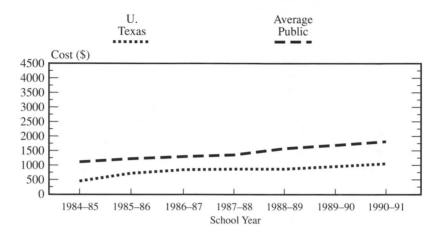

Source: The College Entrance Examination Board

tracks, the Humanities Honors Program and the Liberal Arts Honors Programs, tend to get better reviews. As much as these programs hope to attract better-motivated students, their more important ambition is coaxing senior faculty into the classroom by offering the prospect of better, more engaged students. Thus far, success is mixed. Individual departments also offer honors opportunities, but generally students report that they are seldom more inspirational than the standard fare, and that the main advantage—the opportunity to write a senior thesis—often runs afoul of the problem of getting a faculty advisor who will pay sustained attention.

There is a faction at Texas which hopes to leapfrog all of these difficulties on the cheap by assuming that undergraduate "quality" means aping the fads of the moment and that if the school places itself in the avant-garde, it can somehow compensate for deep-seated structural problems. But sometimes, this backfires. Recently Texas called national attention to its required "Rhetoric and Composition" course by basing the work on a left-wing sociology text. Aside from being a crude venture into political indoctrination, the episode strips bare the now institutionalized laziness of faculty members and administrators who have lost interest in the real work of teaching. It is better to encourage students to chant slogans and, if called up short, to holler about political repression.

Another way of finessing the real problems of Texas students is to focus on manufactured ones. In recent years, the university has created a large staff whose purpose is the theory and practice of "multiculturalism." As at other institutions, there is now a built-in lobby with a vested interest in these issues as they affect "student life." No doubt, the transition of an all-white university to a "diverse" one (29 percent of the university are minorities) in the course of a generation would not have been easy under any circumstances. But students report that minority groups and those inside the administration who are responsible for their well-being have managed to introduce even greater strains into the situation. Predictably, the controversies seem never to be concerned with the content and quality of Texas education as such, but with a host of ancillary matters.

But it may be that these activists are among the few who really pay much attention. Back in March 1990, only 3,400 undergraduates

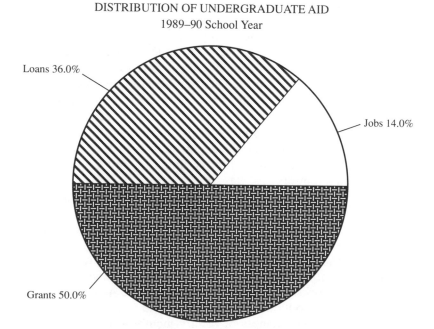

DISTRIBUTION OF UNDERGRADUATE AID
1989–90 School Year

Loans 36.0%

Jobs 14.0%

Grants 50.0%

Source: The College Entrance Examination Board, 1990

bothered to vote in the student government election and these, by a margin of 400, elected Toni Luckett as their president. Ms. Luckett, a campaigner for lesbian rights, headed a coalition which included not only the campus's homosexuality advocates but also the student organizations of blacks, Mexicans, women, environmentalists, and the University Democrats.

It is easy to sympathize a little with serious causists at Texas, for you can imagine their frustration as they compete with the campus's other distractions. A traditional football rivalry and its cast of thousands will blot out all other noises. The famous Longhorn Marching Band seems to have more brass players than the average liberal arts college's total enrollment. But one consequence, perhaps even a benefit of such gigantism, is that many different campus subcultures are able to survive. There is, after all, sometimes an advantage in the ability to live unnoticed. Thus, within the boisterous life of the University of Texas, there are enclaves of space and time for serious pursuits of serious interests—but students will need to make them. In fact, students need to make their own way in other practical respects. Only about 10 percent are able to live in university housing; the rest fend for themselves in the usual ways.

Still, it remains undeniable that all of that oil money buys *something* of use to undergraduates. The facilities are excellent. The university has the seventh largest academic library complex in the country. There are also numerous student computer facilities, an on-campus observatory, impressive new recreational installations, and plenty of places to relax and study. The on-campus Student Union features delis, a cafeteria, a tavern, a cantina, billiards, and a bowling alley.

The university itself is built with a Southwestern architectural flair—red-tile roofs and decorative stonework. It is surrounded by the beautiful, oak-filled city of Austin, with more parks per capita than any other Texas city. Austin lies on both sides of the Brazos River and is also very close to lakes and public springs. Excellent opportunities for outdoor activities, from spelunking to water-skiing, can be found inside and just outside the city. And Sixth Street is the site of the famous music scene and night life. The city, one of the fastest growing in the nation overall, manages to combine a small-town atmosphere with big-town excitement.

Like any large land grant institution, the University of Texas is as much a phenomenon as a university. And, like its peers, it can be a self-contained world unto itself, with its students turning to the outside when they feel overwhelmed by the university's sheer mass and energy. Texas is therefore an ''experience' as well as an education; indeed, it is one of those places that defines what ''higher education'' really means for millions of average Americans—in itself a reason for reflection.

Tufts University

Dean of Admissions, Tufts University
Medford, MA 02155 (617) 381-3170

Type: Private and Secular			**Costs and Aid:**	
			Tuition and fees	$15,920
Students:			Room and Board	5,170
4,683 undergraduates				
2,421 men			Scholarships:	
2,262 women			Academic	Yes
3,037 graduate students			Athletic	No
			Minority	No
Applications:			Financial Aid:	
Closing date: January 1			Freshmen	44%
39% of applicants accepted			Upperclassmen	41%
Applied	*Accepted*	*Enrolled*		
men 3,757	1,509	556	**Library:**	689,000 titles
women 4,028	1,501	556		
SAT or ACT required (SAT preferred)			**ROTC:**	Yes
Score reported by: March 1			**Study Abroad:**	Yes
Mid 50% of freshman scores:				
SAT-Math 610–700				
SAT-Verbal 560–640				

Tufts, founded in 1852 by a clergyman of the Universalist Church, began life as a small liberal arts college, which was intended to be non-sectarian but not antireligious. Now a prestigious university of more than 7,000 students, Tufts employs just one full-time professor of religion. Yet, other special-interest groups—particularly blacks and women—are favored with departments of their own and with university-sponsored centers and salaried administrators. On a student level, the Afro-American Society and the Women's Collective, as well as the Lesbian, Gay and Bisexual Community enjoy funding from the student government. Tufts, which has climbed high in recent years on the American academic ladder, likes to lean it leftward.

Nevertheless, in spite of its political tilt, the university has gained an impressive reputation for the quality of both its eight graduate and two undergraduate schools, the College of Engineering and the College of Liberal Arts, both located on the Medford campus. Often in the vanguard, Tufts went coeducational in 1892, long before most of its peers thought about mixing the sexes, and in 1933 established the now world-famous Fletcher School of Law and Diplomacy. In 1955, Tufts was officially constituted a university and hasn't looked back since.

355

Bulletin of Tufts University, 1990–1991:
English 170—Sexuality, Literature, and Contemporary Criticism.
Professor Lee Edelman

"An introduction to contemporary approaches to literature that concern themselves with the relation between sexuality and the textual production of meaning. Consideration of current feminist, gay, psychoanalytic, and deconstructive theories of literature in conjunction with the reading of a variety of literary works. Texts for the course will include novels, poems, critical essays, case studies, and films."

For the past 15 years, the university has been led by Jean Mayer, one of the world's leading nutritionists. President Mayer, who is French, has been credited with elevating Tufts's academic reputation, especially at the graduate level. As he had spent most of his previous academic career working in graduate programs, upon arriving at Tufts he immediately began an impressive drive to improve and expand them. His achievements in this regard include the creation of the USDA Nutrition Institute on Aging, the Tufts School of Nutrition, the Sackler School of Graduate Biomedical Sciences, and the Tufts School of Veterinary Medicine—along with increased funding for the existing Medical, Dental, and Fletcher Schools. In the fall of 1991, Tufts opened the Olin Language Center, a new arts center, and a new dormitory. In 1990, the university inaugurated its Science and Technology Center. This monumental effort to transform Tufts into a leading research university, however, has not been without cost.

Because Tufts traditionally claimed to be committed to undergraduate education above all else, both professors and students now express discontent over the apparent shift in priorities. There is dissatisfaction about faculty salary levels and massive financial aid shortfalls. These worries culminated in a class walkout in February 1990 by about 500 students; many faculty members also protested against the administration's neglect of undergraduate concerns. The irony was that at the same time Tufts was pleading poverty to the students, the university was planning a multimillion-dollar research development in downtown Boston in conjunction with an outside developer.

The difficulties facing undergraduate education at Tufts do not center solely on resource allocation. The events of the 1960s fundamentally transformed the university, not only practically, through the 1969 closing of the Crane Theological Seminary, but also in a philo-

TUITION AND FEES INCREASE
Average Increase/Year: Private = 11.15%, Tufts = 8.88%

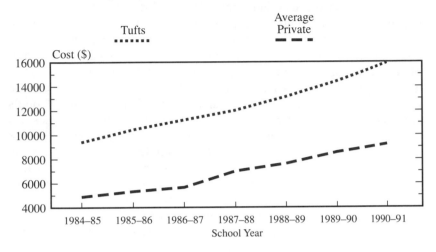

Source: The College Entrance Examination Board

sophical sense; radical students of the 1960s have become the professors of the 1980s and 1990s. Unable to overturn American society in their youth, in middle age they have settled for revolutionizing the university instead.

Let it be noted, however, that in spite of the continuing radicalization of the curriculum, Tufts can still be proud of a selection of excellent liberal arts departments, including the International Relations Program and the impressive political science, classics, drama, child study, and biology departments. Several disciplines in the College of Liberal Arts, however, are subject to the political agendas of their faculty—the Peace and Justice Studies Program, which includes such courses as "Toward a Just World Order," "Racism and Social Inequality," "Topics in Income Distribution," and "Class, Status and Power." In the sociology department, students may delve into "Theories of Sexual Inequality," not to mention "Marxist Sociology." Serious history buffs are treated to such intellectual necessities, if not niceties, as "Sexuality, Gender and Economy in Preindustrial Europe," and "Witchcraft and Society."

Although Tufts has developed an intricate array of distribution requirements, there is nothing that resembles a core curriculum with a

Western civilization accent. The only mandatory courses are two
semester courses in English. Distribution requirements include two
courses each in the mathematical sciences, the natural sciences, the
social sciences, the humanities, and the arts. In addition, the college
asks students to take three courses in a foreign language and then to
continue the study of the language until two courses have been completed at the third-year level. Alternatively, they may study a second
language for three semesters or take three courses in a single culture
not native to their own. It is possible to place out of part of one's
language requirement through a proficiency test, and some courses can
fill two or even three requirements at the same time; but, with the
exception of these few loopholes, the university strictly enforces the
academic guidelines. There are honors programs in all liberal arts
departments, as well as a number of interdisciplinary programs including Environmental Literacy; Social Psychology and Biopsychology;
and Engineering Psychology and Community Health.

In order to help students negotiate the requirements, Tufts has

DISTRIBUTION OF UNDERGRADUATE AID
1989–90 School Year

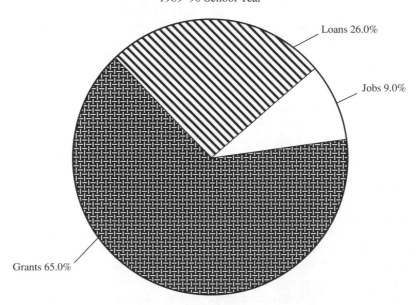

Loans 26.0%

Jobs 9.0%

Grants 65.0%

Source: The College Entrance Examination Board, 1990

developed a partially successful advisory system in which students are allowed to choose their own academic advisor. Tufts also operates the Academic Resources Center, which provides guidance and tutoring assistance. The quality of the advising system depends largely on the determination of the student and the disposition of the professor. Since most Tufts classes are small and teaching assistants are used sparingly, professors are used to working closely with students, so the advising system can work well.

The Tufts experience may also embrace Boston College, as well as Boston and Brandeis Universities, where students may cross-register. They may also spend a semester at Swarthmore College in Pennsylvania, or work in Washington, D.C., or go farther afield to study abroad. There is plenty to do at home in the Medford area, however, with its vibrant social and extracurricular atmosphere. Situated only two miles from Harvard Square and six miles from downtown Boston, the university offers an environment rich in cultural and social opportunities. Life on the small (150 acres) but well-groomed campus is very appealing for the approximately 4,700 undergraduates who come from all over the United States and from more than 50 foreign countries. Approximately 20 percent are members of minority groups.

Almost 70 percent of the student population live on campus in the coed dorms, Greek houses, or in university-owned co-op apartments. Freshmen are guaranteed accommodation, and the rest take their chances by lottery. Tufts has a very active Greek community, which currently claims 20 percent of the students; they participate in philanthropic as well as social activities. The Greek system may not last for long, however, because elements of the faculty and administration would dearly love to see it abolished in the near future.

In addition to Greek-sponsored events, there are about 140 extracurricular activities and organizations to engage all interests, from music and drama to photography and chess. A vigorous and varied student culture results, and it finds its voice in no fewer than 16 media organizations. The athletically inclined play on a full range of intercollegiate and intramural teams, which attract about 70 percent of the student body in spite of an old and decaying gym, and minor budget cutbacks in club sports. President Mayer is now energetically raising money for a new athletic complex, as well as for renovation of the gymnasium. Outdoor facilities include a 400-meter track, and soccer and football fields.

The political complexion of the student body tends to be liberal, but remains solidly more mainstream than the faculty. Many of the most active and vocal organizations swing left, including the Tufts Gay, Lesbian and Bisexual Community, MassPIRG, and the Afro-American Society. There have been no major racial incidents at Tufts in the last few years, but the atmosphere surrounding "diversity" issues in general is highly charged and emotional. Yet, the student body has resisted administration attempts to regulate campus dialogue and debate by supporting, in the fall of 1989, a protest led by campus conservatives against a new policy restricting free speech in class-rooms or residence halls while permitting it in newspapers, on the radio station, and during public lectures and debates. The theory behind this distinction was that minority students need more protection from jokes and insults in intimate settings than they do in public places. The protesters mocked the policy by drawing chalk lines on the ground marking out a "free-speech zone," a "limited-speech zone," and a "twilight zone." The result was national press coverage and the suspension of the policy, at least for the time being.

As Tufts enters into the 1990s, some fundamental decisions about the course and nature of the university need to be made. On the one hand, Tufts is teetering between its research ambitions and its commit-ment to undergraduate education; on the other, it is seesawing between its long marriage to Western civilization and its new passion for diversity. The increasing frustration of its students, who are caught in the middle on both issues, may tip the scales if they continue to let the university know where they themselves draw the line.

Vassar College

Director of Admissions, Vassar College
Box 10, Poughkeepsie, NY 12601 (914) 437-7300

Type: Private and Secular				**Costs and Aid:**	
Students:				Tuition and fees	$15,190
2,436 undergraduates				Room and Board	4,980
1,042 men				Scholarships:	
1,396 women				Academic	No
4 graduate students				Athletic	No
				Minority	No
Applications:				Financial Aid:	
Closing date: January 15				Freshmen	43%
42% of applicants accepted				Upperclassmen	53%
	Applied	*Accepted*	*Enrolled*		
men	1,363	704	256	**Library:**	675,000 titles
women	2,969	1,131	359		
SAT or ACT required				**ROTC:**	Yes
Score reported by: January 15				**Study Abroad:**	Yes
Mid 50% of freshman scores:					
SAT-Math	N/A				
SAT-Verbal	N/A				

In 1969, Vassar College declined an invitation to merge with Yale and instead began to admit men on its own. Twenty-one years later, the liberal arts school that earned fame as one of the nation's first and best women's colleges is still adjusting to the trials of coeducation.

With roughly a 55:45 female to male ratio, Vassar's student body of about 2,400 is now thoroughly mixed, but the school retains the unmistakable flavor of a women's enclave. The college is devoid of what one feminist called "the traditional institutions of male domination such as football teams, cheerleaders and fraternities." There is, however, a women-only student lounge, a women's dorm, an ambitious women's studies program, and a wide variety of women's clubs ranging from the Lesbian Feminists League to the Future Housewives of America.

Yet, by and large, Vassar men manage to survive the snickers when they name their alma mater and rather enjoy the male to female ratio, not to mention an improving sports program which, while lacking varsity football, includes relatively solid rugby, lacrosse, crew, and basketball teams. There are 9 intercollegiate sports each for men and women, in addition to 11 intramurals and 14 club sports. Although the college has excellent facilities, team sports never have been and still aren't a big deal at Vassar, for men or women. Ninety popular extra-curricular activities help compensate for the lack of team spirit, including a radio station, a jazz band, chorale and drama groups, an orchestra, social service organizations, and chess and computer clubs.

Catalogue 1990/91:
Sociology 342b—Women and New Technology (also Science, Technology and Society 342b)
Professor Eileen Leonard

"This course explores the relationship between women and technology by focusing on three types of technology that are particularly relevant to women: reproductive technology, household technology, and office automation. Students study specific technologies while examining larger issues related to technology and of concern to both men and women, including the quality of work, life, equal opportunity, and the social control of technology. The course is framed by an analysis of the social construction of gender and the relationship between technology and society in Western civilization. Alternative technology, utopian fiction, and ethical dimensions are also considered. Readings included Mumford, Bell, Ellul, Merchant, Cowan, Braverman, Ehrenreich, Gordon, Hayden, Dickson, and Piercy." "Not offered in 1990/91."

On the social side, since sororities and fraternities are taboo, nightlife centers around a pub called Matthew's Mug (after the college's brewer-founder) and the nine college dorms, each of which gives two big parties a year complete with bands and dancing. There are also several houses on the fringes of the campus where students live and occasionally make merry. Some also travel into New York City, about two hours away, in order to escape the insularity of the campus. To compensate for the lack of fraternities, the men have established a secret, male-bonding society called the Royal Order of the Moose.

The presence of so many males on the campus, whether men or moose, may well have set the college's founder, Matthew Vassar, to spinning in his grave; for in the mid-19th century the far-sighted British-born brewer and businessman conceived the then radical notion of starting a liberal arts institution devoted exclusively to offering women an education equal to that of the most rigorous men's colleges of his day. In 1865, as the Civil War ended, this unlikely advocate for

TUITION AND FEES INCREASE
Average Increase/Year: Private = 11.15%, Vassar = 9.02%

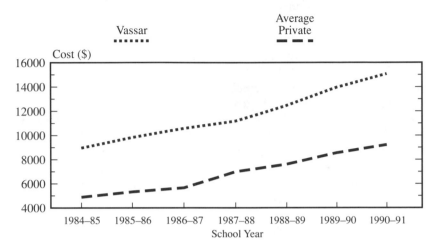

Source: The College Entrance Examination Board

women's rights realized his vision when he opened Vassar's doors to 353 eager young women from across the re-United States. Their successors and their college have been enthusiastic harbingers of change ever since, always ready to slip into the latest in educational and social fashions.

Situated on 1,000 scenic acres near the Hudson River, the romantic-looking Vassar campus, which is circled by a stone wall insulating it from dreary Poughkeepsie, features traditional Gothic architecture, a nine-hole golf course, two small lakes, an umbrella of beautiful old trees, and a blanket of daffodils in the springtime. But the peaceful atmosphere can be deceptive.

As the college catalog points out in its history of the school, during the 1920s and 1930s, "The social consciousness and the sense of social responsibility that are characteristic of the Vassar community were becoming visible to the world. Students and alumnae paraded for causes, organized meetings and committees, raised money, and devoted themselves to the issues of the day." Sixty years later they still do, and the campus often rings to their excited voices.

Vassar therefore remains a school on the move, with a first-rate, if leftward-leaning, liberal arts faculty and student body. Its strongest points are those associated with a small college, i.e., often intimate classes and a friendly, accessible professorate that encourages student consultation and often attends social functions. Although there are occasional introductory lecture courses with more than 100 students, most classes contain between 10 and 30. Teaching assistants are used sparingly, and never for introductory courses.

There is, however, no core curriculum at Vassar, and distribution requirements are minimal, confined to a "freshman course," which concentrates on "effective expression of ideas in written and oral work," and a year of a foreign language. Even the latter may be waived by advanced placement credit or a proficiency test. For the rest, a student may freewheel, concentrating from the freshman year in one department, or two or more departments, or on a single problem or series of problems, or on an independent program not covered by any of the above. In other words, Vassar students do their own thing. A more disciplined program is not in the offing, because the Vassar ethos rejects making anybody do anything—which some observers believe is

DISTRIBUTION OF UNDERGRADUATE AID
1989–90 School Year

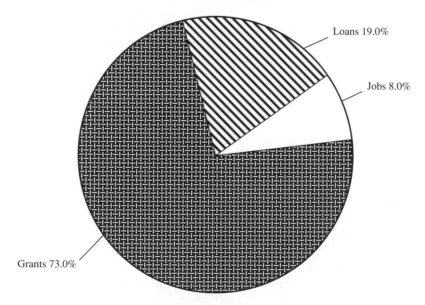

Loans 19.0%

Jobs 8.0%

Grants 73.0%

Source: The College Entrance Examination Board, 1990

the only reason students on this liberal campus escape formal "sensitivity" training and course requirements in ethnic and feminist studies.

Without a core program or distribution requirements worth the name, students are tempted to wander aimlessly though a curriculum an English professor calls "a bit like a supermarket." Of course, the supermarket offers some fine produce, and with guidance it is quite possible to assemble a solid liberal arts program in four years at Vassar. The college features outstanding English, art, history, philosophy, and drama departments, in addition to the heavily funded natural sciences. There are also promising interdisciplinary programs that attempt to provide the kind of integrated general education which should exemplify the liberal arts.

Most notable among the interdisciplinary courses is "Comparative World Views," an innovative and popular Great Books derivative. The course features an ambitious reading list, guest lectures by the college's top faculty, and student led "great conversations" in the dormitories. Comparative World Views should not be missed by any student attending Vassar College.

The administration, as well as the faculty, is congenial, accessible, and reasonably responsive to student concerns. Heading the college management team is Vassar's ninth president, Frances Fergusson, inaugurated in 1988. As Vice Provost of Academic Affairs at Bucknell, she had initiated a highly successful Great Books program and served on the National Endowment for the Humanities advisory board to William J. Bennett's *To Reclaim A Legacy* report. President Fergusson has proven to be a first-rate fund raiser (Vassar recently concluded a successful drive to raise $100 million), but after three years under her leadership, the school still offers a fragmented, often idiosyncratic curriculum, and an environment in which free speech comes under attack.

Senator Daniel Patrick Moynihan's spring 1990 visit to Vassar served as a bitter reminder that freedom of expression is not secure on this campus. The choice of the senator from New York as a guest lecturer caused a campus uproar, which culminated in the militant takeover of the college's main building. Moynihan came under fire for his 25-year-old report on the black underclass and a remark he allegedly made to a black woman after his lecture. Moynihan denied the remark, but a group of students invaded the building, demanding everything from his resignation from the Eleanor Roosevelt Guest Lecturer Chair to the construction of a black student center to the institution of a Kosher deli on campus. Minorities constitute about 17 percent of Vassar students, but often sound like more.

During Commencement exercises in 1991, black students decided they wanted to be seen (separately), as well as heard. Instead of participating as individuals in the traditional "Daisy Chain"—sophomores selected by the senior class to assist in the ceremonies—blacks insisted upon forming their own group, which they named the "African Violets."

In 1990, free speech was threatened when three editors of the conservative *Vassar Spectator* were taken to college court and charged with political harassment because of an editorial the paper had published about the vice president of the student government. After being told by the chair of the college court that harassment can carry the penalty of expulsion, the editors were dragged through a tedious three-week process of threats and delayed hearings. During this time, a group of students formed the Vassar Coalition for Free Speech and collected more than 400 signatures on behalf of the beleaguered editors. Charges were dropped two days before the trial, and although the "harassment" policy remains in place, it has expunged the clause pertaining to political speech.

This campaign reflects the general intolerance for moderate and conservative political views on campus. Two years earlier, the paper had been "de-authorized," thrown out of its office, and denied the use of school facilities for failing to abide by a student government censorship order. Currently, however, the situation on campus actually seems to be improving. Both the Moynihan affair and the charges against the newspaper have evoked sustained protests against censorship in favor of free speech and reasoned political debate. The college has reauthorized the *Vassar Spectator*, and President Fergusson, in a public address, has affirmed the sanctity of freedom of speech in the academy.

The student government continues to take itself all too seriously in its efforts to interfere with the affairs of students. Not long ago, however, a group with a sense of humor—a quality often lacking at Vassar—captured the student body's attention. Running on the platform, "You won't even know we're there," the "Indifference Party" diffused the tense political atmosphere and won more than 15 percent of the vote in the student elections.

When they're not out politicking or socializing, Vassar students retreat to their cozy lairs, which include dorms that are single-sex and coed by floor or room, one all-female house, and on- and off-campus apartments. Guaranteed for all four years, housing is comfortable, and in some cases borders on the luxurious. Upperclassmen prefer the college-run townhouses or terrace apartments.

In spite of its sybaritic aura, Vassar can be academically rigorous. With a plethora of demanding and inspiring professors at his fingertips, an enterprising, hard-working student can put together a respectable liberal arts program; but the lazy or undisciplined can graduate knowing little about the liberal arts or the Western civilization from which they sprang. Students can, instead, fill up on trendy courses like the "Sociology of Sociability," "Women and the New Technology," "Confrontations with Diversity," and "Sex, Gender and Society,"— and far too many do. Vassar is a prime example of that growing American paradox: a college of the liberal arts that often fails to teach them.

Villanova University

Director of Admissions, Villanova University
Villanova, PA 19085-1672 (215) 645-4000

Type: Private and Catholic

Students:
8,249 undergraduates
  4,500 men
  3,749 women
3,139 graduate students

Applications:
Closing date: January 15
46% of applicants accepted

	Applied	Accepted	Enrolled
men	4,949	2,405	864
women	4,613	2,041	733

SAT or ACT required (SAT preferred)
  Score reported by: January 31
  Mid 50% of freshman scores:
    SAT-Math   N/A
    SAT-Verbal N/A

Costs and Aid:

Tuition and fees	$10,850
Room and Board	5,220

Scholarships:
Academic	Yes
Athletic	Yes
Minority	Yes

Financial Aid:
Freshmen	45%
Upperclassmen	43%

Library:	570,000 titles
ROTC:	Yes
Study Abroad:	Yes

Today, Villanova University, founded in 1842 by the conservative Roman Catholic Order of St. Augustine, has largely shed its Roman identity and strives to be merely catholic instead. Witness a portion of its current mission statement: "As a Catholic institution, Villanova both emphasizes the values of the Judeo-Christian humanistic tradition and concerns itself with all value systems." The statement would make more sense if Catholic were written with a small "c," although the university remains officially affiliated with the Roman Church.

As a result of its attempt to be both Catholic (with a capital "C") and all-inclusive, Villanova loses its distinctiveness if not its cohesion and tends to attract a student body about 85 percent of whom are nominally but not doctrinally Roman Catholic. (For example, there is an active pro-choice movement on campus, as well as a strong pro-life contingent.) Of an undergraduate population of approximately 8,000, 35 percent are from Pennsylvania, and most of the rest come from the Middle Atlantic region, although 39 states and 17 foreign countries are represented. Seven percent of students are minorities.

The university consists of four undergraduate and five graduate

369

schools. The graduate schools serve 3,200 students in Business Administration, Engineering, Law, and Nursing. Undergraduate colleges also offer degrees in those fields (with the exception of law). Almost 50 percent of undergraduates, however, enroll in the College of Liberal Arts and Sciences.

In spite of efforts to dilute its Catholicism, Villanova's long ties with the Church still manifest themselves in a Western-oriented core curriculum that insists upon a few specific, semester-long courses, as well as a fairly well-defined choice of courses that fulfill supplementary distribution requirements. Forty courses are needed for graduation. The core consists of two semesters of "Introduction to Philosophy"; two in the "History of Western Civilization"; and two of a foreign language, ancient or modern. Distribution requirements also include: three more semesters of religious studies; a further semester of philosophy; two additional semesters in the humanities; three in at least two departments of the social sciences; two in the mathematical sciences; and two in two different natural sciences (with laboratory). The introductory courses in English, history, philosophy, and religious studies are fulfilled during the first year by two semesters of freshman seminars in the humanities.

The honors program, by invitation only, focuses on small sections to complete college distribution requirements, as well as advanced seminars in various subjects. A senior thesis is required. To remain in the honors program, students must maintain a 3.25 GPA. Honors students may or may not elect a major field of study; if they do they receive two certificates, one for completion of the honors program and another in the major field.

All the distribution requirements are strictly applied and students may bypass them only with advanced placement credits. By and large, the student body seems to value the requirements and is currently mounting no serious effort to alter or eliminate them. Outstanding departments in the College of Liberal Arts and Sciences are few by most reckonings, but astronomy, psychology, and philosophy are better than most. History and modern languages are considered weak, while the Program in Peace and Justice Education receives the booby prize for academic demerit.

Although in general the students may be satisfied with the academic status quo, the same cannot be said for many of the faculty. Behind the scenes, the university's politically correct moles are busy gnawing away at the pillars of Western civilization upon which the university has traditionally stood. In 1990, the committee to study the

TUITION AND FEES INCREASE
Average Increase/Year: Private = 11.15%, Villanova = 10.42%

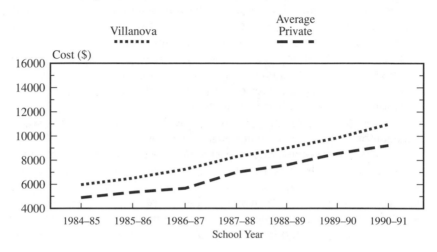

Source: The College Entrance Examination Board

core curriculum released a report recommending a five-year "enrich-ment" program for members of the arts and sciences faculty. "The themes to be explored for the five years include: (1) postmodernism/deconstruction . . . ; (2) women's studies including feminist educa-tion . . . ; (3) . . . recent models for looking at ethical issues; (4) minorities/third world studies . . . ; and (5) . . . positivist vs. alternative models [for studying the social sciences]."

The report goes on to point out that the Western civilization course is now "far too restrictive," and that "there should be greater variety in course offerings," so that faculty can "empower the students with . . . different ways of knowing," and "increase student sensitivity to cultures and groups other than the prominent mainstream hegemon-ous Western culture with which they are most familiar." Predictably at this point, the report also recommends initiating a "diversity re-quirement," designed "to liberate one's self [sic] from the inherent constraints of one's experience . . . . The study of cultures and social groups different from one's own is a powerful antidote for ethnocen-trism, racism and sexism."

On the positive side, Villanova has traditionally been oriented toward teaching, and its professors are generally approachable and concerned about students. Teaching assistants are rarely employed. Class sizes are generally small, even in introductory courses. Faculty members are required to teach 12 credit hours per week with no exceptions made for stars. However, a proposal has been introduced to cut the mandated teaching load to nine hours in order to free professors to do more research and publishing. Thus, as so many others have done, the administration may yet succumb to the temptation to let its undergraduates down as it tries to raise the university to the giddy heights of national prominence.

Meanwhile, back on the ground in Villanova, lack of campus housing provides headaches for administration and students alike. The university can accommodate only slightly more than 3,000 on its small, 240-acre oasis, a long stone's throw from downtown Philadelphia (12 miles). The campus is pretty, however, and revolves around a neo-Gothic chapel with tall, twin spires. The 18 residence halls are single-sex (with one experimental coeducational house) and range from small 20-person houses to modern multilevel buildings for 400. Freshmen are

DISTRIBUTION OF UNDERGRADUATE AID
1989–90 School Year

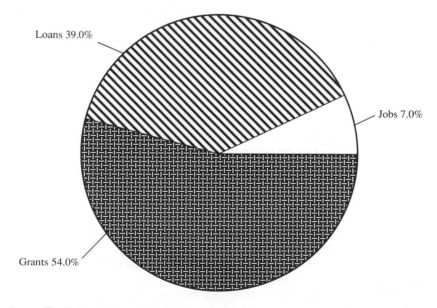

Loans 39.0%

Jobs 7.0%

Grants 54.0%

Source: The College Entrance Examination Board, 1990

accommodated on a first-come, first-served basis, and upperclassmen are selected by lottery. Fortunately, many commute from their homes in the area, but the rest find living quarters with difficulty, a situation that should ease when planned construction of 2,000 apartments is completed.

Relations between town and gown are uneasy at best and hostile at worst. Villanova is surrounded by affluent Main Line communities that do not rely on the university's purchasing power and are therefore unsympathetic to its needs. Nearby Radnor Township has stymied student housing construction, contributing to the problem. It took the university years of proposals and dozens of town meetings to persuade the township to agree to the latest construction of student housing. Villanova's plans to build a state-of-the-art athletic center were radically altered by the township; the beautiful DuPont Pavilion, slated to seat more than 10,000 for Big East basketball play, was reduced to a capacity of only 6,500—the absolute minimum for Big East games. Radnor residents also constantly complain of students' drunken antics as they return from weekend bar-hopping, but tend to ignore their numerous service and charitable contributions to the area.

Because the Villanova campus is officially dry, social life centers around the presence of top-notch, nationally ranked sports teams and the proximity of the fleshpots of Philadelphia. Athletics are immensely popular, with nearly every student participating in individual team sports. There are 12 intercollegiate sports for men and 9 for women, plus 11 intramurals for each. Villanova's nationally ranked basketball team receives a tremendous amount of support from the university community; basketball games become social happenings and often dominate campus conversation. Sporting facilities include a 13,500-seat football stadium, 200-meter track, weight rooms, a pool, and tennis courts.

Although the Greek system draws membership from about 30 percent of both male and female undergraduates, it does not have on-campus facilities and students tend to run off to Philadelphia for entertainment between basketball games. Those who remain on campus have 125 clubs and organizations at their disposal. Musical activities are particularly popular and frequent; they range from concerts by locally known performers to campus-grown singing groups. The university theater shows cultural films during the week and recent releases on the weekends. Active student theater groups perform several plays each year. Safety on campus is a non-issue, as the school is ringed by wealthy, well-policed residential communities.

The student body at Villanova tends to be conservative in both ideology and action. Enrollment in the Navy ROTC is the largest in the country and its cadets constitute a potent force for traditional values, as do the College Republicans, who form the most powerful political group. The College Democrats, traditionally strong on many college campuses, are weak and ineffectual here. Homosexuals generally stay in the closet at Villanova, and feminists speak with soft voices, though there is a women's studies program. Visiting speakers, however, represent all shades of the political spectrum.

Villanova is currently a sound if unexciting academic institution, which still respects the tenets of Western civilization and teaches them to a largely middle-class and homogeneous student body. But this is changing as the school becomes more ambitious for national recognition, and the politically correct among administration and faculty begin to wield the big stick of diversity. If they have their way, the university, in scrambling to the pinnacle of prominence, will sacrifice the bedrock of principle upon which it has steadfastly stood for 150 years.

University of Virginia

Dean of Admissions, University of Virginia
P. O. Box 9017, University Station, Charlottesville, VA 22906
(804) 924-7751

Type: Public

Students:
11,199 undergraduates
  5,594 men
  5,605 women
  6,245 graduate students

Applications:
Closing date: January 2
37% of those applied accepted

	Applied	Accepted	Enrolled
men	6,425	2,314	1,297
women	5,950	2,247	1,277

SAT required
  Score reported by: February 15
  Mid 50% of freshman scores:
    SAT-Math   590–700
    SAT-Verbal 520–640

Costs and Aid:

Tuition and fees	
In state	$2,970
Out of state	8,140
Room and Board	3,150

Scholarships:	
Academic	No
Athletic	Yes
Minority	Yes

Financial Aid:	
Freshmen	35%
Upperclassmen	28%

Library: 3,091,445 titles

ROTC: Yes

Study Abroad: Yes

Percentage of courses that can be used to fulfill distribution requirements: 45.7

The Rotunda . . . the Lawn . . . Mr. Jefferson's academical village . . . Wahoos . . . Cavaliers. These all conjure up images of the University of Virginia, one of the oldest, most traditional, most beautiful, and certainly best public universities in the country. Even without a core curriculum or rigorous distribution requirements, "THE university," which is all the identification it needs for many, manages to do a responsible job of passing Mr. Jefferson's torch of knowledge on to each new generation of students. The secret probably lies in the accent UVA has always placed on teaching, as well as in the comparatively conservative nature of the faculty and student body, who take the value of their Western heritage for granted. Indeed, it would be difficult for Mr. Jefferson's heirs to do otherwise.

After he retired from the White House to his beloved Monticello, the author of the Declaration of Independence decided to concentrate all his enormous personal gifts on what he hoped would be his greatest legacy, the creation of an "academical village" in rural Charlottesville to educate future citizens not only in the classics, but also in practical matters and public service. He personally designed the buildings, supervised construction, planned the curriculum, and engaged the first faculty. Founded in 1819, the university began its educational mission six years later with eight faculty members and 68 students. Today, his university has expanded to nearly 1,700 faculty and more than 17,000 students, but it has not outgrown Mr. Jefferson.

The academic community he designed more than 175 years ago is still the soul of his school and the subject of international acclaim. In 1976, the American Institute of Architects designated it one of the outstanding achievements in American architecture, and in 1988 it was named to the prestigious World Heritage List. A rectangular green, terraced on several levels, "The Lawn" rises at one end to the university's famous Rotunda, which is a half-scale model of Rome's Pantheon. The other end was originally left open to obtain a view, now obscured, of the distant mountains. The sides of the green are bordered by colonnaded walkways giving access to identical rows of continuous one-story rooms that are occasionally punctuated by larger Pavilions in different classical styles. Behind each of the rows are public gardens with serpentine brick walks, plus another row of rooms known as the "Ranges."

Jefferson drew his architectural plan to allow faculty to reside in the Pavilions, students to live in the rooms, and classes to take place in the Rotunda. Today, distinguished students are awarded rooms on the Lawn in their fourth year, some faculty still live in the Pavilions, and the Rotunda is used for dinners, meetings, ceremonial occasions, and student activities.

The university's sense of continuity and community is also based on its entrenched academic honor code, in effect for 150 years and still going strong, in principle if not always in practice. Examinations are unproctored and students may leave the classroom to take their tests wherever they feel most comfortable, so long as they pledge that they have neither given nor received help. Belongings are left undisturbed in libraries and classrooms; trust prevails. If, however, a student is convicted by his peers (the Honor Committee) of a violation of the code, he receives only one punishment, known as the "single sanction," immediate dismissal from the university.

Virginia's students come from all the states and 75 foreign countries. Only 65 percent are from the Old Dominion; the university is proud of being a nationally known institution and regularly matricu-

TUITION AND FEES INCREASE
Average Increase/Year: Public = 8.30%, Virginia = 8.24%

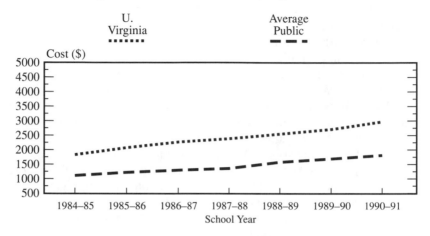

Source: The College Entrance Examination Board

lates 35 percent of students from outside the state. This policy is not universally popular, however, drawing frequent criticism from state residents (particularly those from the heavily populated Washington suburbs), who resent outsiders filling so many of the available places. Partly in response to this, the university is planning a modest expansion, to begin in the mid-1990s.

Virginia sponsors three professional schools, all highly regarded: the School of Law, consistently ranked in the nation's top 10; the School of Medicine; and the Darden School of Business Administration. Schools awarding both graduate and undergraduate degrees are Architecture, Commerce, Education, Engineering and Applied Science, and Nursing. But the College of Arts and Sciences, for which the university has always been justly famous, is far and away the most popular, enrolling 8,300 of more than 11,000 undergraduates.

Virginia operates on the semester system, requiring 120 credits for graduation. Unlike most liberal arts schools, the College of Arts and Sciences mandates that the degree program be completed within four years. This policy was adopted to avoid the perpetual-student syndrome, and most candidates do manage to finish in the time specified. Those who have legitimate reasons for not doing so are granted extensions.

Distribution requirements are: six to nine credits in English composition (six hours may be exempted by examination); a flexible number of credits in a foreign language (depending upon proficiency on arrival); nine credits in natural science and/or mathematics; six credits in the social sciences and/or history; and six credits in the humanities and/or fine arts.

The Echols Honors Program, by invitation to about 8 percent of entering freshmen, allows students of special ability to pursue independent study under the supervision of departmental faculty and a committee on special programs. All candidates for honors degrees (including Echols Scholars) are evaluated by visiting examiners from other colleges and recommended for degrees with honors, with high honors, or with highest honors. The prestigious Jefferson Scholars Program provides generous scholarships each year for 18 applicants who must survive a rigorous selection process.

Teaching assistants are widely used, but most are competent. Because of the university's tradition of excellence in teaching, faculty heavyweights carry their share of the classroom load, often lecturing to large introductory courses and teaching smaller advanced courses and seminars. Strong departments are English (rated superior but still with its share of deconstructionists), history, art history, French, and German. The hard sciences tend to be weaker.

While politically correct faculty members do not yet possess a stranglehold on the curriculum at UVA, they have begun to tighten their grip. The English department is about to put in place a "multicultural" course requirement for the major, and there is talk about instituting a similar "Cultural Perspectives" requirement college-wide, even though there are no Western civilization requirements. So far, there is no verbal antiharassment code, but again there is a growing movement among faculty and militant students to initiate one. As one professor recently put it, "Politically, UVA is left of the American political mainstream, but right of the academic mainstream. There is a gentlemanly aura here, so disputes don't get aired openly, but there is nevertheless a strong cloud of political correctness on the horizon. Traditionalists are definitely an embattled species."

Although Virginia students are generally more conservative than faculty, they too are beginning to succumb to the new orthodoxy. Small groups of feminist, black, and homosexual groups are active and label those who disagree with their agendas "homophobic, racist, and sexist." Students understandably shrink from these epithets and often withdraw from debate on the issues. Minority students comprise nearly 18 percent of undergraduates, with blacks and Asians predominating.

As on most campuses, the majority of students is less interested in politics than in personal agendas. Getting a degree and having a good time in the process are at the top of most lists. UVA students have always been expert at the latter, and today the Greek system is still an integral part of campus life. About 30 percent of students belong to 39 fraternities and 22 sororities, which set the pace for the social scene. The drunken bashes on Rugby Road have quieted down in recent years, since the Charlottesville community demanded that the Greeks "close" their parties. Guest lists now determine who will and will not be admitted to the one-time free-for-alls. This presents problems for non-member, first-year students (never called freshmen), who once relied on fraternities as their main social outlet.

In March 1991, fraternity row made national headlines, which sent shockwaves throughout Virginia and the academic community nationwide. A dozen members of three fraternities were suddenly arrested and indicted on charges of selling drugs ranging from marijuana to LSD Law enforcement officials seized bags of the illicit drugs along with the students. Later, police said the raid was the first of its kind in the country, and was meant to send a message that college campuses are not sanctuaries for drug activity. The federal government then began proceedings to take over the houses under a federal drug law allowing confiscation of assets involved in drug trafficking. Students were allowed to continue residing in the seized houses until the end of term if they agreed to rules set by law enforcement officers.

Many of the two-thirds of UVA undergraduates who don't join the Greek scene (and were probably glad of it in the spring of 1991) gravitate for their social life toward a cluster of restaurants and bars known as the "Corner": the Virginian with its dim lighting, forest-green walls, and Bohemian wait staff attracts English major types; Macado's lively atmosphere hosts the younger crowd; St. Martaan's and its all-you-can-eat seafood nights lure the beer-drinking crowd (you eventually earn your own pewter beer mug handed to you when you come in); the College Inn tempts anyone on a starving-student budget who's hungry for lots of good food. For those who want to go farther afield, Richmond and Washington, D.C., are an hour and two and a half hours' drive respectively.

Lots of Wahoos work off the beer by joining one or more of the 300 extracurricular organizations, or participating in 12 intercollegiate and 27 intramural sports for men and 11 intercollegiates and 24 intra-murals for women. Basketball is the big varsity sport, though football has always drawn loyal fans and, after years in the doldrums, is now improving. Facilities on the 2,440-acre campus include a 44,000-seat stadium, a 9,000-seat gymnasium, recreation centers, and the usual assortment of courts and playing fields.

Only slightly more than half the student body can be accommo-dated in the comfortable on-campus housing, which is guaranteed for first-year students and includes coed dormitories, apartments, honors, and language houses. For the last six years, only 30 percent of upperclassmen have elected to live on campus, so there is no over-crowding; off-campus rooms and apartments are easily available and affordable. Nevertheless, Virginia is constructing additional quarters.

The university, however, is finding that it can afford to do less and less, due to the state's budget difficulties, which are affecting appro-priations. More than $3 million are being cut from the university budget and faculty salaries have been reduced by 2 percent. In only the second year of his presidency, John Casteen (formerly a member of Virginia's own English department and later president of the University of Connecticut) has his hands full with damage control. With any luck, Mr. Jefferson's university will survive not only material deprivations from state legislators, but also intellectual contagion from those who would transform his academical village into just another province of the politically correct.

Wake Forest University

Director of Admissions and Financial Aid
Wake Forest University
Box 7305 Reynolda Station, Winston-Salem, NC 27109
(919) 759-5201

Type: Private and Protestant				**Costs and Aid:**	
				Tuition and fees	$9,700
Students:				Room and Board	3,550
3,444 undergraduates					
1,942 men				Scholarships:	
1,502 women				Academic	Yes
1,856 graduate students				Athletic	Yes
				Minority	Yes
Applications:				Financial Aid:	
Closing date: January 15				Freshmen	66%
32% of applicants accepted				Upperclassmen	61%
	Applied	*Accepted*	*Enrolled*		
men	3,054	1,070	491	**Library:**	518,963 titles
women	3,221	910	416		
SAT required				**ROTC:**	Yes
Score reported by: February 1				**Study Abroad:**	Yes
Mid 50% of freshman scores:					
SAT-Math	530–690				
SAT-Verbal	520–620				

    The New South meets the Old South just outside Winston-Salem, North Carolina, at Wake Forest University. Blending more than a century of tradition with an entirely new physical plant, and an old-fashioned curriculum with modern academic liberalism, Wake Forest has emerged as one of the premier regional universities in the southern United States.

    As you pass through its gates, the first thing you will notice is the utter lack of "Southern charm" at Wake Forest. Modernity is everywhere on the 490-acre campus. The buildings are new, the grounds are obviously young; even nearby Winston-Salem, a growing city of 150,000 souls, seems youthful.

    It is not, of course, the same Wake Forest University that opened its doors in 1834. Founded by the Baptist State Convention of North Carolina, Wake Forest retains a decidedly religious atmosphere. In 1956, the school was relocated from Wake Forest, North Carolina, to Winston-Salem. Although the university lies just beyond the urban stretch of the city, the move cost the school the tranquil, isolated comfort of a small Southern town.

Formal ties with the Baptist convention were severed in the early 1980s, but the Campus Ministry, as well as the numerous individual religious organizations which exist under its umbrella, provides ample opportunities for the pious student to continue in his traditional Christian lifestyle—and many students do just that. While some bemoan the moral provincialism of their more religious peers, it is clearly part of the school's appeal. (One junior at Wake Forest complained that there is a widely repeated aphorism among the male student population, "Sex kills. Come to Wake Forest and live forever.")

The past decade has been marked by enormous growth and improvement for the university. Since 1980, undergraduate enrollment has increased to 3,400, with more than 40 percent of the student body coming from North Carolina and the rest from 45 other states and several foreign countries. A campus-wide building boom that has lasted almost 30 years has given birth to more than a dozen new structures. The main library is approaching one million volumes, and students wander the halls of a brand-new 100,000-square foot student center. Much of this growth has been made possible by the tobacco fortune of the Reynolds family. Indeed, the Reynolds name is everywhere. Wake Forest is located on the Reynolds Campus, administrators work in Reynolds Hall, students study in the Reynolds Library, play in Reynolds Gymnasium—and the list goes on.

Amidst the changes, the basic academic requirements in Wake Forest College have remained steady for the last 20 years. (The only other undergraduate division is the School of Business and Accountancy.) Although there is no formal core curriculum, the college's broad range of distribution requirements does provide students a limited knowledge base in a variety of disciplines. All students are required to take 15 semester courses that include basic composition, an intermediate foreign language and a foreign-language literature course, as well as three courses in each of four divisions—literature and the arts; the natural sciences and mathematics; history, religion and philosophy; and the social and behavioral sciences. Two courses in health and sport science are also mandatory.

A somewhat unusual aspect of Wake Forest's distribution requirements is that they cannot be satisfied through politicized courses like "Humanities 121—Introduction to Woman's Studies." Should students wish to take these nontraditional courses, they must do so with electives. However, it is not difficult to fulfill the general requirements

TUITION AND FEES INCREASE
Average Increase/Year: Private = 11.15%, Wake Forest = 9.76%

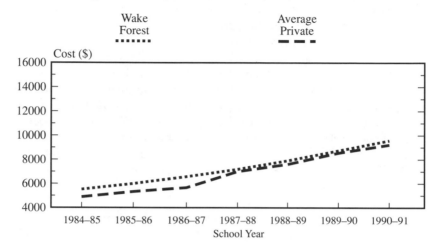

Source: The College Entrance Examination Board

without having taken a course in any number of fields. For example, you may complete the basic and divisional requirements while successfully bypassing mathematics, physics, economics, politics, and American literature. Additionally, there is no requirement to take a specific course in Western civilization or American history. In fact, the only specific requirement is English composition, and even here there is some choice.

The requirements for most majors suffer from the same license. With a little effort, for example, a student can graduate with a degree in politics while completely bypassing the works of John Locke, Adam Smith, Machiavelli, Alexander Hamilton, and others. On the positive side, many of the trendy departments and majors, like women's studies and homosexual studies, have not yet reached Wake Forest. Although you can minor in the interdisciplinary field of women's studies, no such major is offered. Nor is there a major in any of the various "Third World" fields. But consistent pressure is being applied by the younger faculty to include more majors in what has elsewhere been called "victims' studies." It would not be at all surprising if these found a home at Wake Forest in the near future.

At present, a careful advising system helps to balance the university's loose requirements. Each student is assigned an advisory team for the first two years, made up of one student and one professor. Each advisory team serves only 10 students. After a major is declared, a faculty advisor in that field is appointed.

Despite all of its progress, Wake Forest is not without significant problems. It has yet to shake its image as a "fall-back" school for freshmen who apply to Duke University—despite the fact that it is much less politicized and its curriculum is at least as good. The presidential debates of 1988, one of which was held at Wake Forest, provided a significant boost to the university's reputation. However, Wake Forest's graduate programs in business and law are still considered "second tier," overshadowed by more prominent neighbors—UNC-Chapel Hill and especially Duke. Even Wake Forest's excellent Bowman-Gray Medical School must play second fiddle to Duke's world-class medical program.

The teaching staff has also undergone radical change during the past decade. Most of the younger faculty came of age in the late 1960s

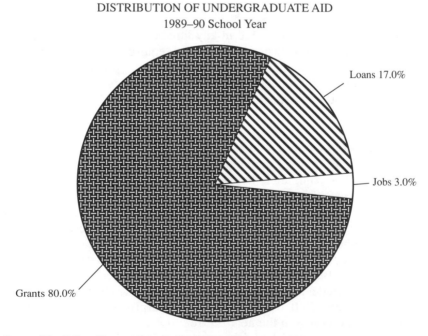

DISTRIBUTION OF UNDERGRADUATE AID
1989–90 School Year

Loans 17.0%

Jobs 3.0%

Grants 80.0%

Source: The College Entrance Examination Board, 1990

and early 1970s, and still swing to the left. As a result, the political views of the younger faculty are usually 180 degrees out-of-phase with those of the average undergraduate. Students, who are generally conservative, often find little common ground with some of their appointed mentors. With much of the older, more traditionally minded faculty reaching retirement age by the turn of the century, this disparity will likely become even more pronounced.

The administration, however, has so far given short shrift to the leftward leaners. (In the past few years, both Jack Kemp and John Sununu have received honorary degrees from Wake Forest.) But with some senior administrators leaving soon, this too may change. For now, the students and administration seem to act as brakes on the more politically correct faculty. However, this does not prevent the administration from showcasing them when it suits university purposes.

Among the best-known academics to hang their hats in Winston-Salem is Maya Angelou, author of a book about oppression called, *I Know Why the Caged Bird Sings,* often assigned to middle and high school students. As one of the most prominent black academics in the country, she is used by the university to attract black students. And while she rarely teaches, the admissions office has eagerly promoted her as a role model and mentor for minorities.

Among the most effective of the university's other minority recruiting tools are the Gordon Scholarships, which provide money to black students regardless of financial need. The goal of this and other recruiting programs is to bring the black population up to 10 percent of the student body. However, the efforts to increase black enrollment have been largely unsuccessful and the black student population still hovers around 7 percent. Unofficially, the university attributes this small percentage to the specter of racism which haunts the school. "They're big on racism here," reports one senior, "everybody is always talking about it, it's the big thing."

The optional Wake Forest "Preschool" for incoming freshmen is one way the administration attempts to cope with the issue. A week before registration begins, the school spends a weekend "sensitizing" students to race and gender concerns. The more conservative students regard it as indoctrination and, in early 1990, the conservative student magazine blasted the ritual as a throwback to Woodstock. Beginning with the freshmen class of 1991, the university will be adding a day of mandatory "sensitivity training" to freshmen orientation.

The most active minority student organization is the university-sanctioned Black Student Alliance, considered the official student voice for Wake Forest's small black community. In keeping with the practice at many universities, the Alliance automatically considers all black students members. White students are allowed to join the organization, but only after they have been approved. In April 1991, this policy resulted in a white student journalist being physically ejected from a "closed" meeting. This type of incident, along with high-profile activities like "Blackfest," often causes resentment among white students. As at other schools, the Wake Forest administration's attempts at social engineering seem to be exacerbating the problems of race relations.

The feminist faction also occasionally speaks out in campus debates, but wields less power. Of practically no significance is the Gay and Lesbian Alliance. In fact, it is more accurate to say that there is no homosexual group to speak of, and students seem to prefer it that way. At Wake Forest, most students still regard homosexuality as sinful and unnatural.

Social life generally revolves around a large and active fraternity system. More than 40 percent of students are affiliated with one of the dozen national fraternities, or seven national and two local sororities. Most unaffiliated students also enjoy Greek parties and functions. There are two black Greek organizations which remain largely segregated, by choice, from the white fraternities. This practice serves to further discourage genuine interracial relationships.

Unlike many other schools, the administration at Wake Forest supports the Greek organizations. Although there is only one off-campus fraternity house, the Greeks find homes in the dormitories. Whole sections of the campus dorms are dedicated to each of the recognized societies and fraternities. Not surprisingly, however, the system enjoys less support among the more liberal faculty. But for the time being at least, the Greek system at Wake Forest is likely to escape the persecution that has plagued fraternities at so many other schools.

As if by design, the campus preoccupation with race seems somewhat leavened by a charming Southern innocence which may also be found at Wake Forest. One female freshman recounted how shocked she was to find the student health organization distributing condoms during orientation week. It was the first time she had seen one, she confessed in midblush. Her response was not typical, but not rare either. That innocence is soon lost as the public discussion of sex, abortion, and AIDS dulls the conscience and emboldens the libido.

However, the conservative mores of the students often seem to survive campus life.

As is the case at almost all ACC schools, basketball is an important part of collegiate life at Wake Forest. The Demon Deacons display their roundball prowess at the Joel Coliseum, which the university shares with the city of Winston-Salem. Football is also a campus-wide activity, but does not command the near-universal allegiance basketball enjoys. These sports play a significant role in helping the university maintain excellent relations with the city. Both the city fathers and the local population seem to take great pride in "their" university.

There are also a dozen other intercollegiate sports teams, many of which have a substantial following, and more than 30 intramural sports. The university boasts several indoor basketball courts as well as a pool, tennis courts, and weight facilities. The athletically inclined student will find more than enough outlets at Wake Forest for any excess energy.

Extracurricular life can also be intense. The university's debate program is highly regarded, well coached, and well attended. Religious life is taken very seriously by many students for whom regular Bible study meetings are an integral part of campus life. A weekly newspaper, which varies in quality from year to year, as well as a biweekly conservative paper and a literary journal offer students a chance to develop their writing and editing skills. Campus radio and television facilities are available for future broadcasters. Altogether, there are more than 100 groups and organizations on campus.

Theme houses reinforce both extracurricular and academic interests for many students. Italian, Russian, French, and Spanish houses, as well as a Radio House and several other special-interest dorms allow like-minded students to get together. All freshmen are generally required to live in the dormitories, and most upperclassmen choose to stay in them as well. Housing is both single-sex and coed and guaranteed for all four years. The residences vary in quality and spaciousness. The newer dormitories, on the southern part of the campus, offer spacious air-conditioned rooms. The older houses, in the Quad, are less roomy and lack air conditioning, but their central location makes them more desirable for many.

All in all, Wake Forest University is just what you might expect to find on the outskirts of Winston-Salem, North Carolina—a decent if not yet academically rigorous, generally conservative school struggling to achieve national recognition. It is also a school at a crossroads. If the administration continues to be fixated on becoming a national university, it may succumb to many of the more pernicious trends in American higher education. As the more conservative professors retire, greater influence will surely be exerted by the more radical young faculty members. How much and to what effect remains to be seen.

University of Washington

Executive Director, Admissions and Records
University of Washington
1400 Northeast Campus Parkway, Seattle, WA 98195
(206) 543-9686

Type: Public		**Costs and Aid:**	
Students:		Tuition and fees	
22,897 undergraduates		In state	$1,940
11,705 men		Out of state	5,420
11,192 women		Room and Board	3,800
8,796 graduate students		Scholarships:	
		Academic	Yes
Applications:		Athletic	Yes
Closing date: February 1		Minority	Yes
65% of applicants accepted		Financial Aid:	

Applied	Accepted	Enrolled
10,168	6,629	3,362

Freshmen	28%
Upperclassmen	29%

SAT or ACT required
Score reported by: February 1
Mid 50% of freshman scores:

SAT-Math	520–650	
SAT-Verbal	440–570	

Library:	4,800,000 titles
ROTC:	Yes
Study Abroad:	Yes

All you have to do to get a sense of the prevailing ethos at the University of Washington these days is glance at the front cover of its *General Catalog (1990–92)*. The artwork features smiling students of different races against a background festooned with symbols representing both male and female homosexuality, as well as various racial and ethnic groups. The caption reads, "The University of Washington Values Diversity." How much it values undergraduate academics, however, is an open question, though it certainly can't be accused of discrimination there, either: One of the more stimulating courses the university offers for academic credit is the dance department's "Exploring the Articulate Body."

When Washington isn't glamorizing race, sexuality, or body language it often boasts about its dependence on the federal government. A profile of the institution proudly declares that, "For two decades the University has been among the top five institutions in the amount of federal grant and contract funds attracted by its faculty . . . [and is]

389

part of an elite group of research universities whose contributions to American life are unique because they generate the basic knowledge upon which practical innovations are based.''

Some may wonder, however, whether the university is too busy generating basic knowledge to teach it on the undergraduate level and whether there is even a consensus about what "basic" knowledge is. No core curriculum exists, and students frequently satisfy distribution requirements by enrolling in watered-down, introductory courses. Liberal arts students take huge lecture courses, often enlisting hundreds, although discussion groups and seminars do exist, especially when students move into their major fields.

The university, which operates on the quarter system, consists of 16 major schools and colleges including the College of Arts and Sciences and the Graduate School. Others specialize in Architecture and Urban Planning, Business, Dentistry, Education, Engineering, Forestry, Law, Medicine, Nursing, Pharmacy, Public Health and Community Medicine, Ocean and Fishery Sciences, Public Affairs, and Social Work.

Founded in 1861 on 10 acres of wilderness (which are now part of downtown Seattle) and staffed by a single overworked faculty member, the university was forced to close several times during its early years due to lack of funds. Picking up steam by the time statehood arrived in 1889, the school chugged along until after World War II, when it began to add branch lines in all directions, as the federal dollars rolled in. The university is now enormous, with around 33,000 students, more than 3,000 faculty and no fewer than 12,000 administrators and support staff, a triumph of bureaucracy by any standard. Many of these people are employed, of course, to unravel the tangles of government-generated red tape, which so often enslaves those who succumb to Uncle Sam's siren song.

To graduate from the College of Arts and Sciences, students must present 90 course credits (five are earned per course) outside the major. Two of these must be chosen from designated courses that emphasize writing (in a number of disciplines). Twenty credits each are required in the humanities, the social sciences, and the natural sciences. The humanities are subdivided into (a) language and literature and (b) the fine arts. The social sciences are subdivided into (a) social sciences and (b) history, philosophy, and civilization. At least five credits must be selected from each subdivision. The foreign language and quantitative/symbolic reasoning requirements may be

TUITION AND FEES INCREASE

Average Increase/Year: Public = 8.30%, Washington = 7.12%

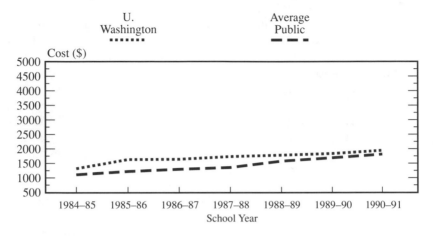

Source: The College Entrance Examination Board

---

satisfied through the language and literature and natural science requirements or by proficiency examination.

An honors program for approximately 700 fortunate students presently provides the best hope for those seriously interested in the liberal arts. On the whole, "U-Dub" (a corruption of UW) is much more successful on the graduate than undergraduate level, which itself succeeds best in the preprofessional fields. In the university's race for primacy, the liberal arts finish last.

The advisory system also lags behind. Professors are usually too busy with their research to bother with students on a personal level, so advising is largely left to teaching assistants, who in turn are often preoccupied with their own graduate studies.

The university community convenes for form-filling, meetings, counseling, and even classes on 690 acres about 10 minutes from downtown Seattle, in a scenic setting on a lake not far from pretty Puget Sound. Almost 90 percent of the approximately 23,000 undergraduates hail from Washington State (which is probably the reason the school is not well known in the other 49 despite its size); but there are many foreign countries represented among the rest. Roughly 20 percent of students are black, Hispanic, or Asian, with the last predominating. About 85 percent of the entire population commutes, enabling the university to guarantee on-campus housing for all four years to those who wish it.

Campus accommodation can put a roof over the heads of 4,400 students, and includes seven well-appointed, coed residence halls, as well as studio apartments for singles and married-student quarters. Minorities do not have their own houses. Slightly under 20 percent of undergraduates belong to around 50 national fraternities and sororities, which also offer some residential space.

Because so many students live in Seattle or nearby, the Greeks reign over the campus social scene despite their relatively few numbers. Social life is fragmented at best and lacks a sense of community; each individual must go his own way and try to find a niche where he can. Those interested in the art or the history of the American West like to browse in the university's art gallery and state museum. The Henry Art Gallery was the gift of a philanthropist who made his money in railroads and real estate. His contribution to the university included

DISTRIBUTION OF UNDERGRADUATE AID
1989–90 School Year

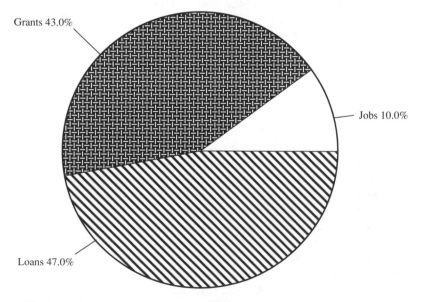

Source: The College Entrance Examination Board, 1990

both the funds for the gallery building and his own art collection of about 200 paintings. The Burke Memorial Washington State Museum, opened in 1885, is the oldest university museum in the West and houses extensive Indian collections as well as fascinating anthropology, geology, and zoology exhibits from mainland and island nations around the Pacific rim.

More than 250 clubs and organizations provide an enormous range of activities, but the most popular seem to be intramural sports, with about a third of undergraduates playing on nearly 60 teams. The university also fields 10 intercollegiate sports for men and 9 for women in the PAC 10. Because of its location and soft climate (U-Dubbers insist it doesn't rain as much as everyone thinks in Seattle), outdoor activities rank high, and there are a lot to choose from. The university has all kinds of athletic and recreational facilities (an advantage of its bigness) including a 72,500-seat stadium, baseball diamond, track and field complex, tennis courts, swimming pool, golf range, and even a climbing rock.

But water sports are many students' real passion (along with the famous Division I Huskies football team which mesmerizes almost everyone). With two lakes to splash in, enthusiasts kayak, canoe, sail, windsurf, and scuba dive to their hearts' content and, when they want a change, pop up a few thousand feet to the nearby mountains to ski, climb, and backpack. If land and sea don't provide enough adventure, highflyers can always take to the air with the skydiving club.

Students are not limited merely to campus-related activities. Seattle is rich in cultural opportunities. Those who enjoy the arts appreciate the student discounts offered by the Pacific Northwest Ballet, the Seattle Opera, the Seattle Repertory Theater (one of many acclaimed theater groups in the area), and the Seattle Symphony. On a more populist level, professional sports teams abound and, depending upon the season, UW students join other spectators at Sonics's basketball, Seahawks's football, Mariners's baseball, Stars's soccer, or Thunderbirds's hockey.

But all is not fun and games in the playground of the West. Crime often rears its ugly head in the form of theft, rape, and assault, which are not always committed by students. The urban setting contributes to the uneasy atmosphere, but so have the campus police, who two years ago overreacted to football fans threatening to tear down the goal posts after a game with rival Washington State. The goal posts remained upright, but the students were felled by squirts of Mace in the face. Relations with security forces haven't been the same since.

Oppressive tactics on campus are not limited to maintaining law and order. Practitioners of the new morality like to bully believers in the old morality; anything goes at UW except traditional behavior. Militant Marxist lesbians frequently shout down moderates, and the Student Task Force on Minority Affairs and Racism busily enforces its own orthodoxy. Asians, who are the largest minority group, are too occupied with their studies to join in the majority-bashing. There have been several incidents in recent years involving sensitivity issues about women and minorities, one of which resulted in the expulsion of a white male student who was deemed "insensitive" to instructors in women's studies. The administration maintains that the student was expelled for threatening violence.

Overall, the University of Washington is a great place for graduate students, jocks, fresh air addicts, and homestate residents who wish a college degree at a subsidized price. Those seriously interested in a broad-based, traditional liberal arts education, however, had better look farther afield.

Washington and Lee University

Dean of Admissions and Financial Aid
Washington and Lee University, Lexington, VA 24450
(703) 463-8710

				Costs and Aid:	
Type: Private and Secular				Tuition and fees	$10,970
Students:				Room and Board	3,900
1,665 undergraduates				Scholarships:	
1,110 men				Academic	Yes
555 women				Athletic	No
346 graduate students				Minority	Yes
Applications:				Financial Aid:	
Closing date: February 1				Freshmen	29%
29% of applicants accepted				Upperclassmen	29%
	Applied	*Accepted*	*Enrolled*		
men	1,862	622	280	**Library:**	257,121 titles
women	1,355	307	145		
SAT or ACT required				**ROTC:**	Yes
Score reported by: March 1				**Study Abroad:**	Yes
Mid 50% of freshman scores:				**Percentage of courses that can**	
SAT-Math	600–690			**be used to fulfill distribution**	
SAT-Verbal	550–640			**requirements:**	37.5

In the summer of 1865, the Confederate General of the Army of Northern Virginia accepted the presidency of a small school in Lexington, Virginia, called Washington College. Robert E. Lee had thought long and hard about the offer fearing he, a symbol of the Confederacy, might embarrass the school in a period of bitter national discord. Instead, he expanded the college's enrollment, strengthened it academically, and left a permanent mark upon its spirit. Today his devotion to duty, integrity, and honor still echoes throughout the Washington and Lee community.

One of the 10 oldest institutions of higher learning in the nation, dating its founding to 1749, W&L instills in its graduates an almost palpable pride in their alma mater, a sentiment that often lasts a lifetime, at least for male graduates. It is too early to tell yet about the women, as W&L went coeducational less than a decade ago, and men still outnumber females by approximately two to one in the 1,700 member undergraduate student body, most of whom come from the South and Southwest.

W&L's crest combines the family emblems of Generals Washington and Lee, the two most influential men in the university's history. This symbol serves to remind students constantly of the enduring influence of these two sons of the South. The seal's upper portion comes from the Washington family coat of arms. General Washington's gift of $50,000 of James River Kanawa Canal stock in 1786 saved the school (then known as Liberty Hall) from almost inevitable closure, due to financial collapse; the funds remain a part of the university's endowment today, and income from it has exceeded $500,000. Thus, W&L students still benefit from the first president's largesse. The seal's lower section (including the school's motto) belongs to the Lee family. This roughly translates as "Not unmindful of the future." Inherent in the phrase's meaning, however, is that preparing for the future involves learning from the past.

While General Washington's donation enabled the school to remain open, General Lee's presidency revolutionized it and determined many of the principles upon which it now functions. Lee's institution of the honor system, which permeates student life today, was perhaps his most important legacy. If you asked a W&L student to define what distinguishes his school from others, he would undoubtedly reply, "the honor system," which was an outgrowth of the General's injunction that W&L men should always act as gentlemen. Gentlemen do not lie, cheat, or steal and, in the old soldier's time, if they did they were so ostracized by their classmates that they were forced to withdraw.

Robert E. Lee's simple injunction that students should behave like gentlemen replaced the numerous regulations and restrictions that had governed the student body before his arrival. He believed in a highly structured academic environment, undoubtedly a carry-over from his military career and tenure as superintendent of West Point. He expected W&L men to respect authority, to refrain from crude behavior, and to treat a woman like a lady.

In the century and a quarter since his presidency, the honor code has developed into a single sentence, "On my honor, I will neither lie, steal, nor cheat." A student's word is never questioned by professors; tests and examinations are scheduled by students and administered without proctors. In town, students may write checks without carrying identification. This reliance on trust does have a price, however; once a person has been found guilty of a violation, he is removed from the community by a student executive committee—no excuses, no exemptions, no fine print. Out.

During his brief tenure (he died in 1870), General Lee also left his

TUITION AND FEES INCREASE

Average Increase/Year: Private = 11.15%, Washington & Lee = 8.82%

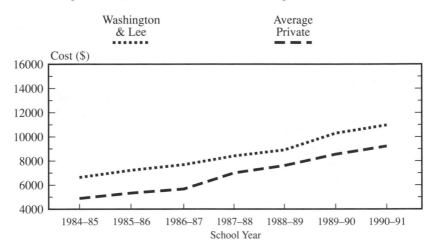

Source: The College Entrance Examination Board

imprint on the university's academics, establishing a School of Law, and programs in business instruction that resulted in the foundation of the second undergraduate school, now called the School of Commerce, Economics, and Politics. Together with the original undergraduate liberal arts college, they form the nucleus of W&L. Further, the general introduced studies in journalism and communications. These courses and those in business were the first of their kind offered in U.S. colleges. After General Lee's death, when the school was re-named for him, the presidency was conferred upon his son, G. W. Custis Lee, who followed in his famous father's footsteps for 26 years.

Like most colleges and universities, Washington and Lee has distribution requirements (known as general education requirements) as opposed to a core curriculum. Students, therefore, can get by without ever taking a United States history course or even a course in Western civilization. However, most students do choose a course in the latter. Beware though—a recent push for increased "multicultur-alism" by student and faculty members may weaken the distribution requirements in years to come.

Presently, students in both undergraduate schools must take an English composition course, unless they are able to place out through an examination; they must also take two literature courses. In addition, undergraduates must demonstrate ability in a foreign language equivalent to third-year level. Other requirements are: four courses in fine arts, history, philosophy, and religion, with one in at least two of these areas; three courses in the social sciences, again covering at least two different departments. Finally, in science and mathematics, 10 credits are required (not all of these courses give the usual three credits), at least four of which must be in a laboratory science and three in math or computer science. Courses required for the major may be used to fulfill the distribution requirements.

Strong departments are the pre-professional programs in the business school, English, history and journalism; math and science are weaker, but on the road to improvement. A recently introduced interdisciplinary program in Russian and East Asian studies shows promise, as does one in cognitive studies that combines computer science, philosophy and psychology. A new performing arts center

DISTRIBUTION OF UNDERGRADUATE AID
1989–90 School Year

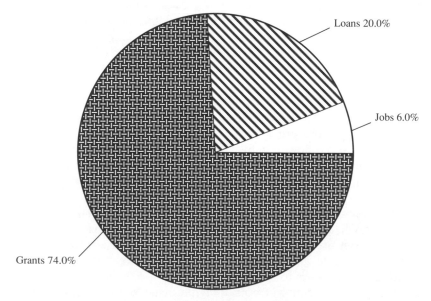

Loans 20.0%

Jobs 6.0%

Grants 74.0%

Source: The College Entrance Examination Board, 1990

should strengthen theater and the fine arts. There are honors programs available in 24 departments.

The administration at W&L is largely invisible on campus, as the honor system replaces policing. One of the few ways the administration does contact the student body, however, is through periodic questionnaires. Various deans chart the political and ideological beliefs of the student body, its social activity and consumption of alcohol and, since the admission of women, its sexual activity. (On the assumption, presumably, that neither gentlemen *nor* ladies tell lies.)

Unlike other universities, W&L does not boast about the high percentage of faculty members that teach, because most classes are taught by faculty, not graduate students. The university comes heavily down on the side of teaching as opposed to research and publishing. While this means that the school does not receive as many federal research grants as other universities, it has created an environment in which the professor's primary concern and responsibility is the student. Most professors keep generous office hours, and nearly all will schedule an appointment with a student at a mutually convenient time. Classes usually have between 15 and 25 students, with the largest rarely exceeding 30.

Contact between teacher and student often continues outside the classroom. Dinners and other social gatherings attended by both students and professors are fairly frequent, and casual contact with faculty in the Lexington shops and on its streets contributes to the informal atmosphere. Student-faculty friendships not only add to the sense of community which distinguishes Washington and Lee, but they also serve to blur the distinction between classroom knowledge and the broader scope of life. Very often, it is not only a professor teaching a class or grading a paper, it is a respected friend—a respect that often runs both ways.

Every student has a faculty advisor. Because the student-faculty ratio is low, students share advisors with no more than 12 to 14 others. Beside the usual functions, advisors often notify students of potential scholarships and awards for which the student might not otherwise know to apply. Especially during the freshman year the advisor provides encouragement and support when grades are released.

Washington and Lee uses a trimester system, one somewhat out of the ordinary. The trimesters are divided into two 12-week terms, concluding with a final six-week "spring term." During each of the 12-week terms, the average study load consists of 12 academic hours, with students enrolled in lab courses taking an additional hour or two.

Even though the majority of classes are taught during these terms, most of the campus would agree that the short spring term is the most exciting of the year, for a number of reasons.

For some students it offers the opportunity for study abroad. Undergraduates have the opportunity to visit almost any nation in Europe (including the Soviet Union), the Far East, or closer to home, New York and Washington, D.C. Other students take advantage of special seminars. Finally, nearly everyone enjoys the relaxed atmosphere which characterizes this term. The weather is usually fine and the always beautiful setting, in the small mountains of the lower Shenandoah Valley, takes on added splendor during the final month before summer vacation.

Despite recent efforts by the admissions office to liberalize the campus's conservative bent, the political attitude remains staunchly mainstream conservative. There is not much "activism" because students generally take common principles for granted and prefer social to political parties, except during presidential elections, when they traditionally hold a mock convention for the party out of power and regularly predict the winner with startling accuracy. While the newer recruits to the faculty tend to bring some of their political ideology into the classroom, the older and more beloved faculty members appear largely apolitical, more interested in the process of education than indoctrination.

Lest traditionalists think W&L is collegiate heaven, however, it must be noted that—like much of academia—W&L has succumbed to the limitation of free speech in favor of enforcing political correctness—through the Confidential Review Committee composed of faculty and students. The committee is responsible for evaluating and punishing "allegations of sexual assault, ethnic, racial, religious or sexual harassment." There is no written code covering specifics, however, and for most students the only relevant issue is the opposite sex, since homosexuality doesn't seem to exist at W&L, and minorities comprise only about 7 percent of the student body. Race relations are generally good, though there are attempts by blacks and some faculty to lay guilt trips on white males, which cause resentment. In this context, however, it is heartening to note that recently a black served as president of the student body.

This racial harmony may not endure for long, however, if some of the more radical faculty have their way. In March 1991, two female professors took it upon themselves to contact local businesses which advertised in the conservative student newspaper, the *W&L Spectator*.

They demanded that the advertisers withdraw their support, accusing the paper of being "blatantly racist, sexist, and offensively conservative." No substantiation of these charges was offered. At this writing, the reaction of the administration to the professors' actions is unknown. Much will depend upon it.

Social life centers almost exclusively around the Greek system. The 16 national fraternity houses, now under renovation, provide the location for parties and for other events during W&L's major social weekends. Indeed, Fancy Dress is one of the most famous social weekends in American college history. Attracting thousands to the campus, it was once described by *Life* magazine as the largest social event in academia. W&L also has four national sororities, as well as other social groups for those who choose not to participate in Greek life; but it is the fraternities that dominate with about 80 percent of the men affiliated. Alcohol flows freely and frequently both in the fraternity houses and local watering holes, the most popular of which is called, unsurprisingly, the General's Pub.

Although Washington and Lee sports lack the luster of larger schools, the athletic department fields teams in 13 intercollegiate sports for men and 8 for women, as well as 14 intramurals for men and 4 for women. Lacrosse is to W&L what football or basketball is to many other universities; nearly all are fans of the championship team. Other popular sports, in which W&L teams excel on a national level, are water polo and tennis, the former played in a pool with a 500-seat gallery. Other facilities include a 2,400-seat arena, a 7,000-seat stadium, exercise and weight-training rooms, as well as an outdoor track and numerous playing fields.

Housing on the 320-acre campus—which has been designated a national historic landmark—accommodates half the students in coed dorms, including all freshmen, who are required to live on campus. Most upperclassmen prefer fraternity houses, or share houses and apartments in picturesque old Lexington. Crime is no problem there, and the lovely Shenandoah district provides lots of fun for nature lovers, including hunting, fishing, and camping, with skiing not far away in winter.

Although the W&L stereotype of upper-class, skirt-chasing, hard-drinking, macho *gentlemen* may be too strong for some to take, the school is now highly ranked academically and is diversifying socially and economically, although there are no present plans to admit more women. At the same time, W&L has succeeded better than most in preserving its heritage, tradition, and devotion to honor, a word all too often rendered meaningless on other campuses.

Washington and Lee remains, therefore, under the watchful shadow of its beloved General Lee, an institution where his presence may be felt everyday—from the classroom to the colonnade to his resting place in Lee Chapel. He is still the school's shining knight, an example and a comfort to those who believe that some things never ought to change.

Wesleyan University

Dean of Admissions and Financial Aid, Wesleyan University
High Street and Wyllys Avenue, Middletown, CT 06457
(203) 344-7900

Type: Private and Secular

Students:
2,672 undergraduates
  1,396 men
  1,276 women
  665 graduate students

Applications:
Closing date: January 15
36% of applicants accepted

	Applied	Accepted	Enrolled
men	2,372	872	330
women	2,751	978	354

SAT or ACT required
  Score reported by: January 15
  Mid 50% of freshman scores:
    SAT-Math   630–730
    SAT-Verbal 590–690

Costs and Aid:

Tuition and fees	$15,770
Room and Board	4,850

Scholarships:
Academic	No
Athletic	No
Minority	No

Financial Aid:
Freshmen	40%
Upperclassmen	43%

Library: 1,100,000 titles

ROTC: No

Study Abroad: Yes

Percentage of courses that can be used to fulfill distribution requirements: 62

Wesleyan University was founded in 1831 and named after the famous Methodist evangelist, John Wesley, who would certainly pound the pulpit in dismay if he could see his namesake today. Although Wesleyan has earned a solid reputation for academic excellence over the years, the school's image was seriously tarnished in 1990 following the drug-related murder of a student, two firebombings on campus, one in the president's office, as well as a number of shots allegedly fired at an administration building. In the spring of 1991, the motives for the firebombings and the shots were still unclear, although a local high school student had been arrested in connection with the former.

In addition, frequent student demonstrations for South African divestment and more minority faculty, among other causes, have disrupted campus life, if much less violently than the other incidents. All of the turmoil has contributed to Wesleyan's reputation as a hotbed of radicalism, violence, and dissension.

In the eyes of many, the university's new president, William Chace, hasn't helped much. Inaugurated in 1989, he has not so far proven a strong leader. He takes a long time to make decisions, loves to form "task forces," and comes down in the middle on everything, satisfying no one. One impatient student commented, "A group comes to Chace with demands and he turns around, stresses total sympathy with the cause, meets one demand, rejects another, and forms a study group on the rest." Some of the causes he sympathizes with include relaxing the Eurocentric curriculum, a university racial-harassment policy, and still more affirmative action.

Announcement of Courses & Academic Regulations, Fall 1989 through Spring 1991:
American Studies 213—Toward a Socialist America: Approaches to Radical Change in Society. (identical with Women's Studies 223.)
Taught by staff

"A collectively taught and student-organized course, TSA confronts the traditional character of teacher-student relations by rotating teaching responsibilities. The course challenges the hierarchy, oppression and exploitation in modern American culture with a variety of critical analyses and alternative proposals. With the guidance of two student facilitators, groups of eight to twelve students will plan the course's agenda: They will educate themselves. Topics cover an introduction to current trends in leftist thought, including anarchism, ecology, feminism, Marxism and ethnic perspectives. The class will deepen its understanding of these views with an analysis of sexuality, heterosexuality, gender, family, race, community, society and liberalism. TSA integrates the personal with the political. Projects have included guerrilla theater, community organizing and campus activism."

Chace presides over a campus which has been riven by discord, where racial epithets are tossed around like rotten tomatoes, and where the militant hold hunger strikes to demand more student "empowerment." They also regularly protest against "homophobia, sexism, and racism." Even the animal rights groups get into the act and want to add "Specieism" to the list of Forbiddenisms. So far, they, at least, have been polite about it.

In Wesleyan's defense, the administration claims that things have recently quieted down on campus and, in February 1991, President Chace wrote, that "we are no longer riven by discord. And we really do not have racial epithets at all . . . If anyone were to issue racial

TUITION AND FEES INCREASE

Average Increase/Year: Private = 11.15%, Wesleyan = 8.41%

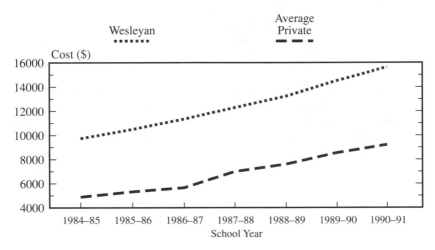

Source: The College Entrance Examination Board

---

epithets that person would suffer greatly from alienation, and would doubtless be brought before a tribunal on campus."

Happily, there is less rigidity in intellectual development than there is in campus politics. Academically, Wesleyan's course choices, professors, resources, and intelligent, questioning student body make learning easy and fun. The grading is not lax, but grades are de-emphasized so students can concentrate on analyzing, discussing, and learning, as opposed to memorization and taking long notes. Under-graduates, except for the premeds, do not compete aggressively with one another. Wesleyan enrolls about 2,700 undergraduates from all over this country and a number of foreign nations; most do come from the northeastern United States. Although nominally a university, there are fewer than 200 full-time graduate students. About a quarter of the student body is comprised of minorities.

Wesleyan has no core curriculum. Students are "encouraged" to take three semester courses in each of three areas (science/math, humanities, and social sciences), but they cannot take more than two of these three courses in any one department. There is no language requirement and there are no mandatory placement tests for new students. Professors are quite fair in lectures and grading.

The best departments at Wesleyan lie at the two poles of academia. At the one end, the art, art history, theater, and English departments have lots of money, generally excellent professors, and topnotch facilities. There are weekly plays, a well-endowed archives, a famous art gallery, and several theaters and concert halls. English is the most popular major and this often leads to long waiting lists to get into desired courses.

The other excellent area lies at the opposite end of campus in the Science Tower. Chemistry and biology are tough but well-respected. Wesleyan's premed program is strong and well counseled. Like their physical location, most other departments lie in between. Government, history and economics all have an excellent faculty. The sociology department often strikes a leftist note. Psychology and astronomy operate with good facilities (such as the largest telescope in Connecticut), but do not have a reputation as truly outstanding departments. Overall, there is no notably weak department, so students should shop for courses by subject and professor preference. Most courses are

DISTRIBUTION OF UNDERGRADUATE AID
1989–90 School Year

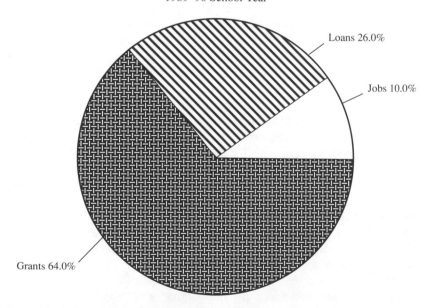

Loans 26.0%

Jobs 10.0%

Grants 64.0%

Source: The College Entrance Examination Board, 1990

small, interactive, and personal; many classes contain fewer than 15 students. Teaching assistants are rarely employed to instruct, but do help out with grading and student assistance.

The "best of the best" (around 165 freshmen) can compete for places in one of the special colleges (such as the College of Letters and College of Social Sciences) where intense courses, oral comps, weekly papers, and evaluations in place of grades are the rule. These colleges have the best professors in every department and are known to offer the most challenging and objective education on campus.

While Wesleyan's sports teams do not have a reputation for winning records, good facilities and fields capped by a new $22 million athletic center open up vast athletic potential. The school fields 15 intercollegiate sports and 10 intramurals each for men and women, and students participate energetically. Matches with chief rivals Williams, Amherst, and Trinity generate greatest enthusiasm.

Off the playing fields, Wesleyan takes on its unique flavor. The campus itself is small (120 acres) but well-kept, with beautiful libraries housing more than a million volumes, an observatory and generally modern classrooms. Computers and media equipment are plentiful and up-to-date. Flower children and PIBs (people in black) are commonly seen wafting around campus. There is great pressure to be politically correct, which means espousing fashionable causes and expressing complete solidarity with every "oppressed" group in society. Needless to say, this pressure can itself be oppressive. More moderate students quickly get used to relentless, leftist propagandizing. Such peer pressure leads many frosh (the PC word for freshmen) to get caught up in whatever cause is on the docket that week.

This climate makes activism easy at Wesleyan. The most popular groups are the competing environmental organizations, the Central American Network, Students for Reproductive Choice, Divest Now!, the Wesleyan Animal Rights Network, and the Democratic Socialists. Homosexuals can choose from the Coalition for Lesbian and Gay Awareness, Bi-focal, Men's Progressive Union, and the powerful Gay, Lesbian, Bisexual Alliance. There are special-interest houses for blacks, Asians, and womyn [sic]. For students wanting alternatives to the above, there is a College Republican chapter, a libertarian/objectivist club, and a conservative newspaper, the *Wesleyan Review*. PC sympathizers may revel in the leftist *Hermes*, the feminist *Iahu*, the all-minority *Ank,* or the main campus newspaper *The Argus* (less radical than some, but still generally PC).

Because of the conflicts stemming from so many inflexible viewpoints, students have become accustomed to running to the administration to have their fights refereed. The administration usually responds by promising more funds, or a new policy. But new policies seem in short supply these days (the old ones keep getting recycled), and funds are growing more scarce. Dining services, maintenance, and endowment have been reduced accordingly. Campus security has remained excellent (and friendly), however, even with rising crime in Middletown.

Socially, Wesleyan has much to offer. Although feminist pressure has almost completely wiped out traditional Greek life, there is still a fair party scene. Hartford and New Haven are about a half-hour away and even Boston or New York can be reached in three hours. Middletown has all the small shops needed, as well as several large stores, although there is a shortage of restaurants. Malls are accessible with a car. Formal dating is rare but when couples do get together, they generally become what students refer to as "fully attached."

Dorm life is quite good. Most dorms are close to campus and Wesleyan provides a very high percentage of singles, since it owns many houses around the perimeter of the campus. Drug use, which has received national publicity, presents no problem for the vast majority. Public pressure may, however, force the university to tighten up soon on its lenient drug and alcohol policies.

In the longer term, it remains to be seen whether Wesleyan can maintain its academic reputation and quality in light of an active and vocal "oppressed group" coalition that is encouraged by the administration. Wesleyan is still well respected in graduate schools and many of its students end up as academics themselves, even as they learn lessons in ideological excesses as well as in the liberal arts.

The College of William and Mary

Dean of Admissions, The College of William and Mary
Williamsburg, VA 23185 (804) 221-4223

Type: Public		
Students:		
5,404 undergraduates		
2,510 men		
2,894 women		
2,138 graduate students		

Applications:			
Closing date: January 15			
27% of those applied accepted			
	Applied	Accepted	Enrolled
men	3,881	1,204	576
women	5,565	1,334	690
SAT required			

Score reported by: February 15
Mid 50% of freshman scores:
SAT-Math 580–690
SAT-Verbal 540–650

Costs and Aid:

Tuition and fees	
In state	$3,400
Out of state	9,250
Room and Board	3,750
Scholarships:	
Academic	Yes
Athletic	Yes
Minority	No
Financial Aid:	
Freshmen	44%
Upperclassmen	46%
Library:	792,785 titles
ROTC:	Yes
Study Abroad:	Yes
Percentage of courses that can be used to fulfill distribution requirements:	19.7

The College of William and Mary, now entering its fourth century, still offers its students a robust liberal arts education, though some say its traditional dedication to teaching over research is weakening. The college also offers students a unique sense of tradition and timelessness, as they meander through the restored colonial capital of Virginia where so many early American giants walked before them. Thomas Jefferson was graduated from the college in 1762. George Washington and John Tyler both served as its chancellor, and James Madison was its president. Currently, former chief justice Warren Burger fills the post of chancellor while Princess Margaret of the Netherlands and Prince Charles of Great Britain are its two honorary fellows.

Founded in 1693, William and Mary, the second oldest college in the country, was private until 1906 when it became a public institution. State law currently mandates that 65 percent of its more than 5,000 undergraduates be Virginia residents; the rest represent all the other states and more than 40 foreign countries, with a good number from the northeastern United States. Eleven percent are minorities.

Technically a university (although the college never uses the term), William and Mary has four graduate schools—in Business, Education, Law, and Marine Science (whose campus is located on the York River). It also offers graduate degrees in the arts and sciences. The college is the site of the first chapter of the Phi Beta Kappa Society, which was started as the American Revolution began, in 1776, by a group of students that included the future first chief justice of the Supreme Court, John Marshall.

Academics are still taken very seriously at W&M by most students and professors alike. Most faculty, including stars, carry a full course load; graduate students never teach, although they occasionally conduct science labs. Professors participate in an advisory program that assigns freshmen and sophomores to their mentors and allows juniors and seniors to choose them. Some students say they don't get enough help but admit that there is logic to the prevailing attitude that if you are smart enough to get into the college, you should be smart enough to work out your own course schedule—particularly in a medium-sized institution that has not yet been taken over by hordes of rule-makers and form-lovers.

Undergraduate Program Catalog 1990–91:
Comparative Literature 490—Topic for Spring 1991: Psychoanalytic and Feminist Approaches to Literary Theory (same as French 450)
Professor Martha M. Houle

"A study of issues of representation, semiology and narrative strategy, with a focus on psychoanalytic and feminist approaches to the text. Literary and theoretical works will be considered."

As in the majority of schools throughout the nation, there is no common core curriculum at W&M, but the distribution requirements are at least adequate from the viewpoint of Western civilization advocates. The level of instruction is generally high and relatively objective; many courses are structured to embrace aspects of Western civilization and most students are tradition-minded and choose courses accordingly. This is not to say that determined students can't fall through the cracks with silly offerings such as "The Sociology of Sports and Leisure," and the politically correct "Gender and Change in Modern Africa," whose description says it "dispels the erroneous notion of the passivity of African women."

TUITION AND FEES INCREASE
Average Increase/Year: Public = 8.30%, William & Mary = 9.30%

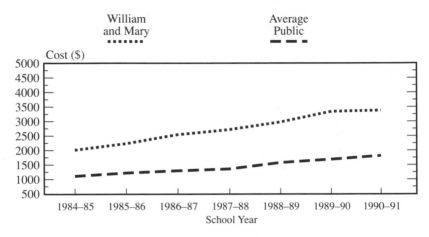

Source: The College Entrance Examination Board

One hundred and twenty-four credit hours are necessary for graduation, of which four must be in physical education. For the purpose of its distribution requirements, the college divides courses into three areas—the humanities, the social sciences (including history), and the natural sciences. Courses usually carry three credits each. Students must take at least three courses in each area (including a lab course in the natural sciences) and then two additional higher-level courses in an area outside the major. Students must also study two years of a foreign language (or pass an examination). Lastly, they must pass a writing course if they have not achieved a combined score of 1300 on the SAT verbal and English Achievement tests, or an advanced placement test score of four or five.

Fulfilling these distribution requirements poses one significant problem. At times it is almost impossible to gain admission to a course, even one needed for graduation. All seminar classes are supposed to be limited to 15 students, but frequently numbers are jacked up to insure timely graduation. Professors tend to be very understanding about bending the size limits, perhaps because they are reluctant to teach additional sections. Class size at W&M ranges from one-on-one tutorials to large, introductory lecture courses (200–250 students), but the latter are rare, and 20 to 25 is the norm. A freshman honors program exists in selected departments, but most honors students join the program as juniors with GPAs of 3.00 or better.

Majors at W&M are called "concentrations." Outstanding departments at W&M are history, government, physics, chemistry, and English. On the whole, the natural sciences, the social sciences, and the humanities are excellent; the latter two tend to be favored by students, as the sciences are known to be very difficult and demanding. Special opportunities include study abroad and Washington, D.C., internships. W&M operates on an honor system, which works well, so cheating is uncommon.

Until quite recently, William and Mary's reputation has been large in the American South but limited in the North. Now the college is attempting to widen its base of appeal. The current administration has been trying to increase academic standards and create a new national image for William and Mary. The danger inherent in this otherwise laudable ambition is that the college may, in the words of one of its

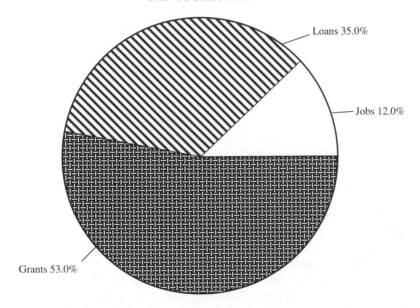

DISTRIBUTION OF UNDERGRADUATE AID
1989–90 School Year

Loans 35.0%

Jobs 12.0%

Grants 53.0%

Source: The College Entrance Examination Board, 1990

former professors, change "from a first-rate teaching institution to a third-rate research institution." Apparently the pressure is on to "publish or perish," so that teaching ability is beginning to weigh less heavily than research when faculty appointments and tenure decisions are made. In spite of this worrying trend, the pervading intellectual atmosphere is still student-centered and fairly serious. Most W&M students are far more concerned with their grades than with any sort of extracurricular activity. Although students generally appear serene and calm, there is underlying competition for intellectual achievement, spurred on by W&M's reputation for tough marking.

In and out of the classroom, campus life is generally conducted with civility. Debate which might lead to abrasive argument elsewhere tends to be frowned upon at W&M. There are accepted standards of polite behavior on campus, and deviation from this norm raises eyebrows, because most students wish to maintain the college's pleasant, convivial atmosphere. This, combined with the strong work ethic, explains the general lack of political activity on campus. As a result, the school has not suffered the disturbances so prevalent recently at more politicized schools,

One of the few uproars in recent years occurred in the fall of 1989 when then Democratic gubernatorial candidate, Douglas Wilder, visited the campus. The College Republicans managed to summon up energy to shout him down, and in an attempt to make amends, the college president invited him to address the graduation class the following May.

The conservative student body lines up enthusiastically when the CIA comes to recruit. Anti-apartheid activities and shanty-buildings do not distort the placid William and Mary horizon. The only issue which has sparked spirited dialogue recently is abortion. But even this usually volatile question led only to a few speakers and several educational films.

Besides the College Republicans, the most conspicuous campus organization is "Alternatives," which supports homosexuality. It is not, however, widely accepted on a campus which has little tolerance for any deviation from the norm. For the most part, the group is regarded by the majority of students, who are too immersed in their own affairs to pay much attention, as the "lunatic fringe." Alternatives did manage, though, to garner $628 from the Board of Student Affairs for the 1990–91 school year.

The idea of an officially established speech or behavior code at W&M would be considered bizarre. This is a school where members of a certain fraternity dress up in Confederate uniforms and sing "Dixie" to their dates. If students are racist or sexist they would consider it exceedingly rude to air their views. There are no "thought police" at William and Mary. The faculty overall tend to be more liberal than the students. Yet, their political inclinations are rarely if ever mentioned in class. Professors do not utilize their podiums as soap-boxes to indoctrinate their students; personal political views are not considered relevant information for class lectures.

In one concession to political correctness, however, an interdisciplinary minor and major are being developed in women's studies, although there is as yet no department as such. In the spring of 1990, a student could sign up for Honors 205—"Perspectives on Women and Culture"—and read such works as *The Feminine World of Love and Ritual* by Carroll Smith-Rosenberg and *The Myth of the Vaginal Orgasm* by Ann Koedt.

Black students comprise the only highly visible minority group on campus. There are black fraternities and sororities, although they are not part of the Greek system and they do not have housing on campus. Instead of agitating for their "rights," these organizations occupy themselves with worthy community-service projects such as renovating low-income housing and assisting orphans. It appears that, as more and more black students join predominantly white social organizations, the black Greek system is dying out. There is also a Black Student Union which sponsors various events and serves to unite the black campus community. The school does run an extensive freshman orientation for minority students, who spend about three weeks at the college the summer prior to their freshman year.

When asked whether academic standards are waived or modified to admit students based on race, ethnicity, or gender, an administration official noted the following: "Sort of. Applicants are ranked one to eight, with one to three almost certain to be accepted. While the rank has no component of race, a minority student rated a five has a better chance of admission than a white four. I would point out that all of the students we accept are capable of doing good work. The white and minority graduation rates differ by less than 5 percent"

Housing at W&M is limited, but guaranteed for freshmen and distributed by lottery to the rest. It is both coed and single-sex, and ranges from history-laden halls to modern dorms. About 1,200 undergraduates must find accommodation off campus, but two new houses are presently under construction which should shortly ease the crunch. The 1,200-acre campus is beautiful, both naturally and architecturally, and is divided into three sections—the Ancient Campus, which consists of three colonial structures, one of which is the famous Wren building, in continuous use since 1695; the Modern Campus, which was built in the 1920s and 1930s; and the New Campus, which dates from the 1960s.

Social life, which is not scintillating by most accounts, generally stays on campus, because historical Williamsburg is so busy catering to its mobs of tourists that it pays little attention to the college, and students return the compliment. Richmond and Norfolk, not social beehives themselves, are an hour's drive away, and Virginia Beach a little farther. Approximately 50 percent of the population are involved in a fraternity or sorority. Rush is fairly competitive, but membership is not so important to student life as it is at many other schools. There is no tension between Greeks and independents, as people appreciate that the Greeks are responsible for most of the parties and free beer. In spite of the fraternities' hospitality, not all the drinking, which is considerable, is done with the Greeks. Many students make regular trips to the nearby Anheuser-Busch brewery to quench their thirst. Drug use is not widely discussed, but it is clear that there are large numbers of students who smoke marijuana with some regularity, albeit discreetly.

Extracurricular activities and organizations number over 180. Although 12 intercollegiate teams are fielded for men and 13 for women, sports are not very important at William and Mary. Many students are, in fact, quite resentful of the exorbitant sums of money spent on a lackluster football team. Students attribute the high level of spending on football to an effort to attract alumni dollars. Teams which are not favorites of rich alumni receive little or no attention. Attendance at sporting events is quite small and people usually only go to be social and get some fresh air on a beautiful day. There are a number of club-level sports like rugby and men's lacrosse to add to the 22 intramural leagues for men and 19 for women, which include archery, badminton, basketball, bowling, golf, handball, softball, swimming, tennis, track and field, volleyball, and wrestling. These, some of which are coed, do attract a high level of student participation.

Recently, William and Mary built a large and attractive gymnasium. The absent-minded administration, however, forgot to install air conditioners—a particular problem since the walls are glass and allow the sun to turn the rooms into infernos. It also failed to construct regulation-size racquetball and squash courts. Better thought-out facilities include a stadium that seats 14,500, a basketball arena for 9,000, a swimming pool, tennis courts, playing fields, and an indoor track.

In the early 1990s, William and Mary definitely does not make a comfortable launching pad for soapbox orators, social malcontents, or for rebels with (or without) a cause—although it must be acknowledged that, in days gone by, the college certainly did propel its share of all three into the pages of American history.

Williams College

Director of Admissions, Williams College
P.O. Box 487, Williamstown, MA 01267 (413) 597-2211

Type: Private and Secular			**Costs and Aid:**	
			Tuition and fees	$15,790
Students:			Room and Board	4,980
2,061 undergraduates			Scholarships:	
1,166 men			Academic	No
895 women			Athletic	No
47 graduate students			Minority	No
Applications:			Financial Aid:	
Closing date: January 1			Freshmen	40%
28% of applicants accepted			Upperclassmen	35%
	Applied	*Accepted*	*Enrolled*	
men	2,409	644	280	**Library:** 655,855 titles
women	1,920	582	243	
SAT or ACT required			**ROTC:** No	
Score reported by: February 1			**Study Abroad:** Yes	
Mid 50% of freshman scores:			**Percentage of courses that can**	
SAT-Math	650–740		**be used to fulfill distribution**	
SAT-Verbal	610–730		**requirements:** 93	

Williams College is tucked away in the purple mountains of the Berkshires, way up in the northwestern corner of Massachusetts. In spite of the lack of both a core curriculum and stringent distribution requirements, a motivated student can and often does acquire a sound grounding in the liberal arts at secluded Williams, which is home to about 2,000 undergraduates. How long this will remain the case, however, is open to question now that the protected, isolated college is moving away from traditional Western values and toward modern relativism.

Consistently rated among the top private colleges in the nation, Williams—along with Amherst College and Wesleyan University—forms part of a group nicknamed the "Little Ivies" or the "Little Three." While Williams lacks the instant, national name recognition of Harvard, Princeton, or Yale, its reputation for undergraduate excellence rivals that of the Big Three. Williams alumni, who are noted for loyalty to their alma mater, include James A. Garfield, the 20th president of the United States (who was assassinated on his way to his college reunion), and, more recently, an eclectic group including

417

former secretary of education William Bennett, baseball commissioner Fay Vincent, directors John Sayles and Elia Kazan, songwriter Steven Sondheim, historian James MacGregor Burns (also a professor emeritus at Williams), journalist Hedrick Smith, and economists Lester Thurow and Herbert Stein.

1990–1991 Course Catalog:
Political Science 244—The Caribbean, Grenada, and the United States
Visiting Professor Dessima Williams

"This course focuses on the relationship between the Commonwealth Caribbean region and the United States. It examines the politics, economics, culture and ideology of the region and the links between each of these and the United States. The nature of these relationships is specified in terms of a theory which distinguishes between policies based on economic and military domination and those based on cultural and ideological hegemony. The course also addresses the question: what happens to small Caribbean states when they attempt to break the hegemonic grip of modern capitalism and imperialism? Grenada will serve as our case study."

[Dessima Williams was an official in the communist New Jewel Government of Maurice Bishop in Grenada in the early 1980s.]

Williams will celebrate its bicentennial in 1993 and has maintained an outstanding reputation for most of that period, in spite of some trying times. The college managed to survive the defection in the 1820s of its president, who made off with portions of the library and the student body to set up what became Amherst College (thus creating one of the fiercest, if least known, rivalries in college sports). In the 1960s, Williams abandoned tradition twice over by admitting women and abolishing the fraternity system. In eliminating fraternities, Williams hoped to come closer to creating an ideal college community devoid of the divisiveness which sometimes occurs on fraternity-dominated campuses.

Although demanding, the academic atmosphere at Williams is not cutthroat. Classes are small, averaging about 15 students, and there are only a few large, introductory lecture classes with more than 100 students. Recently, the college has instituted a system of tutorials, intensive seminars formed to emphasize writing and the close reading of texts, with one professor teaching three or four students. These are proving very successful and popular with students and faculty alike.

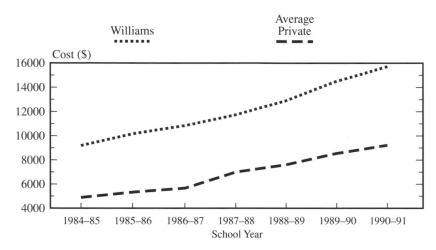

TUITION AND FEES INCREASE
Average Increase/Year: Private = 11.15%, Williams = 9.26%

Source: The College Entrance Examination Board

Professors are easily accessible to students and since Williams is such a small community, many take an active role in college activities. The faculty is mainly devoted to teaching, not research. Although almost entirely dedicated to undergraduate education, Williams does have two small graduate programs, one in developmental economics solely for students from the Third World and the other a well-respected program in art history.

While most departments are solid, the history, art history, English, Russian, and German departments stand out. Romance languages and sociology and anthropology are somewhat weaker than average. One disappointing feature of academics at Williams, however, is the lax advisory system, a problem shared by many colleges and universities today. Freshmen are assigned a faculty advisor who is supposed to guide their academic choices during the first year, but with rare exceptions most advisors do little more than sign course schedules once a semester—which is one reason students need to be motivated to achieve a well-rounded liberal arts education at Williams. The career office, however, gets high marks for helping with summer employment opportunities and postgraduation plans.

There is neither a core curriculum at Williams nor any kind of

Great Books program. Indeed, there are only three requirements
(besides those for the major) for graduation: students must complete
eight credits of physical education; they must take one course, of the
many available, that studies the culture of American minorities or the
peoples of Africa, Asia, Latin America, Oceania, or the Caribbean.
The final requirement involves picking three courses from each of
three designated divisions—languages and the arts, social studies, and
science and mathematics. A laboratory course is not required, and
departments often settle for "gut" courses that have grown up in the
sciences to fulfill the last of these requirements.

  In leisure hours, if city life and the allure of its bars, restaurants,
clubs, and shops are what appeals, then Williamstown is sure to
disappoint. It is out in the "boonies," far from the bright lights of both
New York and Boston, 150 and 130 miles distant respectively. But
Williamstown itself is an attractive, small New England community,
with plenty of shops, fast-food places, and restaurants, all within a

---

DISTRIBUTION OF UNDERGRADUATE AID
1989–90 School Year

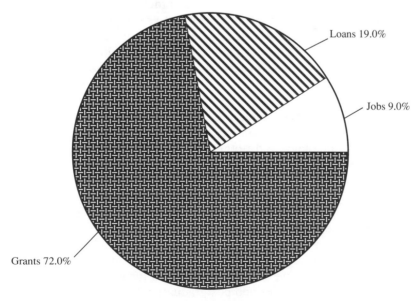

Loans 19.0%

Jobs 9.0%

Grants 72.0%

Source: The College Entrance Examination Board, 1990

short distance of the college. The campus is wooded, with expanses of green lawn between the traditional, redbrick and newer, contemporary-style buildings, which are all within walking distance of one another.

Williams students, it has been said, work hard and play hard. Because of the college's physical isolation, this translates into a social life heavily influenced by athletics and weekend parties. Most of the college community is very much addicted to personal fitness, which is probably a good thing considering how much beer the students drink. A majority participates in vigorous sports, which include skiing, rugby, crew, water polo, tennis, squash, and ultimate frisbee. There are 16 intercollegiate sports for men and 14 for women, as well as 16 men's, women's, and coed intramural teams. Facilities are first rate, and feature a 7,000-seat stadium, a 50-meter pool, rowing tanks, a boat-house, and a golf course. The newly renovated fitness center is always crowded and the campus is overrun with student joggers.

The night life at Williams is largely confined to the Purple Pub, for those over 21, and keg parties in individual dorms. Some have criticized the "totemic keg culture" on campus which they feel detracts from the academic mission of the school. The college itself is tightening up on its alcohol policy. Security has cracked down on parties in freshman dorms and limited the amount of beer served at large, all-campus parties. It's doubtful that Williams will become a dry campus, but the college has valiantly tried to curtail some of the excesses.

Housing is almost luxurious and begins with freshmen assigned to either single-sex or coed "entries" of between 20 and 30 persons. Suites within entries are single-sex, and three or four freshmen usually share a suite, which consists of two or three bedrooms and a living room. A number of entries are located within each dormitory. Sharing the entries are several junior-class advisors, who are meant to act as big brothers and sisters in helping the neophytes adjust both socially and academically to college life. There have been some complaints that segregating freshmen is stifling for the individual and sometimes oppressive to minorities, who compose a little more than a fifth of the student body. Despite these objections, the college has decided to stay with the present system, which seems to work well for the majority.

After the first year, students choose one of five housing units on campus, and usually remain there until graduation. They can opt for either singles or suites in groups as large as seven. Seniors are given the choice of remaining on campus, or living off campus in pleasant, nearby accommodation. Everyone at Williams is assured campus housing for four years, and more than 90 percent of students select singles, many of them within suites. The cozy atmosphere is enhanced because each residential group has its own dining hall; but students have the privilege of eating at any of the other dining halls. The food is well above average as the college does not contract out, but provides its own service. Some of the dining rooms are small, so that the meals are prepared with a more personal touch. Upon occasion, favorite professors traditionally join students for informal dinners.

The cultural life at Williams is not as barren as you might expect, given its location. Williamstown is home to two quality art museums, the Williams College Museum of Art and the Clark Art Institute which house, among many things, a fine collection of impressionist paintings. Theater is also popular in Williamstown. During the summer months, the Williamstown Theater offers star-studded plays, and during the school year, students produce and act in several, which are well attended by gown and town.

Extracurricular activities abound. One hundred and fifty groups and organizations gratify interests that range from jazz and marching bands to photography and international relations. In addition to several literary journals, there are four newspapers on campus: the official, weekly school paper, and left-wing and conservative publications that appear sporadically.

Politically, Williams is best termed apathetic. Those on the left are quick to condemn the complacency and lack of activism of their fellow students, but in reality this lethargy masks a liberal, although not radical, political position. Surveys found that more than 90 percent of Williams students voted for Michael Dukakis in the 1988 presidential election. Many have also embraced environmentalism, reflecting the concerns of students who often choose Williams because of its bucolic location and opportunities for outdoor occupations. The Bisexual, Gay and Lesbian Union is another activist group, small but vocal. Not surprisingly, it inhabits a campus house on the same street as the Black Student Union and the college's new Multicultural Center.

If the student body appears to be decidedly liberal, the faculty is almost unanimously left-liberal. In the 1988 presidential election, according to a survey, 96 percent of the faculty voted for Dukakis. In some departments, notably history and political science, older, more conservative faculty have lost influence and given way to younger, left-wing professors, who were the student radicals of the 1960s.

This is not to detract from the quality of the teaching which is usually excellent and not especially doctrinaire, but it does mean that a measure of balance, fairness, and a true pluralism of opinion have now been subtracted from the Williams equation.

University of Wisconsin at Madison

Director of Admissions, University of Wisconsin at Madison
750 University Avenue, Madison, WI 53706 (608) 262-3961

Type: Public

Students:
29,248 undergraduates
  14,442 men
  15,806 women
  9,848 graduate students

Applications:
Closing date: February 1
72% of those applied accepted

	Applied	Accepted	Enrolled
men	7,647	5,423	2,475
women	7,875	5,700	2,518

SAT or ACT required (ACT preferred)
  Score reported by: March 1
  Mid 50% of freshman scores:
    SAT-Math   520–660
    SAT-Verbal   450–570
    ACT composite 22–27

Costs and Aid:
Tuition and fees

In state	$2,140
Out of state	6,490
Room and Board	3,450

Scholarships:

Academic	Yes
Athletic	Yes
Minority	Yes

Financial Aid:

Freshmen	35%
Upperclassmen	40%

Library:	4,500,000 titles
ROTC:	Yes
Study Abroad:	Yes

First-time visitors to the University of Wisconsin at Madison see a wide-screen spectacle before them—a galaxy of impressive brick buildings, rolling green hills, sparkling blue lakes, and colossal crowds of milling students who turn the vast still life into a fast-moving picture. In fact, the scene has brought a number of movie directors to the area in recent years to capture it all on film—the visual beauty, the vibrant student lifestyle, and the carnival atmosphere of the ever-present street performers. But the cameras don't catch the currents of tension inside the picturesque halls, where educational traditionalists and potential moderates are fighting to keep their heads above water. The University of Wisconsin, founded as public land grant institution in 1849, first moved left of the political center back in the early 1900s when it became a think-tank for the Progressive Party of Senator Robert LaFollette. In the twentieth century, the school continues to pride itself on leading the forces of social, as well as academic, reform.

The tradition of academic innovation began in the nineteenth century, oddly enough under the influence of authoritarian Germany,

many of whose solid citizens had emigrated to Wisconsin. Their emphasis on the commercial and public applications of research—which was more revered than teaching in the old country—started the school down the path which ultimately led to its becoming the nation's number one public university in research fundraising. A result of this aggressive emphasis on research and its money-generating spinoffs has been to make Wisconsin an excellent provider of graduate education, but an often weak supplier of undergraduate instruction.

Correcting this imbalance has been a priority of Chancellor Donna Shalala, formerly president of Hunter College in New York City. Since assuming office in 1988, she has sought to beef up undergraduate education by decreasing class sizes and hiring new faculty. Wisconsin still has a very high percentage of dropouts, however, with almost a quarter of each year's freshman class falling by the wayside. This embarrassing failure is traceable in part to the research megalith's impersonal nature, which overwhelms many of its neophyte undergraduates.

Bulletin, College of Letters and Science, Effective 1990–92:
History 261—Gender, Race, Ethnicity, Class in Comparative Perspective.

"The problem of 'difference' and the designation of groups as 'deviant' is examined by using three case studies: the Ancient Near East (second millenium [sic] B.C.), medieval France, and 19th century USA. Focus is on the connection between gender, race, ethnicity, class and their incorporation into the values and ideas of Western Civilization."

Other challenges facing Ms. Shalala are a bloated university bureaucracy and a state legislature terrified of taxes. Ms. Shalala has presided over tuition increases for the past several years, although expenses are still modest in comparison with most private and some public institutions. In an effort to restrict spending, enrollment cuts have recently been adopted to reduce student numbers (but not administrators) on the main campus in Madison from approximately 45,000 to 38,000, of whom more than 29,000 are undergraduates. (On the 26 campuses of the university system, there are a staggering 162,000 students; by law, out-of-state residents are restricted to 25 percent of the student population.)

Wisconsin's abiding interest in social reform—some would say social engineering—attracted national media attention in 1988 when

TUITION AND FEES INCREASE
Average Increase/Year: Public = 8.30%, Wisconsin = 8.70%

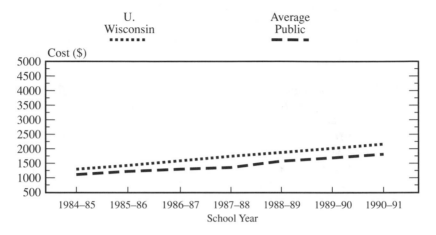

Source: The College Entrance Examination Board

Chancellor Shalala also promulgated its Madison Plan, a policy designed to increase the numbers of minority students and faculty, and to educate the campus in multiculturalism. The plan was generated after several racial incidents on campus that offended blacks.

The underlying spirit of the plan also led to a student code that prohibits the use of "intimidating" speech based on race, ethnicity, sex, sexual orientation, or religion. (This code is now the subject of a court challenge.) Offenders are subject to various penalties, including expulsion. Since the code was instituted, several complaints have been filed against professors who allegedly had made racist or sexist comments in the classroom. One female staff member complained that a professor had used the demeaning word "girls" inappropriately, and another moaned that a coworker had greeted her with a disrespectful, "Hi, Babe." Both women demanded and received explanations from the offending parties.

A part of the Madison Plan mandates that all undergraduates take three hours of credit in ethnic and gender studies, which "may encompass issues of gender and class and . . . reflect the minority experience and minority point of view." A choice of courses is offered to fulfill this requirement. The irony is that minority enrollment has been falling since the plan meant to boost it was instituted. The total minority enrollment on the Madison campus was approximately 6.5 percent in 1990. The university's goal is to double between 1988 and 1993 the number of black, Hispanics or American Indians enrolled as freshmen or transfer students. As the state of Wisconsin has a small minority population, observers are not surprised that the university is not meeting its goals, since it must compete for scarce minority students with other institutions in and out of Wisconsin. Undaunted, zealous administrators now plan to increase efforts to recruit minority students from out of state.

Chancellor Shalala claims that body count is not the only goal of the Madison Plan and that programs to increase awareness of diversity among the entire student body are now largely in place. She also notes that, on the Madison campus, half of the minority students now graduate, a considerable improvement over a few years ago. Still, about a year after the school started its drive to diversify, a fraternity held a mock slave auction in blackface and Afro-wigs, an incident that

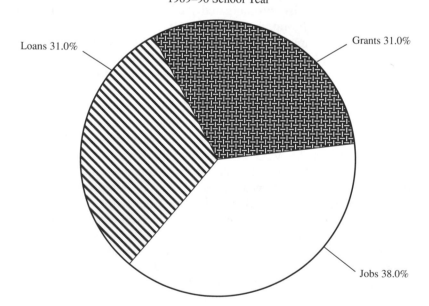

DISTRIBUTION OF UNDERGRADUATE AID
1989–90 School Year

Loans 31.0%

Grants 31.0%

Jobs 38.0%

Source: The College Entrance Examination Board, 1990

signals to some that the Madison Plan is ineffectual, if not counterproductive, in its aim of encouraging acceptance of diversity.

A segment of the faculty has been stirred to more dignified action by the university's clarion call for political correctness. In 1990, historian Theodore Hamerow, one of its brightest stars, accused the university of promoting a political agenda that has tainted scholarship, the curriculum, faculty-hiring policies, and campus life. He and a few others then formed a campus chapter of the National Association of Scholars, which seeks to further the study of Western culture and offers a platform to professors who oppose faculty hiring quotas, mandatory courses in diversity, and other matters associated with the new academic orthodoxy. Professor Hamerow, who says he is no right-winger and voted for George McGovern in 1972, takes particular issue with Wisconsin's drive to hire faculty based on their race or ethnicity, which he feels often sacrifices scholarship on the altar of diversity.

While students and faculty debate the implications of Wisconsin's latest excursion into uncharted waters, students continue to try to acquire an education in these undergraduate schools and programs— agricultural and life sciences; business; education; engineering; family resources and consumer science; journalism; letters and science; library and information studies; pharmacy; music; nursing; and social work. These also offer advanced degrees. Graduate schools include law, medicine, and veterinary medicine.

By far the largest of the schools awarding the bachelor's degree is Letters and Science, which enrolls two-thirds of Madison's undergraduate population. Operating on the semester system, L&S requires 120 hours for graduation, 100 of which must be taken in L&S courses. In an effort to avoid over-specialization, Wisconsin mandates that two-thirds of the credits a student offers for graduation be taken outside the major department(s). There is no core curriculum; distribution requirements include 12 credits (four courses) in the humanities, including 6 in literature; 12 in social studies; 16 in the natural sciences, including 3 in physical and 3 in biological science. There are also foreign language, expository English, and mathematics requirements, all of which may be satisfied by sufficient high school credits.

The political science, English, and history departments are strong, but the last two are so popular that students often fail to get into desired courses. Because of the preoccupation with research, the natural sciences are also excellent; astronomy is particularly interesting because the star professors regularly teach beginning courses, which are often handled in other departments by teaching assistants. The usual arrangement, as at so many big universities, is for faculty to lecture to huge student audiences of hundreds, with the teaching assistants leading smaller sections once or twice a week. How much students get out of these courses often depends upon the teaching abilities of the section leaders, and this naturally varies.

Another typical big-school shortcoming is Wisconsin's weak advising system. Although professors do hold office hours, they are insufficient for the numbers of students; most faculty are too busy with their research and publication to pay much attention to the problems and programs of individual undergraduates. Registration used to present a further pitfall for students, who had to wait for hours in long lines to sign up for their course selections. Recently, however, the university has initiated registration by telephone, a system that saves time and avoids stress, even if it doesn't guarantee first choices.

One excellent program, the first choice for some students, is Integrated Liberal Studies, a well-coordinated series of interdisciplinary courses on Western civilization. The ILS program, one of the oldest in the country, nearly died during the 1970s due to lack of interest. In the last decade, however, it has made a strong comeback and now has a loyal following. On the reverse side of the philosophical coin, African studies are also fashionable these days, especially a course in African storytelling, popular because of both the intellectual and histrionic talents of its professor.

Back in the U.S.A., housing on Madison's 900-acre campus is available for only 6,660 students in dormitories ranging from relatively small buildings along Lake Mendota to large towers closer to downtown. Residences are both coed and single-sex, and also include fraternities and sororities, language houses and married-student quarters. Most students live in private off-campus housing, which has become more available since the enrollment cuts.

The Madison campus is famous for its social and extracurricular life. *Playboy* magazine used to list it annually among the top "party schools," and until a few years ago the Halloween party on State Street attracted up to 80,000 students from across Wisconsin. The Memorial Union, along with the newer and smaller Union South, provides food, games, live bands, and more. Social life seems to revolve around alcohol consumption in Madison. Beer drinking is almost a rite of passage; fake IDs are taken for granted both by students and barkeeps. Only about 10 percent of students affiliate with fraternities and sororities, but there are no fewer than 600 social and special-interest organizations on campus, which is certainly a tribute to diversity.

Just in case all those activities pall, however, students liven things up with a popular sporting event, charmingly dubbed the "Condom Olympics." Attracting hordes of eager participants every autumn, this modern version of the ancient Greek contests involves only one major game. Students laughingly fill condoms with water and toss them playfully in the air, or at one another like snowballs. When they run out of ammunition, they resupply from the many barrels dotted around the Library Mall, where the fun takes place. When it's all over, students carry off the extra supplies to put them to more serious use. The university administration doesn't interfere with this famous frolic, no doubt from a protective sense that it's better for the fun-loving to be safe than sorry.

Despite the flagging fortunes of the Badger football team, the school's many Big 10 sports teams are still a focus of student interest. There are 11 intercollegiate sports for men and 9 for women, as well as 29 and 24 intramurals respectively. Facilities include several gymnasiums and swimming pools, a tennis stadium, and a field house. One arena seats 12,000; the football stadium seats 77,000.

For many students, the extensive facilities do not compensate for worries about their personal safety on campus, specifically rapes and assaults. Although lighted walkways are provided on major streets, and free rides for women are available, the university has dragged its feet in publishing information on the number of crimes, and promised to do so only after strong pressure from the student government. The sorry fact remains that safety is a growing concern, especially at night, with women feeling particularly at risk.

Student participation in campus politics is an exciting if often less risky business. The student government is not *always* dominated by the left, and two daily campus newspapers, one conservative and one leftist, provide a dynamic forum for debate. The administration reluctantly respects the rights of both leftist and conservative student groups, though it prefers the former and these predominate. In the summer of 1990, for example, the female copresident of the Wisconsin Students Association used student government funds to attend a peace conference in North Korea. Although there was later some talk of impeachment by the Student Senate, nothing could be done because the woman was a senior and had graduated. So far as is known, the administration winked an eye and did nothing to help recover the funds. But why should the administration object to the appropriation of student money for trips to North Korea when it sponsors a formal if inactive relationship with Ho Chi Minh University in Vietnam?

The University of Wisconsin at Madison certainly doesn't lack for stimulation on many levels. The politically minded, and especially the politically correct, will find plenty to keep them busy. Those who want a well-balanced education, however, will fare better treading water elsewhere, while Wisconsin's radicals swim with the tide in turbulent Madison and traditionalists fight against it.

Yale University

Dean of Undergraduate Admissions, Yale University
P. O. Box 1502A Yale Station, New Haven, CT 06520
(203) 432-1900

Type: Private and Secular			**Costs and Aid:**	
			Tuition and fees	$14,000
Students:			Room and Board	5,310
5,217 undergraduates			Scholarships:	
2,949 men			Academic	No
2,268 women			Athletic	No
5,622 graduate students			Minority	No
Applications:			Financial Aid:	
Closing date: December 31			Freshmen	41%
19% of applicants accepted			Upperclassmen	38%
Applied	*Accepted*	*Enrolled*		
men 6,697	1,317	744	**Library:**	9,143,727 titles
women 5,366	947	542	**ROTC:**	Yes
SAT or ACT required			**Study Abroad:**	Yes
Score reported by: March 1				
Mid 50% of freshman scores:				
SAT-Math 650–740				
SAT-Verbal 610–710				

Along with Harvard and Princeton, the very word Yale sends sparks flying through the educational ether. Always one of the brightest beacons in American higher education, Yale long ago expanded into a world-class research university. But, unlike many research institutions, Yale continues to focus on its original intent—excellence in undergraduate education in the liberal arts.

Founded as the Collegiate School in 1701 by Congregationalists, the future university started life in Branford, Connecticut, moving to nearby New Haven in 1716. Two years later the school was renamed after a distinguished benefactor, Elihu Yale. President George Bush currently tops a long list of distinguished graduates.

Now enrolling close to 11,000 students of whom about half are undergraduates, the university consists of graduate schools in: Architecture; Art; Divinity; Drama; Environmental Studies; Law; Medicine; Music; Management and Organization; Nursing. However, Yale's defining institution is still the undergraduate liberal arts unit, Yale College.

Life there revolves around the Oxbridge system of residential colleges, of which there are 12—Berkeley, Branford, Calhoun, Davenport, Timothy Dwight, Jonathan Edwards, Morse, Pierson, Saybrook, Silliman, Ezra Stiles, and Trumbull. Each student is assigned to one before he arrives, although he doesn't move in until sophomore year, because most freshmen live together on the Old Campus. The Gothic-looking colleges are small, self-contained communities with dining halls, libraries, courtyards, and common rooms. Each organizes its own intramural athletic teams and social and cultural events throughout the year. At the head of every college are a resident master and a dean who advise students on both academic and non-academic matters. About 50 members of the faculty, known as fellows and drawn from different departments, are associated with each college; some live on the premises and others maintain offices there.

Yale College Programs of Study, Fall and Spring Terms, 1990–1991: Sociology 180b—Development and Underdevelopment.
Professor Kim Blankenship

"Analysis of global power structures in the development and underdevelopment of societies. Films, lectures, and readings cover the role of multinational corporations in the Third World, population control, world hunger, and non-capitalist strategies of development."

Sociology 225a—Women and Public Policy.
Professor Blakenship

"An examination of the role of women in the policymaking process and the impact of public policies on women; how and why state policies create and perpetuate relations among gender, class, and race; feminist policy analysis."

Because their campus is decentralized, with no student center or principal gathering place, Yalies tend to become extremely attached to their colleges and, when they graduate often earmark donations for them, as well as for the university itself. College accommodation is coed and guaranteed for all four years. About 10 percent of upperclassmen elect to live off campus, but even they retain their college affiliation on a non-resident basis.

Yale's reputation for excellence in scholarship and teaching is well established. Several departments stand out, however, as exemplars of the good and the bad. The comparative literature major, for example,

TUITION AND FEES INCREASE
Average Increase/Year: Private = 11.15%, Yale = 7.67%

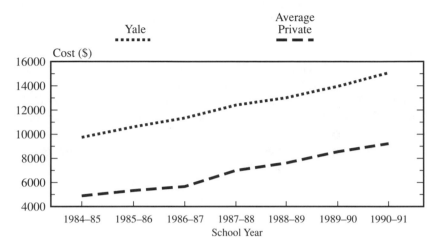

Source: The College Entrance Examination Board

is attempting to recover from a bout with deconstructionism, and is in confusion. In fact, the whole English department has suffered from the deconstructionist virus. The classics department, on the other hand, is one of the best in the country and appears likely to remain so for some time. History and foreign languages, music, drama, and religious studies are also very good. History and English are traditionally the most popular majors.

Overall, Yale is better known for the liberal arts than for the natural sciences, although the present administration appears eager to change that. Currently, the science departments can boast some first-class teachers and scholars, including the Nobel Prize-winning chemist Sidney Altman, a former dean of the college. Science enthusiasts are quick to point out that they get more attention from the faculty than they would in more popular departments.

Yale has no core curriculum, but it does insist upon a series of general distribution requirements and exhorts all to put Western civilization at the top of their academic agendas. In the autumn of 1990, Donald Kagan, the distinguished classical scholar and dean of Yale College, firmly declared:

It is both right and necessary to place Western civilization and the culture to which it has given rise at the center of our studies, and we fail to do so at the peril of our students, our country, and of the hopes for a democratic, liberal society emerging throughout the world today.

He has also pointed out that Western civilization is the tie that binds all Americans, because it originally formed and has always informed the American way of life. Whatever citizens' national, ethnic, or racial origins, Dean Kagan has said, all are now Americans and need to understand what makes them so, what they have in common as well as how they differ.

Accordingly, the college offers to 80 freshmen, who are selected competitively from those who apply, a "Directed Studies" series that provides an introduction "to the fundamental ideas of Western civilization viewed from the perspectives of several intellectual disciplines." Students choose three courses from a short list; class size is about 15, and they seem to love the program.

DISTRIBUTION OF UNDERGRADUATE AID
1989–90 School Year

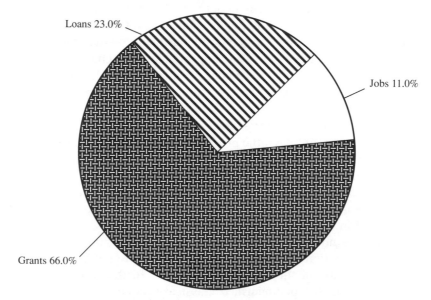

Loans 23.0%

Jobs 11.0%

Grants 66.0%

Source: The College Entrance Examination Board, 1990

Traditional liberal arts studies received a further boost in April 1991, when a Texas oil family bestowed $20 million on the college to endow special teaching positions for an elective series of courses in Western civilization. The program, planned for sophomores, is expected to begin in the fall of 1993, and will take up about half of students' academic schedule for that year. In commenting on the gift's objective, Dean Kagan took pains to point out that the new program would examine the flaws, as well as the triumphs of Western civilization. A few months earlier, a member of the same family had given a similar sum to support humanities teaching at Yale.

Yale divides its departments into four groups for the purpose of its general distribution requirements—languages and literatures; history, religion, philosophy and the fine arts; the social sciences (including archaeology); and the "hard" sciences and forestry and environmental studies. In addition to a language requirement (two years of a language or passing an examination), students must take three courses in each of the four divisions by the end of their sophomore year (including two in the natural sciences) and, by graduation, 12 courses outside the division that includes the major. The current administration appears to be attempting to increase the requirements both overall and for specific majors, though it is not yet clear how much further it intends to go. President Benno Schmidt, Jr., speaks up for the liberal arts and encourages faculty to develop fresh approaches to traditional learning, one example being a newly established undergraduate major in ethics, politics, and economics.

The typical humanities major requires 12 or 13 semester courses and a senior essay or project. The typical science major requires 14 or 15 courses including prerequisites. All undergraduates must pass 36 semester courses to graduate, an average of nine each year. Interestingly, there is no separate honors program, but approximately 30 percent of each senior class graduate with honors, with no more than 5 percent achieving *summa cum laude*.

Teaching at Yale is excellent. The college has always treated its undergraduates like precious natural resources, with the result that very few courses are taught by teaching assistants; some professors even lead their own discussion sections. Lecture courses are never limited in audience size and, with the exception of a few popular seminars, Yale students are almost never denied admission to courses. Classes range from quite small (5 to 15) to extremely large (500), though most lectures are in the range of 50 to 100 students. Seminars are typically restricted to 15 or 20.

Yale's advisory system is extensive—at times cloyingly so, students complain. Freshmen and sophomores are assigned advisors who have offices in the residential colleges and must approve student course schedules. Because most professors are genuinely interested in passing the liberal arts torch to the next generation, they often steer students to an integrated series of courses within the broad-based distribution requirements. Orientation programs and support systems abound to mitigate the stress and complexities of life at a competitive school. There are, however, no codes defining forbidden speech or mandatory sensitivity-awareness sessions, and not likely to be any in the foreseeable future. President Schmidt recently came out with a statement defending freedom of speech even when some deem it "offensive."

In fact, he and Dean Kagan are primarily responsible for the institution of the university's Free Speech Law, which warns that "the university must do everything possible to ensure within it the fullest degree of intellectual freedom." In addition, the code declares that "secondary social and ethical responsibilities must be left to the informal processes of suasion, example and argument." In other words, the right to freedom of speech must not be curtailed to assuage hurt feelings; civility must be voluntary and not enforced. Yale's Free Speech Law also serves to sharpen the important distinction, all too often blurred elsewhere, between the freedom to speak as you please and the freedom to act as you please.

Politics at Yale are generally low-key. The residential college system probably contributes to the apathy on campus. During the stormy late 1960s and early 1970s, Yale was one of the least politically active campuses in the country. (Its one great outbreak occurred during the trial of the Black Panther, Bobby Seale, which was instigated at least as much by external activists as by Yalies.) The division of the undergraduate population and their loyalties among the 12 colleges has made Yale's a difficult campus to unite or to stir up, though the radicals try. Black and feminist groups have been quoted in the *Yale Daily News* calling Dean Kagan a "racist" and a "sexist." Some blacks demand a thorough review of Yale's "racist curriculum" to destroy any implications of white superiority.

Most students fail to respond with enthusiasm. This may be due to the general character of the undergraduate body. As a rule, Yalies look forward to rewarding and remunerative careers—a great many go on to law or business schools. Although the college does not promote competition among students (it does not calculate GPAs or class ranks), students generate their own competitive spirit. Such political activity as there is drops drastically as exams approach. In sum, Yalies are more interested in their careers and their transcripts than they are in what's happening in the world around them, and if this detracts from the excitement quotient, it adds to the tranquillity serious students need to learn about the world before they try to reform it.

All of which is not to say that Yale isn't a predominantly left-of-center campus; it's just not very far left of center. The Black Student Alliance (BSAY) and the gay-lesbian groups are more active than any other organization. In both cases, however, their successes are partly due to failures of courage on the part of successive Yale administrations. BSAY and other minority groups have succeeded in imposing a system of minority deans and "peer" counselors on Yale undergraduates, with the result that black students can scarcely help feeling "different" and "special" from the moment they arrive. The sense of apartness thus engendered encourages them to disengage from the white community. Were it not for this, Yale would be rapidly moving toward complete integration—already most minority students room with members of other minorities or members of the white majority, even after their freshman year when rooming arrangements become voluntary. Yale has a relatively large minority population of about 25 percent, of whom nearly half are of Asian descent.

The homosexual groups are dominated by lesbians, probably because they function out of the feminist Women's Center—which receives support from the university. Having gained recognition, the homosexuals now seek moral equivalence. Although Yale has had a reputation for gay activism, in reality no one pays homosexuals much attention these days and they are not, in fact, as militant as they appear to be on other campuses.

On the whole Yale's population is as cosmopolitan as you would expect at one of the world's best-known universities. In addition to the large minority representation, students come from all 50 states and more than 50 foreign countries. It is also a relatively tolerant campus—more than 30 journals of various kinds represent just about every point of view from the most radical feminist-lesbian to the extreme right. Most publications reflect the opinions of the average student, a moderate left-leaning "liberal" who likes to hear the occasional conservative argument, if only to remember why he disagrees with it.

Social life is also fairly low-key at Yale and, like so much else, tends to be self-contained in the colleges. Fraternities and sororities do not officially exist, though several have sprouted up informally since Yale went coed in 1969. Every spring, Yale's famous secret societies still tap the next year's chosen seniors on the shoulder and, although most of these clubs turned coed and egalitarian, two (including President Bush's Skull and Bones) remained just as exclusive and mysterious and male as ever. In the spring of 1991, however, senior class "Bonesmen" finally voted to admit women; but the Bonesmen's alumni board quickly moved to change the locks on the "tomb," as the clubhouse is called, excluding the rebellious students—and any women they tapped. This effectively closed down the society on campus until a majority of its 800 alumni members voted to open the sacred portals to Bones*women*.

Other Yalies, happily unaffected by the battle of the Bonesmen (of whom there are only 15 in any given year), usually spend weekends attending small parties or entertainments sponsored by several film societies and drama clubs. The Yale Repertory Theater, a professional company, and Yale Drama, a big undergraduate group, are the most active and best known. In 1991, the repertory theater won a Tony Award as the best regional theater in the country. Then, there are the singing societies, including the famous Whiffenpoofs who still hang out down at Mory's, and dozens of other organizations catering to most interests.

When students tire of all this, they take off for New York or Boston (each about two hours by Amtrak); they definitely do not prowl around New Haven, which is unattractive and crime-ridden, though currently undergoing gentrification. Although the town surrounds the small 175-acre campus and crime has frequently spilled over onto Yale property, students have felt relatively safe, partly because the university runs efficient escort and minivan services. In February 1991, however, the entire community was jolted by the murder of a 19-year old student just a block from the president's house. The young man was shot in an apparent robbery attempt. President Schmidt immediately responded with a vow to "take whatever steps are necessary to protect our campus." Neither drink nor drugs seem to be a big problem at Yale, though plenty of elbow bending goes on, just as it always has.

Sports are strong for those who like to play (many couldn't care less) with 16 intercollegiate teams for men and 17 for women, and more than 20 intramurals for each. Soccer, hockey, golf, and tennis are usually good, and football fans still shout themselves hoarse every year as the Bulldogs try to roll back Harvard's Crimson Tide. Facilities include the 71,000-seat stadium, an enormous athletic complex, a pool, skating rink, sailing center, and riding stables.

Although Yale athletics are competitive by Ivy League standards, it is intellectual exercise that the college has always put first. This tradition of excellence, based on the guiding principles of Western civilization, is still alive and well despite assaults by the politically correct on both the curriculum and student life. That these have so far been largely overcome is due in great measure to the resolve—and political skill—of the present administration.

Dictionary

Below is a list of words or terms that are commonly used at colleges and universities across the country. Some of these are defined straightforwardly, for example, **core curriculum** or **distribution requirements;** others are defined as current, collegiate fashion dictates, for example, **conservative** or **open-minded.** Look for them in course descriptions, as well as in official school policies, social life, and extracurricular activities. The frequency of their use can illuminate, in a general way, the character of the school in question.

Ableism   "Oppression of the differentially abled, by the temporarily able." [Quoted verbatim from definitions given by the Office of Student Affairs at Smith College.]

Awareness   As in "awareness day" or "awareness organization." Knowing, and/or the process of teaching others the current politically correct line.

Capitalist   One who believes in exploiting both workers and the Third World for his own benefit. Hostile to the natural equality that socialism will provide. Pressures the U.S. government to use the military to defend monied interests around the world. See **Multinational Corporation.**

Classism   "Oppression of the working-class and non-propertied, by the upper and middle-class." [Quoted verbatim from definitions given by the Office of Student Affairs at Smith College.]

Conservative   One who supports or contributes to the suppression of minorities, women, and the poor. Supports imperialist U.S. military aggression around the world, solely for the benefit of American capitalists. Supports policies that help the rich at the expense of the poor. Unwilling to accept that the U.S. is at least as guilty, if not more so, as the Soviets for the Cold War.

Core Curriculum   A set list of courses that all students must take in order to graduate. Schools that have a true core tend to give students a common background in Western civilization and culture. Those supportive of multiculturalism see the requirement of Western civilization as evidence of continued oppression of minorities.

Deconstruction A technique of reading literary "texts," most closely associated with Jacques Derrida and the late Paul DeMan, which holds that an author's attempt to communicate always breaks down because definitions are constantly shifting and meaning is always unstable. Used to demonstrate that the "canon" of classic works of Western philosophy and literature are internally self-contradictory (and, by implication, that the authors of these works are more obtuse and less perceptive than deconstructionist critics).

Differently Abled "Term created to underline the concept that differently abled individuals are just that, not less or inferior in any way (as the terms 'disabled', 'handicapped', etc. imply). Physically challenged is also accepted." [Quoted verbatim from definitions given by the Office of Student Affairs at Smith College.]

Distribution Requirements A list of courses from which students must pick a certain number to fulfill general education requirements for graduation. Often the list will include well over half of all courses offered in the college. Schools can use these requirements to mandate diversity courses. Not to be confused with **Core Curriculum.**

Diversity Chief goal of the politically correct. The need to widen the curriculum to include multicultural studies and eliminate the dominance in the curriculum of Western culture. When referring to the student body or faculty, as in "diversify the faculty," it often implies more or less hidden quota policies.

Eurocentrism Undue emphasis on European culture and history in the curriculum.

Fascist Anyone who is not politically correct; anyone who advocates capitalism, liberty, and individual rights.

Hegemony Complete control of ideas, people, society, the economic system, nations, and/or the world. For example, "The United States' military and economic hegemony keeps Latin America underdeveloped."

Heterosexism "Oppression of those of sexual orientations other than heterosexual, such as gays, lesbians, and bisexuals; this can take place by not acknowledging their existence. Homophobia is the fear of lesbians, gays, or bisexuals.'' [Quoted verbatim from definitions given by the Office of Student Affairs at Smith College.]

Imperialism   While this term can refer to sixteenth through twentieth century European expansion, it is most often used, in a Leninist way, to describe the current international political and economic system as it negatively affects the Third World. See **Neocolonialism.**

Individual   "This is a 'RED FLAG' phrase today, which is considered by many to be RACIST. Arguments that champion the individual over the group ultimately privaliges [*sic*] the 'INDIVIDUALS' belonging to the largest or dominant group." [Response from a University of Pennsylvania administrator in charge of writing the school's diversity education requirements to a student representative on the diversity education committee who expressed a "deep regard for the individual."]

Insensitivity   Ideas and behavior that are not understanding, compassionate, and supportive of politically correct causes. See **Sensitivity.**

Liberation   Freedom from European colonialism, neocolonialism, capitalism, or, in the case of the United States, from domination by white males. Tied in closely with nationalist revolutionary movements, movements that tend to value equality more than liberty.

Logocentrism   The belief that words can in principle accurately describe the real world, that communication is both possible and worthwhile. This concept is used by deconstructionists to disparage those who believe that words have consistent meanings.

Lookism   "The belief that appearance is an indicator of a person's value; the construction of a standard for beauty/attractiveness; and oppression through stereotypes and generalizations of both those who do not fit that standard and those who do." [Quoted verbatim from definitions given by the Office of Student Affairs at Smith College.]

Multiculturalism   A creed that holds there should be no dominant culture in the United States and that no one culture is better than another. The traditional "European" dominant culture is seen as inherently evil, as it is racist, classist, homophobic, and sexist. Courses on feminism, the Third World, homosexuality, sexism, classism, racism, etc., would all come under the term multicultural. Also known as cultural diversity.

Multinational Corporation   A company based in the First World that exploits Third World countries. It extracts profit, abuses workers, and generally impoverishes the host country for the benefit of a handful of white, rich capitalists. It does this with the support of the military, and often the government, in both the First and Third World countries. See **Capitalist.**

Neocolonialism   The idea that the First World keeps the Third World poor and powerless through the workings of the international capitalist system. Often used by those critical of U.S. policy and apologetic for Third World economic and political policies.

Open-Minded   "Possessing a willingness to consider *all* Politically Correct points of view" and "having enough self-control to refrain from reading, listening to, or considering anything which might be called close-minded." [Quoted from the Harvard *Peninsula*, September 1990, Vol. 2, No. 1.]

Oppression   The subjugation of those who are politically correct. For example, denying the intellectual importance of feminist studies would be an attempt to oppress women. Only those who are politically correct, i.e., women, blacks, homosexuals, Hispanics, the working class, etc. can be oppressed. It is impossible for those who are oppressed or those who are politically correct to oppress others; oppression is only possible with institutional power.

Peace Studies   A field ostensibly centered around the pursuit of peace in the world. Topics include nuclear holocaust and disarmament, militarism, racism, sexism, poverty, justice, violence, etc. U.S. defense policy based on deterrence is seen as threatening the world with nuclear holocaust.

Phallocentrism   The domination of society by males, suppressing the rights of females. For example, "Western civilization is inherently phallocentric."

Pluralism   The belief that all voices and ideas on campus have a right to be expressed and heard, that is, all voices and ideas that are politically correct. Those questioning multiculturalism are to be censured in the modern pluralistic community. Society is becoming more "pluralistic," consequently, the curriculum must become more pluralistic.

Political Correctness   The belief in all or most of the following: multiculturalism, diversity, animal rights and environmentalism, cultural relativism, equality over liberty, Third World nationalism and liberation, affirmative action, radical feminism, homosexuality, etc. Usually hostile to one or more of the following: free market capitalism, traditional liberty, Western culture and core curriculum, a strong national defense, U.S. foreign policy, the CIA and ROTC, Republicans and conservatives, heterosexuals, etc. Also known as PC.

Progressives   Those who support and advocate politically correct causes. Often used in the titles of student groups on campus; for example, "Progressive Student Union." See **Open-Minded.**

Reactionary   See **Fascist** or **Conservative.**

Sensitivity   The state of being understanding, compassionate, and supportive of politically correct causes. For example, freshman orientation often includes political sensitivity sessions, explaining to students the "proper" way to view politically correct issues. See **Insensitivity.**

Socialist   One who believes in and acts to create a "just world," where there is no exploitation, racism, sexism, classism, etc. Believes in the underlying inequality and oppression of capitalism and its concomitant, individualism.

Tolerant   "Accepting the Politically Correct view on a given subject." [Quoted from the Harvard *Peninsula*, September 1990, Vol. 2, No. 1.]

U.S. Military   "It sucks the economy dry, is grossly inefficient, has done little of value since World War II, and is run by idiots." Used to support fascist regimes around the world, as well as the interests of American capitalists. Drains the budget of funds which could be used for more politically correct causes. [Quoted from Robert Weissberg, "Safe-Bashing," in *Academic Questions*, Winter 1989–90, Vol. 3, No. 1.]

Western Civilization   "A conspiracy dead white males to oppress the world. To be spoken of as if it were a toxic virus spread to the defenseless. Thus, one can say: 'The people of X were fortunate not to succumb to Western civilization.' " [Quoted from Robert Weissberg, "Safe-Bashing"]

White Males   "A class of humanity whose guilt is self-evident. Even their alleged accomplishments—art, literature, science, philosophy—are really thinly disguised mechanisms of oppression." [Quoted from Robert Weissberg, "Safe-Bashing"]

Womyn   Spelling of woman or women sometimes used by feminists in order to remove the 'man' or 'men' from the word.